FROM
TOKEN
TO
TRIUMPH

FROM
TOKEN
TO
TRIUMPH

The Texas Republicans
Since 1920

Roger M. Olien

SMU PRESS • DALLAS

Library of Congress Cataloging in Publication Data

Olien, Roger M., 1938-
    From token to triumph; the Texas
  Republicans since 1920.
    Bibliography: p.
    Includes index.
    1. Republican Party (Tex.)—History. I. Title.
JK2320.A8T4   1981   324.2734'09764   81-13589
ISBN 0-87074-180-2   AACR2

Contents

Illustrations are grouped following page 134

Preface

NOT SO LONG AGO, many Texans might have reacted to mention of the state's Republican party with amusement: "What Republican party?" was a common response. In 1981 it is no longer necessary to apologize for discussing the Republicans in Texas. The election of Ronald Reagan to the presidency, with massive and effective support from Texas, the election of Texan George Bush to the vice-presidency, and William P. Clements's tenure in the governor's mansion in Austin have stemmed the once inevitable jokes about the paucity of Republicans in the state. The most ardent Democrat might wish, but he could hardly believe, that all the Republican voters in Texas can meet in a telephone booth and rent spare space within it. For the GOP a new day has dawned—though it was a long time coming.

Charlie Goldsmith, a Midland old-timer, recalled that during the 1920s there were only two Republicans in Midland County, the local postmaster and Taylor Brown, a local rancher. The postmaster obviously owed his job to a political appointment. As for Taylor Brown, "it was just his way." Allowing for the customary blanket-stretching to which every accomplished storyteller is entitled, Charlie Goldsmith was closer to the truth than one might believe.

Like the majority of states in the U.S.A., Texas was a one-party state for most of the twentieth century. The Republican party in Texas, like its counterparts in Mississippi and South Carolina and the Democratic parties in Oregon and Vermont, has only in recent decades offered serious electoral challenges to the permanent majority party. During most of this century its token candidates waged minimal campaigns and attracted fewer adherents than the nominees of minority factions in the Democratic party. Hardly credible as a political party to either the electorate or its opposition, it and the other Republican parties in the South were lampooned by V. O. Key, Jr., a native Texan, as "wavering somewhat between an esoteric cult on the order of a lodge and a conspiracy for plunder."

Born out of scattered Unionist sentiment in 1860, the Texas Republican party held power from 1865 to 1874; for nearly a century thereafter it failed to win another statewide election for a Texas post. By 1914, the Republican party was so weak that it mustered fewer votes than the Socialists in Texas. In 1920 the party was, for all practical purposes, a historical vestige, long past challenging the permanent majority party for control of the state. The Republican party defied the conventional wisdom of Texas observers, however, and lingered on. It enjoyed some local success during the 1920s, survived the long patronage-dry years of the Roosevelt and Truman administrations, and attracted new adherents who took over the party and renewed it during the 1950s. During two decades of growth under skillful and aggressive leadership, which succeeded in erasing the party's public image of a perpetual loser, the GOP built highly efficient grass roots operations in the expanding cities of Texas. By 1970, it turned its corner. Texas turned with it, into the modern arena of two-party politics.

Some elements of this important revival have been explained adequately by other writers. James R. Soukup, Clifton McClesky, and Harry Holloway more than a decade ago showed the relation of social and economic change to the increasing strength of Republicans. Numerous scholars, including Numan V. Bartley and Hugh Graham, have traced the rise of Republicanism as a conservative ideology in the modern South. The role of strong Republican candidates, such as John Tower, George Bush, and William P. Clements, has been fully described by well-informed Texas journalists. Though attractive candidates, conservative ideology, and underlying causes have deserved the attention they have received, a number of significant aspects of the history of the Republican party call for further consideration.

Proper estimation of the recent success of the party should include examination of the darker days that preceded it. In that context, the turning point in party affairs, the victory of the Eisenhower faction in 1952, represented a dramatic break with the habits and preoccupations of the past. The conventional pictures of party affairs, however, wherein party bosses deliberately sacrificed electoral success to insure control of patronage, is a gross caricature, as the relationship of R. B. Creager, Republican national committeeman for nearly thirty years, to Congressman Harry Wurzbach indicates. The party's past is not entirely what it is assumed to have been.

Some measure of correction is equally necessary in the more recent history of the GOP in Texas, mainly to give proper weight to the important role of planners, strategists, and party workers. Party leaders, such as Peter O'Donnell, Beryl Milburn, and Ernest Angelo, raised funds, recruited candidates, and directed volunteers. Party workers, especially the members of Republican women's clubs, deserve considerably more credit for the party's victories than they commonly receive. Through work in nonpolitical voluntary organizations and local campaigns, for example, Republican women learned canvassing and other techniques, which they applied energetically in Texas politics. In the ranks of the Republican women and local campaign organizations, effective managers, such as Florence Atherton, Rita Clements, and Nancy Palm, rose to leadership positions in state and national party affairs. Considered to be ornamental during the Creager era, Republican women became the arms, legs, and often the brains of the GOP in Texas.

The absence both of substantial printed literature on the Texas Republicans and of R. B. Creager's papers took me to numerous collections and libraries in an effort to fill in the story. In the process, I was greatly aided by the Ohio Historical Society, the Herbert Hoover Presidential Library, the Dwight D. Eisenhower Presidential Library, the Sterling Library of Yale University, and the Republican Party of Texas. Robert Taft, Jr., Mike Nolte, H. J. Porter, Mrs. George S. Atkinson, and Senator Barry Goldwater generously permitted me to use letters and other documents in their possession. Dorothy Bosch, of the Fondren Library, Southern Methodist University, efficiently and cheerfully secured numerous items through the interlibrary loan system.

Personal debts for exceptional consideration are too numerous to list completely, but special thanks are due to Helen Ackenhausen, Bayard Ewing, and Senator John G. Tower for helping me gain access to

interviewees and research materials. J. Conrad Dunagan and Professors
Forrest McDonald, Elmer E. Cornwell, and William G. McLoughlin
provided valuable advice and encouragement throughout the project.
My greatest debt of gratitude is owed to Diana, my wife, my most pa-
tient supporter and my best critic.

Roger M. Olien

Midland, Texas
October, 1981

FROM
TOKEN
TO
TRIUMPH

1

Bossism in Sunday Clothes

ON THE AFTERNOON of September 18, 1920, an impressive parade wound its way through the streets of downtown Dallas. Its marching bands, decorated automobiles, and fanfare alone would ordinarily have attracted local notice, but what made the procession remarkable was that it was organized by members of the Republican party. No one could have guessed that there were enough Republicans in all of Texas to stage a parade. At the end of the procession lumbered its prize entry, Queenie, an elephant borrowed from the Forest Park Zoo. The entourage proceeded down Elm Street without a hitch until it stopped to permit photographers to take pictures of Queenie standing next to Jefferson, the scrawny Democratic donkey. And then, as the *Dallas Times Herald* reported, "Something about the donkey, presumably not his politics, apparently offended the symbol of Republicanism: she broke away from her keeper, bellowed, and took out after the frightened Democrat." Bystanders scattered down side streets, some climbing telegraph poles to escape the charging beast. "Meantime the Democratic donkey did not pause to arbitrate Queenie's onslaught, which looked like a landslide to him, and turning on one hoof, he broke from his custodian and bounded up the street with a terrible hee-haw...Queenie followed in hot pursuit." The stampede ended when the elephant's keeper stopped her with

3

vigorous applications of the gaff. The donkey disappeared down a side street and out of politics.[1]

The parade was a reversion to the ebullient electioneering of earlier decades, when Texas Republicans orchestrated the conventional hoopla of American politics to accompany the predictable election of Republican presidents. From William McKinley to William Howard Taft, the GOP held the White House and federal patronage, until members of the party fell out among themselves in 1912 over the contending candidacies of Taft and Theodore Roosevelt. On the heels of disunity came disaster in the form of Woodrow Wilson and eight years of Democratic control of the federal government. Tantamount to a lifetime in conventional politics, Wilson's two terms saw the temporary decline of Texas Republican activity, most notably in San Antonio and the German counties; and realignments in local politics as once-powerful Republicans, such as R. B. Creager in Brownsville, made separate peaces with Texas Democrats, gave up the fight, and accepted the rewards of tactful surrender. In local rites around Texas, Republicans expunged the memories of defeat, unemployment, and collaboration with the new-found optimism which the Harding campaign evoked.[2]

To any reasonably superstitious Republican in Dallas, Queenie's charge could only be a favorable portent of events to come on the first Tuesday of November. Tradition triumphed over the omen; when election day arrived, Texas went Democratic, as it had regularly since 1876. But if Harding's performance on the presidential ballot did not amount to a runaway showing, still his part of the vote in Texas, 28.5 percent, represented a considerable improvement over the 15.6 percent won by Charles Evans Hughes in 1916. Dallas, Houston, Fort Worth, El Paso, and the other urban counties remained in the Democratic column, but the Republican national ticket carried twenty-one counties, including the rural "German" counties and San Antonio, the state's largest city. Thus, even in Texas, Republicans had cause for postelection celebration. No more concerned with the philosophical ambiguity of "Normalcy" than their counterparts in other states, the leaders of the Texas Republican party quickly became absorbed in schemes for distribution of federal patronage and favors, to be realized as soon as the pomp of the presidential inauguration was completed.[3]

Four prominent Texans were among the new President's guests at the ceremony in March: the Honorable Henry F. McGregor, a wealthy Houston businessman and veteran Republican national committeeman for Texas;[4] Rentfro Banton Creager, an enterprising Brownsville attorney and Republican state vice-chairman; Frank E. Scobey, a San Antonio businessman and the new President's friend and longtime political associate; Harry M. Wurzbach from Seguin, the Republican congressman-elect. Around these men and their mutually incompatible ambitions, the affairs of the Republican party in Texas turned for the next decade.

The four Texans were not particularly conspicuous during the round of official events and official celebrations, nor were they singled out for special preferment or notice by the party hierarchy. After all, no Republican miracle had been conjured up and no political tradition broken in the recent election. Texas held with James M. Cox, and the Democratic nominee had a larger proportion of the vote in Texas than he did in eight other southern states. However, Harding's election soon effected changes within the small Texas Republican party—changes which began with a minor flurry over patronage and which stirred up rough waters in the internal affairs of the party for the next thirty-one years. During the first stormy decade of this period, in response to a variety of local and national political developments, the Texas Republican party showed occasional signs of outgrowing its passive preoccupation with patronage. From 1922 through 1932 party candidates made serious if sporadic attempts to gain state offices, but in the years following the election of Franklin Delano Roosevelt, serious exertions in electoral politics ceased, and the party reverted to the southern Republican predilection for patronage and pelf. As old habits and ingrained attitudes lived on, the federal paycheck, or the prospect of it, loomed larger in the calculations of party leaders than victory at the polls.[5]

Given his position in the state party, the Republican national committeeman for Texas, Colonel McGregor, should have been able to look forward to dispensing several thousand federal jobs within the state, following the election of a Republican President. In the absence of a Republican from Texas either in the United States Senate or in a high-ranking administrative position, and with a Democratic governor in Austin, McGregor should have been arbiter of federal favors for Texas. But what should have been a sunny political vision for the elderly "colonel" was obscured by a cloud from the recent political past which cooled relations between the new President and himself: his party's victory increased the likelihood of his own decline because McGregor made the calamitous error of being stubbornly loyal to Governor Frank Lowden, one of Harding's principal rivals at the Republican National Convention.[6] His miscalculated adherence to Lowden was a fatal blunder by the recognized rules of southern Republican politics. A southern national committeeman had to deliver the national convention vote of his state to the winning candidate to maintain his potential patronage rights and his standing with the Republican national leadership. McGregor, though evasive with the press, was generally known to have been a staunch Lowden man during the tight convention, a matter which Harding's friends had not forgotten. Worse yet, he had publicly identified General Leonard Wood as his second choice, passing over Harding, Coolidge, and Hoover, among the hopefuls at the convention and all in the executive circle in March, 1921. Both Harding and his political manager, Harry Daugherty, knew full well that it was contrary to McGregor's wishes, and despite his arm-twisting, that nineteen and one-half of the twenty-three votes in the Texas delegation went to Harding on the decisive ninth ballot.[7] This partial victory was fairly credited to Creager and Scobey, who led the movement for Harding in the Texas delegation and worked on the convention floor to secure additional support from other southern delegations. Though their campaign for Harding produced substantial results only after the Ohio senator emerged as front runner at the convention, their loyalty would be rewarded. As rival claimants for federal favors, Creager and Scobey were now powerful enough to threaten to usurp McGregor's powers and destroy his influence.

The man who gained most by McGregor's presidential miscalculation was the state vice-chairman, R. B. Creager. Long a powerful figure in Republican "customshouse" politics in the Rio Grande Valley, he had achieved wider prominence in the party hierarchy thanks to McGregor, who tapped him for the Republican gubernatorial nomination in 1916. Creager had had the lucky intuition not to follow his impresario in support of Lowden; he had instead enthusiastically backed the winning political dark horse from the beginning. Early in 1920, he openly joined the small Harding faction in Texas and worked thereafter with political associates on the Republican State Executive Committee to organize delegate support for Harding, thus abandoning McGregor. With Harding elected, Creager could well expect the new President to reward him for the great political risk he took in breaking openly with McGregor, and his following in the Texas party could reasonably look for patronage consideration, if necessary at the expense of Colonel McGregor's faction. Creager was clearly a man to watch.[8]

With all his ambition, Creager was not the only claimant for Harding's favor. When the newly elected President thought of his Texas political friends, the first man in his consideration was not Creager but the creator of the maverick Harding movement in the Texas Republican party, Frank E. Scobey. Though Creager's political maneuvers delivered the convention votes to Harding, Scobey was responsible for having brought Creager into the Harding camp long before the national convention. Scobey's connection with Warren Harding, morever, was strong, personal, and of long duration. Old political cronies, the two men had known one another from the days of Scobey's tenure as sheriff of Miami County, when he supported Harding's debut in public office, his election to the Ohio State Senate. Scobey's migration to Texas in 1906, undertaken to improve both his health and his finances, did not sever their connection. Scobey speculated in Mexican mining and American real estate ventures with the Ohio senator and exchanged political badinage and anatomical jokes in frequent matey letters. Both crony and friend, Scobey gradually became a political informant and advisor, but he carefully maintained his personal intimacy with Harding; he entertained Harding and his wife as casual guests in his own home before, during, and after the presidential campaign of 1920. With his friend finally in the nation's highest office, Scobey had no intention of being forgotten.[9]

The new President owed Scobey a debt of gratitude, for Scobey's work for Harding in Texas had been more than ordinarily difficult. By reputation a fiery-tempered, hard-drinking hothead, Scobey was not the sort of man to ease effortlessly into local prominence. As a transplanted Yankee, he found San Antonio Republican circles closed to him. From the viewpoint of local leaders, Scobey, the political "high roller" from Ohio, was a potentially threatening newcomer. He had little to offer Bexar County Republican leaders apart from his knowledge of big-time politics, Ohio-style: and if this knowledge were activated it could only generate a new faction in local politics.[10] Had he been a wealthy man, Scobey might have secured his position in the ranks of party leaders. By San Antonio standards, Scobey was only moderately well off; his profitable cold storage company was under the financial control of ball-bearing magnate H. H. Timken, who refused to sell the controlling interest in the firm to Scobey until Warren Harding strongly urged him to do so in 1922.[11]

Failure to make a mark in county politics did not deter Scobey from trying to influence state political transactions. In 1915 he began a strenuous campaign to stir up interest in Harding as a candidate for the Republican presidential nomination. He predictably met with no success in San Antonio. In Houston, he talked up Harding to H. F. McGregor, who held undisputed control of the Texas party and hence controlled the forthcoming state convention, at which delegates to the 1916 national convention would be chosen. McGregor was not interested in Scobey or his candidate. Frustrated in this attempt to promote both himself and Harding, Scobey then tried and failed to gain a seat on the Republican State Executive Committee.

Finding himself checked at every move by McGregor's strong influence over party leaders and the reluctance of the old crowd in San Antonio to admit a choleric newcomer, Scobey next tried to bring national pressure on McGregor to gain admission to the party leadership circle. In 1916, at Scobey's request, Senator Warren G. Harding set Harry Daugherty in action. Daugherty persuaded national chairman Charles H. Hilles to put in a word for Scobey with McGregor, and himself approached McGregor on Scobey's behalf at a meeting of the Republican National Committee. All of this maneuvering came to nothing. Sensibly enough, McGregor was not interested in bringing a newcomer with apparently few Texas resources into the party leadership. Scobey's demonstration that he had influential national connections, moreover, could only strengthen the national committeeman's resolution to keep a potential rival out of Texas Republican politics.[12]

Pulling national political strings having brought him no closer to prominence in the Texas Republican party, Scobey tried yet another strategy, constructing a base of support among state Republicans. He began by cultivating R. B. Creager. In the circle of state party leaders, Creager was the only man who was approachable, for he was the only man who had anything to gain by doing business with Scobey. Creager, a Bull Mooser in 1912, was stalled at the middle level of party leadership, and his prospects for advancement in the McGregor organization were decidedly unpromising. After some negotiation, Scobey won Creager's commitment to Harding's—and hence his—side in December, 1916. For the next few years, Scobey promoted Creager to Harding as the principal Republican political craftsman in Texas, and Harding in turn acknowledged that he was impressed with Scobey's ability to recruit potentially valuable political allies. Establishing himself as a political impresario, a purveyor of political talent, Scobey moved Creager's political stock high on the market with Harding and his friends. Scobey identified Creager as the entering wedge in Texas for Harding's projected candidacy in 1920, as the most effective organizer for the Harding movement in the South, and even as the principal Texas fund-raiser for Harding.[13]

Scobey was not content, however, merely to bring Creager to Harding's attention. He was determined to make his protégé one of the senator's pals, an ambitious project for which he could expect Creager to be appropriately grateful. Thus, in August, 1919, he persuaded Harding to invite Creager to Washington so they could make one another's personal acquaintance. The meeting was a smashing success. Creager played golf with Harding, shooting the first four holes at par, on an unfamiliar course, thus impressing Harding with his self-control and skill: he then did badly on the next five holes, neatly enabling Harding to win the short friendly match. Harding was charmed. Though the two players discussed little in the way of politics, Harding shortly thereafter sized up the adroit Texan as an impressive and useful politician, and he told Scobey that he wanted to see more of Creager. In his early search for possible delegate strength, candidate Harding saw in Creager the likely developer and leader of whatever firm support he might muster in Texas for his own nomination at the 1920 Republican National Convention. The events of the following year did nothing to alter Harding's assessment.[14]

When the election of 1920 brought triumph to their candidate, Scobey and his protégé could at last expect reward for their risk and effort. Creager's rise was rapid; he advanced to the vice-chairmanship of the state committee in September, 1920. In April, 1921, he became state chairman. Scobey, by contrast, had gotten himself into an ambiguous position. By mutual agreement, he gave way to his "best friend" and remained outside the formal circle of party leaders. Thereafter, Creager's rise was nothing short of meteoric. Within two years he became sole patronage referee in Texas and created a new state headquarters organization which effectively shut out McGregor from management of the party. When the national committeeman died in 1923, Creager succeeded him, encountering only feeble opposition from the McGregor group on the Republican State Executive Committee. But, at the same time he stepped into McGregor's place, Creager succeeded in establishing his own independence from his former mentor; in the process of doing so, in less than two years, he finally eased Scobey out of an active role in politics.[15]

Notwithstanding Creager's machinations, the prime author of Scobey's plummeting fortune was Scobey himself. Having taken the dubious step of giving way to his friend Creager in state politics, Scobey still expected to enjoy influence with the President: he was, after all, the President's friend.

Even before Harding's inauguration, Scobey pressed for personal favors. Looking to reward a loyal political supporter, Scobey proposed P. J. Lucas for postmaster in San Antonio, the best available patronage position in town. This nomination would ordinarily have been confirmed with little delay on account of Scobey's influence with the President-elect. Under pressure from Republican congressional leaders, however, Harding gave way to the traditional view that members of Congress should receive preferential patronage consideration when a member of their party was chief executive. Congressman-elect Harry M. Wurzbach, of the Fourteenth Texas District, which included San Antonio, understandably advanced this view of congressional privilege and pressed for the appointment of August Brian to the postal position. Thus, the lines of political battle were drawn. Scobey was adamant in his support of Lucas because his newly established political standing was at stake. He secured Creager's support. Colonel McGregor accordingly supported Wurzbach's candidate throughout the long and bitter controversy, which lasted until 1922.[16] The dispute ended in a pyrrhic victory for Scobey. President Harding settled "this disagreeable business in San Antonio" by giving the appointment to his nominee. At the same time, however, Scobey lost the friendship of the President by pressing the issue, thereby placing Harding in a difficult position with the Republican leadership of the House of Representatives. According to Harding, the dispute over the postmastership in San Antonio was "the most unfortunate and troublesome question" of his early months in the White House because it undermined his initially cordial relations with the congressional leaders of his own party.

Harding felt put upon. He had expected Scobey to give in on the issue for the sake of their friendship, a fair expectation, while Scobey expected Harding to pay off for past political favors, a reasonable request. But fair expectations and reasonable requests were both irrelevant to the situation. Scobey failed to realize that his poker-playing friend was now the President, that table rules had necessarily changed, and that the game was not being played between equals. Beyond physical distance, an affinitive gulf separated the former cronies. Harding's letters grew less frequent and the former tone of intimacy disappeared from them. When Scobey's man was finally appointed, on the spurious grounds that Lucas was a personal friend of the President, Harding's notification letter to Scobey was cold and formal.[17]

Frank Scobey does not seem to have sensed the deterioration of his friendship with Warren Harding. He continued to play at local politics, using Harding's presumed support as his political stake. As if the scrimmage over Lucas's appointment were not enough, Scobey blocked yet another of Wurzbach's nominations and weakened his own position still further. Wurzbach wished to see Judge C. K. McDowell of Del Rio appointed collector of internal revenue for the South Texas District. Colonel McGregor supported the judge, an old political ally who had opposed Scobey in West Texas. In an attempt to break the deadlock between Republican contenders, once again Scobey pressed the issue with Harding. This time, Scobey was forced to trade on more than his own standing with Harding. He won only after he brought Creager to promote his side of the controversy, and not coincidentally, shut McGregor out of patronage politics. In the course of this battle, Scobey suggested to Harding that Creager be made head of a Texas patronage-dispensing triumvirate whose other members would be McGregor and himself. But with the San Antonio postmastership rankling in the President's mind, he turned Scobey down and decisively shut out both McGregor and Scobey by making Creager sole patronage referee in the Texas party. Harding did not completely ignore Wurzbach, for Wurzbach's recommendations were for the most part honored: only Wurzbach's objection to the appointment of David A. Walker, Harry Daugherty's son-in-law, to be United States attorney for the Western District of Texas was flatly overruled. As for the cause of contention, a place on the federal payroll for McDowell, the judge from Del Rio was made U.S. assistant attorney general. As if to signal his own indifference to the furor which preceded his appointment, McDowell held this Washington post for no more than a few weeks. He resigned, he explained, "because he didn't care for the town."[18] The charms of Del Rio were irresistible.

With the cooling of Harding's friendship, all chance Scobey ever might have had for a leading role in Texas politics vanished, though he still had a few powerful friends within the Texas GOP. There remained his protégé, Creager, state Republican chairman. With his unerring gift for political mishap, Scobey managed to break this connection as well, giving Creager final independence of him in Republican politics. As luck would have it, the final occasion for Scobey's downfall was once again the San Antonio postmastership. P. J. Lucas was retiring, and Creager decided to use the opportunity of Lucas's replacement to mend his relationship with Congressman Wurzbach. He nominated William Hansen, one of Wurzbach's campaign workers in 1920. Scobey was outraged. Both Wurzbach and Hansen sided with Colonel McGregor in his rebuffs to Scobey before 1920, and Scobey determined to keep the best federal job in the fourteenth district from Wurzbach and Hansen.

Matters proved more complex than Scobey imagined. In opposing Hansen's appointment, he clearly thought he was thwarting Wurzbach. Unknown to Scobey, however, Hansen had split with Wurzbach after his nomination, and the congressman belatedly and unsuccessfully tried to block Hansen's confirmation. Having enlisted Hansen in the ranks of his own supporters, Creager naturally stood by his nominee. Hansen's appointment drove Scobey to a unilateral break in political relations with Creager. He refused to answer the state chairman's conciliatory letters or even to return his long distance telephone calls. Politically isolated, Scobey accepted Harding's offer of a job, promised in 1920, and became the director of the mint in Denver, serving with no particular distinction from 1922 until the President's death in 1923.[19]

Scobey did not immediately realize what had happened to him, or indeed, that his political influence had ended. Shortly after the congressional election of 1922, he joined forces with Harry Wurzbach, his former adversary, largely because Wurzbach constituted the only potential challenger to Creager in Texas and Washington. Following his resignation as director of the mint, in 1923, Scobey returned to San Antonio and importuned President Coolidge on behalf of Wurzbach, to no apparent effect. Several years later, in 1928, Scobey traveled around the state stirring up opposition to Creager, by supporting Congressman Wurzbach's attempt to seize control of the Texas delegation to the Republican National Convention. Scobey tried to blacken Creager's reputation with national Republicans. In correspondence with Vice-President Charles G. Dawes, Scobey demeaned Creager as overvaluing himself by aiming at the vice-presidential nomination, and, ultimately, at the presidency. Political acquaintances and old friends were sent frequent reminders of Creager's "unbounded ambition" and disloyalty. Right up to the time of his death in 1928, Frank Scobey never forgave Creager for the double cross of 1922.[20]

What kind of person was the new leader of the Texas Republican party? It is no easy matter to get a fair measure of Rentfro Banton Creager. Political enemies, such as South Texas *jefe* Jim Wells, accused Creager of a wide variety of crimes, including election fraud and murder. Surviving friends and former employees offer uniformly loyal opinions of the man. His principal political adversaries and allies are now dead; at his direction no significant papers survived the execution of his estate; and the papers of Jim Wells and other foes fall short of supporting the persistent allegations of criminality. It is clear that Creager's reputation suffered at the hands of opponents and that he did his best to leave no personal data behind. Even in the absence of substantial biographical data, it is important to reconstruct aspects of Creager's personality and style as they relate directly to his political activity.

Recollections of his acquaintances and photographs permit only a spare reconstruction of Creager. Even the camera failed to capture Creager in a candid fashion; he used the camera lens to sustain and perpetuate a more general kind of image. His photographs are surprisingly similar. He appeared with his left foot forward, making him look taller and slimmer. Carefully tailored suit jackets and coats emphasized vertical lines and hid his emerging stomach; long-collared white shirts drew the viewer's eye away from his square and somewhat chubby face. A custom-made hat with an extended crown gave the illusion of added height. These surviving photographs do reveal a man who gave great attention to his appearance and who was highly conscious of the importance of "image" in politics and business. A group photograph taken at Hoover's inauguration in 1929 shows Creager standing with Orville Bullington and John Philp, and nowhere is his image-making more obvious. All of Creager's height-emphasizing devices, elevated hat crown, carefully tailored clothing, and position—squarely in front of the two men on either side—make him seem nearly as tall as Orville Bullington, who was in fact several inches taller. Creager's poses and habits suggest that he was somewhat vain. In any event, set apart from fellow party members, who look like the small town bankers and big city lawyers they are, Creager appears polished and elegant. Latter-day recollections of Creager suggest that pose and vanity were not merely attributes of his behavior before the camera: they were hallmarks of his political style. His public posture was highly contrived. Though the absence of personal data prevents any penetrations of his private reflections on politics, nothing about Creager's handling of political business indicates the careless expression of an unselfconscious personality. His manner had practical political purpose. Creager's polish, his "class," impressed less sophisticated folk. The tailored look conveyed the image of the wealthy, well-connected, skillfully manipulative politician—an image useful to both Creager's political position and his financial interests.[21]

A highly compatible mixture of business and politics boosted Creager's career. He was born in Waco, Texas, on March 11, 1877, received the bachelor of science degree from Southwestern University, Georgetown, Texas, in 1898 and a law degree from the University of Texas in 1900. Little more is known of his early life; in later years, Creager was not given to sentimental revelations of his prepolitical life. Beginning in politics in 1900 as the collector of customs at Roma, Texas, a picturesque, dirt-road town at the head of navigation on the lower Rio Grande River, he sought and won the support of Judge James O. Luby of San Diego, in Duval County, for appointment to a more lucrative post. His efforts were rewarded in 1902, when Creager was named as collector for Brazos de Santiago District, which included Brownsville, at a salary of $1,500 and fees per year. In the Gulf Coast city, Creager made useful business contacts, speculated in land in Hidalgo County, and enhanced his social and political standing. With the steady income and security of his federal position, the ambitious young attorney launched out confidently into town and courthouse politics. He soon became a major force in local politics, as the leader of the "Customs House Republicans" and of the so-called Red Party—opponents of the Democratic Blue Party, which was led by Jim Wells and Archie Parr.

One of Creager's few miscalculations, his support of Theodore Roosevelt in 1912, resulted in a temporary setback to his ambitions; President Taft fired him. By 1912, however, Creager was firmly established in Brownsville. His first political error actually worked to his advantage. He turned to the private practice of law in Brownsville and enjoyed considerable success. By 1920 he had acquired land and mineral lease holdings, served as president of the First National Bank of Brownsville, and represented powerful clients, including the Missouri Pacific Railroad, and D. W. Fordyce of St. Louis. When he became vice-chairman of the state executive committee, he was a man of considerable stature in the lower Rio Grande Valley. His mansion on Elizabeth Street, the symbol of his prominence, is still the largest house in Brownsville.

The real financial dividends from Creager's political connections, however, came after he became national committeeman in 1923. Creager probably never sold federal offices for outright personal gain, as other southern Republican national committeemen such as Perry Howard of Mississippi were alleged to have done, but he did not need to. Political connections paid dividends of their own. As the court-appointed receiver for both the W. E. Stewart Land Company, whose principal holdings were in the lower Rio Grande Valley, and the Houston Oil and Gas Company, Creager was awarded more than half a million dollars in attorney's fees. As a large-scale real estate speculator—a category which might almost be stretched to include nearly every Anglo-American in the Rio Grande River Valley before the Depression—as a man of great influence, and as a skillful attorney, Creager could generally cope with the high-handed courthouse gangs in Cameron, Hidalgo, and Starr counties, where his real estate tracts were located, though he took the precaution of using Gus Jones, a local customshouse employee, as an armed bodyguard. In Brownsville, Creager profited handsomely when he obtained the easements for the International Bridge, which was privately financed and owned.[22]

Creager's cozy arrangements with local Democrats drew attacks from dissident Republicans in the Rio Grande Valley, who charged that he deliberately stunted the growth of the GOP in South Texas in exchange for favors from the Democratic machine.[23] Other critics alleged that not all of Creager's prosperity had been gained legally. In 1928, Frank Scobey told Vice-President Charles G. Dawes that Creager had received large fees for practicing law before federal agencies, especially the Bureau of Internal Revenue, whose local officials were appointed upon his recommendation. According to Scobey, Creager received $25,000 from the Sanger Estate in Dallas, $25,000 from Karl Hoblitzelle, Dallas, $30,000 from Lutcher Stark, Orange, Texas, for intervening in tax disputes, and $15,000 from the Missouri Pacific Railroad for a single appearance before the Interstate Commerce Commission with his partner, George Hill, an influential Houston attorney. Scobey's damaging allegations were given widespread circulation, though his informants were never identified.[24]

During the 1920s, there was no doubt of Creager's considerable wealth, though the speculative nature of his business ventures did not come to light until 1935, when he declared bankruptcy, with liabilities of $494,139 and assets of $460,894. After earning nearly a million dollars during the 1920s, Creager invested almost $750,000 in real estate and retained few assets which could be converted to ready cash when he needed it in 1935. After he went through bankruptcy proceedings, Creager effected something of a recovery when he acquired oil and gas leases in Illinois and Kentucky. He consolidated his recovery when he became the president of the Illind Oil Corporation in 1939, and he seems to have been comfortably off thereafter, managing to hold on to his Brownsville mansion until several years before his death in 1951.[25]

It is clear that political prominence brought a large measure of R. B. Creager's fortune during the 1920s, and that wealth sustained his political position. Thousands of Texans were wealthier than Creager, but few were as adept at conveying the impression of polish, prominence, and respectability. With successful contrivance, Creager fostered magnified views of his influence in Washington and of his dominance of Republican politics in Texas, though in neither place was his power what he induced people to believe.

During the early 1920s there was little question but that Creager's political position was solid. Though McGregor and a few old-guard Taft men opposed him, he was elected state chairman in April, 1921, by a thirty-one-to-six vote of the state committee. The newly elected "Red Fox of the Rio Grande," as he liked to be called, operated with a considerable political asset, the generally held belief that he was a personal friend of President Harding. In this regard he owed a debt both to Scobey and to Scobey's techniques. Texas newspapers speculated that he might be Harding's postmaster general and reported on several occasions that Creager had turned down the appointment as ambassador to Mexico,[26] though there is no reliable evidence of his receipt of any offer of appointment, either to the cabinet or to a diplomatic post. Creager, however, generated the bulk of his political assets after his election to the state chairmanship by organizing a local power base. He created the Headquarters Committee, which he chaired. Colonel McGregor was admitted *ex officio* to the committee, but he was only one member among seven, four of whom were appointed by Creager. As Creager construed it, the Headquarters Committee assumed the organizational prerogatives which had formerly been the national committeeman's. In effect, Creager assumed operating control of the GOP in Texas. On the heels of his loss of patronage power, McGregor found that the new Creager-dominated party apparatus left him with little more than his title, Republican national committeeman for Texas.[27]

With his Headquarters Committee, the vehicle of his control, Creager established a full-time, year-round, professional headquarters staff, which supervised party operations. A full-time headquarters was a political novelty in Texas. Before Creager's chairmanship, the party had been run through the business offices of Colonel McGregor and Phil Baer, former United States marshal and Creager's predecessor as state chairman. This was a common enough way of handling party business throughout the nation and was a customary mode of operation in the South; Republican leaders like McGregor and Baer simply assumed that there would be little ongoing party business and acted accordingly. Nor were they alone in their attitude toward organization within the state. In Texas the Democratic party continued—and, to a remarkable degree, still continues—to operate with far less permanent and professional organization than its counterparts in many other states. But Creager sensed how useful a permanent headquarters could be in his own control of party fortunes, and on September 1, 1921, Republican Party Headquarters was officially opened in Dallas where McGregor had no following. To serve as director of organization, at an attractive salary of $7,500 per year, Creager hired an experienced Dallas businessman, William E. Talbot. In addition to the director, party headquarters was staffed with the director's secretary, Mrs. Ruby Erdwinn until 1926 and Miss Helen Ackenhausen from 1926 to 1932 and from 1936 to 1947, and a typist-stenographer. In nonelection years, the regular staff operated on an annual budget of about $25,000.[28] The total party payroll naturally increased during election campaigns; for example, additional workers were employed by the Hoover Headquarters in Fort Worth in 1928 and a full-time accountant joined the headquarters staff in Dallas.

Some staff reorganization was necessary in 1924 when William Talbot resigned as director of organization to become the sales manager of the American Rio Grande Land Company, in which Creager and a fellow Republican, Clarence Linz, a major stockholder and officer of a Dallas life insurance company, were major investors. Clinton S. Bailey, a young Dallas attorney, succeeded Talbot, but was removed after the 1924 general election because, according to one employee's account, the party leadership thought he lacked sufficient organizational experience. Bailey's successor, Fort Worth editor Leonard Withington, served from December, 1924, until his death in 1930. Like Talbot, Withington displayed considerable interest in developing the party's formal organization. His main service to the party, however, and especially to Creager, was drawn from his long experience as a journalist. During the days of intermittent intraparty warfare, Withington wrote polished apologies for the Creager organization and kept the Texas press solidly behind Creager while local rivals, congressional leaders, and crusading journalists launched attacks against the management of the Texas party.[29]

From an organizational viewpoint, the permanent minority party in Texas, unlike the run of Republican parties in the South, appeared to

operate with a strong sense of professionalism; fund-raising, press relations, and liaison work with county leaders were handled in a generally
businesslike way, though the last received desultory attention. Even
patronage, the bane and boon of political leaders, was ordinarily handled
in a methodical manner, with at least the appearance of routinized cooperation between county and state leaders. In theory, nominations for
all federal posts in Texas originated with county leaders, were considered by the headquarters committee, and were promoted by Creager
in Washington. In actual fact, such an arrangement was neither entirely
realistic nor workable because county organizations were often more
apparent than real. In most instances when he wished to reward a loyal
follower, Creager planted the suggestion for his nomination with a local
leader, who obligingly endorsed it and passed it along to the headquarters committee. On other occasions influential Republicans, such as
T. P. Lee or Clarence Linz, both substantial contributors to the party,
were consulted on patronage decisions outside of formal channels.
Though he enjoyed seeming to be powerful solely in his own right,
Creager rarely moved on major appointments before consultation with
both party leaders and influential Republicans.[30]

At the same time that he consulted widely on patronage matters,
Creager maintained the useful public fiction that he was a party czar
and that his approval was the essential support for an appointment to
a federal post in Texas. Creager thus enhanced his own standing; his
political charade kept potentially dissident party members in line, as no
one willingly took on a party leader who appeared to be in his prime.
At the same time, Creager's pose also caused considerable confusion and
resentment on occasions when he was unable to deliver promised appointments or when several influential claimants sought the same position.
Thus, in 1929 Orville Bullington nearly broke with Creager over the
boss's failure to secure a federal judgeship for him. Bullington, accepting
the fiction of Creager's vast influence in Washington, assumed that he
had been led up the garden path, a mistaken notion which Creager could
not dispel without destroying the illusion of his own vast power.[31]

Financial problems were as difficult to avoid as those connected with
patronage. Political leaders have generally found that it is relatively
difficult to sustain continuous headquarters operations, because most
donors prefer to contribute funds directly to the campaigns of specific
candidates. Housekeeping funds are hard to come by. For this reason,
political organizations have long searched for methods of sustaining

party headquarter operations between elections. In 1921, Will Hays, who served as postmaster general in the Harding administration, proposed a fund-raising system which aimed at solving the recurrent financial problems of the Republican party. The Creager organization adopted its own variation of Hays's scheme. Republicans, including federal officeholders, were urged to sign unsecured personal notes, in nonelection years, payable in equal installments over a two-year period, for sums ranging from $25 to $5,000. Creager and other party leaders traveled over Texas, speaking at rallies at which the party faithful signed these promissory notes. The notes were subsequently forwarded to the party treasurer, Dr. F. L. Thompson, a San Antonio oilman, who frequently discounted them to commercial banks; the banks arranged payment schedules ranging from $2.50 to $50.00 per month and relieved the party of the burden and possible embarrassment of collecting on the pledges.[32]

The Hays system offered the party obvious advantages; it provided a continual flow of funds to support the permanent headquarters operation, and it did not interfere with fund-raising during political campaigns. Moreover, it did not involve raising funds immediately after elections, when patronage decisions were made; and it thus deflected the recurrent charge that the party in power essentially extorted funds from federal officeholders and sold federal posts. The scheme would presumably work even when the party was out of power; still, it was wiser to solicit funds on the eve of national elections as long as potential contributors, who were prospective federal employees, thought that the party's presidential candidate had a reasonable chance to win.

With all of its advantages, Will Hays's fund-raising program produced some undesired and unforeseen problems for its managers. Given the lucrative potential of this fund-raising arrangement, it is not surprising that it attracted considerable attention, especially from persons not fond of state bosses like Creager. The charge of outright coercion of federal employees in Texas—a common enough allegation long before Creager assumed control of the party—was made a number of times during the 1920s in the course of intraparty feuds. Congressman Harry Wurzbach, Senator Smith Wildman Brookhardt of Iowa, and two journalists, William H. Shepard and Owen P. White, charged that the scheme was corrupt and illegal. By the end of several congressional hearings and various journalistic attacks on Creager and the Hays scheme, no one had succeeded in proving that federal employees were ever actually threatened with the loss of their jobs for their failure to sign notes, or that jobs had ever actually been promised to signers. But the taint of suspicion of scandal lingered. Although the scheme operated within the letter of federal and state law, Creager found it difficult to lay these allegations of illegality and impropriety to rest, largely because the Hays system did contain obvious opportunities for coercion and corruption.[33]

By contrast, however much malcontents grumbled, the Republican party of Texas had little difficulty staying within the letter of state law. As defined by the Terrell Election Law of 1905 and modified in 1907, 1911, and 1925, laws governing political parties were designed with the Democratic party in mind and generally were not germane to the operation of the Republican party. The law, for example, mandated specific procedural behavior for political parties whose candidates for either governor or United States senator polled two hundred thousand or more votes. Thus it ordinarily applied to the operations of the Democratic party alone; only in 1924 and 1932 did the Republican gubernatorial candidates poll enough votes to require their party's conformity for the following two-year period. On various occasions, as established through opinions of the attorneys general and Texas courts, the Republican party was considered a private association, "subject to Party rather than statutory control."[34]

For reasons of its own the Republican party chose to conform to the letter of the law regarding party organization and structure, though it was normally exempt from the election statute. By generally conforming to the law when not specifically required to do so, the party leadership successfully altered the relationship between local, county, and state organizations from that which was intended. The Terrell Law provided for broadly based party government: it required both precinct-level and county organization; party officials were to be chosen by the rank and file of party adherents, from the grass roots upward, through precinct, county, district, and state meetings. In actual fact, the Creager organization reversed this relationship in a manner which strengthened its hold on Republican organization on the one hand and exploited political reality on the other. Barely one-fifth of the 254 counties in Texas returned enough Republican votes to warrant the support of any formal party organization. The German counties, together with Bexar, Harris, Dallas, Tarrant, Nueces, Cameron, El Paso, and Jefferson counties, generally accounted for the large majority of Republican votes. In some counties, such as the thinly populated "prairie dog" counties of West Texas, elections came and went without the appearance of a corporal's guard of Republicans. Even local postmasters were politically apostate. On the face of it, under these conditions the Republican party would have been unable to meet the law's specific requirement of county organizations. In some parts of Texas, there simply were no Republicans available to hold precinct or county meetings, and thus only a nominal state and local organization was possible.[35]

Creager's solution to the question of organization was legalistic and simple: the Headquarters Committee appointed county chairmen directly where they could find takers for the job. By securing a large number of presumably loyal, if otherwise useless, county chairmen, the Creager organization gained a strong hold on the entire party apparatus. Controlling the appointment of a majority of the county chairmen, the Creager group effectively controlled the county conventions which chose delegates to the state convention; and control of the state convention guaranteed control of the GOP in Texas.

Unlike Creager's tightly organized state meetings, county party conventions were proverbially loose in their regard for the niceties of regular procedures. In 1934 party counsel Carlos Watson discovered that one county chairman kept his "meeting" going all day so that Republicans could vote when they found it convenient to come to town. When the chairman was asked where he actually held the convention, he replied that he held it outdoors in the courthouse square and kept moving it to stay on the shady side of the street. At the same state convention, in 1934, the embarrassed credentials committee was forced to throw out the delegates from eleven counties after it was discovered that the primary election returns from these West Texas counties were all in the same handwriting. The state committee could find no reliable evidence to prove that either primaries or conventions had actually been held in these counties, though state convention delegates arrived with proxy votes for them. Creager and his associates disdained maneuvers like this as flagrantly fraudulent—unlike their own clever adherence to the letter of the law. Complete inactivity was preferable to potentially embarrassing shenanigans. The ingenuity of local leaders guaranteed a constant supply of the latter, while their general lack of sustained effort moved in the direction of the former.[36]

The state convention, which Creager controlled directly and indirectly, was the only party assembly from which a direct threat to his leadership could come. Moreover, under the bylaws which governed both county and state conventions, a majority of the members of the convention elected all of the delegates to the national party convention at which the exchange of support for promises and favors was carried out. State conventions were easily managed on most occasions. Safe delegations, moreover, could be expected from strongly Democratic backwater areas of East Texas and West Texas to offset an occasional challenge from the strongly Republican urban areas and German counties. Such challenges were not frequent. Indeed, it is questionable how active and enterprising the more thoroughly organized urban counties actually were. For example, on July 13, 1926, on the eve of the party's first primary election, the Dallas County Republican Executive Committee met to appoint election judges and carry out other preparations. Of a possible 116 delegates (one per election precinct), 17 members appeared in person, 45 were represented by proxy, and 53 were unaccountably absent. Heber Page, a federal postal employee in Dallas, moved that County Chairman George Atkinson, a tax lawyer, appoint the election judges. John A. Kettle, an employee of the Bureau of Internal Revenue in Dallas, held most of the 45 proxies, and seconded Page's motion. When the 17 delegates in attendance and the 45 proxy votes were tallied, Chairman Atkinson declared the motion carried and proceeded to read a prepared list of election judges, and then adjourned the meeting. This variety of party activity on the county level scarcely demonstrated enthusiastic grass roots activity.[37] Several years later, Mrs. Sarah Menezes, who served as president of the Dallas County Republican Women and held a post in the United States attorney's office, called the Republican chairman in Dallas County to notify him that a new lawyer, a Republican, had moved into Dallas. The county chairman's reply was: "Oh, yes. I know that, but we already have a Republican in that precinct." This mode of doing business in the relatively vital urban counties was certainly conducive to Creager's dominance of party operations from above.[38]

Documents related to the 1926 primary election provide a useful indication of the type of membership and the level of organizational activity of the Republican party in Texas, most particularly in Dallas County. In spite of considerable publicity and advance work by the state headquarters, the turnout was slight: only fifteen thousand ballots— about 5 percent of the vote cast for the Republican gubernatorial candidate in 1924—were cast throughout the state. Dallas County Chairman

George Atkinson kept a "List of Republican Voters Voting in Republican Primary Election, July 24, 1926." The list groups the 386 voters by precinct and provides information regarding the residence, occupation, race, age, and length of residence for each voter: 11 voters (3 percent) were black, nearly one-fifth of the total number were federal employees, and more than two-thirds of the Republicans were not native-born Texans. The list includes Creager associates who were on the federal payroll: Samuel L. Gross, state committeeman, was U.S. marshal; George C. Hopkins, highly active in Dallas Republican politics and state chairman during the 1940s, was collector of internal revenue; John Philp, onetime county chairman and state chairman at a later date, was Dallas postmaster; Heber Page, occasionally county chairman and member of the state committee, was fourth assistant postmaster general. Other information concerning length of residence reinforces the commonly held notion that in urban areas a large number of regular Republican voters were probably transplanted Republicans. Thus 69 percent of the primary election voters were not born in Texas, whereas in the whole adult population of Dallas County three-fourths were natives of the state. Moreover, 56 of the voters had lived in the state less than ten years, with the greater number earning a living through business, law, or government employment. These party loyalists were easily managed, and Creager gave at least the appearance of governing the party in a most businesslike way, through a central office which was filled with pin-dotted maps and staffed with paid party workers.[39]

The approach of R. B. Creager and W. E. Talbot, the GOP's first executive director, to party organization was the result of a coalition of nonpolitical experience: the former's experience as a real estate promoter and the latter's experience as a Dallas area sales manager for Hupmobile and other automobile manufacturers. The Hays scheme for fund-raising, for example, involved practices such as the installment payment program which were common in both mail-order real estate and automobile sales. The pin-on-the-map approach to political organization, in which a chairman in every county was the goal, was also generalized from business practice: before one organized the sale either of automobiles or of the Republican party, local agents had to be recruited. But in contrast to the automobile business, where a dealer might work to hold his franchise, in the Republican party organization Creager and Talbot often had to be content to locate a postmaster (frequently a Democrat), who would agree to nominal service as Republican county chairman. Though a county chairman might make no move to build electoral strength for the party, he would still be a necessary part of party organization, as occasionally required by law, and he would hold down a post which could, potentially, be won by an opponent of the Creager organization. Such county leaders were scarcely the most desirable of subordinates. Creager and Talbot seem to have held the hope that a pep talk, an admonitory letter, or a friendly phone call would stir local men to some show of activity on special occasions. Thus in 1922 Creager wrote Charles Hubbard, a member of the Republican National Committee:

The Director of Organization is constantly hammering our county chairmen to compel them to keep their county committees at full strength. The tendency, as by experience you doubtless know, is to permit county organizations to go to pieces, through death, moving away, or entire inattention to the political affairs of the precinct chairman.

Creager carefully avoided telling Hubbard that the prairie-dog county postmasters who formed a significant part of his paper organization and enabled him to control county and state conventions did not normally care about county committees or precinct affairs. Nor did Creager expect them to do so.[40] Yet when special occasions warranted some semblance of action, Creager and Talbot usually had most success in urging activity from federal employees who swelled the rank of party officialdom. A look at the list of Republican officials of 1928 indicates the party's reliance on federal jobholders.

In 1928, thirty-six county chairmen were postmasters and thirty-two other county chairmen were married to postmasters. In the Thirty-First Senatorial District, the Panhandle, perhaps a political microcosm of the Republican party in the South, thirteen out of twenty-six chairmen were either postmasters or married to postmasters. At least six members of the Republican State Executive Committee were in this employ. Inadvertently, Roy B. Nichols, postmaster at Houston, Texas, told Senator Smith W. Brookhardt that he had made the acquaintance of "most of the postmasters in Texas holding, at least, offices of the first and second class" by attending Republican state conventions since 1916. Nichols had not intended to suggest that the state organization was effectively run through the manipulation of patronage and control of federal officeholders, but he gave the game away.[41]

Strict adherence to the legal guidelines for party organization also worked to Creager's advantage in regard to the Republican State Executive Committee, which functioned in the name of the state party between biennial conventions. According to state law, executive committees of *regulated* parties contained two members from each of the state's senatorial districts; the members were nominated in district conventions and confirmed by the state convention, sitting as a committee-of-the-whole. In the event of vacancies on the committee between conventions, the committee itself was empowered to appoint members from the various districts. The state executive committee, after the state convention, was the group which Creager, or any party manager, for that matter, had to work with and through. The executive committee elected the state chairman, who was theoretically the head of the party in Texas. In fact, the national committeeman was normally more powerful by virtue of his real or presumed connections in Washington. The national committeeman's presence at state committee meetings was not provided for by law. He functioned as an official of the national committee which appointed him; and he was not, strictly speaking, an official of the Texas Republican party. There was nothing in the law, however, to bar the national committeeman from attending state executive committee meetings. Creager usually did so.[42]

The election of two members to the state executive committee from each state senatorial district effectively placed the control of the party in the hands of the back-country delegates. Drawn in 1921 by the Thirty-Seventh Legislature, the Texas senatorial district lines were not redrawn until 1951. The result was the continued proportional overrepresentation in state conventions and on the state committee of rural and strongly Democratic areas, at the expense of urban areas and German counties, which contained the bulk of Republican voters. The effect of this basis of selection on Republican organization is clearly reflected when census data are introduced. The census of 1940 serves as a reasonable example. The Tenth Senatorial District, which consisted of Collin, Hunt, Rains, and Rockwall counties, had a population of 110,368; the Eleventh District, Dallas County, 398,564; the Sixteenth, Harris County, 528,961; the Twenty-Sixth, Bexar County, 359,140; and the Twenty-Seventh, Hidalgo, Nueces, and Cameron counties, 463,684. Each district had the same representation on the Republican State Executive Committee. Representational distortion is more pronounced with regard to the Republican vote than to the entire vote because the overrepresented rural areas were strongly Democratic. Thus, in 1920, 56.2 percent of the whole vote for the Republican gubernatorial candidate was cast in Bexar

County, the Twenty-Sixth District, whereas in the rural counties (Bell, Bosque, Coryell, Erath, Hamilton, and Cos) which made up the Twenty-First District, the Republican candidate received less than 5 percent of the statewide total.[43] As one of Creager's opponents charged before the Republican National Committee in 1924: "The control of the Republican convention of Texas is turned over to rattlesnakes and Democrats of West Texas . . . . I use the terms in the order of their venom."[44]

The election of members of the Republican state committee on the basis of state senatorial districts produced a committee whose membership could be easily managed. Though Republican votes and donors were concentrated in Bexar, Dallas, and Harris counties, and in the twelve rural German counties, these areas sent only ten members to serve on the committee. With the national committeeman's control of federal patronage ensuring the loyalty of back-country committee members, the state executive committee was not likely to pose any threat to his leadership of the party. Such a threat would have to involve the unlikely combination of committee members from both the urban and the prairie-dog counties: this happened only once, in 1946.[45]

Under Creager's guidance, the state committee had broad functions. At its meeting in Dallas on June 14, 1926, for example, it set up the first Republican primary in Texas. Nineteen members were present—eighteen by proxy. State Chairman Eugene Nolte, who had formerly earned $4,000 per year as a U.S. marshal, presided; the lone member present, postal employee Heber Page of Dallas, successively moved to certify Republican candidates in the primary election, set a date and location for the state convention, appointed fifteen new county chairmen, and appointed W. E. Parsons of Port Neches to the state executive committee to succeed Dr. W. T. McAlpin, who resigned. All motions were routinely seconded by Creager as an *ex-officio* member of the committee, who also cast eighteen proxy votes. This was, to say the least, a tidy way of doing business.[46]

State and district conventions were handled with similar dispatch. According to the letter of the law, district conventions should have been important. Some of the delegates to the national conventions and members of the state convention were chosen in these conclaves. Yet district meetings were, in fact, sparsely attended because they were often held at the conclusion of the more important business of the state convention. They were generally as cut-and-dried as state meetings. Creager and other party leaders lined up support for their candidates by controlling the selection of a substantial number of delegates to the state convention through the appointive power of the state committee. The night before the state meeting convened, Creager, Eugene Nolte, T. P. Lee, and a score or so of other close associates customarily decided the business of the state and district conventions at a preconvention, invitation-only party. When the party was over, the business of both conventions was effectively transacted.[47] Yet all this fit the letter of the law. Framed with the Democratic party in mind, Texas election laws produced a Republican party which was open to narrowly based control by its top officials. More specifically, the allocation of one county delegate to the state convention for each three hundred (or major fraction thereof) votes cast in the county for the party's gubernatorial candidate in the preceding general election gave the prairie dog counties and other strongly Democratic areas a large vote in the Republican convention.

The influence of the urban Republican and rural counties in the party was further diminished by the representation system within the state convention, unchanged from 1901 to 1951. The 1946 state convention, in which Creager received a rare setback, is an important example of a "stacked" convention. Delegates were allotted on the basis of the vote cast for B. J. Peasley, the party's gubernatorial candidate in 1944. Under the delegate selection formula, one-delegate counties held 222 of 449 seats. From this group of counties, Peasley had received less than ten votes in each of eight counties, which sent 10.3 percent of the convention delegates. Loving County accounted for .000,004 percent of Peasley's vote, but the county chose .02 percent of the delegates to the convention. Four voters selected Peasley; presumably, one of their number attended the state convention two years later, as the Loving County delegate. In terms of convention representation in 1946, one Republican voter in Loving County weighed equally with seventy-five voters in Bexar County. This situation produced the possibility of an easily managed convention, as long as patronage and finesse were used to control back-country delegations. Perhaps the most accurate assessment of "Creagerism" was offered by an editorial writer of the *Dallas Morning News* in 1932: "It is bossism in Sunday clothes."[48]

In 1927, Representative Harry Wurzbach turned to the Democratic legislature for reform of the GOP. He persuaded sympathetic Democrats to introduce the so-called Eichenrodt bill which proposed a radical readjustment of the apportioning formula. The measure provided that no county would receive representation at Republican district or state con-

ventions if fewer than fifty voters had cast ballots for the party's gubernatorial candidate in the preceding general election. The proposed measure
would have both diminished the post office vote and enlarged the delegations from Wurzbach's district and from Dallas County, both of which
Creager frequently failed to control. Had the measure passed, one-quarter
of the counties would have lost representation altogether; and the three
largest metropolitan counties would have obtained a clear majority in
the state convention. Creager's system of party management and control
would have collapsed. Not surprisingly, Creager worked to defeat the
measure. He warned Democratic State Senator Thomas B. Love of Dallas
that the bill "would very probably lead to retaliatory legislation in Republican states." Though it is not certain that Creager's warning led the
Democratic legislature to defeat the Eichenrodt Bill, one may safely assume Creager's sincerity when he expressed "sincere appreciation" to Love
for the Democrat's aid in killing the reform legislation.[49]

With a firm hold on party apparatus, Republican party leaders
strengthened their grip on the party by utilizing the practical advantages
which followed from adhering to the unreformed law even when their
party was not subject to regulation. Equally important, especially in
terms of overcoming the rowdy image which Reconstruction politics and
the subsequent leadership of E. H. R. Green had given the party, was
the orderly management by Creager and his associates which made the
Republican party seem respectable. By the standards of Texas politics,
it was. The scruffy days of Black-and-Tan shenanigans were over, and
respectable conservative Democrats might potentially be attracted to the
Republican party. The refinement and action of Republican organization,
moreover, would be of tremendous importance in decades to come.[50]

Disunity in the Democratic party made it possible for the Creager
group to develop a friendly relationship with the conservative factions in
that party. Creager occasionally appointed a few Democrats to federal
jobs. In 1929 he recommended former governor O. B. Colquitt to the
U.S. Board of Mediation, in exchange for Colquitt's support of Herbert
Hoover. Creager proved to be especially considerate of Democrats when
the candidates for a federal post were well connected to the Texas press
(the sister of *Dallas Morning News* reporter W. H. Kittrell received a
post office job), or when the candidate was connected to the Democratic
leadership in Texas, as was the brother of State Senator Thomas B. Love,
who received Creager's endorsement for a seat on a federal board. In
turn, Creager's group was spared rough treatment by state regulatory

agencies and occasionally received small favors from Democratic state administrations: Eugene Nolte was appointed to several state commissions and Orville Bullington, the party's candidate for governor in 1932, was later appointed to the board of regents of the University of Texas.[51] Creager, in fact, made capital within Republican ranks of his "personal and intimate friendships with many of the leading Democrats." Presumably, his connections were widespread and powerful.

More important, the cooperation of some conservative Democrats brought the Republican party reasonably close to winning statewide office on three occasions. In 1922, George B. Peddy, thirty-year-old Harris County district attorney and a Democrat, received about one-third of the total vote for United States senator, running as the Republican candidate in opposition to Earl Mayfield, who received the Democratic nomination with Klan backing after a bitter primary election. Under the circumstances of his race, Peddy's showing was unusually strong. The state party raised only $10,000 for Peddy, and he was not even listed on the official ballot and had to be written in. In 1924, University of Texas law professor George Butte ran well, with covert Klan backing, against Mrs. Miriam A. Ferguson. In 1932, when Orville Bullington opposed Mrs. Ferguson, he ran more than three hundred thousand votes ahead of Herbert Hoover's electors in Texas. It is not surprising, then, that Creager and most other Republican leaders often claimed that Republican victories would only result from occasional temporary coalitions with disgruntled Democrats like Thomas B. Love and Oscar B. Colquitt and that the long-term growth prospects of the Republican party rested on its ability to woo conservatives away from the Democratic party.[52]

In the short run, Creager's political and personal fortune depended on his ability to maintain his control over the Texas Republican party and to gain patronage and favors from the federal establishment. In actual fact, the two factors were interrelated. Without patronage and influence, Creager would have been forced to rely on his control of the party apparatus and on his own considerable skills to keep his hold on party leadership. During the 1920s, his heyday, Creager's regime was subject to severe attacks from some unhappy Republicans, several highly influential members of Congress, and two muckraking journalists, but these attacks failed to bring Creager down. They did, however, inflict serious political wounds, though he skillfully concealed this damage from public view. Control over the Texas Republican organization, which he developed to his taste, survived attack.

2

A Fight over Tangible Benefits

BY 1928, ONLY ONE MAN presented a challenge to R. B. Creager's hold on the Texas Republican party. This was Congressman Harry Wurzbach. Wurzbach, however, was quite enough opposition for any politician to manage. From his election in 1920 until his death in 1931, Wurzbach kept Creager from resting comfortably in the apparent security of his position and power. More important, the Creager-Wurzbach rivalry critically retarded the political development of the party. Energy, intelligence, and money which might well have bolstered Republican organization during the 1920s were dissipated during the bitter factional dispute. Wurzbach enlisted the aid of allies in Congress and won the support of sympathetic journalists; but in the end, he was no match for Creager. The Red Fox of the Rio Grande maintained tight control over the state party, harassed Wurzbach's allies with the help of loyal supporters in the Internal Revenue Service, and dogged Wurzbach with a lawsuit, which the politically compliant Justice Department pressed to the day of the congressman's death. For more than a decade, Creager and Wurzbach waged intraparty battles, to their mutual disadvantage.

As the first Texas Republican in Congress in twenty years, Wurzbach was, at least initially, the exception to the Texas political rule; but for his time in office, Democrats held all Texas seats in Congress until 1950.[1]

The election of the short, stocky, gregarious Wurzbach in 1920 was an unforeseen consequence of the Harding landslide in Bexar County, where party operation headed by Frank E. Scobey brought in the strongest Republican vote in all of Texas. Wurzbach had been a county judge in rural Guadalupe County before his election and was unknown to leaders of the Republican state party and voters outside his area. After he was sworn in, however, he became difficult to ignore. He pressed aggressively for pork barrel legislation for his district and for control of a sizable share of the federal patronage in Texas. With one significant exception Wurzbach controlled all post office appointments in his district, and he had a voice in appointments to federal judicial positions in the Western District of Texas; this arrangement followed established precedent for recognition of patronage rights of congressmen. Had Wurzbach been a less ambitious person, this distribution of power might have held up; and he might never have run afoul of the Creager group.[2] On the other hand, had Creager and his friends been more generous in patronage matters, Wurzbach might not have ended up in opposition to them.

Despite his warfare with Creager, in Congress Wurzbach seems to have accepted the prescribed modest status of the freshman representative with little difficulty. As something of a novelty—a southern Republican—he received a post on the Military Affairs Committee, a special advantage because of the economic significance of army installations in San Antonio. In Congress, Wurzbach loyally voted and, more rarely, spoke on his party's side of two principal issues—tariffs and the Muscle Shoals project. After pork barrel legislation, protective tariffs were Wurzbach's most durable interest during his congressional career. He campaigned on a high tariff platform in 1920 and in every campaign thereafter; in so doing, he won the support of John Henry Kirby and of his Southern Protective Association for the duration of his time in Congress. The issue was sufficiently important to the congressman to make debate on the Young Tariff Bill the occasion for his maiden speech. Wurzbach's verbal effort was given over to the addition of hides to the tariff bill as "proof that the Republican party cares about the South!" A good party man in Washington, Wurzbach aimed invective at the leader of the opposition, fellow Texan John Nance Garner, and took particular delight in telling the House of his discovery that the Democrat had once given a protariff speech, which he later had expunged from the *Record*:

You know when I came here, a green boy from the sticks away down in

Texas, I had an idea that everything a man said on this floor was recorded against him, and that if you made a speech on the floor you would certainly find it in the *Record*. I have looked into the *Record*, and on December 22, 1920, I found a note in the Congressional Record to the effect that "Mr. Garner addressed the Committee. His remarks will appear later." (Laughter.) I chased around here foolishly, I find now; I went to see the reporters, and everybody else, and they told me that the speech was not on record at all. (Laughter.) But I will say this: I am so anxious to read a good Republican tariff speech made by a man like John Nance Garner that I will give $50 to any Washington charity if John Garner will give me a copy of that speech. (Laughter and applause.)

According to the record, Wurzbach's wit was appreciated by his Republican colleagues, who interrupted his address seventeen times by applause and nineteen times by laughter. Seven years later, Wurzbach was still warm on the issue of the tariff and hot after John Nance Garner. Garner had abandoned his efforts to include Angora wool on the duty list, and Wurzbach went to the attack:

Think of it, gentlemen of the House, John Garner, of Angora goat fame, left entirely shepherdless and forsaken, the goats upon which his former fame rested. Not only the goats, but the sheep of his county, district, and State were left to their sad fates, so far as the gentleman from Texas was concerned or seemed to care. Little Boy Blue, oh where were you. (Applause.) I wonder what happened to John. I wonder who got John Garner's goat?

The final query is easily answered: Harry Wurzbach. Small wonder that when Wurzbach and Creager locked horns, Garner took care to insert Creager's rebuttals to Wurzbach in the *Congressional Record*.[3]

Wurzbach's rhetorical efforts on the floor of the House did not extend to many subjects. Four times, between 1922 and 1930, he supported Henry Ford's proposal for the leasing of the Muscle Shoals project. In 1922, as a function of his committee assignment, he opposed Democratic attempts to cut the size of the army; three years later he carried an army pension equalization plan to the floor and defended it. In consideration of his sizable German-American constituency, Wurzbach spoke for adjustments of the Alien Property Act in 1923 and for German relief in the following year.[4]

Apart from goading John Nance Garner, the bulk of Wurzbach's energy was given to winning federal funds for projects in his district. Thus, he sponsored measures which proposed the construction of federal

buildings in both Seguin and San Antonio, the improvement of the inter-
coastal channel from Aransas Pass to Corpus Christi, federal funding for
the improvement of the Corpus Christi port, the establishment of Randolph Field at San Antonio, and improvements at Brooks and Kelley
Fields and at Fort San Houston. Behind the scenes, he cooperated with
San Antonio businessmen in their contest with Austin and El Paso leaders to secure the site of the Federal Reserve Branch Bank.[5]

On highly controversial issues, Wurzbach tended to say little and
to vote the party line. Thus, he entered the debate over Secretary of the
Treasury Andrew Mellon's tax program only to spar with John Nance
Garner. During his first term, Wurzbach tried to avoid an open vote on
House Bill 13, the so-called Dyer Anti-Lynching Bill, by supporting the
motion of Representative Hatton Sumners of Dallas to recommit the
measure. After this stratagem failed, by a vote of 119 to 228, Wurzbach
voted with the Republican majority as the bill passed the House with
231 yeas and 119 nays. Significantly, Wurzbach was the only Texas congressman to vote for passage—a fact which was to become a topic of
debate when he campaigned for reelection. But the measure which tied
Wurzbach most directly to the affairs of the Republican party in Texas
was a bill forbidding the sale of patronage, which he introduced in 1926.
Though innocuous in the context of national politics, the measure was
part of a significant and heated round in Wurzbach's long contest with
R. B. Creager over the control of federal patronage in Texas.[6]

Wurzbach was snubbed in two patronage matters: not only was his
candidate for the postmastership in San Antonio turned down, but his
candidate for United States attorney was passed over by Creager in
favor of David Walker, son-in-law of Harry Daugherty, the attorney
general of the United States.[7] As their disagreement grew ever more
heated, Creager decided to destroy Wurzbach by denying him patronage
consideration altogether. No man to take such treatment passively, Wurzbach attempted in turn to oust Creager from the state chairmanship. In
1921 he urged J. G. McNary, a wealthy banker and a Republican leader in El Paso, who had been offered the post of comptroller of currency,
to oppose Creager for the state chairmanship. Unfortunately for Wurzbach, for the time being McNary remained loyal to Creager, who had
engineered the offer of the federal position, and McNary passed copies
of Wurzbach's letters on to Creager.[8]

By 1922 relations between Creager and Wurzbach had become sufficiently hostile for the Republican leadership in Congress to press Presi-

dent Harding for action. Writing to Creager from the White House,
Harding accused Creager of being "less than generous" in accommodating Wurzbach's requests for federal jobs. At the same time, however,
Harding complained to Creager about Wurzbach's disruptive activities
within the Texas party. Through an arranged conference in July, 1922,
Harding forced a temporary reconciliation of the antagonists not long
before the congressional election. Shortly thereafter, Creager reported to
Harding that "our lone Congressman from Texas has removed a large
part of his warpaint." As a result, Creager supported Wurzbach and
raised a modest sum, about $1,250, for the congressman's campaign.
Wurzbach halted his public attacks on Creager's leadership of the Republican party, and on the surface all seemed amicable.[9]

It was just as well for Wurzbach that a temporary truce was declared, for he faced a determined Democratic opponent, Harry Herzberg,
a prominent San Antonio businessman. With the help of John Reed, a
former secretary to Wurzbach, Herzberg made a bold attempt to exploit
powerful racial prejudices in San Antonio. On November 2, 1922, in
a public debate with Wurzbach at San Antonio's Beethoven Hall, the
Democratic challenger attacked Wurzbach's vote for the Dyer Bill—a
"second force Bill" in his view, no less than an attempt to reestablish
Reconstruction government. Herzberg had indeed found an issue to which
the audience responded; the crowd booed and heckled Wurzbach when
he rose for rebuttal. Speaking slowly and firmly over the din, Wurzbach
affirmed that he had indeed voted for the Dyer Bill and promised that
he would vote for it again at the next session of Congress because, he
told the restive audience, "Whenever I think of a lynch mob, I think of
that mad mob which cheered at the crucifixion of Jesus Christ." Most of
the audience rose to applaud the congressman, who had clearly won the
first skirmish of debate. But when his turn came to reply, Herzberg released an even sharper arrow from the same quiver.[10]

Herzberg claimed that he had a copy of a letter of Wurzbach's
which demonstrated the congressman's warm feelings toward blacks. A
black schoolteacher, Mrs. Willie Blount, was cited as the object of Wurzbach's favor; Herzberg claimed that Wurzbach had not only tried to get
her a job in Washington but had also suggested that the schoolteacher
pay a social call on Mrs. Wurzbach when she was in Washington. Herzberg's bombshell once again turned the tables against Wurzbach: the
congressman's campaign manager, seated in the crowded auditorium, was
convinced that the election had just been lost.[11] But Herzberg had not

thought his scheme through and was not prepared for Wurzbach's rejoinder: that the letter was a forgery with which Herzberg was trying to dupe the public.

The strength of Herzberg's strategy of attack was that Mrs. Willie Blount had indeed corresponded with Wurzbach. She had written to the congressman while Reed was serving in the Washington office and had asked if Wurzbach could find her a job in the capital. Reed remembered the correspondence when Wurzbach fired him, and he removed the file copy of it from Wurzbach's office. In August, 1922, a mysterious "Mr. Jones" visited Mrs. Blount at her home. "Jones," whose identity was never uncovered, told the schoolteacher that he represented Wurzbach. The congressman, he explained, was trying to develop an appeal to black voters in his district; Mrs. Blount could be of great service to him by certifying that he had helped her secure employment in Washington and had invited her to call on his wife. Mrs. Blount obliged.

At the time of Herzberg's dramatic disclosure, Wurzbach thought that Herzberg had actually obtained Mrs. Blount's letter: he was unaware that his opponent had only the unsigned file copy which Reed had supplied. Thinking rapidly, Wurzbach charged that the presumed signature was a forgery, a fact which could be proved by verifying that no copy of the letter was to be found in his files in Washington. Wurzbach told the audience that he would immediately send a telegram to a fellow congressman, Frederick L. Lehlbach, a Republican from Newark, New Jersey, asking him to check Wurzbach's files for the letter and to send an answer back to several neutral monitors in San Antonio. Wurzbach promised to withdraw from the election if Lehlbach found a copy of the Blount letter. His audience was suitably impressed—unaware of the close personal friendship of the congressmen. The next day, local newspapers picked up Wurzbach's forged letter story, which was strengthened by Lehlbach's report that there was no copy of the letter in Wurzbach's files.[12]

Herzberg's feelings are readily surmised. With the knowledge that he had the genuine file copy of the letter, Herzberg could derive no comfort from Lehlbach's promise to search Wurzbach's files. For his part, Wurzbach knew that his old friend Frederick Lehlbach would certainly destroy the copy if he found it. After he learned from Mrs. Blount that she still had the original, signed copy of the letter, and after Lehlbach informed him that there actually was no copy in the files, Wurzbach suspected that his opponent had an unsigned carbon copy. The copy

alone would never stand as adequate evidence that he had ever corresponded with Mrs. Blount. He then proceded to exploit the "forgery"
issue for all it was worth. He announced the appointment of a committee
of five San Antonio bankers, whose number included several active Democrats, to judge the presumed signature on Herzberg's copy of the letter.

Obviously, Herzberg could not submit the file copy for the bankers'
scrutiny. His failure to do so presumably convinced many voters that
Wurzbach's forgery claim was correct. Several days before the election,
Wurzbach obtained Mrs. Blount's signature on an affidavit to the effect
that she had never received a letter from the congressman; a Mr. Jones
had obtained her picture and her endorsement of Wurzbach under the
guise of working in the congressman's behalf. Herzberg could do nothing. Having created a sensation with the forgery issue, Wurzbach rallied
support by pointing to his success in obtaining Randolph Field for San
Antonio and deep water port facilities for Corpus Christi. With these
accomplishments and an endorsement by General John J. "Blackjack"
Pershing in his favor, Wurzbach defeated his opponent easily, by a margin of more than three thousand votes. As a public demonstration of
Republican unity, R. B. Creager sent him a congratulatory telegram.[13]

The presidentially imposed rapprochement between Wurzbach and
the Creager organization did not outlive Harding. Soon after the President's death, Wurzbach renewed his efforts to exercise strong patronage
powers through the entire state. The congressman openly maintained
ties with the Taft-McGregor faction and with remnants of the Black and
Tan faction, and kept an alert eye on the development of factions in
Dallas County. When McGregor died in October, 1923, Wurzbach attempted to block Creager from the succession to the office of Republican national committeeman for Texas by endorsing the undeclared candidacy of T. P. Lee, a wealthy Houston businessman and erstwhile
Creager ally.[14] His attempt at opposition came to nothing.

Shortly after his appointment to the National Committee, however,
Creager came under a blistering attack from another congressional quarter. Senator James Thomas Heflin, a Democrat from Alabama, chaired a
subcommittee investigating allegations of mail fraud in Texas. Turning
a good cause to a politically useful end, Heflin directed attention at
Republicans and alleged political favoritism in the Department of Justice. Heflin charged that Creager, who was president of the Alamo Land
and Sugar Company and represented both the Rio Grande Land Company and the W. E. Stewart Land Company, had interfered with an in-

vestigation in 1921 by interceding with Postmaster General Hays and Attorney General Daugherty. Heflin claimed that J. M. Donaldson, a post office investigator in Kansas City, was removed because of alleged prejudice against Creager and that his prudent successor, O. B. Williamson, "limited his inquiries to the Lincoln, Nebraska, office of the C. H. Swallow Land Company," in which neither Creager nor his friends held any investment.

Heflin's star witnesses, in a hearing which was generally shy of concrete evidence, were Mr. and Mrs. George C. Brownell of Watertown, South Dakota. Describing their experience in Hidalgo County, the Brownells complained: "We were shown an alfalfa field which they said could be cut eleven times a year." The Brownells claimed that they were liquored up, given a whirlwind tour, and signed up on their return trip to San Antonio. The testimony of the unfortunate Brownells was not sufficient basis for a solid case against Creager, so Heflin took his findings to the press, exclaiming, "If I can get the investigation I want, I believe we can put him [Creager] in the penitentiary," and the details of this scandal "will make the Teapot Dome look like a May morning zephyr." Creager's rejoinder called Heflin's attack "scurrilous, slanderous, and cowardly" and answered that Creager had actually requested a Justice Department investigation. (For the record, it must be noted that there is no evidence of Justice Department action.) Creager further asserted that Heflin was merely a tool of the Ku Klux Klan and of Senator Earl Mayfield of Texas, who wished to discredit him. Not surprisingly, Heflin denied both charges, and Creager never succeeded in making them stick. At the end of Heflin's probe into mail fraud, no legal indictments were returned on the basis of the committee's meager findings. Moreover, Creager's loyalty to President Coolidge, and the President's presumed gratitude, effectively barred inquiry by the Justice Department. Creager thus escaped legal action, but his personal reputation was sullied.[15]

With his problems in Washington, Creager successfully kept his intraparty difficulties from public view. In 1924 Creager included Wurzbach on the Texas delegation to the Republican National Convention. That same fall, Wurzbach won reelection by a margin of more than twelve thousand votes. Creager played no part in this campaign; presumably he was not asked to raise funds or to offer an official endorsement. Having overcome Wurzbach's attempts to gain control of the party, the national committeeman stayed entirely out of the contest.

Creager made no open moves against Wurzbach, though he continued his tacit support of the anti-Wurzbach faction in the San Antonio Republican party.

The uneasy truce in the Creager-Wurzbach rivalry did not last long beyond the election. Without the mediating force of an active President at the head of their party, there was nothing to prevent the recurring collision of the two men's political ambitions. By the time of the first Republican party primary election in Texas, in the spring of 1926, Wurzbach had stirred up Creager, bringing him into open opposition to his candidacy. Wurzbach renewed hostilities by attacking Creager's leadership of the Texas party, using the House of Representatives as his platform and congressional immunity as his chief weapon. He repeatedly charged that Creager was extorting political funds from federal officeholders, referring to the Hays scheme; he asserted that Creager's main political business was the trading of delegates to the national conventions in exchange for patronage and other favors from the party's successful presidential candidate. To highlight his dispute with Creager, Wurzbach introduced two bills which would have required federal officeholders to swear that they had not paid for their positions either with political support for presidential candidates or with cash contributions. (The bills apparently died in committee.) Wurzbach maintained that Creager worked to stunt the growth of the Republican party in Texas in order to facilitate his own influence and to make patronage-mongering less complex. Nor did Wurzbach stop there: he charged both that Creager tried to bring about the defeat of Republicans in Texas to facilitate his control of patronage and that Creager's fund-raising schemes amounted to raids on the taxpayer: "This money comes out of the Treasury and goes into the coffers of the State organization for building up the patronage machine." Creager responded with a thinly veiled threat: "If Mr. Wurzbach, who recently criticized the handling of Texas patronage on the floor of the House fails to be renominated, it will be solely and alone because of his own folly and for no other reason."[16]

Congressman Wurzbach's charges were little more than a repetition of notions broadly held in Congress regarding the functions and leadership of the Republican party in the South. The leaders of the GOP in the House supported Wurzbach's charges. U.S. Representative Will Wood of Indiana, chairman of the Congressional Committee of the Republican party, advised Creager that his committee "condemned without a dissenting vote, your attitude toward Representative Wurzbach." For maximum effect, Wood sent his statement both to President Coolidge and to the press. His action was reinforced by Representative Tilson of Connecticut, House majority leader, who sent a sharp warning to Creager:

If by reason of the course now being pursued by your organization, which calls itself Republican and which is enjoying the direct benefits of a Republican administration, the House shall lose the only Republican member it has had in recent years from the State of Texas, it is our intention to see that the blame is placed where it belongs.

The *New York Times* commented on the dispute between Wurzbach and Creager, attributing to the latter an overriding interest in patronage: "The Federal loaves and fishes must be fed only to the faithful, the national and state committeemen. An intruding Republican Representative like Judge Wurzbach is a superfluous unwelcome hand at the scramble. Keep the grab-bag out of his reach." The *New York Times* gave editorial support to Wurzbach's claim that Creager was merely a patronage wholesaler. Neither Wurzbach nor his charges did much to weaken Creager's position in the Texas party, but the onslaught of congressional criticism did undermine Creager's reputation in Washington, the source of the jobs and favors which maintained his position at home. One way or another, such punishing attacks had to end, either through reconciliation with Wurzbach or through his defeat at election time. The former course had been tried. It had failed.[17]

Led by State Chairman Eugene Nolte, Wurzbach's opponents fought back in San Antonio, and it was soon obvious that physical violence was not ruled out in party warfare. A meeting of the Bexar County Republican Executive Committee on June 23, 1926, was disrupted by fistfights; the meeting was finally adjourned when San Antonio police appeared to quell the burgeoning riot. On the next night, A. A. Luter, Wurzbach's campaign manager and floor leader for Wurzbach at the previous night's meeting, was found unconscious at campaign headquarters. Both the fisticuffs and Luter's condition received attention as far away as New York, where the *Times* reported: "When he was revived, he declared that he had been attacked by two masked men, one assailant beat him with a revolver and the other with a milk bottle. He was severely bruised about the head."[18] Three weeks later, on July 14, 1926, Creager, Eugene Nolte, and other Republican leaders met in San Antonio to plan a strategy for Wurzbach's defeat. On previous occasions the congressman's control over the conventions of the Fourteenth Congressional District had made it impossible for them to push him out of office. But because the Republican party was required to hold its first primary that year, an unusual opportunity to dispose of Wurzbach emerged. Creager and his friends decided to sponsor a Republican opponent to Wurzbach in the primary.[19]

The Creager group's initial move took advantage of a provision of the state law which permitted party officials to set primary filing fees. The group designated $1,250, an unusually high amount, for the congressional seat. Wurzbach offered to pay it; they raised the figure to $7,500. At this point, Wurzbach objected to the attempt by the "machine" to crowd him out of the race and made a major issue of his previous opposition to "Boss Creager." Wurzbach refused to pay the stipulated fee, though he had sufficient funds; and he proposed that his own organization furnish the primary election personnel—election judges and tellers—who would otherwise have to be paid by the party. This clever move, which would have left the electoral machinery in Wurzbach's control, was rejected by his opponent, Frederick Knetsch. Creager and Knetsch had already decided that anti-Wurzbach Republicans would be rewarded with the posts of election judges and tellers, placing the electoral apparatus in their own control. After additional public wrangling between Wurzbach on one hand and Knetsch and Creager on the other, the issue was finally settled in Wurzbach's favor by the district court in Bexar County, which ruled against the levying of the $7,500 filing fee.[20]

Having lost the disputes over election personnel and legal technicalities, Creager, Nolte, Dr. F. L. Thompson, state party treasurer, and Mrs. J. C. Griswold, national committeewoman for Texas, actively entered the campaign against Wurzbach by appearing at a Knetsch rally in San Antonio on July 21. In an attempt to drive a wedge between the congressman and Republican party members, Creager scored Wurzbach as being divisive and claimed that the congressman was really a Democrat at heart and that he became a Republican, in 1912, only after Eugene Nolte told him that he could arrange his election as Guadalupe County judge if Wurzbach would run as a Republican. Appealing to the congressman's practical-minded supporters, Creager claimed that Wurzbach's patronage and pork barrel usefulness in Washington was at an end. For the sake of the party and the district, the committeeman urged the defeat of the congressman in the primary.[21]

Congressman Wurzbach replied at a rally at Beethoven Hall on July

25, the night before the primary election. He retorted that Creager had amassed a fund of $100,000 to defeat him and threatened that if Knetsch backers tried anything dishonest on election day they would all end up in a federal penitentiary. He tarred Creager as the "kept" attorney and political influence peddler of the locally unpopular Missouri Pacific Railroad, whose opposition to the construction of the Southern Pacific lines in West Texas Wurzbach claimed he defeated, single-handedly, as an act of principle. Making a strong appeal to the emotions of black voters in East San Antonio, he claimed that lily-white Republicans such as Creager and Nolte would sell them back into slavery if the opportunity ever presented itself. Wurzbach dismissed Knetsch as a stalking-horse, whose sole function was to knock him out of the race so that the Democratic candidate, A. D. Rogers, would win in November. Wurzbach's personal popularity and his skillful use of the Boss Creager issue decided the contest. When the primary election returns came in, Wurzbach defeated Knetsch by a margin of five to one; and Ed Lyons, a Wurzbach backer, had replaced Karl Holzschuher as Bexar County Republican chairman. Once again Wurzbach turned a tight situation to his advantage. In the general election, which followed "a gumshoe campaign," Wurzbach won easily over his Democratic opponent.[22]

During his attacks on Creager, Harry Wurzbach loudly advertised the sham of Republican organization in Texas. In 1926 Wurzbach told his colleagues in the United States House of Representatives:

Patronage is the beginning and end, the alpha and omega, of political interest and activity of Republican state organizations in Texas and other Southern states. In exchange for the patronage they receive, they deliver the delegate votes to Republican National Conventions. The national committeemen handle one end of the patronage delegate exchange system, and usually the Postmaster General handles the other end. Party loyalty—loyalty to party principles—does not enter into the consideration of the criminal exchange in the remotest degree. It is a spoils system, pure and simple, without one redeeming quality.[23]

In responding to that allegation, Creager jockeyed numbers, changing party statistics from time to time as the occasion demanded. When he became state chairman in 1921, he claimed that only 68 or 85 counties—he used both figures—were legally organized. Later in the same year, he placed "less than forty" and 85 counties in the unorganized category, ante-Creager. By 1922, he claimed to have set up organizations in 238 counties; finally, in 1929, he claimed to have established county organizations in two of the remaining counties. All the pins were in place. Both Creager's juggling of organizational figures and the statistically contrived attacks of occasional detractors were grandly irrelevant to the electoral fortunes of the Republican party in Texas. A majority of the population in Texas, and nearly all the Republican voters, were concentrated in forty counties. Clearly, electoral strategy and organizational attention would have been concentrated on these key counties if Creager's primary goal had been the delivery of the vote. By contrast, his creation of an organization based on prairie dogs and postmasters clearly indicates that his *objet fixe* was control of the party apparatus to insure his tenure as national committeeman. Votes were less important than his position.[24]

It was no surprise that, in response to allegations from hostile Texans, national Republican leaders questioned Creager's organization and drove him to continued assurances. In 1929, reassuring President Hoover of the vitality of the Texas Republican organization, Creager claimed to have held 25 regional conferences in the principal cities of Texas. The meetings were attended by from 50 to 250 "leading Republicans and Hoover Democrats." Such a flurry of activity would have been impressive had it taken place.

Once he developed a defense against the charge of deliberately stunting the growth of the Republican party in Texas, Creager used it for more than a decade. The national committeeman or, more often, his spokesman, Leonard Withington, claimed that patronage had been used to build a highly developed Republican organization in Texas. In 1926, Withington claimed that there were "legal and functioning organizations in two hundred forty-one of two hundred fifty-four counties; while in 1921, before Creager became State Chairman, only forty counties had been organized." Further evidence offered for the effectiveness of Creager's organization was the occasional presence of Republicans in both houses of the Texas legislature and the record high vote cast for Republican gubernatorial candidate George Butte in 1924. In later versions of this argument, Herbert Hoover's victory in Texas was explained by Creager's organization. Replies to charges were generally made by Withington in the name of the headquarters committee, in an attempt to offset the charge that Creager ran a "one-man party" by offering the appearance of collective leadership.[25]

Though clever and energetic, however, the defense of the Creager organization never laid to rest Wurzbach's most damaging charge, that

Creager and his associates worked the state organization to the exclusive end of controlling national convention delegations, whose votes were bartered for political promises and personal gain. Congressmen, national committeemen, some of the delegates to the 1928 national convention, journalists, and Presidents Coolidge and Hoover all seem to have believed Wurzbach's original charges—in part because they were substantially correct.

Though he received little outward sign of agreement from the Coolidge administration, the congressman was well aware that his attacks on Creager attracted the notice of possible presidential candidates, including Herbert Hoover, then secretary of commerce. Hoover found it difficult to ignore the charges of wholesale corruption brought against Creager; nor could he ignore the potential difficulty which the influential congressman could make for an administration. Consequently, when Hoover became a likely contender for the Republican presidential nomination, Creager took special care to supply him with cogent answers to Wurzbach's charges.[26]

More serious than allegations of corruption was Wurzbach's attempt in 1928 to gain control of the Texas delegation to the Republican National Convention. Had he succeeded, the congressman would surely have unseated Creager. Wurzbach drew on pockets of opposition to Creager, most notably among Republicans in Dallas, Fort Worth, San Antonio, and the German counties, and continued to draw support from remnants of the Black and Tan faction. Allies, such as C. C. Littleton of Fort Worth, George S. Atkinson of Dallas, and Ed Lyon and Frank Scobey, traveled to doubtful counties to line up support for the challenge to Creager. For his part, Wurzbach spent his energies on the upcoming challenge at the state convention; he traveled less than formerly in his congressional district and failed to give adequate attention to his campaign for reelection.

In the end, Wurzbach's efforts came to naught; for in the essential political business of tending to local alliances and maintaining contacts, he was simply no match for Creager. Indeed, even in the Fourteenth District the congressman had never shown much interest in or any talent for the organizational side of politics. He relied on resourceful personal friends like Joe Sheldon, on a gregarious disposition, on highly persuasive platform oratory, and on the congressional pork barrel to see him through his various campaigns. Neither an abstract issue nor tangible organization was ever a large part of Harry Wurzbach's individualistic career. Usually sure of his footing in both his district and the House of Representatives, Wurzbach was always off balance in the swifter game of presidential politics. Thus, the congressman found himself in the untenable position of having to oppose Creager in 1928 by heading a delegation which was generally not committed to the nomination of Herbert Hoover, to whom Creager threw his support in the early months of that year. By the time Wurzbach made his challenge, Creager had already attached himself to the most likely candidate. Moreover, Creager served as the spokesman for a group of national committeemen who sought to advance Hoover's candidacy by pressuring President Coolidge into an early and reluctant denial of his own candidacy. When Coolidge finally announced that he would not seek another term, Creager pressed for the advantage, quickly endorsing Hoover and announcing that he would receive all the votes of the Texas delegation to the national convention.[27]

Creager's handsome endorsement did place him in the vanguard of the forces of the man most likely to win, but it also created an avenue of opportunity for the Wurzbach faction. Though the national committeeman's estimate of the Texas party's attitude toward Hoover was probably accurate, he had done little to determine what that attitude was. In fact, he did not even bother to confer with the state chairman, Eugene Nolte, before he issued his sweeping endorsement of Hoover and promise of the Texas delegation's votes. After some objection was made to his cavalier pronouncement, Creager sent explanatory and conciliatory letters to the members of the headquarters and state executive committees; but he did not succeed in offsetting considerable resentment in party ranks. Wurzbach set out to exploit this discontent and to organize opposition to Creager for a challenge at the May state convention, which would name the delegates to the June convention of the national party.[28]

In spite of this activity, however, the elements of opposition to Creager never coalesced into a serious problem for the state organization. Wurzbach's forces carried only his own constituency, the Fourteenth Congressional District, and even this slim victory was lost when the state convention named Dr. F. L. Thompson and other anti-Wurzbach Republicans from his district as delegates to the national convention. Shut out of the Texas delegation, Wurzbach bolted the Texas state convention with his "uninstructed slate"; he left control of the regular convention in the hands of Hoover and Creager forces, but he had not given up the fight.[29]

In June Wurzbach's Texas delegation presented itself at the Republican National Convention in Chicago. Though not unanimous in opinion, the Republican National Committee voted after a lengthy hearing to recommend the seating of the Creager delegation. Not all members of the committee sided with the veteran Texas member. Mark Requa, the national committeeman for California and a close associate of Herbert Hoover, questioned him particularly sharply. Because Wurzbach continued to press his case, the contending delegations then appeared before the credentials committee of the convention. The main argument of the Wurzbach group involved the right of state conventions to name district delegates to the national convention in contravention of the decisions of the district conventions. Denying this right, Wurzbach contested the Creager delegation from his own congressional district. He argued that the precedent of national conventions was firmly on his side and that the state convention was not properly constituted under Texas law; hence its decisions were invalid. District conventions, in his argument, selected delegates to the state convention and thence to the national convention. Creager countered that under Texas law the state convention was required to name all delegates; technically, this included the naming of those who represented congressional districts.

The committee, strongly tied to Hoover's candidacy, decided in Creager's favor by a two-to-one margin, but only after a great deal of highly damaging material was read into the record against him. Wurzbach, for example, once again leveled charges that Creager's organization aimed at controlling patronage and losing elections. In Wurzbach's presentation, the Texas party was a sort of Potemkin village, existing for the most part on paper and solely for political effect. As evidence, Wurzbach offered signed depositions from the clerks of 128 Texas counties; they certified that there was no legal Republican organization in their counties. Through a damaging oversight, Creager's side never challenged the truth of the charge or the reliability of the evidence on which it rested. Yet Wurzbach's charge that Creager misrepresented the number of organized counties was serious: Creager's defense against Wurzbach's barrage of allegations referred time and again to the number of counties Creager had organized.[30]

Congressman Wurzbach's protectionist friends, supported by members of the Progressive wing of the party, then carried the attack against Creager to the floor of the national convention, but with no more success than they had enjoyed earlier. Supported by the southern delegations, including the twenty-six votes of the contested Texas delegation, Creager won out by a vote of $659\frac{1}{2}$ to $399\frac{1}{2}$. The battle finally over, Wurzbach and his friends left for Union Station in Chicago and the train back to San Antonio. They had lost the battle, but the victor had sustained serious wounds in an especially vulnerable area: his relations with the presidential candidate. Fully aware of the possible effect on Herbert Hoover of Wurzbach's convention disclosures, Creager mounted an extensive public relations campaign which attempted, with partial success, to rebuild his standing with his party's nominee. Most of Hoover's close political associates received lengthy personal letters from Leonard Withington, who offered a polished version of Creager's standard defense.[31]

More important than argument was Creager's ability to deliver the vote. If his early and handsome endorsement of Hoover can be explained as enlightened self-interest, there is still no doubt that Creager's action, early in 1928, gave substantial assistance to the presidential aspirant. Creager did not waver in his support of Hoover. Yet the national committeeman from Texas found Hoover much less congenial than either Harding or Coolidge: even the chilly Coolidge acknowledged more commitment to Creager than Hoover did.

It is possible that relative political inexperience contributed to Hoover's aloofness toward Creager. Thanks to Harry Wurzbach, the way in which Creager used his power in Texas had been the subject of public attention and political controversy since 1926. Calvin Coolidge, long acquainted with facts of state-level political life before his election as vice-president in 1920, was neither surprised nor repelled by a powerful national committeeman who used his power as Murray Crane had used his in Massachusetts. By contrast to his stolid predecessor, Hoover had never held elective office before 1928. A brilliant manager of both men and material, Hoover found the mechanics of intraparty politics unfamiliar and somewhat distasteful. Even politics was not to make him a comfortable bedfellow of R. B. Creager. The Texan appeared to thrive on intraparty maneuvers which, if Wurzbach were to be believed, were, at the least, of a rather shady nature. In the forum of public opinion, the questions Wurzbach raised at the national convention in 1928 received no satisfactory answers.[32]

Creager had, however, realistically high expectations of carrying Texas for Hoover with the support of conservative anti-Smith Democrats. Even if Creager's methods and character were suspect, Hoover, once in the White House, would still be bound to carry through on his part of a standard political bargain. There was only one potential difficulty: such an exchange of votes for favors might be difficult for Creager to exploit if Harry Wurzbach were still in Congress building seniority, acquiring additional allies, and pressing for favors from the White House from an increasingly strong and influential position. Worse yet, close Hoover associates such as Walter Newton and Mark Requa were openly opposed to Creager and publicly committed to Wurzbach. From Creager's point of view, it was imperative to retire Congressman Wurzbach in the November elections in 1928, while carrying Texas for Hoover.

The Republican campaign for Herbert Hoover in 1928 was a model of businesslike organization. According to the Hoover-Curtis Organization Bureau, Texas had Hoover-Curtis Victory Club chairmen in 249 of 254 counties; and these clubs had a total enrollment of about 60,000 members. College clubs had been organized on seven campuses, and 2,461 "Hoover Hostesses" had been enrolled from the various Texas towns to brighten campaign rallies. Business and trade organizations produced dozens of Hoover-Curtis Clubs; they included everyone from aviators, clay product manufacturers, chiropractors, and harness and saddle makers to doctors, lawyers, teachers, and advertising executives. On paper, at least, the campaign in Texas produced a record number of voluntary organizations and volunteer workers.[33]

More significant in Hoover's victory in Texas, however, were the exertions of the various groups of conservative Democrats. One faction, led by State Senator Thomas B. Love, formerly Democratic national committeeman for Texas, had earlier refused to support Mrs. Miriam Ferguson, the Democratic gubernatorial nominee in 1924. During the Hoover-Smith campaign, the Love faction again supported the Republican candidate, as did random groups of prohibitionists, anti-Catholics, and leaders of the once-powerful Ku Klux Klan, many of whom supported Herbert Hoover in 1928.[34] The polyglot Democrats for Hoover, "anti-Al Smith Democrats," as they styled themselves, carried their appeal to Democrats apart from that of the Republicans; but the dissidents ran their loosely coordinated campaign from an office which conveniently adjoined that of the Republican Headquarters Committee in Dallas. According to a postcampaign report of expenditures, the Democrats spent $29,157.04 of the $59,805.68 raised for the Hoover campaign in Texas. Much to the dismay of Republican workers and leaders, the anti-Al Smith Democrats spent a great deal more money than they raised and passed unpaid bills along to the GOP, thus placing Republican party finances in sad shape after the election.[35] Nevertheless, following the election the Republican leaders refrained from public criticism of the Hoover Democrats. The dissident Democrats had carried the state for Hoover by bringing over normally Democratic counties such as Jefferson (Beaumont), McLennan (Waco), Dallas, Harris, and Cameron, while Smith's religion and his advocacy of repeal of the Volstead Act had carried him through in important Republican counties, Bexar and Guadalupe. The statewide Democratic defections to Hoover more than offset these losses and enabled Hoover to win the state's electoral votes with 51.9 percent of the presidential vote in Texas.[36] Naturally, R. B. Creager was well pleased by the results. Even the loss of San Antonio had its brighter side: Harry Wurzbach was at last in trouble.

Running against what proved to be a strong wet and Catholic vote for Al Smith, Harry Wurzbach encountered his most serious challenger since 1920, when he defeated then incumbent Congressman Carlos Bee. The Democrats were after all as anxious to regain Wurzbach's seat as Creager was to unseat him. The Democratic nominee for Congress from the Fourteenth Texas District was August McCloskey, judge of Bexar County since 1920. Running in the most populous county of the district, the popular judge would at least hold down Wurzbach's margin in an otherwise safe county and perhaps leave him open to defeat through votes from such strongly Democratic areas as Corpus Christi. McCloskey conducted an aggressive campaign; by election eve he stood a good chance of improving on previous Democratic showings.

Seeing their deliverance in McCloskey, Creager and Nolte gave the Democratic candidate the assurance of their tacit support in the November election. Worth more than it might at first appear, this action kept Wurzbach from raising funds outside of his immediate political circle and tied the Creager organization Republicans in the district to McCloskey's campaign. At the same time, however, Creager's backing was worth considerably less than he claimed. Wurzbach had been renominated and reelected in 1926, despite the exertions of the state organization and local opposition. In fact, Wurzbach's best issue in 1926, and in subsequent campaigns, was the opposition of "Boss Creager."[37] Having already faced repeated charges of cooperation with Democrats in opposition to Republicans in the Rio Grande Valley, Creager could not risk an open endorsement of McCloskey; in any event, McCloskey did not seem to think that he needed Creager's active support to defeat Wurzbach. He had reason to be optimistic, knowing that the presence of wet and Catholic Al Smith on the November ballot gave the Democratic ticket a decided advantage with the German-American and Mexican-American voters in Bexar County.

The degree of association McCloskey struck with Creager was to prove shortsighted for both men. As far as McCloskey was concerned, Creager's support gave renewed life and national publicity to his opponent Wurzbach's winning issue, the underhanded alliance of "Boss" Creager with Texas Democrats. As for Creager, the gentlemen's agreement dragged him into a highly publicized and hotly contested election which ended in a sensational charge of election fraud.

Unofficial election returns, in by Thursday, November 9, showed that Wurzbach had been reelected by the slim margin of 427 votes, about one-tenth of his margin in 1926. On every day thereafter until mid-January of 1929, when Bee County returns were finally submitted to the Texas secretary of state, the figures for each county in the district changed considerably in response to the correction of errors in the reports of precinct election judges, to reports from tardy officials, and to desperate attempts to effect victory through postelection manipulation of returns. Through corrected late returns, Guadalupe County, the home of both Wurzbach and Nolte, added 1,400 votes to Wurzbach's total and about 400 to McCloskey's. McCloskey's margin increased by 800 votes in Nueces County, 320 in Bee County, 500 in Comal County, and 100 in Wilson County. On November 13, one week after the election, Wurzbach held his seat by a margin of 164 votes. Within one week, amended returns were filed from Aransas, Nueces, San Patricio, and Bexar counties; the greatest changes were in San Antonio, where McCloskey continued to gain votes—an even 50 in precinct 13 alone.

Meanwhile, rumors of serious irregularities circulated through San Antonio. In precinct 10, which tallied 481 votes, 471 of them favoring McCloskey, only 475 voters had registered before the election. In precinct 123, Wurzbach lost 147 votes. When the county commissioners returned this tally, according to Wurzbach, it was marred by numerous erasures. Charging widespread alterations in poll records by the commissioner's court, Wurzbach demanded a legal investigation and challenged McCloskey's right to assume the congressional seat, which he had apparently won by about three hundred votes. Undaunted, local officials in South Texas continued to report "errors" in Wurzbach's favor in Guadalupe County and to McCloskey's advantage in Bee County. In fact, the amended reports were still arriving when Representatives Frederick Lehlbach of New Jersey, John E. Nelson of Maine, Carl R. Chindbloom of Illinois, and Loring M. Black, Jr., of New York arrived in San Antonio to hold hearings on the disputed election. Two days of hearings were held, with no apparent aim other than to provide a platform from which Wurzbach could air charges of fraud against McCloskey, Creager, and Eugene Nolte. Though the issue was unresolved for the moment, the charges were given new life by the committee's session. Shortly thereafter, McCloskey, Commissioner's Court Clerk David Dewhurst, and various Democratic election officials were indicted by the Bexar County Grand Jury on charges of election fraud. Nothing came of the indictments, though a considerable amount of testimony alleging election fraud was given under oath.[38]

During the trial of McCloskey, Alphonso Newton, the sheriff-elect, testified that McCloskey had asked him for returns from a number of precincts before the canvass was carried out by the Commissioner's Court. According to Newton, McCloskey later claimed to have lost the returns when the sheriff-elect attempted to recover them. On the basis of this testimony and that of other witnesses, McCloskey was charged with tampering with returns in six precincts. Testifying as a witness for the state in the hope of escaping conviction, David Dewhurst claimed that McCloskey brought election returns to him and an assistant, Charles Ramirez, and watched them make alterations both in the precinct tallies and in the totals. Ernest Altgeld, Bexar County Democratic chairman, had actually instructed Dewhurst to make the changes; according to the clerk's testimony. Altgeld had said, "Get this election: I don't care how in the hell you get it, but get it." Presumably because they carried out the instructions issued by Altgeld, Ramirez was charged with tampering with returns from four precincts and Charles Wernette, an election judge, had been indicted on the charge of altering election returns from one precinct.[39]

The highly publicized trial began on February 21, 1929, in the District Court of Travis County and ended seven days later with the jury's acquittal of McCloskey on the first ballot. Charges against Ramirez and Wernette were dropped. Apart from the tallies and totals for eight precincts, the state had little tangible evidence of fraud or conspiracy. The prosecution even failed to prove that these bits of evidence were sufficient proof that any fraudulent act had actually been committed. The state's case rested largely on the testimony of Dewhurst, Edward Englehart, and Fritz Russi, the latter two having been election officials in Precinct 20.

Their testimony was confounded by alibis, countercharges, and character witnesses for Judge McCloskey, including R. I. Smallwood, a Baptist minister who, according to the prosecution, on a previous visit to the court had been fined $25.00 for a violation of the Volstead Act. With his name cleared legally, McCloskey went to Washington and took his place in Congress.[40]

In the course of McCloskey's trial, Republican party leaders R. B. Creager and Eugene Nolte were identified by David Dewhurst as the instigators of the alleged fraud. Dewhurst claimed that Ernest Altgeld told him and Judge McCloskey that he had conferred with Creager and Nolte at the St. Anthony Hotel in San Antonio and that they had urged him to win the election count at all costs. Altgeld, also under oath, denied all of Dewhurst's claims. Neither of the Republicans was a party to the suit and no legal charges were brought against them. However, the state did introduce the testimony of N. C. Hall, the assistant manager of the St. Anthony Hotel, who testified that Creager and Nolte were guests at the hotel during the week of the November election and during the confusing week which followed. Not party to the suit, Creager was never given the opportunity to refute these damaging charges; because they were not important in the case against McCloskey, his attorney did not bother to contest them.[41] Creager's reputation was muddied again, and not for the last time.

With McCloskey declared victor by the secretary of state, Texas's principal election officer, Harry Wurzbach was out of office, if not removed from politics. The *New York Times* commented, "He will be missed from the House," and added that "his vigorous denunciation of the immemorial practice of swapping Federal patronage for Southern delegates to the Republican National Convention would be particularly untimely in the next Congress. That practice never worked more effectively than in 1928." But Harry Wurzbach had no intention of being missed: he contested McCloskey's seat and his protest was referred to the Special Committee on Elections. This body acted with no great dispatch, perhaps because its Republican majority agreed with the *Times*'s editor that Wurzbach might embarrass the party if seated too soon after the inauguration of Herbert Hoover: the Great Engineer's convention steamroller had been constructed with the considerable aid of southern fabricators, Creager most conspicuous among them. Thus the Committee on Elections #3, chaired by Representative Willis G. Sears, did not report to the House until February, 1930, at which time it reported Wurzbach elected by unanimous vote of the committee. McCloskey promptly resigned.[42]

On February 10, Wurzbach was sworn in as a member of the House of Representatives after that body by unanimous vote declared him elected. With but weeks to run in the actual session of the House, Wurzbach appears to have taken a relatively inactive role in House deliberations. His attention was fixed on the November election, in which he had to defend his regained seat. In this last campaign Wurzbach directed his main attack against the Bexar County and San Antonio city administrations, receiving valuable help from a good government group, the Citizens' League, in San Antonio. Wurzbach's campaign and popular reaction to the "stolen election" issue generated such optimism among Republicans that they ran candidates for state representative and some county offices. When the results of the election were in, Wurzbach had won by eight thousand votes, having carried San Antonio by more than six thousand ballots, the largest majority he ever received there. Unfortunately for his party, Wurzbach lacked coattails; he was the lone Republican victor. Thus, as in previous elections, his candidacy had few direct benefits for the local Republican party.[43]

The congressman's failure to carry other Republicans into office is best explained by Wurzbach's peculiar hold on his constituency. The son of a Confederate soldier who served as Democratic county judge of Bexar County for some years, Wurzbach attracted a considerable number of nominally Democratic voters, particularly in San Antonio. Recognizing the potential danger of close identification with the permanent minority party, Wurzbach wisely chose to emphasize his ancestry, together with other nonpartisan items, principally pork barrel gains for the district. His running feud with Creager was highly useful in disassociating him from the Republican party. Joe Sheldon, longtime Wurzbach supporter, considered the "Boss Creager" issue to be the congressman's strongest argument; it essentially led the electorate to respond to Wurzbach as an individual, apart from his party. Walter Newton, President Hoover's chief aide, was surely correct when he observed: "Congressman Wurzbach had such a personal hold upon his district that I imagine it would be difficult to elect another Republican."[44] Though he vanquished the Democratic challenge to his seat, Wurzbach's troubles were not all behind him, for Creager was not disposed to bury the hatchet.

Shortly after McCloskey's acquittal, United States Senator Smith Wildman Brookhardt, a maverick progressive Republican from Iowa, came to Texas for the ostensible purpose of investigating the dispensing of federal patronage and the alleged interference of Creager and other Texas Republicans with the enforcement of the Volstead Act. In addition to reviving all of the anti-Creager charges of the Heflin and Lehlbach committees, and of the McCloskey trial, Brookhardt subjected the Creager organization to intense scrutiny and bitter criticism.

When the report of the Brookhardt Committee appeared, it charged Creager with extorting political contributions from federal officeholders and using his political power to undermine the development of the Republican party in Texas. Creager might have faced indictment on the former charge if Senator McKellar, the only active member of the Brookhardt Committee apart from the chairman, had not added his brief comment to the committee report. McKellar maintained that Creager's actions were not in fact illegal, but the truth was that they ought to be.[45]

During the hearings, Creager gave a succinct and candid history of his relations with Harry Wurzbach: "Because of underhanded and deliberate efforts on his part to undermine and destroy the influence of myself and my friends in Texas and for many other amply sufficient reasons, I did not support or assist him in his last two campaigns, but openly stated I regarded him as unfit and hoped some Republican might be elected from his district." Moreover, Creager claimed that he had evidence that Wurzbach had accepted illegal campaign contributions from federal employees. Creager's charge brought about the speedy indictment of Wurzbach in Waco, on March 4, 1929. After a change of venue and considerable agitation among Republican leaders in Washington, the action was quashed in San Antonio by Federal Judge DuVal West.[46]

Intent on removing Wurzbach from active politics, R. B. Creager pressured the Justice Department into reviving charges of soliciting illegal campaign contributions against Wurzbach. These charges had earlier been quashed by District Judge West, who was upheld on government appeal to the Fifth Circuit Court. The Justice Department, with full knowledge of President Hoover, took the case to the Supreme Court, which ruled against Wurzbach. At the very least it seemed that Creager had collected from Hoover on past favors due repayment and that, in spite of the intervention of members of Congress, Wurzbach would be dragged through long and potentially damaging litigation. Before the government could ready its case, however, the action was moot: Harry

McLean Wurzbach died in Washington following an appendectomy in November, 1931.

Wurzbach's following in his district, his "personal hold" as Walter Newton had described it, was clearly reflected by the events which followed his death. His funeral was the largest in San Antonio memory. More than fifteen thousand admirers filed past his bier at San Antonio's Municipal Auditorium, and more than twenty thousand persons participated at funeral services in San Antonio and Seguin. There was no doubt that Harry Wurzbach was well liked by the people he represented for nearly twelve years in Congress. But popular affection proved to be nontransferable: Wurzbach was succeeded by a member of the Democratic party, which has held the San Antonio seat without interruption since Wurzbach's death. If Creager succeeded in plaguing Harry Wurzbach's last days with litigation, Wurzbach had had the satisfaction of seeing Creager's reputation sullied by muckraking journalists with a national following.[47]

After the Brookhardt report Creager faced more challenges in June, 1929, when *Collier's Magazine* published two muckraking articles about southern politics. Though he was not the major target of either article, R. B. Creager was seriously compromised by the attacks and the litigation they prompted. In its June 15 issue, *Collier's* offered "the unique correspondence course (positions guaranteed) which Congressional investigators are studying in an effort to locate and punish the job merchants." John W. Martin and Perry Howard, patronage referees in Georgia and Mississippi, respectively, were the principal villains of "Getting a job for Jack," by William P. Shepard. However, Ralph (*sic*) Creager was attacked for running the Hays fund-raising system, which was allegedly providing about $60,000 every two years for Texas party use. Much of Shepard's information was supplied by Senator Brookhardt, whose supposed investigations in Texas had been yet another round in the long-term battle between Harry Wurzbach and R. B. Creager. The article included Creager in the ranks of the job sellers, most of whom, Shepard claimed, had already been cut off from White House influence because of the revelations of the Brookhardt Committee. He implied Creager ought to suffer the same fate.[48]

In the following issue (June 22, 1929) of *Collier's*, Owen P. White, a native Texan and an acquaintance of Wurzbach, offered readers "an advance course in vote-switching, jail-dodging, plain and fancy grafting ... free of charge and very little home study is necessary." The brunt of

White's attack was directed against the Democratic machine of Hidalgo County Sheriff Yancey Baker. With little hard information at his disposal, White described the elaborate highway and school building programs, paid for by public bonds, which were, in turn, sold to loyal bankers at rates highly favorable to them. Only the taxpayer, victim of high valuations and increasingly high tax rates, lost out in the Hidalgo County government. Until 1929, discontented taxpayers had been defeated by Baker's use of Mexican (alien) voters and intimidated by the sheriff's readiness to sustain his power with violence.[49] According to White, discontented Democrats then attempted to reform county government through the Republican party; they attended the precinct conventions and chose delegates to the county convention. In response to this "invasion," the handful of regular Republicans, five delegates, walked out of the convention and held a rump meeting in which they nominated their own candidates. By recognizing the convention and candidates of the "regular" Republicans, R. B. Creager undercut the actions of the "good government" group, thus bringing forth the wrath of both the local reformers and White, for his act of alleged grafting. If White were to be believed, the corrupt Baker machine was kept in office only with Creager's support and at the expense of the real Republican party in Hidalgo County.[50]

The importance of the charges against him in the White and Shepard articles was not lost on Creager. Shepard concluded his piece by suggesting that Creager ought to lose patronage control in Texas; White ended his exposé by claiming that the Republican National Committee ought to look into Creager's activities. It is no surprise that Creager sought to protect his reputation in Washington by forcing the retraction of damaging statements through two libel suits, which he filed in Brownsville against *Collier's* and the authors.

When the case came to court in Brownsville a special trial judge substituted for the regular judge, DuVal West, who excused himself on account of his long friendship with Creager. On the motion of the *Collier's* attorney, jurors were brought in from rural environs of Houston; they argued that Creager would enjoy influence over local jurors because he had promised to donate his damage award to the city of Brownsville for the creation of a public park and recreation system. According to White's description of the trial, the jury found for *Collier's* and White after a bare five minutes of deliberation—an outcome which caused Creager to turn "from a ruddy red . . . to a pale, sickly gray." Creager dropped his second suit, against *Collier's* and Shepard. The news of his defeat, however, was carried in the *New York Times* and the *Washington Post*.[51]

As far as Texas Republicans were concerned, Creager came through Brookhardt's investigation and the journalists' attacks quite well. Creager's opposition to Wurzbach, however, and his involvement in the election fraud charges, placed him in disfavor in the White House circle whence all patronage flowed. Presidential Secretary Walter Newton, formerly a congressional colleague of Wurzbach, convinced President Hoover that Creager's actions could only result in the permanent loss of Wurzbach's seat to the Democratic party. In the face of chilly reception at the White House, Creager was increasingly reliant on the influence of J. F. Lucey, an independent oilman from Dallas and formerly a close aide of Hoover's in war relief programs; indeed, Creager found Lucey's help essential in obtaining a hearing at the White House and continuing his control of Texas patronage. The national committeeman, having thus lost a portion of his independence, had gained nothing in his campaign to unseat Wurzbach.[52]

The extent to which Creager's influence at the White House eroded is well illustrated by his struggle to win a federal appointment for a loyal supporter. He had promised Orville Bullington, a Wichita Falls attorney, a post which had fallen vacant on the United States Fifth Circuit Court. Bullington was a member of the state executive committee and had stuck by Creager during the leader's various bouts with Harry Wurzbach. Bullington was, moreover, an influential man in his section of Texas and was widely known through his activity in the alumni association of the University of Texas. It was no surprise that the Wichita County Republican party approved and endorsed Bullington for the post and that his nomination was supported, through the party, to the door of the Justice Department in Washington.[53] When that door opened, Joseph C. Hutcheson, a Democrat who had been named United States district judge for South Texas by Woodrow Wilson, was elevated to the position on the circuit court by Herbert Hoover.

Creager had, in short, been unable to secure the post for Bullington or for any other member of his party. His own reputation had been damaged as a result of his battles with Wurzbach, attendant congressional investigations, and sensational exposés of his operation of the Texas party. Thus, in spite of his important role in the creation of the preconvention Hoover boom, Creager had little pull with the President. It is worth noting that Wurzbach, temporarily out of office but not out of politics in 1929, opposed the Bullington nomination on the grounds that the candidate carried public stigma as a result of his business association with railroads. Bullington and Creager, charged Wurzbach, were simply two railroad lawyers who were trying to pull off a private deal involving the federal courts. Although it seems unlikely that the White House accepted the substance of Wurzbach's unsupported charge, the publicity given to the charge was sufficient to make the attorney general reluctant to nominate Creager's candidate.[54] At the same time, President Hoover was being pressed by Senator Tom Connally, a Democrat from Texas, to appoint Hutcheson to the circuit bench. The senator made it clear that any nominee other than Hutcheson would find it difficult to secure confirmation because he would act to block approval by the Judiciary Committee.[55]

When Creager learned how matters stood in Washington, he persuaded Bullington to withdraw his name from consideration. Then, to sustain his public image of party boss, Creager claimed that Hutcheson had been his personal choice, following Bullington's "withdrawal," because he and the judge had been friends in law school. But Bullington, sharply disappointed, had had a clear view of Creager's weakness; he began a political flirtation with a strong and dissident faction in Dallas County, a group which emerged in 1927. Creager's face-saving maneuver also angered some members of his party who objected to the high-handed gift to a Democrat of the best federal plum to fall their way since the Republican party regained the presidency in 1920.[56] As this incident makes clear, the appearance of one-man leadership, often misleading in earlier days, was equally deceptive in 1929. Having been more than a first among a few equals, Creager was now highly dependent on the power of other influential men such as J. F. Lucey to maintain his position in the Republican party. And the worst was yet to come.

3

"Are You My Friends Or Ain't You?"

FOR R. B. CREAGER, the end of national Republican hegemony meant the beginning of a new and far less promising era. His reputation and influence seriously impaired by the Wurzbach feud, journalistic exposés, lawsuits, and congressional investigations, the national committeeman faced intraparty challenge to his dominance in 1931 and 1934. During the same period he became increasingly active in the internal struggles of the national party through his service on the Republican National Committee and his involvement with the maneuvering for the Republican presidential nominations in 1932, 1936, and 1940. With the loss of patronage upon the inauguration of Franklin Delano Roosevelt in 1933, the organizational and electioneering activities of the party succumbed to lethargy and indolence during the 1930s. Among the rank-and-file members, party activity reached an all-time low.

Until the death of Harry Wurzbach in 1931, Creager was preoccupied with Texas Republican politics. In 1930, he faced a fight over the party's nomination for governor. Normally, a tightly scripted convention could be relied upon to choose "the right man"; but in 1930 the Republican party was required by Texas law to hold a party primary because its gubernatorial candidate in 1928 had received more than one hundred thousand votes. A primary vote of similar magnitude would have been difficult to control, especially if Harry Wurzbach's followers turned out in force. Wurzbach's undisciplined coalition of dissenting Republicans and maverick Democrats did make a great show of mustering support for C. C. Littleton of Fort Worth, their candidate. As was true of most contests within the Texas Republican party, however, all of the excitement lay in the expectation. On election day, Texans demonstrated their habitual indifference to the affairs of the nominal minority party. C. C. Littleton received a mere handful of votes, thus demonstrating once again that Harry Wurzbach's considerable personal popularity could not be converted into electoral support for his allies. Only 9,717 votes were cast, 5,001 of them going to George Butte, who had been the party's nominee in 1924, even though he had made his lack of interest in the nomination known on a number of public occasions.[1]

Despite the lack of rank-and-file interest in the primary, there was serious unrest within party ranks. The apparent cause of dissatisfaction was the widespread and well-founded rumor, current before the primary election, that under Creager's control the state convention would designate W. E. Talbot, formerly executive director of the party, as the nominee, regardless of the outcome of the primary election. Consequently, at convention time Creager's rivals supported Butte, who was still the front-runner as winner of the nonbinding primary election. After Butte refused the nomination, Hugh Exum of Amarillo, a powerful member of the state executive committee, made a public bid for the nomination at the state convention in San Angelo in September.

In spite of the vote for Butte and Exum for office, Creager ran the convention to suit himself. Once in session, the convention loyally passed a resolution which defended R. B. Creager against the charges of the Brookhardt Committee and went on to declare Talbot the official Republican candidate for governor. Creager's allies argued that Butte's earlier opposition to the Fergusons would be a liability because the party now hoped to attract voters from the Ferguson faction of the Democratic party, which had lost the nomination to conservative Ross Sterling. Talbot's supporters told the convention that his experience in sales, management, and public relations would enable him to wage a more effective campaign than Butte. For his part, Professor Butte continued to make no visible exertions in his own behalf, hoping to maintain friendly relations with Creager. After Butte's earlier service as a candidate, Creager had secured several federal appointments for him in 1930; Butte was not inclined to enter the lists against his former patron.[2]

The assertion that Talbot was an expert in public relations was borne out in the candidate's campaign: Talbot carried out a most colorful campaign based on irrelevant ballyhoo. His general strategy aimed at drawing attention from his Republicanism and emphasizing his own business experience and his devotion to the Lone Star State. He made extensive use of a slogan, "Buy it made in Texas," which had no overt association with regular party politics; he backed up his slogan by telling voters that all of his clothing, from hat to shoe leather, had been manufactured in the state. Though Talbot's abandonment of Arrow shirts failed to excite the electorate, his novel campaign succeeded in gaining more press coverage than conventional Republican candidates normally received, a useful advantage for an underdog fighter. In his corner, moreover, Talbot had one of the scrappier independent oilmen of Dallas, J. F. Lucey, who managed the campaign, made aggressive attempts to raise funds, and tried to stimulate party activity in Talbot's behalf.[3]

Lucey's energy and Talbot's publicity, however, were of little avail. Most Republican county chairmen sat out the election, and in November Talbot's effort brought in a bare 20 percent of the vote. His best showings were in Bexar, Gillespie, Guadalupe, and Kendall counties, where Harry Wurzbach's name was on the ballot for Congress; in Hidalgo County, where both Creager and Talbot had extensive business connections; and in Dallas County, the home ground for both Talbot and Lucey. Elsewhere, East Texas returned its traditional strong Democratic vote; and the Panhandle vote showed the effect of Hugh Exum's pique: the Republican vote simply did not materialize. Long the party chief in this region, Exum was unenthusiastic about Talbot; and he was understandably angry with Creager.[4]

If there were problems in the Panhandle, Creager also faced continued difficulties in Dallas County. The possibility of double trouble took shape in 1931. Exum leaked word to the *Dallas Times Herald* that "Dallas and Tarrant Counties, together with such proxies as H. E. Exum, member of the state executive committee from Amarillo, can control the spring convention in 1932." Fro Creager's perspective, this raised a serious threat indeed. The spring convention would choose the Texas delegation to the national convention; and the delegation would, for all practical purposes, nominate the national committeeman for Texas. Exum was difficult to displace; therefore, something had to be done about the situation in Dallas County.[5]

Trouble had been brewing in the Dallas County Republican party for several years; with the aid of John Kettle, Dallas County chairman in 1930, Harry Gordon, and D. J. Haesley, George Atkinson, county chairman in 1926 and again in early 1930, had been building up a challenge to two factions which exercised control of local party affairs and were loyal to Creager. Federal officeholders formed one group: they included Heber Page, acting postmaster at Dallas; George C. Hopkins, district collector of internal revenue; John Philp, fourth assistant postmaster general and former Dallas postmaster; and United States Marshal Sam Gross. A second group of local Republicans loyal to Creager included J. F. Lucey, E. C. Toothman, director of organization, and Thomas E. Ball, who with Carlos Watson founded the Texas Young Republicans in 1930.[6]

Creager was inclined to accommodate the Atkinson faction. Atkinson was both seated on the state executive committee and nominated for attorney general, while a Creagerite, D. J. Haesley, was nominated for the United States Senate, to stand against Morris Sheppard, the incumbent Democrat. The candidate of the Atkinson faction for Dallas postmaster, George C. Young, received the appointment over Heber Page; and W. E. Talbot became census supervisor with Atkinson's support. Following his usual strategy of minimizing intraparty battles when possible, Creager tried conciliation with the dissident faction. Like Harry Wurzbach, Atkinson was not easily mollified. Once seated on the Republican State Executive Committee, Atkinson threw in with the dissident faction which included Exum and Henry Zweifel of Fort Worth. With Exum's threat of party domination alive and current, Creager began by autumn, 1931, to apply pressure to keep George Atkinson in line. An attorney specializing in tax law, Atkinson was more than ordinarily vulnerable to the kind of political pressure Creager could create. Like their counterparts in Washington, politically loyal party members at the Texas offices of Internal Revenue could presumably be counted upon to question the returns of Atkinson's clients, who would quickly guess that such difficulties might be avoided with a change of attorney. The threat of this sort of action against him probably brought George Atkinson to retire from party office. For whatever reason, Atkinson removed himself from the scene. Following the loss of support in Dallas County, Zweifel withdrew from the fracas. Hugh Exum bided his time.[7]

The resultant lull in intraparty rivalry was of short duration. After a brief period of inactivity, Atkinson resumed free-swinging criticism of Creager, whom he publicly linked with the patronage clique. Atkinson was supported by his friend John A. Kettle, who served as Dallas County chairman. Before long, the Creager faction struck back. In January, 1932, Thomas E. Ball announced he would oppose Kettle for the county chairman's post in July. Refusing to be openly drawn into the dispute, Creager, in a rare public display of wit, dismissed it as "a tempest in a kettle." The decisive encounter was lively and hot: the local press reported that "at one point George C. Hopkins, Collector of Internal Revenue, jumped on the city council table and defied the opposition boos and jeers until he was jerked down by Mr. Kettle." The contest ended with a victory for the Ball-Creager faction at the stormy county convention. Creager, obviously relieved, wrote Eugene Nolte, "I am mightily glad that things went off as they did in Dallas. And I am particularly glad that we got rid of that sore spot in Dallas County." Creager might well have felt some measure of relief. With the Atkinson-Zweifel connection broken up, he could expect to have a smooth state convention in early August.[8]

There were two aspirants to the Republican nomination for governor in 1932, John F. Grant and Orville Bullington. Grant, a wealthy Houston timberman, ran for comptroller of public accounts in 1928 and was a candidate for the Republican nomination for governor in the 1930 party primary. After Talbot's selection in the latter year, Creager offered apparent encouragement to Grant's aspirations by telling him that the party would need a widely known nominee in 1932. Consequently, Grant spent considerable time and money traveling through Texas, meeting local party leaders and journalists, in an attempt to become a "widely known nominee."

In most instances, the Texas GOP might have welcomed the candidacy of a well-financed and respectable industrialist. But in 1932, party leaders supported a second claimant, Orville Bullington, who was better known in the party than Grant though his candidacy was never discussed outside of a narrow circle of party chiefs. Bullington, a prominent Wichita Falls corporation lawyer, had served on the state executive committee since 1926, had sat as vice-chairman on several occasions, and had been chosen as a delegate to the Republican national conventions of 1924, 1928, and 1932. Moreover, Bullington was known throughout Texas because he had served variously as executive director and president of the "Texas-Exes," the highly influential alumni association of the University of Texas. Creager, taking a calculated risk by assuming that Mrs. Miriam A. Ferguson would win the Democratic run-

off primary with incumbent governor Ross Sterling, threw his support
to Bullington; he reckoned that Bullington stood the best chance of
rallying conservative opposition to Mrs. Ferguson. Accordingly, at the
August convention, after Creager made the necessary arrangements, Bullington received the nomination on the first ballot. Not surprisingly, John
Grant was highly incensed. After a heated exchange with R. B. Creager
at the rear of the convention hall, Grant left both the convention and
the Republican party.[9]

Creager's choice of Bullington cost the Republican party the support
of one wealthy backer, but it paid off politically. In the hard-fought Democratic runoff, "Ma" Ferguson won the Democratic nomination with a
scant 50.1 percent of the vote. The Democratic party was deeply divided.
Republicans were increasingly optimistic about Bullington's chances,
especially after Anti-Tammany Democrats such as Cato Sells, Alvin S.
Moody, and Carr P. Collins formed an Anti-Ferguson league. Bullington's chance of election was still further advanced on October 22 when
Governor Sterling announced that he would bolt the Democratic party
ticket to support Mrs. Ferguson's Republican opponent. For his own
part, Bullington waged an intelligent campaign; recognizing the obvious, that clear identification with either the national ticket or the state
GOP ticket would weaken his support, Bullington made the dramatic
announcement that he would quit the race and support Franklin Delano
Roosevelt if Mrs. Ferguson were taken off the Democratic ticket. He
predicted a strong Roosevelt-Garner victory and backed up his predictions by speaking at a Dallas meeting of a so-called Roosevelt-Garner-
Bullington Club.[10]

Though strong on conservative appeal, however, the Bullington campaign was weak on organization. Management of the campaign was in
the hands of Henry Zweifel, who failed to consolidate the various groups
supporting Bullington. Republicans, Anti-Fergusons, Roosevelt-Garner
enthusiasts—each group went its own way with no effective central control. Caught up in the heady spirit of the big-time campaign, Zweifel
recklessly committed funds far faster than they came in. Spending at
least fifty thousand dollars, he raised barely half of that sum, leaving
both himself and his party with a significant postcampaign debt. Even
the $10,000 "rainy-day" reserve fund, kept to insure at least skeletal
headquarters operations between elections, was exhausted, leaving Zweifel stuck with some of the tab. No one came forward to pay the bills:
money was tight, and Orville Bullington lost the election.[11]

Though he did lose the election, Bullington ran well. He led the national ticket by more than two hundred thousand votes. His showing was especially strong in the Panhandle, where he carried most of the counties, in west central Texas, and in far west Texas. As a regional favorite son, Bullington carried Wichita and Dallas counties; and he ran strongly in Cameron, El Paso, and McLennan counties. He did not do as well in the late Harry Wurzbach's fourteenth congressional district; only San Patricio and Guadalupe counties, the former reliably Republican and the latter the home of state chairman Eugene Nolte, fell into Bullington's column.[12]

The relative success of Bullington's gubernatorial race proved to be an isolated event in the history of the Republican party in Texas. The alliance with factions of disgruntled conservative Democrats, a tactic used in 1924 and 1928, proved partially successful in 1932, particularly in Dallas County, where the conservative wing of the Democratic party was strongly entrenched. Bullington's campaign clearly reconfirmed the advantages of occasional combination with dissident factions in the majority party. This opportunistic strategy, implemented three times during the Republican era, was not forgotten through the long electoral drought which followed 1932, when the party entered an extended period of hibernation.

After 1932 respectable men, many of them old party hands, ran nominal campaigns against strong Democratic candidates; they generally received less than 10 percent of the total vote. In terms of popular response, a notably low point was reached in 1938 when Alexander Boynton, running against W. Lee O'Daniel, received slightly less than 3 percent of the gubernatorial vote. Token Republican candidates ran respectably dull campaigns. In sum, from 1932 to 1948, general elections were an insignificant aspect of the history of the Republican party in Texas.[13]

Bullington's mighty effort had failed, and its failure presented R. B. Creager with new liabilities in 1933. Having lived down unfavorable publicity from congressional and journalistic investigations and having outlived Harry Wurzbach, Creager now faced the sacrifice of that convenient device in party management, the state party office in Dallas. Without the "rainy-day" fund, the headquarters committee was forced to close the state headquarters office. It remained closed until the fall of 1936, when it was reorganized to coordinate the Texas campaign for Governor Alfred M. Landon of Kansas. In the meantime, Creager was without one of his most valuable political assets, use of the headquarters apparatus in controlling the party. Between 1933 and 1936, Creager's headquarters operation, like that of the Republican party throughout the South, was a "hip pocket" organization. It had no federal patronage to dispense; it had no election campaigns to run. Creager's young business associates, E. C. "Ted" Toothman and Carlos G. Watson, watched the store for the national committeeman, but no one had much enthusiasm for keeping up even the facade of a functioning statewide party organization. There was no money to do so. At the same time, after FDR's sweep of Texas and Orville Bullington's defeat, no realistic party leader could think that Republicans would pose a serious threat to the Democrats of Texas in the foreseeable future. Most serious for Creager, the wells of federal patronage were dry for Republicans; and the Roosevelt drought was to be a long one.[14]

Political rivals like Hugh Exum assumed that the disappearance of federal patronage and the closing of the state office would mean political eclipse for R. B. Creager. By the fall of 1934, the San Antonio Express regularly referred to Creager as the "titular leader of Texas Republicans," a demotion indeed for the man who had been the "intimate friend" of Presidents Harding, Coolidge, and Hoover.[15] Though down, however, Creager could still not be counted out; the support of political allies and his ability to maintain his influence over the state executive committee kept him ahead of possible contenders for control of the party in Texas. But it was not surprising that the weakening of Creager's position after the Republican defeats in 1932 encouraged rival aspirants to seek party power.

The most serious challenge came from the renascent George Atkinson faction in Dallas County. With control of the Bureau of Internal Revenue in Democratic hands, Atkinson reentered Republican party politics. In 1934, contrary to the policy of the state committee, Atkinson's group in Dallas announced that it would nominate candidates for state and local offices in the November elections as it had in 1932. Not content with this much rebellion, the Atkinson faction proceeded to a direct challenge of the regular party organization by contesting the legality of measures of Creager's state committee, charging that the group had met in the wrong place and at the wrong time to canvass the returns of the Republican primary election. The effects of the misplaced and mistimed meeting, whatever they may have been, were of no concern to the Dallasites; their interest lay in charging that Creager's committee was not operating in compliance with state law. Calling themselves the "Grand Old Party," the Atkinson faction arrived at the state convention in Houston that September spoiling for a fight.[16]

The "Grand Old Party" soon found out that they had underestimated Creager and his friends. With little statewide support, the Dallas faction's revolt was not so much suppressed as ignominiously brushed aside. The convention, firmly under Creager's influence, simply ignored the claims of the antiorganization Republicans. It emphasized the faction's insignificance by naming John W. Philp, a Dallas associate of Creager, as permanent chairman of the convention and by nominating D. E. Waggoner of Dallas as the party's candidate for governor. The lesson was plain. George Atkinson lost his bid against the statewide organization; he was further humiliated by Creager when members of the opposing Dallas faction were singled out for preferment. At the close of the convention, Atkinson bitterly commented that "Creager has just about driven the real Republicans from active participation in party affairs in Texas."[17] But R. B. Creager was not thinking in terms of political participation. Unlike other Republican leaders, who expected the Democratic party to lose seats in Congress in the off-year election, Creager told the Houston convention:

In the November elections we do not anticipate gaining more than fifteen or twenty seats in Congress. We don't want control of the Lower House. If we had control, the blame for the failure of the New Deal would be placed squarely on our shoulders. Let the Democrats have free rein, and by 1936, the people will return to the Republican Party, which they have always turned to in time of trouble.[18]

Creager's attitude was defeatist, but it was realistic: the Republican party lost seats in both houses of Congress and the majority of the contested governorships. The only Republican governor reelected in 1934 was Alf Landon of Kansas. With Republican fortune at its nadir, Landon acquired a special status in the Republican party. Defeated on nearly all sides, the party clearly lacked national leadership—an observation on which both former President Herbert Hoover and Committeeman Creager agreed.

Former President Hoover had not lost hope that he might once again lead the party—a hope that the Republican National Committee did not share.[19] As a member of the national committee, Creager's main assignment, shared by other old guard members, was to "contain" Herbert

Hoover. Accordingly, Creager resumed correspondence with Hoover. Eager for friends wherever they might be found, Hoover responded, frequently at length. The correspondence between Creager and Hoover, rarely cordial even when the latter was in the White House, developed a strained camaraderie. Whatever the former President hoped this correspondence might bring about, Creager offered little encouragement for Hoover's declared intention of seeking his party's presidential nomination in 1936. In July, 1935, Hoover suggested he might make an early announcement of his availability; but Creager advised him strongly against such a move. Seven months later, on February 10, 1936, Hoover asked for Creager's support within the national committee: apparently, he received no reply.

While he steered an unsteady course on the Republican National Committee between the dominant eastern and influential midwestern factions, Creager avoided committing himself either to Hoover or to Governor Landon. Of his valuable allies in the Texas party, some, like J. F. Lucey, were committed to Hoover; others, like State Chairman T. P. Lee, were generally uncommitted. Creager could not risk alienating anyone by delivering an early commitment, as he had done in 1928. The national committeeman had other good reasons, however, not to promote either Hoover or Landon.[20] With the drying up of patronage and of party funds within Texas, Creager's political influence in the Republican National Committee assumed a larger part of his interest and concern. For him, the most interesting arena of political action was in Washington. With "grass roots" rebellions put down at home, Creager hoped to make something of his status in the infrastructure of the party. Second-ranking in terms of seniority, an old hand at delegate-trading at national conventions, he was likely to be influential as long as the national committee controlled Republican party affairs. There was no obvious reason to doubt the committee's continued dominance, in the absence of a Republican President, unless its presidential nominee and a dissident faction in the party attempted to supplant the old professional politicians. In the event of a successful challenge to the preponderant position of the committee within the party, Creager, along with other members of the old guard, stood to lose his last important political asset. Moreover, loss of influence within the national party could encourage opponents within the Texas GOP. It might prove difficult at home to impress knowledgeable party members with an obviously empty title.[21]

Creager was understandably alarmed when Governor Landon attempted to enhance his chances for the presidential nomination in 1936 by promoting "grass roots" regional meetings to revive party activity and heal factional divisions. Such gatherings could only make more work—and problems—for Creager and other state bosses at the same time that they diminished the significance of the national committee in party governance. Creager wanted none of it, but he did attend at least one meeting as an observer, presumably to keep a wary eye open for trouble. Former President Hoover, more hopeful, attended several meetings in the Middle West in a fruitless attempt to rally support for his own candidacy.[22]

As a veteran committeeman, Creager was aware that general proposals for party reform and activity should be assessed in terms of the forthcoming contest for the presidential nomination. Such proposals had little to do with grass roots Republicanism but a great deal to do with the candidacies of Landon and Hoover. The committeeman for Texas warned national chairman Henry P. Fletcher that the emergence of deep-rooted candidate followings outside of party channels could make it difficult to enforce party discipline once the nominee was chosen. If every candidate fostered his own "grass roots movement," the party would be hopelessly fragmented in 1936. Creager argued that the party's chances of electing a President in 1936 rested both on the maintenance of a united Republican party and on the exploitation of discontent in the ranks of conservative Democrats. For this reason, the commitment of the party either to Herbert Hoover or to a liberal Republican would doom the party to another devastating defeat.

Fletcher was urged to undertake his own national tour on behalf of the national committee both to heal party wounds, and more important, to head off the dangerous formation of deep-seated preconvention factions. If Fletcher acted expeditiously and prudently, the reins of party control would remain in the hands of the national committee. By reasserting his power as national chairman, he would be blocking the emerging influence of Alf Landon as an independent operator in national party affairs.[23] This was no small matter. By building support independently of the old guard, and by accepting the backing of powerful outsiders, including the erstwhile Democratic publisher William Randolph Hearst, Landon set himself up as an opponent of the entrenched old guard's control over the national party apparatus. There was, however, good reason for the national committeemen to avoid open opposition to him: the Kansas governor had made important friends by his endorsement of the Thomas "hot oil" bill in 1935 and by his diligent cultivation of a middle-of-the-road image. Without a viable candidate of their own, the old guard found their tactics limited to attempts to check Landon's expanding influence in the party.[24]

Creager, like other members of the old guard on the national committee, played a waiting game. He was convinced that the renomination of Herbert Hoover would be catastrophic for the party. But where was the party to find a widely known and sufficiently powerful affirmative candidate? Members of the weak Republican congressional establishment, such as Senator William E. Borah, were more appealing candidates than Hoover; but Creager, among other national committee leaders, thought it highly unlikely that any Republican could defeat Franklin Delano Roosevelt in 1936. He observed mounting opposition to Roosevelt, from such groups as the utility interests and the American Liberty League; and he counted on a continually mounting opposition to dislodge FDR: but he did not expect this to take place in 1936, regardless of whom the National Convention might nominate.[25]

In the absence of any significant division over contenders for the presidential nomination, Texas Republican politics were placid in 1936. E. C. "Ted" Toothman, Creager's secretary, ran party headquarters and kept in touch with prominent party members. Though a few new faces appeared at party meetings, Republican activities were sustained by a small group of well-acquainted members. One new member of the state committee, Ralph Currie, a young attorney from Dallas, observed that his fellow committeemen were mostly former federal officeholders, who, in his estimation, stuck with the party in the expectation of regaining federal offices.

The August state convention of 1936 was held in San Antonio during stifling 106.5 degree heat. Perhaps the best illustration of the state of the party in 1936 is provided by an episode in the otherwise uneventful convention. A delegation dispute emerged between some spirited young Republicans, led by W. A. Ernst, and Caswell K. McDowell of Del Rio. The young Republicans claimed that when they went to the published meeting place of the county convention, at the stated time, no one was present. Thus, they convened the meeting and, in the absence of McDowell, the county chairman, they selected delegates to the state convention. McDowell, who sat on the state committee, told his fellow committee members that he had actually held the county convention "on the back of a galloping horse," but that the real issue was, "Are you my friends or ain't you?" McDowell's delegates were seated in the convention with their friends.[26] Events were less colorful at the national convention.

Meeting little resistance, Governor Landon made good his claim to the nomination and installed John D. M. Hamilton of Kansas as chairman of the Republican National Committee. More than thirty new members joined twenty veteran members in the party management group. Under Hamilton's probing, it was soon revealed that the party had been ill-managed since its defeat in 1932. The new national chairman found that his office even lacked a list of Republican county chairmen—an indication of the state of disrepair into which county, state, and national organizations had fallen. But with a campaign to manage, the Landon organization concentrated upon fund-raising and publicity, doing little to repair past damage. The campaign was surprisingly energetic, given the broadly pessimistic expectation of veteran party leaders. The party raised slightly more than eight million dollars and spent $9,300,000 in 1936: both sums were all-time high figures for the Republican party. Better at public relations than at either organization or finance, Landon's supporters made the campaign big-time news by enlisting the talents of Cecil B. DeMille, the Sunflower Girls, and corporate advertising: "A balanced budget! That's what *Landon* did for Kansas and a Balanced Budget is what Electrolux can do for you!" Ad writers resisted the obvious temptation of "A Cleaner Sweep With Landon and Electrolux."[27]

The sustained enthusiasm of Landon's devoted backers gradually spawned optimism, which in turn fostered encouraging events. Republicans drew more votes than Democrats in the primary elections in Michigan and New Hampshire. Normally Democratic newspapers, such as the *Baltimore Sun* and the *St. Louis Post-Dispatch*, endorsed Landon. A number of conservative Democrats, like former Congressman Joseph W. Bailey, Jr., of Texas, supported the Kansas governor; Landon and Knox won the September general election in Maine, and the generally reliable *Literary Digest* opinion poll showed Landon maintaining a lead over FDR by 54 percent to 43 percent and predicted that Landon would win the presidential election with more than three hundred electoral votes.[28]

In Texas, R. B. Creager had resisted the youthful optimism of the Landon crowd, who invaded the state with theatrical rallies and organized hoopla. The *Literary Digest* poll, however, changed the veteran politician's opinions. Though neither he nor his associate, Orville Bullington, expected a Republican landslide in Texas, Creager was increasingly optimistic about national victory. Yet there were unpromising indications for Landon's political future. Powerful Republicans, including United States Senators George W. Norris, James Couzens, and Peter Norbeck, defected;

other party leaders, including Senate minority leader Charles L. McNary and Senators William E. Borah, Hiram W. Johnson, and Gerald P. Nye, were inactive. In North Dakota—seemingly safe Landon country—the fusionist Union ticket deprived him of victory. More ominously, according to one historian, the support which had helped Landon win the nomination, the backing of William Randolph Hearst and of the Al Smith Democrats, amounted to the kiss of death in campaigning toward the general election.[29]

The 1936 general election gained little for the Texas Republican party in terms of votes; satisfaction with Roosevelt and the continued presence of John Nance Garner on the national ticket produced a Democratic landslide in the state. The anticipated flood of disgruntled Democrats did not rise to swell the diminished reservoir of Republican voters. When the returns came in, Creager "felt like the man who stood on the bridge at midnight and found someone had moved the bridge." The Texas party's only significant gain came in the person of one conservative Democrat, Marrs McLean, a San Antonio oilman. McLean gave five thousand dollars, his first sizable political contribution, to the Landon campaign, raised more than a quarter of a million dollars for the candidate, and continued to serve as the party's head fund-raiser in Texas until 1952.[30]

After the election, the question of national party governance re-emerged. Members of the old guard like R. B. Creager offered polite condolences to Landon, but they refused to commit themselves to his leadership of the party. Creager, for one, looked for an early showdown and, presumably, for the replacement of John Hamilton as national chairman. At the expense of irritating some of the old guard, however, Landon succeeded in keeping Hamilton in his post. Landon even managed to install two of his campaign aides, William Castle and William Hard, in important staff positions at Republican National Headquarters; he thus insured his own influence in the party, at least until the next national convention in 1940.[31]

Former President Hoover, meanwhile, renewed his efforts to obtain his party's nomination; members of the old guard, like R. B. Creager, chafed at Landon's continued sway in the party and told newspapers that they were "sticking by" Hoover, to avoid premature commitment and to wait for a more promising candidate. Hoover, however, seems to have mistaken these moves for genuine support; and he attempted to consolidate his meager following in the party by proposing a between-conventions meeting of all prominent Republicans to "set the party's affairs straight." Hoover's idea was promptly promoted by his former secretary of agriculture, Arthur M. Hyde. When the scheme came to Landon's attention, he mistakenly thought it an attempt on the part of the old guard to revive Hoover to the end of displacing himself. Actually, the old guard had as little enthusiasm for Hoover's scheme as for the former president, and when Representative Joseph W. Martin moved to derail the Hoover plan, he seems to have done so with the assurance of support from at least a sizable number of the senior members.

Landon made his own political commitments clear by giving support to New York district attorney Thomas E. Dewey, who was battling the old guard for control of the party in his state. With Landon openly in opposition by November, 1938, the old guard set itself squarely against his renomination, though it had as yet found no candidate of its own. Though he was still advertising his availability, Hoover was a drug on the market in the view of candidate-makers. Depression memories and his devastating defeat in 1932 made him an unpromising candidate for the nomination in 1940; but, as a former President, he had to be humored and displayed.[32]

Democratic reverses in 1938 offered encouragement to both Republicans and conservative Democrats. Despite President Roosevelt's attempt to "purge" his party, Democratic Senators Millard Tydings, Walter George, and Guy Gillette were reelected. Republican membership in the Senate increased from seventeen to twenty-three; among Republican newcomers in the Senate were Alexander Wiley of Wisconsin, Leverett Saltonstall of Massachusetts, and Robert A. Taft of Ohio. Pennsylvania and Ohio returned impressive statewide Republican victories; John W. Bricker was elected governor of the latter state. Not surprisingly, then, Creager spoke for a sizable number of Republican national committeemen when he publicly predicted victory over FDR in 1940.[33]

With all of these encouraging signs, only fund-raising had gone badly for the Republicans. Though the $900,000 deficit from the 1936 presidential campaign had finally been paid off, the badly divided national committee failed to raise adequate funds for congressional candidates in 1938: only $133,750 of the $320,000 promised was ever delivered. As a result, titular party leader Alf Landon agreed with the newly selected House minority leader, Joseph W. Martin, that the Congressional Campaign Committee should assume full authority for congressional campaign fund-raising. The agreement indicated, once again, that the Republican National Committee, Creager's main sphere of political operation, was losing its place as the gathering of president-makers, delegation-traders, and fund-raisers. For Creager, this was an ill omen indeed.[34]

During the early months of 1940, Creager had no strong preference for any particular candidate. Field men for Robert A. Taft reported that the Texas national committeeman seemed to be going along with Walter Hallanan, Republican national committeeman for West Virginia and a close personal friend, in offering encouragement to Senator Arthur Vandenberg of Michigan. None of the contenders—Senators Taft and Vandenberg, Thomas E. Dewey, and Wendell Willkie—had captured the field in Texas. Leo Horowitz, a member of the Texas state committee and a native New Yorker, was the lone backer of Dewey, while L. J. Benckenstein expressed sympathy for Vandenberg's candidacy. Taft received increasingly strong support from Marrs McLean, who contributed $4,000 to Taft's preconvention campaign, and from J. F. Lucey. Only with regard to Willkie, who had no significant pre-national-convention following in Texas, was the situation uncomplicated. No one knew the midwestern utility magnate. Indecision was general, and Creager could not afford to be decisive; he dared not repeat the highly publicized and independent endorsement of a presidential candidate he had issued in 1928. By playing the waiting game skillfully in 1940, Creager carefully prevented a challenge to his position in the state party from the newly troublesome "West Texas crowd."[35]

The geographical label applied to these political challengers is somewhat inaccurate. Though West Texas members of this faction regularly included Hugh Exum of Amarillo, Caswell K. McDowell of Del Rio, and Charles O. Harris of San Angelo, they found valuable allies elsewhere in the state. One such ally was Eugene "Mike" Nolte, Jr., of San Antonio, who successfully contested the state committee position of Dr. F. L. Thompson, a longtime Creager ally, who had gone bankrupt in the oil business. Perhaps because of the hard feelings held against Creager from the Bullington campaign in 1932, Henry Zweifel of Fort Worth was also on good terms with this group. The West Texas crowd, with its public and its presumed allies, became both loud and powerful. Word of this emerging faction eventually leaked out of the state. In 1940, the Taft field workers reported to their chief that the Exum group held twenty-four of sixty-two votes on the state committee—eight short of a voting majority—and this figure did not include possible support from Nolte and Zweifel. The truth of the situation was simple: the West

Texans could supplant Creager by Hugh Exum if they could find any issue which would swing a handful of votes.[36]

The first opportunity for launching an attack on Creager's control over the party structure emerged in early 1940 with the death of State Chairman T. P. Lee. Ready for a decisive battle, Exum declared for the vacant post, only to find that Creager was willing to accept him without a fight. Presumably, the national committeeman could count votes as quickly as the Taft field men. In any event, he was not about to give Exum the assistance of a "cause" by fighting over a position with little real power. Exum's second opportunity to challenge Creager never materialized. Having no candidate for the presidential nomination himself, Exum waited for Creager to declare himself; he could expect that the national committeeman would antagonize supporters of the other candidates by a declaration and thereby lose additional support to Exum. If they could control the state committee, the state chairman and his allies would control the state convention, choose the delegation to the national convention, and, in all probability, replace Creager as national committeeman. No novelty, this plan had been brooded on by Creager's rivals since 1928, but it had never hatched.[37]

Creager thus did not attempt to settle a candidate on the state party: he kept out of the limelight while the Taft field workers and the senator's Texas allies clinched the Texas delegation and, consequently, saved his own political position. In private, "the Red Fox of the Rio Grande" assured Taft workers that he was fully behind the senator; he indicated, however, that no public statement would be issued before the state convention. Soon afterward, Senator Taft learned to his surprise that Thomas Dewey had been invited to speak at the state convention in May. The Texas party was still openly uncommitted. Behind the scenes, Creager did some self-serving persuading in Taft's behalf: Mike Nolte's declaration for Taft in early spring derailed the West Texans and gave the national committeeman renewed liberty of action. Even so, Creager left the hustling to the recognized Taft forces. Marrs McLean, the acknowledged leader of the pro-Taft group, brought over L. J. Benckenstein to the Taft side. J. F. Lucey and John Philp rounded up delegate support. All the while, Helen Ackenhausen, secretary to the director of organization, kept Taft's lieutenants informed of developments in Texas, with Creager's knowledge. By the time the May convention was held, Taft workers had lined up a state convention majority. It only remained for Creager graciously to accept "the will of the convention" and to head the state's delegation to the national convention. And so he retained control of the Texas delegation with a minimal effort and was off to Philadelphia. Hugh Exum tagged along.

Once the choice of the Texas convention had been made, Creager had worked zealously for Taft's nomination. A veteran delegate-trader, he urged Walter Hallanan and Harrison E. Spangler, fellow members of the national committee, to hold their delegations from commitment to a candidate until the three men could confer before the national convention.[38] When the convention opened, Taft could count on the loyalty of about two hundred delegates, including more than sixty from Ohio and forty-one from Texas. Beyond that number, Taft hoped to pick up additional support as the uncommitted delegates and those pledged to Dewey and Vandenberg swung to him in order to keep the nomination from going to Willkie.

Creager, an old hand at convention business, was enlisted to serve as one of Taft's principal floor leaders and to work within the infrastructure of the party to gain delegate votes as well as to hold those of Texas, Louisiana, and Mississippi. He succeeded at his task, but the general Taft strategy failed. On the sixth and final ballot, though Taft's southern support held up, the Willkie bandwagon psychology, promoted by his floor manager, Governor Harold Stassen of Minnesota, brought uncommitted delegations into the camp of the apparent winner. For his part, Creager made strong protests against various tactics which Willkie managers employed. He charged that Samuel F. Pryor had improperly issued visitors' passes to thousands of Willkie supporters, who packed the galleries and provided noisy support for their candidate. Creager took his complaint about Pryor to the press, but to no avail. From the point of view of Texas Republicans, though their candidate had lost, their national committeeman had nonetheless fought hard for him; Creager gained favorable public notice and was unanimously reelected to his post.[39]

After the convention, the Texas party abided by the meeting's choice and worked for Willkie's election, albeit none too zealously. Within Texas, if not in other states, the Willkie campaign was managed by the regular Republican organization. Willkie may not have preferred this, but there was no one else to deal with: Creager had seen to that. A group of disaffected Democrats, headed by Joseph W. Bailey, Jr., supported the Willkie Clubs, which were not, in theory, connected to the state Republican organization, for the state organization had charge of the campaign. In fact the regular organization maintained a measure of control over the

Bailey group by arranging for the appointment of party employee Helen Ackenhausen as assistant treasurer of the group.[40]

Willkie created no great stir in the Lone Star State. He appeared in Texas once, paying court in Hugh Exum's hometown of Amarillo on his way through the state. Republicans, however, expected considerable gains in the upcoming election. Above all, they expected negative reaction in Texas to Roosevelt's rift with John Nance Garner; they also hoped that the third-term issue, the Utilities Holding Act, and the court-packing scheme would swing a strong protest vote behind Willkie. This expectation was not altogether unrealistic. Though relatively few people seemed to have great interest in Willkie, anti-Roosevelt feeling ran high. Mike Hogg, whose father had been a Democratic governor of Texas; other Houston oilmen, including John Blaffer, Hugh Roy Cullen, and H. J. Porter; and Marion R. Knight all joined in the campaign against Roosevelt. Marrs McLean, who had supported Landon in 1936 but stuck with the Democrats on the state level, came over fully to the Texas Republican party in 1940.[41] The new support of conservative Democrats and oilmen was doubly important to the Texas party. At the same time that it brought a strong financial force within the party, whatever the Republican vote in Texas, the new group also tended to reinforce the strongly conservative cast of the Texas party: it set the party in a long-term pattern of reaction against the various measures of the New Deal. Though old placemen like George Hopkins and Henry Zweifel might be fairly flexible in accepting candidates from Taft to Dewey to Stassen, the wealthy conservatives would go down the line for the most conservative candidate. That candidate was Robert A. Taft in 1940 and 1948 and John W. Bricker in 1944.

With the new conservative support, the Willkie campaign in Texas was encouraging—until the election returns were in. Though his vote was twice as high as that given Alf Landon in 1936, Willkie still received only 18.9 percent of the statewide vote; he carried only six counties, all of them rural. Some encouragement was found in his stronger showing in urban counties, including Dallas, Harris, Nueces, Potter, Tarrant, and Travis, and in a good showing in the Panhandle. But, as usual, the loss left little for the party to do except wait for another try at the White House and pick up the pieces.[42]

Wendell Willkie, meanwhile, was busy rearranging the pieces; indeed, he even discarded a few scraps. During the campaign, he had downgraded the importance of the Republican National Committee and its old guard members like Creager and Walter Hallanan. Volunteer groups, the Democrats for Willkie and the Associated Willkie Clubs, carried the brunt of the national campaign, with little regard for the national committee. A substantial proportion—some 45 percent—of Willkie's campaign funds had been raised outside of party channels; eight eastern industrial families contributed about 17 percent of the revenue. After his nomination, Willkie replaced John Hamilton as national chairman because Hamilton was committed to Alf Landon. House Minority Leader Joseph W. Martin was Willkie's choice to replace Hamilton. The choice was significant. With the new national chairman busy with Congress and identified with the congressional wing of the party, the national committeemen would be less important as a group. In line with the de-emphasis on the national committee, national headquarters all but closed down after the election of 1940. Even press releases stopped.[43]

The old guard fought back. Creager, for example, attempted to generate a rift between Martin and Willkie. He appeared at the national committee meeting in March, 1941, armed with a resolution praising Martin's vote against lend-lease, and thus implying opposition to Willkie's support of the measure. Only after Martin himself talked to Creager was the committeeman persuaded to withhold the resolution. For all Creager's hopes, that meeting and subsequent gatherings brought no renaissance of the old guard. It was clearer than ever that the congressional Republicans and eastern party financiers were the new power bases in the party; and the national committee had to recognize that fact.[44]

But Creager did much better than passively accept a diminished role; changing his directions, he made the most of the new situation by becoming the liaison between the wealthy new "Republicans" in Texas and the congressional wing of the party. In assuming this new role, he tended to downgrade the importance of the Texas old guard, a group largely composed of former federal officeholders, leaving them in their places and disgruntled. By going over to a "new guard," which included wealthy former Democrats, Creager necessarily accepted their view of the Republican party in Texas: its proper function was to bankroll candidates in the East and Middle West, where expectations of electoral success were realistic. To the new guard, little could be gained by reviving William Talbot's and R. B. Creager's unrealized schemes for a popularly based Republican party. Such efforts would be futile, given the entrenched strength of the Democrats in Texas: and the new Republicans had no quarrel with the dominant conservative wing of the Texas Democratic party. In this comfortable arrangement, the existence of a popularly based party—which had never actually been built during the palmy twenties—might even threaten the position of the moneyed group as the dominant element in the Texas party. There was no reason, then, to concentrate effort toward building broad popular party support in Texas.[45]

There was never anything conspiratorial or planned in the emergence of the moneyed interest in the Texas party. From the beginning, the party was a small circle of friends and business associates. Onetime state chairman T. P. Lee employed Hugh Exum to manage his land holdings in Kansas. Exum succeeded Lee as state chairman. Lee did business with both Marrs McLean and L. J. Benckenstein, who was also an attorney for Marrs McLean. Lee was a friend of Hugh Roy Cullen, J. S. Cullinan, and H. J. Porter, all Houston oilmen and occasional contributors to Republican campaign funds.[46] John Philp, secretary of the party and later state chairman, had been appointed to federal posts at Creager's nomination. Philp was associated in the Huey and Philp Hardware Company with Alvin Lane, a member of the state executive committee. Roy Jones, an oilman from Wichita Falls, did business with the Houston oilmen and employed Orville Bullington as his attorney on occasion. Bullington's campaign manager in 1932, Henry Zweifel, conducted his banking business with Eugene Nolte, Sr., when the latter was state chairman; did legal business for Fort Worth oilman Sid Richardson; and was for a time a law partner of Joe Ingraham, who became Harris County Republican chairman in 1946. The inner circle in the Texas Republican party consisted of old friends and of business associates who had learned to work together on nonpolitical transactions, sharing general political views and making political decisions.[47]

The emergence of the new guard Republicans, and of future dissenters to their management of the party, was thus not the result either of sheer accident or of concerted planning. The new view of party finance and organization was irresistibly sensible. Thus, in 1938, it could be argued that if the party had supported an expensive campaign against W. Lee O'Daniel in the gubernatorial contest, the effort would probably have done little more than double Alexander Boynton's vote, leaving it at less than 10 percent of the Democratic vote. Party funds might help elect Republicans in the North while they would be wasted in Texas. There was little sense in challenging incumbent Democrats either in Congress or in the county courthouses. Funds spent to make the party competitive in Texas would yield little return; in the view of the new guard, Texas was a "dry hole"; its assessment of Texas politics and its opinions did little to advance the cause of two-party government, but this perspective was realistic. Conservative Democrats, moreover, showed an inclination to cooperate with pragmatic Republicans. State vice-chairman Orville Bullington, for example, was appointed to the board of regents of the University of Texas in 1940. To take another example, there is no indication that oilmen, the dominant element in the new guard, had any special complaint against the Texas Railroad Commission, which regulated oil production at the wellhead. As far as these Republicans were concerned, all was well in Austin.[48]

The money men did more politically than sit on their haunches. While giving support to northern Republicans, they accepted a long-term strategy for Republican party growth in Texas. Drawing on the party's historical experience in the state, leaders assumed that their main efforts would be aimed at drawing voters away from the majority party when suitable opportunities appeared. After the disappearance of the Fergusons from the gubernatorial ballot, there were fewer opportunities for the Republicans to exploit factional divisions within the Texas Democratic party. From 1940 on, however, the new guard sought advantage in the falling-out between the conservative Democrats in Texas and the national Democratic administration. Reacting against the court-packing scheme, the third-term issue, and the imposition and continuation of price controls on oil and gas, small but influential groups of Democrats became "Presidential Republicans," and generous donors to national campaigns in 1940, 1942, 1944, 1946, 1948, and 1950. Though these halfway converts, like Hugh Roy Cullen, were always more important financially than numerically, their support made it possible in 1940 for Marrs McLean to oversubscribe the Texas quota for the Willkie campaign. "Presidential Republicans" who served Creager's purpose by counterweighting the West Texans did little to revive the Republican party in the state of Texas, but they enhanced the influence of the fund-raisers in the state party and their generosity made the Texas Republican party increasingly important in the business of party finance and in presidential nominations. Moreover, the involvement of most of the members of the inner circle of the party, including Creager, with the petroleum industry gave the Texas party a strong issue orientation which conformed to that of the state's dominant economic interests. Therein rested the future of the party in Texas.

4

"Our Crowd Are Firmly In the Saddle"

BETWEEN THE PRESIDENTIAL ELECTION of 1940 and the maneuvers in 1943 and 1944 for the presidential nomination, there was little purposeful electoral activity to suggest that the Republican party had a future in Texas. Caswell K. McDowell was the weakest GOP gubernatorial candidate of the century, polling only 9,202 votes in 1942 and losing all 254 counties to Coke Stevenson, the Democratic nominee. Even in his hometown, Del Rio, McDowell trailed by a six-to-one margin. It is not surprising that once-active party workers saw scant merit in either McDowell's candidacy or the nonfunctional party apparatus which R. B. Creager continued to head. One longtime party worker, Mrs. Sarah Menezes, told Senator Robert A. Taft that the Texas group was "dead from the bottom up," a reasonable opinion in 1942. Only in occasional tiffs between Creager and former federal officeholders and in the party's connection with the larger world of national Republican affairs did the Texas party show any sign of life. The Texas GOP might have sunk entirely from view had it not been for candidates and would-be candidates for the presidential nomination. These men and their lieutenants sought campaign funds and delegate support in Texas, thereby stirring interest in the otherwise dormant Texas party. For his part, R. B. Creager looked to maintain support within the Texas party and labored to shore up the positions of the old guard within the national committee. Both efforts required increasing measures of energy and skill.[1]

From December, 1940, to November, 1942, Wendell Willkie and his associates contended with the allies of Robert A. Taft for control of the national party organization, by carrying on a drawn-out campaign whose maneuvers were suggestive of a tedious chess game. A new competition from New York appeared in 1942 following the party's gain of thirty-six seats in the United States House of Representatives and ten places in the Senate. Would-be candidates, including Governor Thomas E. Dewey, took heart at the off-year and mid-War setback to the Democratic party. Republican victories and persistent rumors of FDR's ill health seemed to weaken the Democratic hold on the White House and improve Republican prospects of regaining it. But the grand goal was often obscured by apparently petty events, by disputes over committee and staff appointments, reactions to Wendell Willkie's support of Roosevelt's foreign and military policies, and intermittent threats of resignation from the national chairman, Congressman Joseph Martin of Massachusetts.[2] Though these incidents seemed to lack an obvious relationship, all of the minor forays were directed at the GOP's quadrennial nominating convention.

When factional struggles erupted, there was little doubt as to which group R. B. Creager would support; he had served, as everyone remembered, with great diligence as Taft's floor manager at the 1940 national convention. In the politics of the 1940s, he fell back on the Taft connection to attempt to regain a place on the prestigious executive committee of the national committee, a post he had lost in 1938. Thus, in 1942 he solicited support from Taft, though he failed to gain the desirable post: Creager was ignominiously defeated by Mrs. Pearl Waters of Alabama. The friend of late and former Presidents was in obvious decline, his diminished status clearly marked by an appointment to the distinctly minor post of chairmanship of the subcommittee on convention badges. Creager was relegated to the sidelines of the intraparty contest.[3]

The pace of factional activity within the national committee picked up considerably after the election of Thomas E. Dewey to the New York governorship, the first Republican to hold that post since 1920. Boosted by the aggressive management of Herbert Brownell and by the likelihood of a sizable homestate vote in the forthcoming 1944 national convention, Dewey was a growing power in the national politics of the

Republican party. His waxing influence was manifest in 1943 when he withheld support from National Chairman Joe Martin, enabling Harrison E. Spangler, a Taft man since 1940, to assume leadership of the national committee. Dewey's exertions effectively undermined Wendell Willkie, a rival for nomination and party leadership.

But Willkie, already declining in power by 1942, was not Dewey's principal potential opponent. Clearly, Senator Robert A. Taft of Ohio was the man to beat. As it happened, the peculiarities of Ohio Republican politics had produced an accommodation between Senator Taft and Governor John W. Bricker, which kept Taft out of the race. In 1940 Taft and Bricker, each powerful in his own right, had determined to keep the large Ohio delegation to the national convention intact and supportive of a single favorite son. By covenant, Bricker agreed to withdraw in Taft's favor in 1940 in return for Taft's reciprocation in 1944. Thus, the stronger of the Ohio candidates did not take to the field in 1944, a situation which greatly smoothed Dewey's course to the nomination.[4]

In the meantime, as Dewey and Taft-Bricker forces jockeyed for advantages within the national committee and sought support within state parties, R. B. Creager maintained his ties with the Ohio group, though he gave the appearance of dealing in an evenhanded manner with both factions. His public appearance of neutrality was enhanced when he permitted both Governor Bricker and a Dewey representative, Oswald D. Hicks, speaker of the New York State Assembly, to address the Texas Republican convention in May, 1944. Several months earlier, however, Creager confirmed his commitment to Bricker when he sponsored a conference of "some forty-five or fifty of the outstanding party leaders" of Texas with Bricker. Delegate strength and financial support, in fact, were lined up solidly for Bricker before Hicks traveled to Texas. What seemed like support for Bricker was in reality somewhat reluctant support for the Taft-surrogate. The Texans were not willing to risk future standing in the party by taking an uncompromisingly pro-Bricker position. Texas party leaders prudently decided to send a publicly uninstructed delegation, free of the unit rule, rather than enter the lists for Bricker, who in May looked like a fading star. Prudence dictated abandoning a stalwart stand for Bricker, but nothing generated great enthusiasm in Texas for Dewey. In the view of some Texas delegates, Dewey was nearly as liberal as Wendell Willkie, which damned him to the company of "that man in the White House."[5]

On arrival at the Chicago convention, R. B. Creager fell back on one of the durable clichés of American politics to find a safe position. He informed reporters that he was "prepared to accept the will of the party." The remaining Bricker supporters, after assessing their own strength, made no determined effort to halt the Dewey bandwagon. Consequently, the convention settled into a lackluster sequence of speeches and indifferent applause. By the time Texas was called on the first ballot, Dewey had enough cast or committed votes to secure the nomination. The Texas delegation yielded gracefully to the general feeling and cast its votes for Dewey. Despite having beaten a graceful retreat, the Texans were on the losing side in still another convention; there were no victory celebrations for them. The high point of the delegation's activities in Chicago was unquestionably the lavish six-course banquet given by party angel Mike Nolte at the Palmer House; once the party was over, the delegates returned to Texas, saddled with a presidential candidate who was little to their liking and unlikely to attract much support from Texas voters.[6]

Though Dewey's candidacy, like those of Landon and Willkie before him, was no fillip to the GOP in Texas, the prime opportunity for party growth was in the recruitment of disgruntled Democrats who held FDR in no higher esteem than did die-hard Republicans. Back in 1940, growing numbers of disaffected Democrats had become "presidential Republicans" in reaction to New Deal programs and proposals. Four years later, Roosevelt's notice of intention to seek a fourth term seemed likely to precipitate a major split in the Texas Democratic party. Sam Rayburn, speaker of the United States House of Representatives and leader of the proadministration "loyalist" faction in Texas, foresaw an attempt by conservative Democrats, led by Governor Beauford Jester and E. Wilson Germany, Democratic national committeeman for Texas, to take an anti-Roosevelt delegation to the Democratic national convention. As usual, "Mister Sam" was well informed. The same cannot be said of members of the Roosevelt administration. Alvin J. Wirtz and Harold Ickes were self-proclaimed experts on Texas developments. Wirtz naïvely described the division of Texas Democrats as falling between loyal Democrats, on the one hand, and the Texas oil interests on the other. If Wirtz's thinking had been correct, Tom Connally, Sam Rayburn, and Lyndon Johnson would have fallen into the category of those hostile to Texas oil interests —a conclusion whose political naïveté is stupefying.[7]

The Democratic State Convention in May 1944 did business in a continual uproar. Loyalists and conservatives exchanged catcalls and recriminations and split into two rival conventions. Each meeting observed the customary practice of ignoring the GOP and concentrating fire on rival Democrats; each group settled the "rump" label on the other and readied its case for the national convention. Once at the national convention, however, the dispute was settled expeditiously. Democrats who were politically loyal to the President controlled both the national committee and the convention. They promptly seated the loyal Rayburn group. Angry conservatives returned home, in no mood to bury the hatchet. Thus, in a few weeks a conservative splinter movement within the Democratic party developed, with two aims in view: the first was to perpetuate conservative control of the state party organization—hardly endangered as long as the courthouse "gangs" remained loyal. The second was to establish an anti-FDR organization which would keep Texas's electoral votes out of Roosevelt's column.[8]

The open rebellion of conservative Democrats immediately presented Texas Republican leaders with the alluring political prospect of drawing large numbers of Democrats into their camp as presidential Republicans. State leaders, including Creager, Marrs McLean, J. F. Lucey, and Walter F. Rogers, state director of the Dewey-Bricker campaign, quickly entered into private negotiations with the "Texas Regulars." The Republicans proposed the formation of a Democrats for Dewey organization, after the practice of the gubernatorial election of 1932 and the presidential campaigns of 1928 and 1940. The Regulars, however, were not satisfied with their designation, "the caboose on a short train," and held out for more political leverage with the Dewey forces. Recognizing the difficulty of agreement with GOP state leaders, Democratic National Committeeman Eugene B. Germany went to New York to confer directly with Dewey and Herbert Brownell. In response to this rebuff, the Texas Republicans gave ground and offered to replace twelve of their twenty-three electors with Regular electors, who would cast their votes for Dewey.[9]

Here indeed was the rub: though out of sorts with Roosevelt, the Regulars were reluctant to take a step which would openly identify them with their enfeebled local opposition and give little firm promise of tangible gain if the coalition were instrumental in electing Dewey. For the Regulars, union offered few advantages. Creager was willing to give them political recognition if they would agree to assimilation by the Texas Republican party. In the event of victory, he would still control access to the White House and patronage, and he had not been notably generous in either regard after earlier collaborations with dissident Democrats. It was still remembered that though Thomas B. Love and his faction had helped Creager in electing Herbert Hoover, they found many subsequent requests for patronage answered with gift boxes of Texas Ruby Red grapefruit. Citrus had been no fit substitute for the anticipated bread-and-butter rewards for cooperation. Consequently, negotiations in 1944 broke down. Creager, under increasing pressure from other old guard Republicans and looking to appear to leave the Regulars at the altar, thereby avoiding the embarrassment of being dumped by them, declared on October 18, "It is now too late for a mixed ticket." His maneuver saved face for the moment, but his apparently precipitate action brought splintering in Republican ranks: Hugh Roy Cullen, J. S. Cullinan, and Albert Buchanan, all major contributors to the Willkie campaign in 1940, defected to the Texas Regulars.[10]

Even with the failure of statewide collaboration, some Dallas Republicans met with success in obtaining the support of local Regulars. J. F. Lucey, Ralph Currie, and Sam Cummings recruited a Regular, Charles D. Turner, law partner of Mayor Woodall Rogers, to run as the Republican opponent of veteran congressman Hatton Sumners, who had stuck by the national Democratic party. A modest campaign was undertaken. Turner delivered half a dozen talks in rural towns—Garland, Carrollton, and Farmers Branch—while his managers worked up scattered support among the "downtown crowd" and bought radio spot announcements for him. Funds trickled in slowly. Though J. F. Lucey pried $2,500 loose from the Republican Congressional Campaign Committee, more likely winners elsewhere were given more generous support. With all of its shortcomings, Turner's campaign was both a rebirth for Dallas Republicans and a signal indication of potential opportunities for cooperation across party lines. Some optimists even scented victory in the air.[11]

The electoral results of Turner's campaign were not encouraging: while only 65 percent of the vote was cast for Roosevelt electors, 74 percent of the voters stuck with Hatton Sumners. Dissatisfaction with FDR was not transferable to loyal Democratic candidates. Out of an unsuccessful campaign, however, two prominent party members emerged with an activist bent—not a common posture for GOP leaders in the South. Disappointed at the outcome of their efforts, Lucey and Currie nonetheless thought that Dallas might emerge as a center of Republican strength if a more effective GOP organization were created.[12]

Throughout the region, however, party chiefs found comfort in Dewey's relatively strong showing. The national vote totals showed Dewey capturing only one percent more of the vote than Willkie had received in 1940. In the South, however, he did at least twice as well, except in South Carolina. In Arkansas, Kentucky, North Carolina, Tennessee, and Virginia, Dewey ran considerably better than Willkie, picking up from 5 to 9 percent more of the major party vote. Clearly, there was good reason for optimism among Republican leaders in the South.[13]

Within Texas, election returns contained considerable encouragement for the GOP. Republican electors received about 5 percent more of the whole vote statewide than their Regular counterparts—a situation which also pleased Democratic loyalists, such as Speaker Rayburn. Dewey ran particularly well in South Texas, with better than 40 percent of the vote in Bexar, Cameron, and Guadalupe counties. In most of the major cities of Texas, Dewey's showing represented a return to pre-New Deal days, as Dallas, for example, cast more than one-quarter of its votes in the Republican column. Clearly, it would seem that the fortunes of the GOP were on the mend. At the same time, the unexpectedly weak showing of the Regulars, who garnered only 11.79 percent of the major party vote, suggested that Democratic splinter movements had little likelihood of success. In several urban counties, notably Dallas and Harris, the combined Regular and Republican vote (42 percent in Dallas and 37 percent in Harris) reflected significant divisions within the Democratic party. In several other urban counties, notably El Paso, Lubbock, Midland, and Taylor in West Texas, Tarrant and Wichita in North Texas, Smith in East Texas, and Travis, the seat of the capitol, strong Regular votes signaled dissidence within the Democratic party, a situation which an aggressive Republican party might exploit.[14]

Even in the Panhandle, which FDR carried handily, the improved Republican showing and the Democratic disunity encouraged Frank "Tim" O'Brien to make a heroic effort to win a seat in Congress in 1946. Having returned to Chicago, his hometown, after World War II, O'Brien decided to move to Amarillo to manage the large Bush estate, his wife's inheritance. After he had lived in the Panhandle only one year, a group of friends, including Dallas insurance executive Carl Weichsel and Amarillo attorney George Shannon, persuaded O'Brien to oppose veteran Congressman Eugene Worley. Shannon headed the campaign committee in Amarillo; and Gerald Cullinan, a livewire Dallas journalist, was lured by Weichsel to manage the campaign. J. F. Lucey raised funds for a campaign which the *Amarillo Daily News* described as "the most expensive . . . ever conducted in the panhandle." Money was spent on half-hour radio broadcasts, but more especially on newspaper advertising:

readers of the *Daily News* were advised by O'Brien's ads to vote for all Democrats except Worley. Apart from media, O'Brien waged an energetic campaign, speaking in nearly every town and crossroads in the vast congressional district.[15]

Eugene Worley, the incumbent, had intended to carry out a front porch campaign. Right up to election eve, he claimed that he had made no strenuous effort to secure reelection. However, O'Brien's diligent beating of the bushes for voters in such places as Dawn, Friona, Sunray, and Dumas prompted Worley to more activity than he had intended. While O'Brien assaulted the record of the Democratic administration in scores of Panhandle towns, Worley toured the larger settlements, delivering a well-received attack on "Communism and left-wing radicalism" in Amarillo, where the *Daily News* blessed him with its endorsement. The newspaper handsomely "found no fault with Frank O'Brien," though it reminded its readers that he was a newcomer, a Chicago lawyer, and presumably unacquainted with Panhandle people and problems. The endorsement concluded: "It would be unlike the Panhandle to desert a man who has labored night and day for six years for the district."[16]

True to the editor's word, the electorate defied snowstorms and sleet to return Worley to office with a three-to-one margin. But the election returns contained some encouragement for O'Brien and fellow Republicans: he carried Gray County and received about two-fifths of the vote in Amarillo. Previous Republican candidates, a rare species, received about 5 percent of the vote in congressional races. Along with this encouragement, Republicans in Amarillo and elsewhere began to wonder what might be accomplished another time with more organization, more money, and more support from the state party. Their speculation never reached R. B. Creager.

Out of touch with electoral politics, Creager had taken no part in the campaigns of Turner in 1944 and O'Brien in 1946. During these years, he was preoccupied with the internal politics of the Republican National Committee, which engaged in seemingly endless rounds of internecine contention. After the defeat of Thomas E. Dewey in 1944, party factions again contended for control of the party apparatus. National Chairman Herbert Brownell, Dewey's principal manager, delayed an immediate confrontation: he did not bother to convene the national committee for four months after the election. Even then, he succeeded in fending off rivals for another year, until in February, 1946, supporters of Senator Taft and Governor Harold E. Stassen replaced Brownell with

Representative Carroll Reece of Tennessee. In the fast-moving game of chair occupancy, Reece was ousted in turn by Hugh Scott of Pennsylvania, Dewey's candidate, at the national convention in 1948. Throughout these changes in national party leadership, R. B. Creager kept his place as chief of the Texas Republicans. Indeed, he regained his seat on the national executive committee in 1944 and retained it during the subsequent changes of upper-level GOP leadership.[17]

Perhaps the length of time Creager had served on the national committee gave weight to his claims to preferment. By 1946 he was second in seniority to Perry Howard of Mississippi, albeit that gentleman was hardly a symbol of Republican vitality. Unaware of Creager's loss of contact with important elements of the GOP in Texas, outsiders frequently remarked at his ability to maintain influence in Washington and control at home. In fact, though Creager's position of state leadership appeared impregnable to outsiders, between 1944 and his death in October, 1950, he needed all his skill to cope with an interrelated series of powerful assaults on his preeminence in the Republican party of Texas.[18]

Hugh Exum's death in the spring of 1944 created the first set of problems Creager faced. While Creager no longer had to reckon with Exum's ambitions, a new set of accommodations had to be reached with the West Texas Republicans who had backed Exum. Lacking Exum's leadership, Creager calculated that C. K. and Hobart McDowell of Del Rio and C. O. Harris of San Angelo and their allies might be managed in such a way as to present no threat to his position in the party. If, on the other hand, they aligned themselves with other dominant factions in the party—those of Dallas and San Antonio, for example—they might succeed in using coalition pressure to place another West Texan in the state chairmanship. Finding a candidate would prove no difficulty; at first call Hobart McDowell appeared ready to take Exum's place. Wishing to head off a showdown over the position, Creager acted before the potential opposition could rally. He summoned up overwhelming support for the appointment of party veteran John Philp of Dallas to the post. By the time the state executive committee met in Houston on May 22, the dim prospects for a challenge to Creager's action were so clearly evident that McDowell himself nominated Philp, who was elected by a unanimous vote.[19]

Defeated but still determined to gain control of the party, the West Texans renewed maneuvers the following November when it was rumored that Creager was seriously ill. W. C. "Collie'" Briggs, of Paducah, both believed and exploited the credibility of the rumor; he encouraged speculation about control of the party "if his [Creager's] illness should prove fatal." Briggs was no idle dreamer: he did his speculating in letters to Hobart K. McDowell and Mike Nolte. Considering Dewey's defeat and Creager's alleged illness, Briggs concluded: "I think Creager's influence is largely waning and with new faces coming on I do not fear him as in the past." Here was ample encouragement for ambushing and upsetting Creager. If, as Briggs told his correspondents, the Dallas crowd was already grooming a successor for Philp—and ultimately for Creager —and if Mike Nolte brought the San Antonio party into an anti-Creager alliance, there was reason to hope that a challenge to Creager would finally succeed. Despite Briggs's hopes, nothing happened. Creager was closemouthed about his health; he left for a vacation in Mexico, indicating only to Herbert Hoover that his trip was connected with his physical condition. John Philp, though ailing, continued in the state chairman's office, thus leaving no occasion for a showdown in either 1944 or 1945.[20]

While the efforts of the West Texans to regroup and increase their influence after Exum's death remained unsuccessful, the leaderless faction had made one advance in its frustrated efforts toward conspiracy: it attracted the interest of Mike Nolte, who followed his father's political footsteps. He did not appear to aspire to party leadership outside of Bexar County. With ample funds derived from inheritance and income from a beer distributorship, a nightclub, and other properties, Nolte was far wealthier than any of the regular West Texas crowd. Nolte, moreover, was eminently likable: he was gregarious, generous, and well regarded. Party old-timers had a special liking for him, for the son of Creager's late political ally frequently did financially pinched delegates such personal favors as providing hotel accommodations at state conventions. While Creager devoted his attention to oilmen and national politics, Nolte maintained personal contact with local Republican leaders through business-related travel and his function as the party's "angel," paying for parties, luncheons, and rallies. Consequently, after Hugh Exum died, Mike Nolte emerged as the only man around whom enough support could be rallied to mount a new threat to Creager. A challenge would bring little advantage to the West Texans unless Nolte was willing to sign on as their man. After several cautious soundings, they approached Nolte directly, but he cleverly avoided a binding commitment to the ambitious malcontents. Nolte kept in touch with the McDowells and

Collie Briggs, thereby offering them some encouragement; but he took no unequivocal stand against Creager's leadership.[21]

Job-hungry West Texans were not the only Republicans who by 1946 wished to see some changes in the Texas party. Their sentiment was shared by Governor Thomas E. Dewey, whose backers had to deal with the wily Texan on the Republican National Committee. Tightly tied to the Taft faction and loosely connected with the congressional wing of the party, Creager was totally opposed to the Willkie and Dewey factions. To Dewey's supporters, he had to be enlisted or eliminated—or at least neutralized. Enlistment was highly unlikely. Apart from his own ties to the Taft faction, similar commitments from such influential Texas Republicans as J. F. Lucey and Marrs McLean would have made it difficult for Creager to align himself with Dewey. Dewey's accommodation of the moderate-internationalist wing of the party represented by the following of Willkie and Senator Vandenberg, moreover, made the governor scarcely more tolerable than Truman to Texas conservatives.

Thus, in Texas, Dewey had to travel off the main road of the Republican party for support against Creager. Herbert Brownell found this support on the dirt-scoured streets of West Texas in Del Rio, San Angelo, and Paducah, where the McDowells, C. O. Harris, and Collie Briggs held sway in the party. Taking additional help where it could be found, Brownell picked up the support of irascible George C. Hopkins, former collector of internal revenue for the Northern District of Texas, who was making a political comeback in the faction-ridden Dallas County Republican party. Brownell's appeal to Hopkins and the West Texans followed an obvious line: in the event of Dewey's nomination and election in 1948, he would reward his followers with patronage and the other federal favors at the President's disposal. With presidential support, Deweyites in Texas would naturally assume leadership of the state party. Obviously, before they could become primary claimants for anticipated rewards, Hopkins and the West Texans would have to gain sufficient influence in the state party to be useful to Dewey's campaign, and, ideally, to deliver the Texas delegation to the 1948 Republican National Convention. For the strategy to work, Creager would have to be either pulled along, as he was by the Taft forces in 1940, or pushed out of the way. In the latter event he would be replaced by a member of the Hopkins–West Texas group and set aside at the national convention.[22]

A "grand strategy," the principal property of the aggressive minority faction, was clearly in Hobart McDowell's mind as early as 1944. With state convention votes from Dallas and Bexar counties, the West Texans would control the May convention in 1948 and name a pro-Dewey delegation. Like many grand strategies, McDowell's lacked only the dimension of reality: no one had successfully put together the necessary Dallas–San Antonio–West Texas combination. Harry Wurzbach tried and failed in 1928; and Wurzbach had enjoyed the advantage of the prestige of elective office, had personally secured the most important corner of the triangle, and had exploited a serious division in the Dallas County party. But by throwing his weight to a reliable group in Dallas, Creager had dismissed this challenge. With any warning, there was every likelihood that the national committeeman would successfully block the formation of a menacing coalition, and Texas party affairs would remain as tranquil in 1946 as they had been for the past fourteen years.[23]

In the early months of 1946, there were no signs of impending danger. Good-natured, quiet, and loyal John Philp of Dallas, as state chairman, casually tended Creager's interests in the county and state parties. Following Philp's pacific example, no one in Dallas County had the stomach for an extended and divisive fight: even George Hopkins —a man with powerful enemies—reentered county politics with little opposition. In San Antonio, Mike Nolte and Joe Sheldon joined forces to defeat a pro-Dewey faction led by Mrs. Walter Groce, president of the Bexar County Republican Women, Neil Beaton, Walter Baird, R. H. Band, R. W. Paterson, and James Crenshaw—all officers of the insurgent Republican Citizens' Committee. After Nolte's support of the Taft faction, the issue of party control was settled in San Antonio, and there seemed no reason for Creager to doubt Nolte's reliability, though he might well have been uncertain of the loyalty of county chairman Joe Sheldon, who had fought Creager as a campaign manager for Harry Wurzbach during the 1920s.

Had the malcontents looked to Houston, they would have discovered, as did the new Harris County Republican chairman, Joe Ingraham, that functional party organization existed in only nineteen precincts and that no significant support for a party rebellion existed. By midsummer of 1946 there seemed to be no challenge to the national committeeman. The West Texans seemed fated to remain a colorful, noisy, and ineffectual faction in the party—barring unforeseen events or erroneous political calculations. By the time of the state convention in August, 1946, the improbable had come to pass: Creager, the past master at party and convention control, suffered his first and only public defeat in Texas Republican politics, at the hands of a coalition of Deweyites and West Texans and at the end of a highly exceptional series of events.[24]

The initial mishap was the illness and resignation of John Philp in May, 1946. Philp's retirement not only deprived Creager of the active assistance of an old friend and experienced political observer, it also left the state chairmanship vacant at an inopportune time: the Republican State Executive Committee would have to find a successor, who would have to be presented and elected to a full term by the state convention in August. One member of the state committee, George Hopkins, actively sought the interim appointment. Thinking to bring around the Dallas group by accommodating Hopkins, thereby depriving the West Texans of a potential ally, Creager accepted Hopkins; he assumed that a man of more even temperament, such as Orville Bullington or Carlos Watson, might be unobtrusively maneuvered into the permanent post before the end of the year. In the intervening months, however, Creager would have to work with an ambitious and and excitable state chairman.

The second event in the improbable series is difficult to date with accuracy: sometime during 1946, Mike Nolte got the notion that he would like to be the Republican nominee for governor. Likable, free-wheeling, unconnected with oil, banking, and insurance, Nolte was an improbable gubernatorial candidate for Texas. But Mike had friends in the party, particularly among the old hands who regularly voted on the state executive committee and attended the state conventions. Since Creager already had a candidate, Alvin H. Lane of Dallas, in mind for the office, Nolte's aspirations were highly inconvenient; Creager and Hopkins would have to use all their influence to keep party members in line for Lane.[25]

To the media, Lane was "virtually assured" of the nomination before the convention began; Dallas newspapers saw his nomination as sealed and ran front page pictures of the "next Republican candidate for Governor." So he would have been but for one misstep: Lane himself had alienated crucial support by opposing George Hopkins's reelection as state chairman. With Ralph Currie, Walter Rogers, John Philp, and other Dallas Republicans, Lane had had his fill of the unpredictable state chairman. Hopkins, learning of Lane's defection, moved behind the scenes to deny Lane the gubernatorial nomination. The easiest way to effect this strategy was to support Mike Nolte; Hopkins did so, all the while appearing to support Lane, Creager's choice for the spot. The unprecedented result of Lane's decision, Hopkins's reaction, and Nolte's generosity and popularity appeared on August 13: the nominating committee voted to place Nolte's name before the convention. The convention approved him. Caught completely unaware, a thunderstruck Creager grimly faced his defeat and went through the customary ritual of promising wholehearted support for Nolte, claiming that "differences of opinion are very healthy." Thereafter, unsmiling and slightly ruffled, Creager posed with Nolte and Hopkins for convention photographers.

Other leaders reacted more noisily. Ralph Currie, state executive committee member from Dallas County, angrily berated Hopkins for betraying Lane. Hopkins responded in kind. Heated reactions gave way to the more sober observation that though Lane had been the apparent casualty of the convention, the most serious political wounds had been sustained by "the Red Fox of the Rio Grande." Creager had been outmaneuvered and beaten by a highly unstable coalition of curious characters: jovial Mike Nolte, irascible George Hopkins, and the ambitious McDowells of Del Rio. Old age, retirement, or death of old allies and the entry of new challengers left Creager more vulnerable than he had been since 1920. Collie Briggs's observation of Creager's "waning" influence was premature in 1944 but entirely accurate two years later.[26]

Before the convention, following his general practice of attempting to accommodate any faction that did not challenge his own position, Creager supported George Hopkins for state chairman. Now, fully aware of Hopkins's disposition and ambition, he took carefully measured steps to minimize the importance of Hopkins's position. Following the state convention, the Republican State Executive Committee, over which Hopkins presided, proposed effectively to strip the state chairman of his power by granting full powers between its meetings to the Headquarters Committee, which Creager chaired, and by determining that the state executive committee could be convened on the call of any ten members. Both resolutions passed, with Hopkins, Briggs, and C. K. McDowell speaking and voting against them. Hopkins was thus boxed in.

In December, 1946, Creager made another move to separate Hopkins from his West Texas allies. The Headquarters Committee gave H. K. "Hobie" McDowell a two-year appointment as director of organization at a yearly salary of $7,500. With "young" McDowell installed at headquarters in Dallas, Hopkins's influence was diminished; and he was confronted with a rival from the West Texas crowd. Creager, moreover, had mended his West Texas fences by providing a position for McDowell, who, it was reported, needed the job.

Late in 1946, Hopkins was fully aware that he was in political trouble with his backers in West Texas. They thought that their friend Henry Zweifel would try to dump Creager and that Hopkins, by prior arrangement with Zweifel, would seek the national committeeman's post in 1948. Faced with this rearrangement of power, which did not include them, the West Texans dug in their heels. Collie Briggs, writing to the McDowells and Mike Nolte, proposed to leave "Mr. Creager where he is until such time as a satisfactory successor and a number of things besides this are thrashed out." By offering Hobart McDowell the job at headquarters, Creager had succeeded in pacifying the West Texans and had created contention between them and George Hopkins. The state chairman passed off these reversals to the working of "that dirty Dallas bunch," Lane, Lucey, Currie, Rogers, and other longtime party members; he apparently never realized that it was Creager who put the skids to his political advancement. Hopkins should have sized up the situation in December, 1946: Creager felt secure enough to answer Hopkins's appeal for a patronage favor with a chilling letter beginning, "A moment's reflection will cause us to realize . . ." and continuing with a heavily patronizing lecture on the United States Constitution and the power of the executive branch of the federal government.[27]

Beyond his successful project of splitting the West Texans and Hopkins, Creager also intended to restore order and his own influence in the Republican party by appointing Hobart McDowell to head the party organization, such as it was. In this instance, his judgment was uncharacteristically rash: for reasons Creager had not anticipated, the appointment of McDowell precipitated a long and bitter challenge to his control of the party, accompanied by conflicts of personalities, local factional disputes, and the formation of a potentially powerful and threatening citizen's group outside of party organization.

In January, 1947, less than one month after McDowell was signed on by the state party, J. F. Lucey hired Ted Ewart of Dallas to organize groups to be known as the Republican Clubs of Texas, in urban areas. A month later, the promoters of this organization had assembled an impressive group of vice-presidents and directors and launched a large-scale publicity campaign, directed by Gerald Cullinan, against the West Texas faction. The club's stationery listed as officers most of the wealthy and influential urban Republicans and "presidential Republicans" in Texas: from Dallas alone J. F. Lucey, Roy Black, Jake Hamon, Alvin Lane, and Ralph Currie were listed. The launching of the organization was tightly coordinated. Taking advantage of the postholiday dearth of social events and local activities, meetings and newspaper articles were scheduled to attract public interest during the second week of January, 1947. Some Republican Club members performed heroically: for example, in Granbury, a central Texas town whose population was less than 2,500 persons, Henry Zweifel did his part by founding the *Texas River Valley Farmer*; designed to promote the Republican clubs, the weekly paper was without precedent or, for that matter, practical prospect. Gerald Cullinan's belligerent article, "Republican Activity in Texas," which appeared in Peter Molyneaux's *Southern Weekly* on January 18, gained more extensive publicity. Cullinan's first shot was over the bow: "... the Club will not be factional in purpose. It is not *against* any one man or any group of men. It is merely *for* the two-party system and the growth of the Republican Party in Texas."[28]

However reassuring this statement might have been, Creager had been caught by surprise when the clubs were founded. Upon consideration he saw the possibility of a challenge to his management of the Texas GOP, latent in the group's announced intent to form organizations which would parallel that of the party at district and county levels. His initial public comment on the organization was cautious; he indicated that the clubs' objectives had been "the aim of the official Republican organization in Texas for many years." The national committeeman implied, however, that he was not pleased by the failure of the leaders to invite him, Hopkins, McDowell, or the majority of the state executive committee to join the clubs. Within two weeks of his first comment, Creager moved to open opposition to the new organizational enterprise, asserting that he did not "intend to turn over control of the party to any group." He explained away the group's existence by asserting that its leaders were simply sore at Nolte's nomination, Hopkins's power as state chairman, and the appointment of Hobart McDowell. Creager argued forcefully that no larger issues were involved. For the next few months the clubs continued to meet, despite Creager's denunciations. J. F. Lucey placed Gerald Cullinan in charge of operations and hired an additional fieldman to stir up interest around the state; beyond a doubt, Lucey was outorganizing Creager. The national committeeman bided his time.[29]

The first bombshell of the battle burst in April, 1947, when the San Antonio club announced that Republican county chairman Joe Sheldon would sponsor a local club rally on April 10. Creager had not expected Sheldon's defection, which created the threat of a San Antonio-

Dallas-Houston coalition—the only combination of sufficient power and influence to take over the management of the party. Looking to head off statewide desertions to the new organization, Creager announced to the press that he would attend Joe Sheldon's noon luncheon uninvited. Come what may, he would at least seem to be in control of the situation. The much-publicized luncheon came off with no major altercations, but the strained cordiality only masked Creager's determination to respond forcefully. Less than six hours after the luncheon group dispersed, the Bexar County Republican Executive Committee gathered hastily and removed Joe Sheldon from the chairmanship. Creager and his local ally, Mike Nolte, had won the first public fight with the insurgents.

The next skirmish between Creager and the Republican Club faction occurred in May when Creager brought the headquarters committee to remove Alvin Lane from his post as co-counsel of the party and dismissed Marrs McLean as state finance director. In June, George Hopkins ousted Ralph Currie from the chairmanship of Dallas County, appointing R. P. "Dick" Wall in his place, a course of action which, after extensive litigation, proved a Pyrrhic victory for Hopkins. When the Republican Club's official journal, the *Two-Party News*, appeared in September, Lane, McLean, and Currie were referred to as "the happy Martyrs"; indeed, their martyrdom had been endorsed by 131 guests at a testimonial dinner in Dallas. By this time even outsiders noticed that the dispute had reached grave proportions, especially from Creager's point of view. Tom Bowers, a field worker for Senator Robert A. Taft, advised the Ohioan that "Creager may be on dangerous ground." Bowers thought the activists in the Republican clubs were determined to replace him as national committeeman at the 1948 Republican National Convention. While he believed that Creager preferred Taft to any other candidate, Bowers feared that the national committeeman would have to throw in with the West Texans and Dewey forces to save his place.[30]

The conflict boiled in October after a series of frank—and often heated—exchanges of opinion between Creager and Marrs McLean. McLean placed the blame for the intraparty fight squarely on Creager's shoulders: "Bedding down with your enemies is the 100% cause of the messy mess in the Republican party and organization today." Those enemies, in McLean's opinion, were Mike Nolte, the West Texans, and their allies. Nolte, McLean charged, was attempting to take over precinct conventions in Houston by organizing the employees of Howard Hughes's Grand Prize Brewery. As for the West Texans, McLean assured

Creager that his new West Texas friends would dump him at the first opportunity. Offering a kind of "olive branch," McLean assured Creager of support if he broke with Nolte and Hopkins and fired Hobart Mc-Dowell. Creager did not take kindly to McLean's mixture of admonition, threat, and assurance. He showed the letter to Nolte and issued a press comment in which he cynically denounced the attempt of "some fat cats to seize control of the Republican party." This heedless remark not unnaturally enraged "fat cats" and others; all but a few members of the club, Lucey and McLean being among the notable exceptions, resolved to throw Creager out and to take his deposition as the group's primary goal.[31]

Accordingly, attacks on Creager became more frequent and more direct. Gerald Cullinan characterized Creager as "nothing more than a Japanese gardener in the field of politics." Creager and the Nolte-Hopkins group were accused of changing the Texas Republican party into "a midget plum tree which can be guaranteed to bear luscious fruit whenever a Republican President goes to the White House." Cullinan's article added, somewhat inconsistently, that while Creager had remained out of the intraparty dispute thus far, he would have to take a side soon to avoid the possibility of being rejected by both factions. The article and its Japanese gardener image stung Creager to the quick, for Cullinan's horticultural imagery revived the charges made against him by Harry Wurzbach in 1928 and by Smith W. Brookhardt in 1929. In a valiant effort to discredit Cullinan, Creager disdainfully referred to the publication in which Cullinan's article appeared as a "scurrilous little pamphlet out of Dallas." With temperatures rising, an attempt to reconcile differences at a barbecue given in October by Mike Nolte in San Antonio fell flat. Creager used the occasion to denounce the Republican Clubs and the Sheldon faction in Bexar County. He received no applause and quickly left the scene with Nolte. Russell B. Wine, a veteran party leader, summed up the affair as "the darndest love feast I ever attended—if that is what it was."[32]

In spite of Creager's actions, the Taft men in the club, led by Marrs McLean, decided that, in the interests of their candidate, they would head off additional attacks on Creager and attempt to bring Creager to break with the Nolte-Hopkins faction. Though McLean and Orville Bullington thought it was time to end differences, in November the rift still divided the party. For his part, Creager tried to pass off the division to Taft managers as a personality conflict between Nolte and McLean. Seeing no advantage in taking sides in the dispute, the Taft managers blandly urged both McLean and Creager to reconcile their differences. Clarence Brown took up the matter with Creager in Philadelphia in late October and with McLean by mail in November. Brought around by Brown's urgings to close ranks with Lucey and McLean, during late October and November Creager slowly unglued the Nolte-Hopkins alliance, which he had supported less through choice than through desperation. This chore was none too difficult, for the coalition contained major elements of potential discord: Hopkins, McDowell, and Briggs were outright Dewey supporters, while in early November, 1947, Nolte hesitated to support the governor or anyone else. By the end of November, the crucial demolition work was accomplished as Creager brought Mike Nolte around to supporting Taft. Nolte even contributed $250 as good faith money to the senator's campaign fund.

With the assurance of Nolte's support, Creager then tackled George C. Hopkins. First, on December 20, 1947, he moved the headquarters operation from Dallas to Austin, out of Hopkins's easy reach. Taking this action as it was meant, Hopkins split with both Nolte and Creager and set out to build his own organization through the overnight appointment of friendly county chairmen, a course of action which landed Texas Republicans back in court. As with his ouster of Ralph Currie, Hopkins once again won a Pyrrhic victory. Though successful at the bar, deprived of Nolte's backing and operating without adequate hometown support in Dallas, George C. Hopkins could go no further in politics. By 1948, one of Creager's problems was solved.[33]

There remained the bothersome existence of the Republican Clubs; but here, too, Creager's fortunes brightened. J. F. Lucey died in October, 1947; and without his sponsorship, the Republican Clubs withered on the vine. The organization had failed to develop roots in the Texas Republican party, and with the death of its mainstay, the reconciliation of important club members with Creager, and the collapse of the Nolte-Hopkins faction it lost its reason for existence. Marrs McLean still labored to keep the group together after Lucey's death by trying to persuade oilman H. J. "Jack" Porter of Houston to become president of the clubs. Porter, though a member of the organization, was not persuaded to do so; and by January, 1948, the clubs were inactive.[34] Once again Creager seemed in full command of party activity; and during the early days of 1948, he assured Clarence J. Brown that he would work for Taft delegates. Creager corresponded directly with Taft in February, informing him that the Creager-Taft forces had controlled forty-four of sixty-two votes of the state executive committee during its February meeting in Houston. Reacting to the new state of affairs, a delighted Clarence Brown was moved to comment, "You fellows certainly have things under control." Party activity after the February meeting consisted primarily of organizing and counterorganizing on the local level. In Bexar County, for example, Hobart McDowell and Collie Briggs met with the anti-Nolte faction in preparation for the May precinct meetings and state convention. Mike Nolte was happily working for the Taft group, though some of that number, notably Marrs McLean and Joe Sheldon, were none too pleased to be cooperating with Nolte.[35]

With the West Texans safely divided, Creager gave serious attention to the May state convention, which named delegates to the national convention. In an attempt to destroy what remained of his opposition, Creager brought the headquarters committee to discharge Hobart Mc-Dowell, whom Hopkins had designated as his successor as state chairman, and to name county chairmen where vacancies existed. McDowell could not resist dismissal; he had signed a ninety-day notice contract with the Headquarters Committee when he became director of organization. The naming of county chairmen, however, occasioned more litigation. George C. Hopkins claimed that the filling of vacant county posts was the state chairman's prerogative and obtained an injunction in the Thirty-Seventh District Court (San Antonio) against a scheduled April 8 meeting of the headquarters committee. When the group met, one week after its originally scheduled meeting, Carlos Watson voted for Creager by proxy; the group avoided additional legal entanglements with Hopkins by voting to refer the entire matter to the Republican State Executive Committee, which would meet in May before the state convention in Corpus Christi. Watson presented the motion, Mike Nolte seconded it, and it carried with Collie Briggs and Hobart McDowell recorded as "declining to vote."[36]

In late May, when the executive committee met on the day preceding the state convention, Creager and Taft forces were "completely in control," according to the local newspaper, the *Corpus Christi Caller*. Of thirteen contested delegations, which included those of Bexar and Dallas counties, only two small Dewey delegations, from rural Garza and Llano counties, were seated. The committee vote in all cases was forty-five to twelve. Faced with inevitable and crushing defeat, George Hopkins lost his temper and shouted at the committee: "You know what you are going to do already, and there is no use wasting time." Bursting with propriety, Creager responded: "The chairman is out of order in a reflection on this body and I object." Completing the destruction of the Hopkins-West Texas faction, the committee approved a motion by Mike Nolte to reinstate Marrs McLean and Alvin Lane in their party offices; on a motion by Marrs McLean the committee removed R. P. "Dick" Wall, a Hopkins man, from the Dallas County chairmanship and reinstated Ralph Currie. In all, fourteen of nineteen Hopkins appointees as county chairmen were replaced by the state executive committee.

Hopkins was fighting mad. Newspaper reports carried rumors of a state convention bolt by Dewey forces. But though Hopkins and McDowell were sufficiently desperate to stage a rump convention, this strategy seems to have been discouraged by Herbert Brownell, who was in Corpus Christi for several days to survey the action and to confer with Hopkins and Creager. In the end, party leaders worked out a lopsided compromise on delegates. Two Dewey delegates, Hopkins and Enoch Fletcher of Grand Saline, and one Stassen delegate, Ruthelle Bacon, Hugh Exum's onetime employee and successor as state committee member, would attend the national convention in company with thirty Taft delegates. In recognition of his victory, Creager won endorsement for reelection as national committeeman for Texas.[37]

Even with this sweeping defeat, Hopkins and the West Texans continued their battle in the expectation of Dewey's nomination and election. They mistakenly assumed that after Dewey's nomination Creager would step down. The national committeeman was not about to oblige them. Following the national convention, Creager wrote Clarence Brown that the Dewey crowd were "suffering from swelled craniums" as they thought they should be permitted to take over and control the Republican organization in Texas. "They are in for some disappointments," Creager predicted. "Our crowd are firmly in the saddle and I venture to prophesy are going to remain there."[38]

The political showdown came at the August state convention in Waco. On the day before the meeting, Creager's candidate for manager of Dewey's campaign in Texas, Henry Zweifel, defeated Hobart McDowell by a vote of forty-three to thirteen on the state executive committee. Zweifel also defeated McDowell in the contest for the state chairmanship. Voted down four to one on all issues, outgoing Chairman Hopkins cantankerously insisted on a roll call vote on every issue. In his acerbic valedictory address to the convention, Hopkins charged that "Creager anointed [sic] and appointed whomever he pleased. We did not like it and we don't like it and we feel that a majority of the Republicans of Texas don't like it. He threw his orders and decisions in our laps with a take it or leave it spirit." According to press accounts, while Hopkins denounced him to the meeting, Creager "sat nearby, impassively chewing a cigar." On vote after vote, Hopkins was defeated by "a well-oiled Creager political machine." George Hopkins learned to his chagrin that support for the right national candidate was not necessarily a successful substitute for powerful Texas allies and applied political experience. Creager might well have appeared complacent. On vote after vote, his primacy in the state party was confirmed.[39]

The major business of the Waco convention was the approval of a Republican slate for the November election. Alvin Lane, denied the gubernatorial nomination in 1946, received unanimous approval as gubernatorial nominee in 1948. Barring a fortuitous "act of God," however, the governorship was not likely to fall to the Republicans because the Democratic party was more or less united in support of the incumbent, Beauford H. Jester. Major interest was focused instead on the contest for United States Senate, where Texas Republicans had their best chance of electoral success since the Bullington-Ferguson contest of 1932. The division between the conservative and Loyalist wings of the Democratic party in Texas reemerged as former Governor Coke R. Stevenson sought the nomination with the support of both the dominant conservative faction and of organized labor, while U.S. Representative Lyndon B. Johnson, his most powerful rival, was boosted by the Rayburn group.

The primary contest was bitterly fought. While eleven candidates sought the Democratic nomination, most of the vote went to George B. Peddy of Houston, who had once run for senator on the Republican ticket, Coke Stevenson, and Lyndon Johnson. The front-runner, Stevenson, led Johnson by slightly more than seventy thousand votes and Peddy by nearly a quarter of a million votes; but he failed to obtain a majority of the votes cast. The former governor and Lyndon Johnson were forced into a runoff election. In the campaign which preceded balloting, Stevenson and Johnson exchanged ferocious verbal blows: the governor attacked the congressman as the lackey of the White House Liberals in the national party; Johnson replied that Stevenson's pardoning of a liberal Texas labor leader proved he was soft on subversives. The free-swinging battle within the Democratic camp offered Texas Republicans a reasonable chance to win the Senate seat if they could muster sufficient determination to seize the opportunity.[40]

The Republicans, following their long-established if rarely implemented strategy, sought a candidate who could exploit this division in
the Democratic party. The search was long and frustrating. At their
August convention, the Republicans nominated Carlos B. Watson of
Brownsville, with the expectation that he would withdraw in favor of a
better-known nominee, if one could be persuaded to run on the Republican ticket. Party hopes in this regard were particularly pinned on U.S.
Senator W. Lee "Pappy" O'Daniel, who had fallen out of the national
Democratic party in 1944 when he supported the Texas Regular slate
of presidential electors.

O'Daniel apparently considered the Republican offer, tendered by H.
J. Porter, who was delegated to discuss the matter with him. When
pressed for a final commitment just before the Democratic runoff election, however, O'Daniel refused the Republican nomination. In all likelihood, he expected Coke Stevenson to win the contest. This presumption
seemed realistic: both Stevenson and George Peddy had run as conservative candidates in the initial primary election. Peddy's support would
be logically transferred to Stevenson; this was in fact what happened in
Harris and Dallas counties. However, on election day, August 28, 1948,
calculations were upset by a light voter turnout, particularly in areas in
which Stevenson and Peddy had been strong. At the same time, Johnson's hard campaigning in South Texas improved his showing considerably in that region. In Bexar County, for example, Johnson picked up
nearly four thousand votes over his performance in the July primary
election, while Stevenson ran eight thousand votes behind his earlier
figures. As a result of these shifts in votes, Johnson won the runoff
election and the Democratic nomination by a mere eighty-seven votes,
out of a total of nearly a million votes cast.[41]

Conservative Democratic bitterness over "Landslide Lyndon's" victory fed on numerous tales of slow and dishonest counts from Southwest
Texas—particularly from Duval County, which Johnson carried with
4,622 votes to an even 40 for Stevenson. With a known and recognized
candidate, the Republicans hoped to capitalize on just such a development. After O'Daniel refused their nomination, however, the Republicans were left with Carlos Watson on the ballot—and Watson had never
intended to be the party's nominee for more than a few weeks.

The problem of candidate recruitment, always a serious matter for
the permanent minority party, came to rest with H. J. "Jack" Porter.
An aggressive dynamo of a man, Porter had made a considerable for-

tune in the rough and risky competition of independent oil. Like many another businessman in Texas, Porter fell out of sympathy with the national Democratic party during the late 1930s. Along with Hugh Roy Cullen, a business associate and personal friend, Porter voted for Wendell Willkie in 1940 and supported the Texas Regulars in 1944. At the end of World War II, when various wartime restrictions on business were removed, Porter like most oilmen urged an end to price controls on petroleum products and opposed both the proposed reduction of the oil depletion allowance and the federal claim to ownership of the tidelands.

In pursuit of these issues, Porter became increasingly involved in politics, initially directing his efforts at marshaling congressional support to remove price controls from natural gas. For this purpose, Porter and Cullen visited Washington in December, 1946, and talked to various congressmen, including Representative Joseph W. Martin, for whom the Texans had given a reception in Houston following the November congressional elections. Martin's position was newly enhanced by the return of a Republican majority in the House: he advanced from minority leader to speaker, displacing Sam Rayburn, the longtime ally of Texas petroleum interests. But more than oil was involved in the courting of Martin; Cullen and Porter hoped to swing the Republican party in a more conservative direction. Generalizing from their immediate experience, the regulation of oil operators by the Federal Power Commission, and responding to the postwar "Red Scare" which swept Texas along with the rest of the United States, Porter and other Texas businessmen took a strongly conservative line, especially on economic issues. Their political views were at wide variance with those of the Truman administration, and the resultant conflict turned many of them into political activists.[42]

It is difficult to conceive of a more energetic businessman in politics than H. J. Porter. He supported the campaign of Tim O'Brien in 1946; he helped found and later headed TIPRO, the Texas Independent Producers and Royalty Owners, a major Texas interest group; he joined J. F. Lucey's Republican Club, served as a director, and emerged as Lucey's designated successor as head of the organization. By 1948, though he held no significant position in the party structure, Porter was an influential man in Texas Republican circles. Creager generally accommodated rising men in Republican ranks by encouraging them to take on responsibilities within the party. Thus, in 1948 the burden of finding a candidate for U.S. Senate fell on Jack Porter. He was accustomed to getting things done.[43]

Where could a suitable candidate be found? With O'Daniel's refusal of the nomination, the Republican party had no candidate who was widely known in Texas. Past Republican candidates were unlikely choices. With the exception of Orville Bullington, George Butte, and George Peddy, none had done at all well at the polls. By 1948, these three men were out of the running: Butte was dead, Peddy had returned to the Democratic party, and Bullington's health and business affairs kept him from considering another race. In the absence of a known nominee, the Republican party needed a candidate who would work hard to make himself known. It found its candidate in the person of its candidate recruiter, Jack Porter, who was urged by friends to "drop his bucket" where he was. After some persuasion, Porter agreed to run.

Once in the race, however, Porter's efforts were nothing short of heroic. With only two months of campaign time to cover Texas, he hired a professional staff which included Gerald Cullinan, Lucey's manager of the Republican Clubs and Tim O'Brien's campaign manager. Porter traveled extensively in all sections of the state and made large outlays of cash for newspaper space and radio time, though the media did not seem to respond by favoring his candidacy. Fighting as a Republican and as a political unknown, Porter came to believe that the newspapers and radio stations deliberately blunted his campaign, as they gave little coverage to his appearances and freely edited his paid political announcements. In spite of such obstruction, Porter's high-powered campaign attracted considerable popular notice. The *Houston Press*'s characterization of his campaign as "slam bang" accurately represents the intensity of Porter's activity. To the *New York Times*, the Republican party's fight to regain control of the Senate placed Texas as "the main battleground in the south"; the Porter-Johnson contest was the battle worth watching.[44]

Within Texas, Porter's campaign made the senatorial race the object of more attention than that for the presidency. Split between Truman and Strom Thurmond, the States' Rights party candidate, Texas Democrats tended to minimize the importance of national candidates and issues and concentrate on state and congressional elections. The single exception to this settlement was the Senate race. The moderate Lyndon B. Johnson was closely identified with the Truman administration and with the national Democratic party; a vote against Johnson was a second vote against the liberal policies of the Truman administration. The moderate-conservative rift in the Texas Democratic party deepened when Governor Coke Stevenson, reacting bitterly to his defeat by Johnson, endorsed Jack Porter.

Aided by the division in the Democratic party; by good financial support, mainly from Harris County contributors; and by his own almost unbounded energy, Jack Porter campaigned strenuously. Johnson ran a traditional Texas Democratic campaign, in which references to Republican opponents were rarely made. He continued to develop support in South and West Texas, especially in populous Bexar and El Paso counties, picked up support in Fort Worth and Beaumont, where organized labor was strong politically, and made a strong showing in rural East Texas. Lyndon B. Johnson won the Senate seat, but Jack Porter ran well—eighty thousand votes ahead of Thomas E. Dewey. Porter carried two oil-rich cities, Tyler in East Texas and Midland in West Texas, and most of the German counties, nearly won majorities in Dallas and Houston, and attracted about one-third of the vote in the Panhandle. To Porter, the election returns proved that the Republican party in Texas might become effective if it had strong candidates, adequate financing, and aggressive leadership.[45]

But in 1948 all three items were in short supply. Republicans who were willing to seek office had low visibility outside of party circles: Alvin Lane, for example, the Republican gubernatorial candidate in 1948, was a highly respected Dallas attorney and businessman, but he was generally unknown out of town. Lane's campaign was inadequately financed, supported largely by friends in Dallas County and by his own funds. With all this, the reserved, dignified attorney was an unlikely type of candidate for bare-knuckles Texas politics; he ran a gentlemanly campaign, making few references to his opponent, and relied substantially on newspaper advertisements and radio spot announcements. After years of general political inactivity and the nomination of obscure candidates, Lane's campaign gave new and needed respectability to Republican electoral politics in Texas, but respectability was still only a consolation prize. In the general election, Lane received about 15 percent of the vote; he carried no counties against the incumbent Beauford H. Jester.[46]

If the Republican party were to emerge from subsequent contests with anything more than honorable mention, it would, in Porter's view, be obliged to become a party of action. His own campaign indicated that the brightest prospect for the future might lie in large-scale fund-raising, the building of party organization, and the waging of aggressive campaigns against vulnerable Democratic candidates. Porter, accordingly, urged plans for party development on R. B. Creager when the two men met shortly after the November election at the Rice Hotel in Houston. More aggressive than tactful, Porter told the national committeeman that he would raise funds to build the party and to support candidates if Creager would resign as national committeeman, in his behalf. Caught off guard by this combined offer and assault, Creager politely and predictably turned down Porter's package. The proposition was never revived by either man.[47]

The contrast between Porter's blunt proposition and the numerous conspiratorial sapping operations of the West Texans before him is indeed striking: how was it that he rushed in where Hugh Exum and George Hopkins had only stealthily trod? For all his political activity, H. J. Porter was still new to Republican intraparty politics. The ailing J. F. Lucey had urged him in 1947 to lead the drive to gain control of the Texas party. When Creager was sitting on the fence that year in regard to presidential politics, Lucey and other members of the Republican Clubs urged Porter to unseat Creager as national committeeman. On that occasion, however, a number of persons counseled restraint. Speaker Joseph W. Martin advised against the move, for Creager's longtime contacts within the national party would make him a difficult man to oust. Within Texas, Marrs McLean advised Porter against a coup on the grounds that Porter lacked sufficient support within the state party and held no position in the statewide organization, despite his successful leadership as finance chairman for Harris County. Ever the man of action, Porter then proceeded to remedy what McLean saw as deficiencies: he attended his first Republican precinct convention in the spring of 1948 and was elected to the state executive committee in August of that same year. By taking on the race against Johnson, Porter added the finishing touch to party recognition; however unknown he may have been in 1947, by November, 1948, all state Republicans knew who Jack Porter was. Notwithstanding his rise to political prominence, however, when Porter asked Creager to resign from the national committee, Creager could reject the proposition with little fear of an immediate challenge. Even when Porter joined the state committee, his support was limited to Dallas and Houston; control of the party rested in the back country, where Creager was again on a solid footing. He was in no immediate danger.

True to his long-established practice, Creager attempted to find a prominent if harmless role for Porter in party activities. Thus, when in early 1949 Porter suggested that the party create a Committee for Two-Party Government in Texas, Creager and the state committee supported the proposal and named Porter to head the new organization. Proceeding with vigor, Porter commenced his labors by trying to resuscitate the Young Republican Club of Texas, which had lapsed into inactivity in the hands of men who were nearer to retirement than to college days. He traveled extensively and spent liberally in an attempt to interest college students and young professional men and women in the organization. Nor did his energies stop there.[48]

When he attended his first state convention, in 1948, Porter quickly identified the basis of Creager's power, his ability to marshal support of the country delegates, who held control of the meeting. Until this situation was changed by amending the sections of the state election law which allocated delegates, Porter could never mount a successful challenge to either Creager or his second-in-command and presumed successor, State Chairman Henry Zweifel. After the convention Porter returned to Houston, where he raised the subject of changes in the law with County Chairman Joe Ingraham and Malcolm McCorquodale, both attorneys. Over lunch, the three men sketched out reform legislation regarding delegate allocation and precinct and county conventions. Shortly after this meeting, Porter conferred with former State Senator Walter Moore, a Houston Democrat, and discussed strategy which would be followed in steering such a measure through the legislature. Then, in several subsequent meetings, Moore, Ingraham, McCorquodale, and Porter hammered out a legislative proposal.[49]

The bill which the Houstonians drew up was introduced on Monday, January 15, 1951, by freshman Republican Representative Edward T. Dicker and by veteran Democratic State Senator Rudolph Weinert of Seguin, whose acquaintance with Jack Porter dated from the oilman's leadership in TIPRO. The Weinert-Dicker Bill attracted considerable attention, particularly from the capitol press corps, which gave it highly favorable coverage. Editorially the *Dallas Morning News* worked to create a favorable reception for the measure by calling for electoral reforms a week before the legislature convened. Following the introduction of the bill, the *News* strongly endorsed this "Republican bill," observing: "Democratic conventions are notorious for shady dealings. But the Republicans do their share. Republicans vote dozens of county delegations that are phony as a three-dollar bill."

The Weinert-Dicker Bill reformed regulations for announcing and holding conventions and stipulated that each county would have one delegate at the state convention for every one hundred votes cast for the party's gubernatorial candidate in the most recent general election. The existing law allotted one delegate for three hundred votes. Both measures guaranteed every county at least one delegate. Though the proposed changes were limited in number, they were likely to effect widespread changes in the state party. The proposed numerical basis for the allocation of state convention delegates would have given preponderant voting power in the meeting to the delegations which represented Dallas, Harris, Tarrant, and Bexar counties, in which the majority of Republican ballots were usually cast. Fairly enough, Henry Zweifel objected that the bill would give "practical control of the Republican party" to party leaders in four urban counties, where Zweifel and the rural faction had little influence. Members of the party's old guard, including Orville Bullington and Enoch Fletcher, supported Zweifel's attacks on the Weinert-Dicker Bill while it was in committee hearings; and Mike Nolte lobbied strenuously against the measure.

After a day of hearings and several days of Nolte's activity, Senator Weinert feared that the measure might not receive a favorable committee report. To bar an unfavorable report, he bottled up his bill in committee. Strong and influential opposition to the measure made it necessary to settle on some compromises if any reforms were to be made. When the bill came to the floors of the houses, it was evident that compromises had generally favored the Zweifel-Nolte position. The numerical change in allocation of delegates to the state convention—the key provision of the original reform measure—was eliminated. Only the procedural sections which concerned the holding of precinct and county conventions emerged in the regular bill. Minor as it might seem, this small victory was important; by regulating convention procedures, it made the holding of snap conventions "on the rear end of a galloping horse" illegal.

The most immediate gains for the Porter group from the Weinert-Dicker bill, however, were received in the form of strong support from the urban press. Porter was now consistently identified as "a leader in the movement to make Texas a two-party state," an identification which he affirmed through his determined support for party reform and his energetic participation in election campaigns. Indeed, he did work to reestablish the Republican party as a credible political entity in Texas.

Entering party activity wherever opportunities appeared, Jack Porter worked mightily and successfully in the Panhandle to elect a Republican to Congress. Following Frank O'Brien's groundbreaking campaign in 1946, an unexpected opportunity for the Republican party came along in February, 1950, when Congressman Eugene Worley resigned his seat to accept a federal judicial position. A young schoolteacher and war veteran, Ben Guill of Pampa, decided to run in the special election to fill the seat. Running a vigorous campaign in opposition to the Truman administration, Guill traveled throughout the Panhandle denouncing socialized medicine, federal seizure of the tidelands, and Truman's veto of the Kerr Natural Gas Bill. Guill drew political support from Panhandle Democrats, such as oilman Eugene Green, a delegate to the 1948 Democratic National Convention, and Richard A. Young, chairman of the board of American Zinc; the most important support, however, came from Jack Porter, who raised about one-quarter of Guill's campaign fund in Houston and "practically closed up his office" to muster support for Guill from independent oil operators. The money was well spent on newspaper and radio exposure, both handled by Gerald Cullinan. At the same time, Guill received no financial support from either the state party or the Republican Congressional Campaign Committee. Creager was not interested in helping Guill get to Washington. Former Congressman Worley, a personal friend of Guill, obligingly stayed out of the contest.

With nearly adequate financing, an efficient campaign, an appealing personality, grassroots campaign work by his former students, and a light turnout in strongly Democratic cotton counties, Guill won the seat as the front-runner in a field of seven candidates—the first Republican to sit in Congress for Texas since the death of Harry Wurzbach in 1931. Having little to gain from Guill's victory, Creager had little to say on the subject. Other party leaders were not as closemouthed. In Washington, Representative Hugh Scott took the occasion as an opportunity to even the score with Creager, the "Boss of a paper organization." Scott observed, "The recent election of Ben Guill . . . shows what can be accomplished in Texas." In a possible showdown with Creager, Porter now had a valuable ally in Guill, if the congressman could win again in November.[50]

As it happened, Ben Guill did not hold the seat long. A novel set of circumstances, most notably the candidacies of six Democrats who divided the vote of the major party, accounted for Guill's election in May; by November, at the time of the general election, significant changes had occurred. Running against only one Democrat, Guill faced a more difficult contest, though the editorial support of some of the area's newspapers boosted his hopes. With support from both Creager and Porter and a hard-driving campaign managed by Mickey Ledrick, the freshman congressman waged a tough campaign which attempted to convince voters to split their ballots by supporting Guill, though not necessarily any other Republican candidate. On election day, cotton farmers, "with nothing else to do, came to town and voted Democratic, as usual." Guill's strenuous effort came to nothing.[51]

While R. B. Creager was occupied with the battles within the national committee—in January, 1949, over the continuation of Representative Hugh Scott in the national chairman's post, and in August of that same year over the succession of Guy Gabrielson—Jack Porter was making contacts and building potential support in the ranks of the Young Republicans. He prepared for a challenge to Creager in August, 1950, when, in accordance with Texas law, a party convention would be held. The immediate occasion for contention between Creager and Porter forces was the appearance of two delegations for Galveston County. County Chairman Morris Schreiber, supported by Mike Nolte, claimed that "Porter's youngsters" tried to pack the county convention in Galveston. Porter's Young Republicans rejoined by demanding to be seated in preference to the "old guard" delegation. The dispute became hot enough to keep R. B. Creager from taking a stand; he negotiated a compromise whereby both delegations were seated, splitting the county's vote equally between them. Schreiber was to remain as Galveston County chairman; and T. E. Workman, from the Young Republican faction, would be seated as the district's member of the state executive committee.

Porter's friends lost the next round as Nat Friedman, a Houston attorney, received the party's nomination for attorney general over the determined opposition of the Harris County delegation. By virtue of Creager's managerial talents, however, these open feuds reached an uneasy settlement. Though tired and ailing, the seventy-three-year-old politician could still mediate party disputes: he brought the remaining prestige of his long tenure as Texas Republican leader to mitigate the bitterness of factional disputes and sustain a measure of party unity. Soon his talents would be sorely missed.[52]

The tenuous unity Creager maintained in the Republican party in Texas ended when Creager died on October 28, 1950. Within a week of his death, three candidates spoke for succession to his national committee post. Mike Nolte came forward with Bexar County support; State Chairman Henry Zweifel could count on support from Fort Worth and the back country, from party veterans Carlos Watson and Orville Bullington, and from the former Dewey crowd. The third candidate was Jack Porter, who obtained endorsements from county organizations in Dallas and Harris counties, from Marion Enholm, the acting chairman of the Young Republican Federation of Texas, from Congressman Ben Guill, and from newly elected State Representative Edward T. Dicker. Strength on the Republican State Executive Committee was divided evenly between the three contenders. It looked as though there would be political mayhem. But the "real scrap" anticipated by Allen Duckworth of the *Dallas Morning News* never occurred. By the time the committee met, Mike Nolte had withdrawn from the race in favor of Henry Zweifel. When the state committee convened on November 21, Jack Porter calculated that he would be defeated by a two-to-one margin and prudently withdrew from the contest, leaving Henry Zweifel with a unanimous election as Creager's successor. Orville Bullington was chosen to succeed as state chairman; and Mrs. Carl J. Stearns, a Houston opponent of Porter, was designated as successor to Mrs. Lena Gay Moore, Republican national committeewoman, who resigned her post at the time of Creager's death.[53]

If Creager's death did not bring Porter the national committeemanship, it nonetheless brought him much closer to the position. Porter's next chance at the post would come in 1952, when the Republican National Convention would elect a committeeman for Texas for a four-year term. If the Republican party in Texas was to be rejuvenated with new blood, and if Jack Porter was to be elected to the national committee—and the two developments seem to have been inseparable—a great deal of effective organizational work and successful political maneuvering would have to be done. Whatever was done, moreover, would have to be done before the next state convention in May—eighteen months' time. But Porter's energy was formidable and his supporters were energetic: Zweifel and his friends were to find it hard work to deny Jack Porter his place in the sun.[54]

5

"The Texas Revolution"

THE YEAR AND A HALF which elapsed between Jack Porter's defeat in November, 1950, and his victory in July, 1952, was a time of unremitting struggle for control of the Republican party of Texas. In the Lilliputian-scaled scene of Texas Republican politics, factional struggles had been frequent. Creager, the master of smoke-filled-room politics, had beaten back serious challenges to his leadership from Harry Wurzbach and George Hopkins and the West Texans. And indeed, Henry Zweifel's bitter contest with Jack Porter might well have been merely another factional squabble, another episode in the predictable and unedifying drawing-room comedy of Texas Republicanism, if the local struggle had not converged with a more significant contention: that of Senator Robert A. Taft and General Dwight D. Eisenhower for the Republican presidential nomination in 1952. The interrelation of these two political contests, local and national, took the Texas fight into the center ring of national attention, where it had a profound effect on Republican presidential politics.

By 1952, Eisenhower was already well connected in Texas political circles. Eisenhower had tested the ground with an eye to candidacy for the Republican presidential nomination. In 1949 his presidency of Columbia University allowed him great freedom for political maneuver provided, of course, that he act with discretion. The proper vehicle for a shadow campaign emerged in the form of the American Assembly project, which was designed to bring businessmen, politicians, and intellectuals together at an established conference site for discussions of national problems and programs. Though sponsored by Columbia, the American Assembly project was to be funded through direct appeals to influential businessmen.

Therein rested Eisenhower's opportunity. What better way to establish additional connections with useful and important persons? As he traveled across America, waging a fund-raising campaign far more extensive than its relatively modest $500,000 goal warranted, Eisenhower not coincidentally made useful political contacts. In Texas, he met with Sid W. Richardson, Hugh Roy Cullen, Marrs McLean, John H. Blaffer, and other oilmen; publishers Amon Carter and Governor and Mrs. William P. Hobby; and such influential conservative Democrats as Jesse Jones, William H. Francis, Dillon Anderson, and Houston Mayor Oscar Holcomb. To the Texans, the import of these meetings was clear: indeed, they too had the presidency in mind and were not disposed to coyness on the matter. Recalling the meetings, Dillon Anderson wrote: "We talked about the Presidency but you only talked about the American Assembly." Clint Murchison, Dallas oilman, was sufficiently convinced of Eisenhower's candidacy to give five thousand dollars as "safety money" to the American Assembly. And Jack Porter came away from a meeting with Eisenhower convinced that the General would be a candidate in 1952. True to form, Porter set out to do something about it.[1]

Eisenhower's candidacy was exactly what Porter needed for his own purposes. With the Texas Republican organization still firmly in the hands of the pro-Taft old guard, Porter, like Creager in 1920, needed a candidate who would carry him into power. What Harding's election eventually did for Creager, Eisenhower's nomination and election could potentially do for Porter. Of course, the strategy of tying one's fortune to a promising national candidate had not always proved successful. George Hopkins's support of Dewey in 1948 yielded him no dividends because Creager retained control of the Texas delegation at the national convention. Indeed, Hopkins was never even the undisputed chief of the Texas Dewey faction. Porter would have to do more than support Eisenhower; control of the delegation to the national convention was every bit as important as backing the winning candidate.

Porter did things right. The first and necessary step in his strategy was his successful campaign for control of the Eisenhower movement among Texas Republicans by assuming the leading role in Eisenhower's shadow campaign. Raising funds from all corners of Texas and funneling contributions to Columbia University, Porter became a kind of Texas manager for the American Assembly project. By December, 1950, his efforts brought him the reward of a more important place in Eisenhower's calculations; Porter had established his political loyalty to Eisenhower and was relied upon for political intelligence from Texas. No Texas Republican could challenge Porter's prominence in this regard; he was in on the ground floor.[2]

In 1950, while Eisenhower gradually assembled energetic and useful contacts like Porter through the American Assembly project, Republican presidential politics revived. After Governor Thomas E. Dewey's announcement in midyear that he would not seek the nomination in 1952, influential eastern Republicans, including Herbert Brownell and Senator Henry Cabot Lodge, allied themselves with Eisenhower. Later in the year, Senator Robert A. Taft's flagging political fortunes were restored by reelection to his Ohio seat by a margin of more than four hundred thousand votes. Taft's old supporters, strongly represented on the national committee, took heart at this demonstration of the senator's vote-getting ability and renewed their backing for his undeclared candidacy. In Texas, longtime Taft men Marrs McLean and Mike Nolte had made overtures to the Eisenhower camp; now McLean and Nolte dropped tentative commitments to Eisenhower and eagerly waited for David Ingalls, Ben Tate, and Representative Carroll Reece to muster forces for a national Taft campaign. By the end of 1950, it was clear that in Texas and in the nation there would be a lively battle between Eisenhower and Taft in 1952. Supporters of both candidates commenced preparations for the contest.[3]

Ben Tate and David Ingalls, national leaders of Taft's campaign, arrived in Dallas in May, 1951, to build Texas support for the senator. They conferred with George S. Atkinson, again chairman of the faction-ridden Dallas County Republican party, Helen Ackenhausen, and oilmen H. L. Hunt and Roy Black. Traveling on to Houston, Tate and Ingalls tried to pour oil on troubled political waters: they sought out Jack Porter in an effort to keep his rivalry with Henry Zweifel from damaging Taft's attempt to gain the Texas delegation to the national convention. Their peacemaking project was a thorough failure. Porter was alleged to have told Tate and Ingalls that "it was just too bad if Taft got caught in the row between him and Zweifel." Ingalls then attempted to persuade Roy Black and Representative Joseph Martin to back away from an all-out fight. His choice of contacts, however, was scarcely well taken, for Black was already supporting Porter and Martin was biding his time as far as presidential politics were concerned. Taft's managers could only shrug off these rebuffs and hope that Porter would be a minor problem. To Ingalls, it seemed reasonable both to expect Porter to challenge Zweifel, using the Eisenhower candidacy as his vehicle, and to expect Zweifel to put down the challenge with the old guard and Taft backers, who controlled the state committee and the party apparatus. Past politics made this a realistic expectation. Creager had done things that way.[4]

Henry Zweifel, however, was no Creager. An able attorney and a fairly clever politician, Zweifel still lacked the manipulative skill and self-control which saw Creager through challenges to his management of the Texas party. In July, 1951, Zweifel brought the wrath of the Taft faction down upon himself by announcing his support of Eisenhower. With this surprising move, Zweifel undoubtedly intended to weaken Porter's cause by removing the issue of presidential candidates from the situation; he succeeded only in eliciting some hard words from Marrs McLean, who reminded Zweifel that "every member of the organization who accepted Eisenhower is more likely to go to Porter in the finish than would be one who was for Taft . . . the Taft supporters are the ones who will elect you national committeeman." Zweifel read the implied threat and, in full retreat, hastened to assure McLean of his loyalty to Taft.[5]

While Taft supporters had their difficulties and differences, Jack Porter was having problems of his own. To opponents like Marrs McLean, this was no surprise; McLean ungenerously characterized Porter as "a hard stubborn worker with practically no tact and little concept of political values."[6] More seriously, the managers of Eisenhower's campaign seemed to be having second thoughts about Porter; he was not treated with the consideration that might be the just reward of the man who had forwarded tens of thousands of Texas dollars to the general's pet project. Porter hoped that a public stand by the general on domestic issues would boost the Eisenhower boom and himself along with it. Thus, in September, 1951, Porter tried to persuade Eisenhower, who headed North Atlantic Treaty Organization forces at that time, to speak out against socialized medicine, federal aid to education, and the fiscal system utilized to administer the Social Security program. He received no expeditious reply. True, the general's military status barred overt political activity; but Eisenhower's personal aide, William Burnham, attached a memorandum to Porter's letter which advised: "The attached letter from Jack Porter represents to my mind the thinking of Roy Cullen, who has an adjoining office. Advise at least a week's delay in answering this to Jack." Following Burnham's advice, Eisenhower waited nine days to respond to Porter. Porter could find but small satisfaction in the tardy reply: "I shall certainly keep my own counsel with respect to the questions that are being propounded to me; they have nothing to do with the work of the military post that I occupy here." Playing it safe, he was also stalling on making firm commitments to local political figures like Jack Porter.[7]

As sound a strategy as Eisenhower might be pursuing for his own interests, his continuing aloofness offered Porter small reward for expended effort. While Porter tried and failed to obtain open support from Eisenhower, Taft managers pushed national committeeman Henry Zweifel into open endorsement of the Ohio senator. Ingalls reminded Zweifel that the Taft forces would have no part of a scheme to promote an uncommitted Texas delegation. McLean, the able fund-raiser, warned Zweifel that little money would be forthcoming in aid of a contest for an uncommitted delegation and that Jack Porter could easily defeat such a tactic and become national committeeman. These efforts by McLean, and presumably the activity of other Taft men, had their effect. By November, 1951, David Ingalls viewed Zweifel as safely in the fold. Given such persuasion, how could he resist?[8] Publicly, Henry Zweifel supported his own notion of an uncommitted delegation as late as the end of December; at the same time, State Chairman Orville Bullington, Carlos Watson, Mike Nolte, and Marrs McLean were openly campaigning for a Taft delegation.

Thus the Texas Republican party ended 1951 in a state of predictable discord. Confusion within the Zweifel-Taft force and animosity between this group and the Porter-Eisenhower faction were sufficiently strong to cause the cancellation of a Republican "Yuletide Friendship Program" in Corpus Christi—a microscopic reflection of the state of party affairs, for Nueces County Republican Chairman Jim Stickler charged that Zweifel and Bullington intended to introduce a "note of personal enmity and politics" at the scheduled gathering. Given recent developments in the party, no Texas Republican would have been astonished at such action.[9]

During the early months of 1952, factional patterns came into clearer focus as Texas Republicans publicly identified themselves with either Taft or Eisenhower. Jack Porter was finally given public recognition as leader of the Ike forces in the state when Senators Lodge and Duff arrived in Dallas in early February to open the Texas Eisenhower headquarters. Porter had not waited for ceremonial recognition; in January he recruited party veteran Alvin Lane as codirector of the Eisenhower drive, and he soon added Edward T. Dicker and Ben Guill to the leadership of the faction. Well before the visit of Duff and Lodge, Porter and Lane started to plan a grass roots campaign for control of the party, the only such effort since Harry Wurzbach's partial and unsuccessful campaign in 1928. Like Wurzbach, Porter formed his plan with an eye to the press; like Wurzbach, he found valuable allies among reporters and editors. Thus, as early as January 12, 1952, the *Dallas Morning News*, which usually voiced the point of view of the state's conservative Democratic faction, published a front-page editorial asking Senator Taft to withdraw his candidacy in favor of General Eisenhower. This startling development was reported in the *New York Times* on the following day—the first important element of the Texas campaign to be reported in the national press.[10]

Running second, late, and scared, Taft leaders launched their own Texas campaign. Yet from the beginning the Taft campaign was characterized by clumsiness, lack of attention to details, and inferior political intelligence. In February, Senator Taft solicited the support of Texas Republicans in a mimeographed letter over a smudged rubber stamp signature. Among those on Taft's mailing list were Alvin Lane, who was then heading the state Eisenhower office in Dallas, and the late R. B. Creager. Despite inept work by his staff, Taft's prospects in Texas were encouraging. In March, the Ohio senator spoke in a number of Texas towns and was generally well received, especially in Houston, where County Chairman Joe Ingraham worked up a rousing popular reception for the senator. During a visit to Dallas, Taft picked up the support of County Chairman George S. Atkinson, who had been publicly uncommitted until the visit. But Taft's Dallas visit was marred by more front-page editorials in the *Times Herald* and the *Morning News*: he was again urged to withdraw from the running for the nomination and was advised that the rank and file of the Republican party clearly preferred Eisenhower. The Taft campaign was thus launched on a sour note.[11]

In contrast to the Taft campaign's late start, since the previous September Jack Porter had employed three full-time field men. By the time of the Duff and Lodge visit, Porter had added a fourth full-time field man to his staff and, according to a local Taft supporter, was spending at least $7,500 per month to work up grass roots support for Eisenhower and himself. Such unheard-of activity was more than some of the old guard could stomach. A group of old-line East Texas county chairmen, including Dudley Lawson and A. W. Orr, both members of the state committee, protested:

A group of Houston multi-millionaires scent a Republican victory in 1952 and they want control of the party so badly that they are sending their hired hands into every part of the state with instructions to sow the seeds of distrust in the present able leadership of the party and create confusion in the rank and file.

As the tone of their letter grew ever more heated, the old guard leaders added: "Should they prevail, headquarters of the party would be moved to the plushy surroundings of a carefully guarded Houston club where a hierarchy would put the party machinery to work for their own selfish purposes." Like much of the Taft effort in Texas, this letter and its visions of aggravation were ineffectual. It merely rehearsed old charges of "fat cat" efforts to seize the party and conspiracies in Houston, and it was circulated within the meager ranks of the party's "old believers," who were already favorable to Taft and opposed to Porter. But the authors were quite correct in estimating Jack Porter's general intention to take control of the Republican party in Texas. Porter himself made no bones of his ambition when he wrote to Eisenhower: "It is just this simple: if I control the state convention, I can name the delegation, and if Henry Zweifel of Fort Worth controls the state convention, he can and will name the delegation." The goal was clear to both Porter and Zweifel; whoever controlled the Republican National Convention delegation from Texas would head the Texas party for at least four years.[12]

With this, his second task, uppermost in mind, during February and March Jack Porter out-organized the old guard. He established Eisenhower clubs throughout the state, even in such current Democratic strongholds as Lubbock, in western Texas. Though optimistic in March, the Taft forces suspected in April that Porter and the Eisenhower group were likely to run up large majorities in enough precinct and county conventions to control the state convention. Consequently, according to Mrs. R. H. J. Osborne, Zweifel's state vice-chairman, Zweifel began to urge his supporters to bolt their precinct and county conventions. Failing to achieve a clear majority, Taft supporters were simply to walk out and hold "rump" conventions elsewhere.

A concerted bolt of Taft forces at the precinct level, however, required some organization. In Harris County, where chairman Joe Ingraham favored Jack Porter but was publicly committed to Taft, Zweifel sent in several of his own friends to organize precincts. In Dallas County, the *News* anticipated convention bolts as Taft men studied "seven rules regarding bolting." But it took more than such advice to compete with Porter's organization on the precinct level. Taft efforts were tardy and incomplete. George Atkinson, county chairman, used his authority to fill vacancies with new precinct chairmen who were sympathetic to the Taft faction; but he never bothered to complete so much as a survey of the opinions of precinct leaders. Thus, in Dallas County, though most of the old guard, the familiar faces at county executive committee meetings, favored Taft, the senator's campaign never got off the ground.[13]

Quite the contrary was true in San Antonio. Marrs McLean, Mike Nolte, and Nolte's nephew, attorney John Goode, Jr., had a firm hold on the party machinery, adequate funds to mount an effective campaign, and plans to carry the county. Nolte and McLean underwrote a 25,000-postcard poll and followed through with block-level canvassing and electioneering. Looking back on these efforts, McLean observed: "They (the Porter faction) spent money without looking back and so did we." In turn Jack Porter supported Joe Sheldon's efforts to put together an enthusiastic group of Eisenhower supporters in Bexar County, but the results were not encouraging. The convention in Sheldon's and Nolte's precinct was held at the Olmos Club, which Nolte owned. Eighty persons attended, the majority voting for Taft-instructed delegates to the county convention. Even though Sheldon claimed that voting irregularities had occurred in some southern and northwestern precincts, he conceded that "the Taft people simply out-organized us" and that in most instances they won "fair and square."[14]

In Houston, Eisenhower Democrats, independent voters, and new Republicans swamped many precinct conventions. In the exclusive River Oaks precinct, where Jack Porter lived, 684 persons attended in May, 1952: only five persons, including Mr. and Mrs. Porter, had attended that precinct convention in 1948. Record attendance levels near the 900 mark were recorded in some precincts. Surrounded by new and unfriendly voters, Taft supporters organized the walkouts their national committeeman had suggested. Mrs. Carl Stearns was defeated in her own precinct

and bolted the meeting with a handful of friends; much the same action occurred in thirty-five other precincts in Harris County.[15]

A similar pattern of events emerged in Dallas. Again a record number of persons attended their precinct conventions. Nineteen precincts
had more than 100 persons in attendance, with number 72, in the Park
Cities, recording about 750 participants. Of 125 conventions, Taft carried
nine, MacArthur two, and three sent uninstructed delegates to the county
convention: Eisenhower had a clear majority in 111 meetings. As in
Houston, tempers grew and Taft delegates bolted. In precinct 65, Walter
Rogers, state chairman of the Taft organization, led about 65 backers
in a bolt of the convention. After their departure, the Eisenhower faction
elected Alvin Lane permanent chairman of the meeting. In another
North Dallas precinct, State Representative Edward T. Dicker, a leader
in the statewide Eisenhower movement, deposed incumbent chairman
George Atkinson. V. T. Bartley, temporary chairman, in whose home
the 87th precinct meeting was held, reacted to a Taft take-over of the
meeting by summoning police to disperse the gathering. The *Dallas
Morning News* aptly quipped, "Those grass roots became a little seared
from the heat in spots."[16]

Over the state, the pattern of large Eisenhower majorities and bolts
by Taft groups held true. In Fort Worth, state chairman Henry Zweifel
bolted the convention at his home, where he was defeated as precinct
chairman by a vote of 63 to 50. Zweifel crossed the sidewalk and held
a rump convention on the curb. Members of the state committee met
similar challenges. In Lubbock, where 1,500 Republicans attended precinct conventions, M. D. Temple lost by a vote of 19 to 11 in his home
precinct. L. J. Benckenstein, longtime party leader in Beaumont and
close friend of the late R. B. Creager, lost the vote in his precinct convention and at his wife's urging bolted to their two-car garage. Ruthelle
Bacon lost in Amarillo as all thirty conventions went for Eisenhower.
In Carlos Watson's hometown, Brownsville, the Eisenhower group carried eleven of fifteen precincts. In Corpus Christi, the majority of the
local meetings went for Eisenhower; nearly nine hundred voters appeared at one precinct convention. In oil-rich Midland, three times as
many people appeared at the Republican conventions as at the Democratic. Again, Eisenhower carried the day. With the exception of San
Antonio, in the urban areas of Texas, the story was the same: Eisenhower, the popular general, was a wildly popular candidate. Jack Porter
and his friends had done their work well.[17]

As it transpired, the Porter forces did their work almost too well. Where had all those Republicans come from? The Taft forces advanced a theory: after they were outvoted at the precinct convention, the old guard justified its bolts with the claim that the crowds for Ike were made up of non-Republicans, who, naturally, could not properly participate in the business of the Republican party. This charge—actually a revival of a complaint of some months' standing—alleged that for his own ends Jack Porter swamped the meetings with Democrats. The core of the Zweifel case against the Porter faction, this serious allegation deserves close attention.

It is important to note at the outset that Texas had no law which registered voters by party affiliation. Thus, while the matter of party identification of the Ike fans might have been easily settled in Louisiana, which had a party registration system, in Texas the whole matter was largely one of conjecture and arbitrary definitions. For his part, Henry Zweifel correctly maintained that few of the Eisenhower crowd had previously participated in Republican party activities. By contrast, party regulars, few in number, were old acquaintances at precinct conventions. Though this narrow notion of party affiliation—"They're Republican if they look familiar"—came easily to longtime members, according to one study of Texas politics it excluded 95 percent of the actual voters of the state. Presumably, at least those persons who voted for Republican candidates ought to be considered Republicans.

Even this seemingly impartial supposition, however, is fraught with problems in Texas because only 100,000 Texans, "the sinew and fiber of the Republican Party," in George Atkinson's words, regularly voted for the party's gubernatorial candidate, while three to four times that number cast ballots for Republican presidential candidates. Were the "presidential Republicans" to be excluded? They heavily outnumbered the straight-ticket Republicans. Harold K. Van Buren, the MacArthur manager in Dallas, asserted, along with Eisenhower leaders: "We need those newcomers to win elections." Such problems were bruited about at a March meeting of the state executive committee. After some discussion and over the objection of Porter's allies on the committee, the body passed a motion which required participants in the party's conventions to sign a loyalty pledge: "I am a Republican and I intend to participate in the party's activities in 1952." The party-in-the-organization excluded the largely separate party-in-the-electorate.[18]

The pledge quickly became the object of controversy. After the Por-

ter group unsuccessfully challenged it in district court, they sponsored
newspaper advertisements which urged voters to sign the pledge because
it was practically meaningless. Contrary to Henry Zweifel's much-
publicized assertion, the ads assured signers that they would not be
barred from future Democratic party primary elections by virtue of their
signing the Republican pledge in 1952. In fact, the Porter group printed
up extra copies of the pledge to insure that all of their voters would
have the document, which was necessary to secure entrance to the precinct conventions. Zweifel's intention quite clearly seems to have been to
frighten presidential Republicans and new Republicans away from precinct meetings. Just as surely, the Porter faction rested its hopes of success on the turnout of these groups. For all the legal ambiguity of party
identification in Texas, these new elements in the party's politics did
honor the party's standard of identification by signing the required
pledge. Legally confused and logically weak, the dispute over the loyalty
pledge and the new Republicans came down to a certainty: the newcomers signed the pledge, whatever their previous political affiliation
and mental reservations might have been. Under the party rules established by the Taft faction, the new voters were thereby entitled to vote
in primaries and precinct conventions. The Eisenhower faction built its
case on this contention.[19]

The county conventions which followed were for the most part re-
runs of the precinct conventions. In Houston, Eisenhower supporters
controlled 213 of 236 convention votes. After the meeting had been in
session "about two minutes," Carl G. Stearns, the floor leader for Taft,
shouted, "We bolt—all Taft forces to Room 117." In the lower Rio
Grande Valley, Carlos Watson, legal counsel for the state committee, led
a bolt in Cameron County, while Eisenhower supporters bolted in adjoining Hidalgo County. In Beaumont, at the end of a long and emotion-
ally heated convention, Lamar Cecil and L. J. Benckenstein took the exceptional course: they worked out a compromise and split the delegation.[20] In Dallas County, the Taft people walked out ten minutes after
the convention began, went to a parking lot, and conducted their meeting from the rear end of a red pickup truck. Brazos County sent a one-
man black delegation for Taft after County Chairman J. L. Thomas refused to seat white Eisenhower delegates and was subsequently chosen
as Brazos County's five-vote delegation to the state convention. State
Chairman Orville Bullington was denied a seat on the Eisenhower delegation from Wichita Falls, while in Fort Worth Henry Zweifel staged

a walkout at the Tarrant County convention, announcing, "We will withdraw from this convention and hold one of our own." Amarillo sent two delegations because Taft delegates "reconvened" the county convention at 11:50 P.M., after victorious Eisenhower voters had gone home. In Austin, Taft supporters had foregone the nicety of a walkout by never appearing at the duly called county convention; they held one of their own, elsewhere. "Jr." Crompton, Rusk County Republican chairman, added a novel wrinkle to political proceedings by acquiescing in an Eisenhower triumph at his convention and subsequently appearing at the state convention with a Taft delegation of his own.

After the widespread local disputes, it is not surprising that tempers were high on the eve of the state convention. Henry Zweifel, commenting acidly on the precinct and county conventions, accused the Porter faction of having made a pact with the political devil—the Political Action Committee of the CIO. Porter, for his part, accused Zweifel of attempting to shut out needed "new blood" from the party in an effort to facilitate close management of patronage in the event of a Republican victory in November. In the exchange, Zweifel's attack received greater press coverage because it enjoyed the virtue of novelty.[21]

Two weeks before the state convention began, the scenario for the political drama had already been completed. According to the pro-Eisenhower *Dallas Morning News*, Mike Nolte said: "We have 95 percent of the [state] committee. Taft forces are in control and are going to stay in control." Nolte fanned the flames of controversy again at a meeting of the Republican State Executive Committee in Fort Worth by presenting a resolution commending both Henry Zweifel and Mrs. Carl J. Stearns, national committeewoman and an opponent of Jack Porter in Houston. With Porter supporters a minority on the committee and refusing to vote, the motion carried unanimously by a voice vote. At the same meeting, Zweifel increased the hold of Taft forces on the state committee by appointing Don Barnhart of Denton to a vacant position. With firm control of the state committee, the Taft forces appointed the convention committees, including the credentials committee, and insured the seating of Taft partisans in contested delegations.[22]

Though the confidence of the Texas Taft supporters might be as strong as ever, on the same day as the Fort Worth meeting the Eisenhower campaign received a boost with the announcement of the results of the most recent Gallup poll: Eisenhower led Taft nationally by wide margins among all Republicans, except those in the fifty-years-and-over group. In the following weeks, Texas sustained the Eisenhower boom. Traditional conservatism did not prevent the *Dallas Morning News* from running front-page editorials under the banner "Texas G.O.P. Faces Betrayal." The newspaper charged that the Zweifel-Taft group would use its control of the state committee and of the machinery of the state convention to frustrate the "popular voice." Though partisan, this statement correctly assayed the politics of the situation. Outvoted by new Republicans at most precinct and county conventions, the Zweifel faction found that the only alternative open to it was to capitalize on its firm control of the party organization. The political steamroller, venerable through long use throughout the nation, would be the vehicle for a Taft victory in Texas. However much Ike supporters and newsmen might object to these tactics, it would, after all, be unintelligent politics to refrain from using every advantage—and control of party machinery is a highly significant aspect of political advantage. The remarks of a few self-righteous Democratic editorials were hardly cause for worry, let alone adequate cause to throw away an otherwise unobstructed victory. Correctly assessing their own political assets, ignoring the possible importance of a "moral" issue which could be raised by steamroller politics, the Taft forces set out to play the game their way. Seeing an old-fashioned political shutout in the making before the state convention began, Eisenhower leaders made advance arrangements for rental of a meeting hall near the site of the convention.[23]

When the state executive committee met in Fort Worth on June 26, it had to rule on contested delegations from thirty-one counties—including Dallas, Harris, Bexar, Cameron, Tarrant, Travis, Potter, and Rusk. Though the committee sat from 10:30 A.M. until 6:45 A.M. the next day, it predictably emerged with a settlement which was far from equitable. Even before hearings began, Orville Bullington, the usually prudent state chairman, told reporters that there was not likely to be a fair and just resolution of the factional dispute: "They'll barrelhouse 'em through. Whoever controls the [state] committee can always barrelhouse 'em through. You'll see, it'll be the same at Chicago." The committee did just what Bullington prophesied: it recommended the seating of Eisenhower delegates from only Galveston and Lavaca counties. The red pickup truck meeting in Dallas, the black one-man delegation from Navarro County, and "Boss" Crompton's Rusk County delegates were all recognized, as were about 350 other Taft men from disputed delegations. Triumph was accompanied by vengeance. On a motion by Carlos Watson, the committee removed Alvin Lane from the position of party counsel.

Surveying its work, Henry Zweifel proudly asserted that the committee had "rendered a courageous service to all Texas and to its conservative citizenship and to the wives, sisters, and mothers of this great nation. This is a fight for Americanism and the American way of life and will be so regarded by history." With this statement, Zweifel left history to its labors and got on with the political business at hand by appointing an entirely pro-Taft credentials committee for the state convention. However exalted the state committee's crusade for Americanism might be, some members of that body apparently realized that its actions could be seen as anything but handsome. Mrs. Charles Renaud of Fort Worth, a committee member, argued that "the other side would do the same thing if they controlled the committee." Her logic could not be disputed. On the other hand, this opinion offered no consolation for those who had not the chance to do as they had been done by.[24]

The credentials committee, presided over by Mike Nolte, recommended even more extreme action than that taken by the state committee: solid Taft delegations were seated from both Lavaca and Galveston counties. After temporary chairman L. J. Benckenstein ruled that contested Taft delegates, placed on the temporary roll by the credentials committee, could properly vote on the motion to seat themselves, Taft delegations approved Nolte's report by a vote of 762 to 222. The steamroller steered by David Ingalls and Carroll Reece, Taft's national campaign managers, effectively finished the work of the state convention. The die was indeed cast.

At this point in the proceedings, after a plan approved by Herbert Brownell, the Eisenhower delegates bolted the convention, moving to a neighboring auditorium.[25] The Taft convention then named a national convention delegation which included three Eisenhower delegates and thirty-five Taft delegates. Meanwhile, the Eisenhower convention nominated thirty-three Ike delegates and five Taft delegates. The Taft convention delegation was instructed to support Henry Zweifel for reelection as Republican national committeeman for Texas, while the Eisenhower rump convention instructed its national slate for Jack Porter.[26]

Though the two conventions acted in parallel courses, they differed markedly in spirit. All the fervor of righteousness dominated the Eisenhower meeting. In his invocation, the Reverend Mr. N. O. Carrington prayed: "We like Ike. God likes Ike. We will nominate and elect

him."[27] As the Eisenhower cause went marching on after the meeting at
Mineral Wells, it paraded through the headlines of the leading newspapers and magazines of America. Not all publications went as far as
the *Dallas Morning News*, which blandly told Senator Taft that his
delegation was "nothing short of fraudulent." But Taft's hometown
newspaper, the *Cincinnati Post*, advised the senator that he should openly repudiate the action of his supporters in Texas. Clearly, events in Texas
were already affecting Taft's national campaign.[28]

In this one-sided press war, the Eisenhower forces were skillfully led
by Paul G. Hoffmann and Oveta Culp Hobby; the latter was the former
head of the WACs and wife of former Governor William P. Hobby,
publisher of the *Houston Post*. Mrs. Hobby used widespread contacts in
the Texas and national press to stimulate interest and coverage at Mineral
Wells. Hoffmann persuaded nationally known writer Joseph Alsop to
cover the convention at Mineral Wells and convinced both *Time* and
Life magazines and the *New York Times* to send crews to report on
Texas politics. The benefits of national publicity were all Eisenhower's.
Perhaps it was inevitable that even unbiased reporting would show Taft
forces in an unfavorable light to the national readership of leading papers
and magazines.

In Texas, Taft leaders had the dangerous habit of making extreme
and impolitic statements in the presence of newsmen. Following the
lead of Henry Zweifel, former state chairman George C. Hopkins told
the state convention that the Eisenhower movement represented an attempt by the Communists to take over the Republican party. Not content with that charge, he improved on it by adding that he was afraid to
"tell what I know" about the Eisenhower leaders because "I don't know
how soon I might get shot." Unable to resist recording this intriguing
possibility, the *New York Times* commented drolly, "He did not explain
this meaning further." Not to be outdone by Hopkins, Henry Zweifel
revived his alarm that the Eisenhower group represented a "near-revolu-
tionary movement" inspired by organized labor and backed by the *Daily
Worker*. Even jovial Mike Nolte joined the fray by asserting that Jack
Porter would fill the convention with hoodlums. Nolte also distributed
several thousand copies of the *Clover Business Letter* published by Edward Gallagher of the Clover Manufacturing Company of Norwalk,
Connecticut; Gallagher's pamphlet charged Eisenhower was the agent of
a conspiracy which included "the new deal section of the Republican
party, a group of international bankers, and Fair Deal Democrats."[29]

On the issue of party control both Zweifel and Marrs McLean made highly damaging statements in opposition to the principle of majority rule. McLean, for one, was "not in the least persuaded that there is any right in the majority," and Zweifel openly attacked the principle of majority rule. These extremist statements and openly heavy-handed methods did little to enhance the general credibility of the Zweifel faction with the press, which viewed them as local yokels playing old-fashioned political games. But the yokels made good copy.[30] The pro-Eisenhower press made splendid capital of the Zweifel group's moves and pronouncements. The *Dallas Morning News* compared Zweifel's group to "the boys in the politburo" but credited Zweifel for being intellectually honest: "He is merely preaching what the Republican State Executive Committee has practiced through many years. This little group of sixty members has done exactly as it pleased, regardless of the will of the majority of Texas Republicans." Texas Taft leaders left themselves open to such charges. They also made Senator Taft's campaign increasingly vulnerable to the charge of an attempt to impose the will of party kingmakers on the rebellious majority of Republicans. Taft was cast in the unenviable and largely inaccurate role of ruthless machine politician. Such developments eventually spelled disaster for Senator Taft at the Republican National Convention in Chicago in July: no issue was to prove more damaging to the senator than "the Texas steal."[31]

The most significant buildup of the Texas issue for the national convention was made in the press as *Time, Newsweek*, and the national press and wire services kept the issue in the public eye. National columnist Joseph Alsop wrote indignantly: "This steal has been accomplished by a system of rigging as grossly dishonest, as nakedly anti-democratic, as arrogantly careless of majority rule as can be found in the long and often sordid annals of American politics."[32]

During the month which passed between the Mineral Wells conventions and the national convention of the Republican party in Chicago, the bandwagon of Senator Taft slowly ground to a halt. Dwight D. Eisenhower formally resigned from the army on June 2; he immediately took up the issue which Herbert Brownell identified as most embarrassing to Taft—"the Texas steal." Speaking out at Abilene, Kansas, against dishonest party management and the delegate "rustlers" at Mineral Wells, Eisenhower directed public attention—and that of the uncommitted party factions—to a highly expedient moral issue. The Texas steal deflected attention from Eisenhower's own position on various matters of policy, a fuzzy and somewhat more progressive orientation than Senator Taft's. For his part, the senator shrewdly observed: "I think they'd rather have the issue than the delegates."[33]

Preparations for the national convention had begun in the Eisenhower camp well before the Mineral Wells convention. Convinced that the Zweifel-Taft forces would use their control of the state committee and hence of the convention to steamroll opposition, Alvin Lane had long planned Eisenhower strategy with an eye toward future hearings before both the Republican National Committee and the credentials committee of the convention. Thus, several days before the state convention Lane had appealed to the national chairman, Guy Gabrielson, to guarantee fair play by condemning minorities who had bolted previous meetings. Keeping clear of the factional dispute, Gabrielson prudently declined to comment on the Texas situation.[34]

Formal on-site preparations for credentials hearings began on June 29, as "weary-eyed" Henry Zweifel arrived in Chicago with a filing cabinet of "evidence," which had been kept "under guard" during the whole trip. With the cabinet and aides in tow, Zweifel checked into the Morrison Hotel, where the entire Texas Taft delegation stayed. On Monday, June 30, Mike Nolte, Marrs McLean, and Carlos Watson arrived to reinforce Zweifel. Later that same day, the Texas Chief brought Eisenhower leaders Jack Porter, Alvin Lane, Malcolm S. McCorquodale, and Mrs. Ralph Currie into town. Reporters immediately sounded out their reactions to Zweifel and his evidence. Commenting on Zweifel's filing cabinet, Porter said: "The Taft forces couldn't get enough documentation into the hold of the *Queen Mary* to justify their brazen steal of delegates in Texas."[35]

Hearings before the Republican National Committee began on July 1. In a forty-eight-page brief, prepared by Alvin Lane and Malcolm McCorquodale, the Eisenhower group claimed that the convention at Mineral Wells had improperly excluded some five hundred Eisenhower delegates who had been elected by "sweeping majorities." Enoch Fletcher and Neal Beaton of Texas and F. Trowbridge vom Bauer of Chicago and Monte Appel from Washington, D.C., the Taft faction's attorneys, answered that Jack Porter had attempted to mob Republican conventions with Democrats, a course of action that was illegal, unfair, and contrary to the vitality of the two-party system.[36] Though the merits of these arguments were possibly of secondary importance, the contentions deserve closer scrutiny than the press afforded them in 1952.

Weighed on their own terms, the claims of both parties can be accepted as substantially correct. The heavy-handed actions of the Texas state committee, the credentials committee, and the regular convention at Mineral Wells were too well known to be open to plausible dispute. At the same time, Porter's organization could never have swamped the normally sparsely attended precinct conventions if it had relied largely on Republicans who had attended in the past. The argument over the political identification of the pro-Eisenhower crowds is hopelessly tangled. In the absence of a statutory requirement for party registration, there was no solid legal basis for the claim of the Taft group that the "new Republicans" were simply Democrats. On the other hand, it was uncontested that a large part of Porter's support had come from people who were not previously known as Republicans. It is probable that "Porter's hordes" consisted largely of "presidential Republicans"—who had cast more than 150,000 votes for Thomas Dewey in 1948—and voters who were otherwise inactive in any kind of political party. In the absence of clear-cut evidence to substantiate either position, a narrow legalistic resolution of the argument falls to the favor of the Eisenhower faction: the state executive committee, controlled by the Taft faction, had established the signing of the so-called loyalty pledge as the standard of party identification. When the "new Republicans" signed the required statement at precinct conventions, they properly established themselves as "Republicans." In the absence of a genealogical standard for membership in the Texas Republican party, the Porter Republicans surely qualified.[37]

Whatever the merits of the respective cases, newsmen expected a pro-Taft decision from the Republican National Committee: "While the Committee will go through the motions of hearing contested arguments, Taft supporters are talking as if it were all over." Anticipating a negative decision from both the national committee and the credentials committee, Porter vowed to carry the contest to the floor of the convention. Porter's threat, and the possibility that the cases of other contested delegations—those of Georgia and Louisiana, among others— would be decided on the convention floor, had their effect. Unwilling to have the whole "Texas steal" brought before the convention—and, indeed, not certain that he could hold all of his delegates on the issue— Senator Taft offered a compromise which the national committee approved: on the temporary roll the Texas delegation would include twenty-two Taft delegates and sixteen Eisenhower delegates.[38] The senator's compromise in Chicago was, however, to be less important than an attack on his whole position by the Republican governors, who were meeting in Houston.

Four weeks before the governors' unified attack on Taft's position, ten of their number criticized the tactics employed by Taft's forces in Texas. Their statement was doubly useful because it advertised Eisenhower's support among elected officials and also served to keep the "Texas steal" propaganda in the public eye. The issue became so troublesome for Taft that two full weeks before the national convention the senator momentarily agreed that the disputed Texas delegation should not vote on the report of the credentials committee. By the time of the Chicago convention, Taft had retreated from this position in an effort to hold his supporters together. The change of heart, however, only served to weaken his position when the Republicans attending the National Governors' Conference in Houston endorsed the stand taken earlier by ten of their number. All twenty-five GOP governors endorsed Governor Langlie's "fair play" resolution, which provided that no disputed delegation would vote on delegate credentials. Taft's attempt to compromise by dividing the delegation was obscured by the governors' action. Picking up on the argument, a backer of California Governor Earl Warren, United States Senator Richard M. Nixon, said, "A death blow will be dealt the highly important issue of morality and cleanliness in government if the Zweifel delegation is seated." Even Taft's regional lieutenants began to back off the issue: J. Bracken Lee of Utah told reporters, "I am for Taft all the way, but there are lots worse things than defeat. We should take a stand against the Old Guard throwing out those young people." By the time the credentials committee made its recommendation to seat the Taft compromise delegation, the theme of conciliation had been drowned out by the crowds of outraged moralists so carefully conducted by Dewey, Lodge, and Brownell.[39]

For all of Taft's last-minute efforts, the "Texas steal," the governors' manifesto, and Taft's earlier compromise on the Texas delegation came into play as the Republican National Convention opened on Monday, July 7, at the Cow Palace.[40] After the usual patriotic observances and the election of temporary officers, the convention quickly moved to the important business of the temporary roll of delegates. Governor Langlie's resolution was introduced as the first item of credentials business; the Eisenhower forces won the issue by a vote of 658 to 548 as favorite-son delegations from California, Michigan, and Maryland joined uncommitted delegates from Pennsylvania to hand Senator Taft his first defeat of the meeting. Seeking to reinforce his public image of confidence, the natural tactic of the front-runner, Taft announced that his analysis of the vote on the Langlie Amendment made him more sure than ever of a first-ballot nomination.[41] But however confident his comments to the press, Taft knew he had suffered a serious defeat on the roll call vote: he had lost at least temporary use of sixty-eight delegates from Georgia, Louisiana, and Texas. Newsmen noticed that his strategists worked frantically to repair the damage sustained as a result of the victory of the Langlie Amendment by reassuring Taft delegates of a first-ballot victory. Predictably, Eisenhower expressed happy agreement with the vote.[42]

The day after the first Eisenhower convention victory, the credentials committee of the convention began hearings on contested delegations. Chaired by U.S. Representative Ross Rizley of Oklahoma, a Taft backer, the panel settled a few local spats with dispatch and moved on to the more hotly contested Georgia delegation, finding for Taft. After hearings on Texas, on Wednesday, July 9, the group voted twenty-seven to twenty-four to seat the Taft compromise delegation. Jack Porter rejected the settlement and again promised that the fight would be taken to the convention floor. That evening, the Eisenhower camp fed the fires of its campaign of moral outrage; Porter, John Minor Wisdom of Louisiana, and other southern Eisenhower Republicans rented the Blackstone Theater, near the convention hotels, for a protest meeting. The "Dixie Indignation Rally," as it was billed, once again trumpeted old charges of chicanery against the Taft faction and succeeded in fastening the attention of both the convention and the press on the alleged immorality of the "Texas steal." Local Chicago newspapers reported the event, according it nearly as much coverage as the organizational phase of general convention activity. Pressure was thus maintained on the Taft and favorite-son delegations to reach an "honorable" settlement of the Texas dispute: Jack Porter conceded nothing.[43]

In the early hours of the following day, the dispute was decided; but contrary to general expectations, the Texas delegation issue never came to an open vote, and Jack Porter did not need to make good on his promise of a contest. In what both Eisenhower and Taft managers regarded as a key vote, that on the Georgia delegation, Eisenhower forces won by a vote of 607 to 531. Following this setback, Taft's managers foresaw inevitable defeat on the widely publicized and hotly debated Texas delegation. Thus, a Taft delegate moved that the minority report

on Texas credentials be accepted unanimously, thereby seating the entire Porter delegation.[44] With most of the sixty-eight contested votes from
Louisiana, Georgia, and Texas in his pocket, General Eisenhower was
assumed to have pulled alongside Taft with about 550 votes at 1:45 A.M.
on July 11. The presidential showdown came later the same day as
Eisenhower came within a handful of votes necessary for a first-ballot
nomination. United States Senator Edward Thye dramatically announced
that Harold Stassen's favorite-son delegation from Minnesota was changing its vote, giving Eisenhower enough votes to win the nomination.
Porter's delegation had been seated, and Eisenhower was nominated; as
far as Texans were concerned, the important events of the Republican
convention were over. Henry Zweifel boarded the train to Fort Worth.
And Jack Porter, his four-year fight for the national committeemanship
won, returned to his hotel room, fell asleep, and missed the first meeting
of the newly elected national committee.[45]

His own position in Texas secure, Porter now had to unify the Texas
party if his election to the national committeeman's office was to bring
him real power: he had to wage a victorious campaign for Eisenhower in
the state. Ostensibly, the hostile Republican factions buried their political hatchets. Before the dust had cleared in Chicago, both Eisenhower
and Taft groups were talking about party harmony, but such party harmony did not flow freely after months of hot dispute. Indeed, when
State Chairman Orville Bullington announced a "unity meeting" for July
19 in Dallas, his project was viewed with suspicion by some Eisenhower
supporters, a sentiment quickly amplified in the press. One reporter
guessed that Zweifel's followers might be trying to preserve their places
on the state executive committee after Porter vowed to oust all of them.
Suspecting a maneuver, Porter told the press that he would be on vacation on July 19.[46]

Suspicions of a power play by the old Taft faction rested, however,
on an unrealistic assessment of their postconvention unity, for the Old
Guard was in disarray. Henry Zweifel, in full retreat, faded from politics, urging support for Eisenhower; he resignedly told his friends that
he was "just a precinct chairman now." George Atkinson dropped out of
Republican politics for the final time. Following an angry exchange with
Jack Porter before both men left Chicago for Texas, Marrs McLean
bowed out of politics altogether. According to his biographer, James A.
Clark, after the Chicago convention McLean grew "nervous, irritable, and
he lost weight." McLean died less than one year later.[47]

But not all of the Old Guard either retired or died. Indeed, Carlos Watson, former Creager protégé and longtime party official, entered the race for the state chairmanship in opposition to Alvin Lane. With a majority on the state executive committee, the old Taft faction might well have retained control over the state party apparatus had its ranks not been depleted by retirement and conciliation.[48] Perhaps with this possibility in mind, Porter reconsidered his refusal to attend the harmony session and interrupted his New Mexico vacation to travel to Dallas. The meeting at the Baker Hotel was all sunshine: "Porter and Zweifel swore there had never been any harsh words between them." Porter told the group: "I harbor no ill will. I want to live to a ripe old age and I found out long ago that the way to live a short life is to harbor a grudge." Young John Tower of Wichita Falls, an in-law of Orville Bullington, called for a unified campaign to erase the political past: "We have got to remove the shadow of Thaddeus Stevens and Sumner from the Republican party. We have got to convince Texas people that the Democratic party no longer serves their interests." Following Bullington's formal resignation as state chairman, Alvin Lane and Carlos Watson were nominated to succeed him. Lacking a majority on the unreconstructed state committee, Lane withdrew his nomination but indicated that he would run for the post at the state convention on August 26.[49]

Despite the harmony of July, it became clear as the August convention drew near that the deep rifts between party factions had not vanished with the nomination of a presidential candidate. In spite of the public affability and talk of party unity, some members of the old Zweifel faction were determined to win on the issue of party control. The Old Guard was not about to give way without a fight. Retiree Henry Zweifel, reviving some of his former energy, said, "I don't think that the fact that Eisenhower was nominated entitles them to run the whole organization. We've been here through thick and thin carrying on the party." The candidate of those who had been there through thick and thin, Carlos Watson, trimmed his sails to the wind and pledged support for both Eisenhower and Porter. Instead of withdrawing his candidacy, Alvin Lane offered Watson his own brand of compromise: he offered Watson any state party post other than national committeeman or state chairman. Watson did not reply. It was clear, then, that the management of the party would be decided at the August state convention in San Antonio. But the delegates to that meeting would be selected by late July in precinct and county conventions. Though it might seem that the contest should have been one-sided, the Eisenhower forces encountered unexpected and energetic opposition; this time, the Old Guard had its own issue, cross-filing, and they made the most of it.[50]

The election law as revised in 1951 made it legal for political parties to cross-file or cross-list the candidates of the opposition party on their ballot. The Eisenhower chiefs astutely planned to cross-list Governor Allan Shivers, Senator Price Daniel, and perhaps other Democrats; the Republicans hoped that conservative Democrats, solidly behind Shivers and Daniel, would break from the pattern of straight-ticket voting and carry the state for Eisenhower. The strategy proved eminently sound, but it disappointed some Republicans who hoped that the state party might capture congressional and state offices by riding Eisenhower's coattails in November. State Representative Edward Dicker, for example, made no secret of his own wish to run for the United States Senate in opposition to Daniel. Thus, the Old Guard opposition to the Eisenhower faction picked up new adherents; and the battle was joined again.[51]

Local planning and maneuvering for control of conventions began shortly after the Chicago convention adjourned. In Dallas County, Eisenhower supporters backed Walter Fleming, Jr., for county chairman; John C. Strickler held Old Guard support, and John D. Ferris ran as an "independent candidate." Three weeks after Eisenhower's nomination, leaders of his faction in Dallas County organized a preconvention meeting in Alvord's Cold Storage Warehouse, with about four hundred persons in attendance. Ralph Currie, former Taft supporter, urged the election of Alvin Lane as state chairman lest Eisenhower lose Texas at the hands of a pro-Taft party head.

The ensuing precinct conventions brought a new string of Eisenhower victories. Fleming was elected Dallas County chairman by a ten-to-one vote; on the other hand, in Fort Worth Henry Zweifel was again defeated, by a vote of thirty-nine to thirteen, in his race for precinct chairman. On the precinct level, the events of May seemed to be recurring. On the county level, bitter displays of factional animosity were numerous. Disputed delegations from a number of counties, including Tarrant, developed the disputes to be settled in late August at the state convention. The Dallas convention was tied up for six hours in a battle over cross-filing; the body finally decided to run candidates for various county offices. A sort of compromise between the Old Guard and the Eisenhower forces was worked out in Bexar County as Nolte and Porter divided the delegation to the state convention. With a momentarily re-

Rentfro Banton Creager in 1925.

Texas Republicans in Washington for the inauguration of Herbert Hoover, 1929. Front row, left to right: Eugene Nolte, Orville Bullington, R. B. Creager, John Philp, T. P. Lee.

Eisenhower nominated! Texas Eisenhower leader H. J. Porter (standing) and Henry Zweifel, head of Taft delegation, in contrasting moods at the Republican National Convention in 1952. *Copyright © The Houston Post Co.*

Congressman Bruce Alger boosts Senate candidate Thad Hutcheson in 1957. *Dallas Morning News photo by Tom C. Dillard*

Former Governor Allan Shivers and Mrs. Sue Fitch, cochairmen of Democrats for Nixon in 1960. *Photo: Dallas Morning News*

Representative Bruce Alger and Senator Barry Goldwater campaign with senatorial candidate John G. Tower in 1960. *Photo: Dallas Morning News*

Senator Barry Goldwater and Dallas County GOP Chairman Peter O'Donnell confer at Dallas meeting in 1962. *Dallas Morning News photo by Johnny Flynn*

Senate candidate George Bush and campaign workers in Houston, 1964.
Photo: Houston Chronicle

Left to right: Peter O'Donnell, Albert B. Fay, and Fred
Agnich at the Republican National Convention in 1964.
Photo: Houston Chronicle

Governor Ronald Reagan on the stump for Paul Eggers in 1968. *Dallas Morning News photo by Joe Laird*

Congressman James M. Collins pitches at a political picnic in 1969. *Dallas Morning News photo by Jack Beers*

Henry Grover campaigning for governor in 1972. *Copyright © The Houston Post Co.*

Former Governor and Mrs. John Connally on the campaign trail with President Gerald R. Ford in 1976. *Dallas Morning News photo by David Woo*

Congressman Alan Steelman (right) campaigning in 1974. *Dallas Morning News photo by Larry Reese*

President Gerald R. Ford greets a mariachi band in Fort Worth in 1976. *Photo: Dallas Morning News*

The widely reported nonmeeting of Congressman Bob Krueger and Senator John Tower in Houston in 1978. Phase one: Krueger extends a friendly hand to his political rival. *Copyright © The Houston Post Co. Photo by King Chou Wong*

Phase two of Krueger-Tower nonmeeting: a nonplussed Krueger retrieves the offered hand as Tower concentrates attention on his salad plate. *Copyright © The Houston Post Co. Photo by King Chou Wong*

Ronald Reagan and Gerald R. Ford appear at a Houston rally for gubernatorial candidate William P. Clements in 1978. *Copyright © The Houston Post Co. Photo by Fred Bunch*

George Bush speaking in Houston in 1980. *Copyright © The Houston Post Co. Photo by Roger Powers*

Looking ahead: Vice President and Mrs. George Bush at the Inaugural Ball in 1981. *Dallas Morning News photo by David Woo*

surgent Taft faction and numerous disputed delegations, what would happen when the convention met in San Antonio?[52]

The question was open to much speculation. Before the state convention began, Mike Nolte breathed new life into the dispute over cross-filing by threatening to back a movement for a conservative Republican party in Texas, a group which would run candidates across the board for local and state offices. This spectacular suggestion and Porter's prompt rebuff to it prompted speculation that the Old Guard would "bolt the state convention, hold a rump meeting, and nominate a slate of candidates." And statements of various Taft leaders lent weight to such surmise. State Chairman Watson declared against cross-filing: "It is necessary that we nominate our own candidates for state office if we are going to have a two-party state." Tarrant County Republican Chairman Marshall Kennady, earlier an ally of Porter, described cross-filing as "a sell-out of the Republican Party." There was every prospect, then, of lively action in San Antonio.[53]

Yet it was clear that another public bloodbath was in no one's interest, least of all that of the backers of Eisenhower. Some conciliation was in order. On the day of the state committee meeting, which customarily preceded the state convention, Jack Porter held an invitational cocktail party, as Creager had always done, and conferred both with members of his faction and with members of the Old Guard. Earlier that day, he and Republican National Committeewoman for Texas Mrs. Roy Black had been the honored guests at a noon luncheon at the Gunter Hotel which was attended by about five hundred persons; Porter assured the luncheon guests that he held no ill will as a result of past party battles. That same day, the Old-Guard-controlled state committee "played it down the middle" in deciding delegation disputes, seating "old guard, new guard, and Duke's Mixture delegations." The generally fair-minded hearings were so unexciting that about twenty members left the session for their air-conditioned hotel rooms before deliberations had concluded.

For all the political thunderheads had loomed high before the convention, prospects for unifying the party appeared brighter. The only threat to more amicable prospects could be expected from Mike Nolte. Yet by the time the gavel called the delegates to order, Nolte and Marshall Kennady had been talked around to abandoning their scheme for a separate "conservative Republican" state slate; they settled for the promise of a "watchdog committee to keep the conservative wing of the Republican party alive."[54] By the time the issue of cross-filing got to the

floor of the convention, it was defused. Former State Chairman Orville
Bullington, among other party stalwarts, spoke in favor of the measure,
which was approved with the lone dissent of Ruthelle Bacon of Amarillo.
No floor fight occured over the state chairmanship. After counting
heads, Carlos Watson made an appeal for party unity and withdrew in
favor of Alvin Lane, who was elected unanimously. Watson was thereafter appointed general counsel of the new state committee elected by
the convention.[55]

Cross-filing became a reality after the convention. Adlai Stevenson,
the Democratic party's presidential nominee, announced on August 23
that he agreed with the decision of the United States Supreme Court
which upheld the federal claim to offshore areas referred to as "tidelands" and that he also agreed with President Harry Truman's veto of
the Tidelands Bill, which recognized state ownership of these areas. On
the day after Stevenson's announcement, Texas Governor Allan Shivers
announced that he would not support Stevenson; Senator Daniel had
endorsed Eisenhower more than one year earlier. Shivers, Daniel, and
all the statewide Democratic candidates were thereafter cross-listed on
the Republican ticket. The only exception was John C. White, commissioner of agriculture, who was not cross-billed at his own request.[56]

The state convention over, the Republican party was completely in
the control of the Porter faction; and the election was still to be won
in November. Even with a public hero and a "native son" running for
president, and the active support of many conservative Democrats, a
vigorous Eisenhower campaign would have to be waged. The last time a
Republican presidential candidate had carried Texas, in 1928, Herbert
Hoover had the benefit of strong anti-Catholic and anti-Wet sentiment.
More recently, while Harry Truman won a narrow victory nationally,
he had carried Texas in 1948 with nearly three-quarters of the major
party vote, winning handily even in Dallas County. An Eisenhower
victory would require effective organization and an energetic campaign.
Immediately after the August convention had concluded its business,
Porter announced that an Eisenhower organization would be established
in each of the 254 Texas counties. Ben Guill, director of the statewide
Eisenhower headquarters in Fort Worth, conferred with county delegates
to the state convention to accelerate local organization. As with the
Hoover campaign of 1928, volunteer organizations mushroomed. Wo-
manpower for Eisenhower was formed on October 1; Veterans for Eisenhower worked at Democrats-for-Eisenhower headquarters in Austin;

Young Industry for Eisenhower set up a political demonstration at the Texas-Oklahoma football game in October; capitalizing on the Tidelands issue, the Texas Democrats for Ike established a Public School Committee for Eisenhower. Nonpartisan Eisenhower clubs were set up in the leading cities of the state. By one means or another, Ben Guill brought about serious precinct organizations in most Texas counties.[57] Working from Fort Worth, with Gerald Cullinan's assistance in handling public relations, Guill worked to coordinate the efforts of scores of citizens and volunteer organizations. The goal of all these efforts had been set earlier by General Eisenhower: the Republican share of the major party vote would double that cast for Dewey in 1948. A tall order, to carry Texas as handily as Herbert Hoover had in 1928, with even less coordination of effort.[58]

The most significant of the new groups, the Democrats for Eisenhower, was only nominally under Republican control. The organization was formed from the ranks of conservative Democratic supporters of Governor Allan Shivers and did not use the regular Republican party campaign organization. The Democratic group included influential publishers: William P. Hobby of the *Houston Post*, E. M. (Ted) Dealey of the *Dallas Morning News*, Amon G. Carter of the *Fort Worth Star-Telegram*, Walter Humphrey of the *Fort Worth Press*, Charles Guy of the *Lubbock Avalanche-Journal*, George Carmack of the *Houston Press*, and Frank Huntress, Sr., of the *San Antonio Express*. Financiers in the Democrats for Eisenhower included Sid W. Richardson, Jesse Jones, and Carr P. Collins. Democratic politicians signed up in numbers; they included Wallace H. Savage, chairman of the State Democratic Executive Committee, at least thirteen committee members, and the mayors of Houston, Dallas, San Antonio, Fort Worth, Waco, Lubbock, and Tyler. In fact, the list of Democrats for Eisenhower reads like a "Who's Who in Texas Democratic Politics." Not surprisingly, Ben Guill observed in October that "Shivers and Daniel are the 'Number One' factors in carrying Texas for the General." These Texans were moving in September, even before the National Citizens for Eisenhower swung into action under the chairmanship of Oveta Culp Hobby.[59]

Combining their efforts, the Republicans and the "Shivercrats" raised more than a million dollars in Texas for the Eisenhower campaign. With big campaign money and important votes at stake, both Eisenhower and Stevenson spent considerable time campaigning in the state. Ike spoke to large crowds in Houston, Dallas, Waco, and Austin, re-

ceiving a tumultuous welcome at a rally in San Antonio, while Adlai
Stevenson appeared in Dallas, Grand Prairie, Houston, Fort Worth, and
San Antonio. Republican vice-presidential candidate Richard M. Nixon
gave seven speeches in Texas, while the retiring vice-president, Alben
Barkley, appeared once in Texas on Stevenson's behalf. The results of
all of these efforts were obvious on election day: Eisenhower carried
Texas with 53.2 percent of the vote and surpassed the campaign goal
of taking 28 percent more of the majority party vote than Dewey had
received in 1948. Eisenhower carried all of the state's urban centers except Wichita Falls, Waco, Corpus Christi, Beaumont, and Galveston;
he received 71 percent of the vote in Midland, 65 percent in Brownsville, 63 percent in Dallas, 62 percent in Amarillo, 61 percent in Odessa,
58 percent in El Paso, Fort Worth, Houston, and Lubbock, and 56
percent in Tyler and San Antonio. Stevenson's main strength lay in relatively poor areas of East Texas and in the Gulf port cities, where his
support among organized labor held up.[60]

Despite an enhanced vote which might be attributed to cross-filing,
the Eisenhower victory had few locally beneficial effects, in part because
cross-filing deprived Republicans of opportunities to ride Eisenhower's
coattails. In Dallas County, for example, the Republican vote was so
strong that both Senator Daniel and Governor Shivers received Republican majorities; Dallas Congressman J. Frank Wilson received only
seven thousand more votes on the Democratic side of the ballot than
he did on the Republican list. Yet local GOP gains were limited to a
single post as Grover Hartt, a Republican, was elected to the County
Court-at-Law by a margin of nearly eighteen hundred votes. Surprised,
the *Dallas Times Herald* observed that Hartt "may be the first Dallas
County Republican to hold county office in the past fifty years."[61] But
scattered local victories and a brief renewal of the debate over cross-
filing seemed far less important than the fact that Republicans had
their man in the White House for the first time since 1933. On the
prospect of support from Washington and continued efforts by Jack
Porter and the new Republicans rested the future of the Republican
party in Texas.

6

A Decade of Public Relations

DURING THE DECADE that followed the election of 1952, the Republican party made substantial gains in Texas. Many of the young Eisenhower Republicans retained an interest in the party's fortunes. With their help, Jack Porter and other state party leaders so enhanced the effectiveness of state and local organizations that their selective challenges to the Democratic party were no longer taken lightly, especially after a limited number of victories and a great number of aggressive challenges. By 1960, after a decade of public relations and organizational development, the GOP was taken seriously in Texas politics. With the election of John G. Tower to the United States Senate in 1961, it was clear to all observers that the day of nominal minority status had passed.

The first stage of this evolution of the Republican party in Texas occurred in 1954 in Dallas when Bruce Alger, a thirty-six-year-old real estate salesman, carried an upset victory over a veteran Democratic politician, Wallace Savage; Alger thus won the first full term in Congress for Texas Republicans since Harry Wurzbach's final campaign in 1930. Texas Republicans had long been eager for the Dallas seat. Even before the Democratic primary, W. H. Francis, chairman of the Texas Republican Finance Committee, used his considerable influence with Sherman Adams in an effort to persuade Governor Allan Shivers to discourage

Savage from running. There is no evidence of any action taken by Adams in response to Francis's request—a situation which is consistent with Donald S. Strong's suggestion that the Eisenhower administration willingly sacrificed the Republican parties in the South in the interests of better relations with powerful Democrats.[1] Though the White House was no help, the Republicans found that their prospects were inadvertently improved by local Democrats, whose ranks were seriously split by the presence of two major candidates, conservative Savage and liberal Leslie Hackler. The failure of either candidate to receive a majority of the primary vote forced the Democrats into an expensive and free-swinging runoff election. Generally assumed by knowledgeable observers to be the front-runner, Savage nonetheless conducted a vigorous campaign. In the process he overtaxed his campaign funds and antagonized Hackler's supporters to such an extent that when Savage won the nomination, liberal Democrats cared little who won the subsequent general election. The division in his party resulted in Savage's loss of the decisive advantages which normally accrued to Democratic candidates in Texas.

Alger, by contrast, though himself not the first choice of party leaders, had considerable campaign assets. Young, handsome, and articulate, Alger had an appealing personality, a quality which helped his managers recruit a large volunteer staff of debutantes and former debutantes, many of whom had first participated in Republican party work during the 1952 presidential election. They now waged an intensive voter canvass and carried out a highly effective door-to-door campaign for Alger. Caught in the excitement of a new campaign, on behalf of a glamorous local candidate, platoons of energetic women effectively carried out a grass-roots campaign, backed by telephone squads and canvassing teams. The Republican ladies, in short, did shoe-leather politicking for Alger while the local Democratic establishment, early confident of Savage's victory, remained inactive; the Republican ladies took the contest seriously and worked to win. The Savage campaign was undermanned, underfinanced, and totally lackluster; but past experience led Democratic leaders to believe in early October that the seat was as good as won. Savage himself was sure that he had the backing of the people who counted in Dallas. As the campaign progressed, however, Savage received the disquieting intelligence that the leaders of the Dallas business community were not unanimous in their support of him. Several wealthy backers were displeased with his high expenditures during the runoff campaign against Hackler, and they decided that they had already invested enough money in Wallace Savage. Moreover, the financial establishment—insurance men, bankers, and oilmen—was divided politically, and some mavericks contributed to the Alger campaign. With valuable assistance from Jack Porter, Alger's enterprising finance chairman, oilman Jake Hamon, succeeded in raising funds to pay for the door-to-door campaigning, newspaper and billboard space, and radio and television time. By the end of October, it was obvious that Bruce Alger was a candidate who had to be taken seriously.

Too late, Wallace Savage recognized that Alger was no ordinary, ignorable Republican opponent. When the *Dallas Morning News* declined to endorse him, it was clear to Savage that the contest was not in the bag. In desperate recourse, with only a few days before the election, he sought additional public exposure through extravagant employment of the media: but too little was done too late. When the election returns were in, it was clear that the legions of ladies in North Dallas and the antipathetic liberals in South and East Dallas had contrived to bring Bruce Alger a triumph. Local journalists observed that a great deal of the former Eisenhower vote in North Dallas and the Park Cities went for Alger; he won in a number of strong Democratic liberal precincts as Hackler's liberal supporters stayed home on election day. Nor was Alger's the only Republican victory in Dallas, for in a less publicized contest, Republican attorney Grover Hartt won reelection to the County Court of Law. Grass roots organization won the day.[2]

Grass roots vitality was certainly not limited to Dallas. Though the Alger victory was the only remarkable gain, the Republican party throughout the state ran candidates in far more contests in 1954 than was customary. Democrats were challenged for six congressional seats, the United States Senate, the governorship, the office of State Commissioner of Agriculture, and 12 of the 150 seats in the Texas House of Representatives. In the Panhandle, Leroy Lamaster tried to regain for the party the congressional seat which Ben Guill had held briefly several years before. In Houston, veteran Democratic Congressman Albert Thomas, nearly as permanent a fixture in Washington as Sam Rayburn, won over his Republican opponent, William B. Butler, by an astoundingly narrow margin.

Candidates running statewide fared less well. Tod R. Adams, who opposed Governor Allan Shivers, polled about 10 percent of the vote, about par for a Republican. Carlos Watson lost five-to-one to Lyndon

Johnson after an uneventful campaign for the U.S. Senate. Elsewhere in Texas, ambitious Bexar County Republicans contested two seats in the Texas House of Representatives, while their counterparts in rural Zapata and Cherokee counties made strenuous attempts to win local offices. Hoping for a repetition of the strong 1952 vote for Eisenhower, young Wichita County Republicans ran two Texas House candidates; one of the contenders, John G. Tower, waged a fairly aggressive campaign on the Alger model, with few funds but considerable support from housewife volunteers. Though these contests ended without victory, the energy which Republicans showed in the autumn of 1954 was unprecedented. And this show of organizational activity in itself attracted more support for the party; there was reason to think that the Republican party was organizationally vital if not politically triumphant. Above all, it was clear that Texas Republicans were no longer preoccupied with patronage-mongering. The new GOP was bent on winning elections.[3]

After the encouraging efforts of 1954, party leaders decided to make an all-out effort to win state contests in the 1956 general election. As a first step, Jack Porter tried to avert the possibility of future cross-filing by calling for a Republican candidate for governor. He told the state committee in late November, 1954, that the conservative Democrats "like to have a foot in two doors—the Democratic door in Texas and the Republican door in Washington. It's time to put a stop to this!"[4] Closing doors on the Shivers Democrats was more easily said than done. In 1955, Porter informed President Eisenhower that he judged Shivers's political position in the Democratic party and in the state to be weak; accordingly, the Texas Republicans intended to run a strong candidate for governor in 1956, "with some expectation of success."

But if Shivers had powerful political enemies in Texas, he still had influential allies in the White House; sometime between the beginning of 1955 and August, 1956, Jack Porter changed his mind on the matter of cross-filing. Presidential politics had priority over the aspirations of Texas Republicans. Eisenhower needed Democratic votes to carry Texas in 1956, and Shivers and his allies could be expected to deliver them. Far from challenging Shivers, national Republican leaders forged an alliance which was formally confirmed when Attorney General Herbert Brownell traveled to Texas for a strategy meeting with the governor in May, 1956. The two men—Jack Porter was not invited—discussed and settled upon Texas election strategy for 1956, without even giving

Porter notice of Brownell's visit. Under these circumstances, it is not surprising that Porter's reconversion to cross-filing was accomplished with some difficulty. He fired off a vigorous objection about Brownell's cavalier disregard of the Texas Republican party to Sherman Adams but, predictably, received no satisfaction. He was soon obliged to give way to a policy contrary to the interest of the Texas GOP. Allan Shivers and the conservative Democrats remained in unchallenged control of Texas.[5]

Just as Jack Porter and many Texas Republicans were unhappy with the heavy-handed White House control of the state party's actions, some Republicans within Texas were not satisfied with Porter's management of the party. Like most state party heads, Porter ran the Texas Republican organization from his own office, in Houston. Though he made no attempt to run a tight ship, Porter left no doubt that he was captain and that the party's course and the appointment of other officers would rest with him. This attitude toward party governance, generally practiced in the United States, came naturally to Porter. He had learned the necessity of decisiveness and control as an independent operator in the highly competitive oil business. Moreover, Porter had learned the national committeeman's role by observing R. B. Creager, a masterful political manipulator, who had managed to hold the reins of party management for more than twenty-five years by controlling the bodies that made decisions in the party. But Porter was not Creager, and the party was now less amenable to one-man control. Porter soon encountered opposition from other party leaders who had ideas and ambitions of their own. Soon after the general election of 1952, Porter and State Chairman Alvin Lane had a difference of opinion, after which relations between them remained cool. Porter allegedly expected the state chairman to assume a more subordinate role than Lane, a strong-minded and able man, could comfortably accept; in 1954 Lane resigned.[6]

Porter also had political problems with the new activists. Women volunteers, organized into twenty-eight clubs—fourteen of them in Dallas County—had demonstrated through the 1952 and 1954 campaigns that they were the organizational sinew of the Republican party. The men raised the money and recruited the candidates, but thereafter the women did the work that carried the day in Dallas County and nearly won in Houston.[7] Aware of their importance to the party and enthusiastically subscribing to the belief that a two-party system could be supported in Texas with enough tough-minded work for the right candi-

dates, the women's groups occasionally offered the party's leadership
unsolicited advice. Thus, in 1954, the Fort Worth Republican Women
objected to the candidacy of Carlos Watson for the United States Senate
in opposition to Lyndon B. Johnson. A caretaker candidate briefly in
1948 until he was replaced by Porter himself, Watson seemed unlikely
to make much of an effort to win in 1954. Watson, argued the ladies,
ought to be "yanked out" of the race in favor of a "strong candidate."
Jack Porter did not take this advice with equanimity. After pointing
out to the ladies that money was tight and that they had demonstrated
no talent for fund-raising, Porter dismissed them as "backseat drivers."
There is no record of the women's reply, but according to the *San
Antonio Express*, "Porter's reply . . . was considered by gleeful Republican Old Guardsmen to be somewhere near the top-blowing category."[8]
The newly active Republicans also expected to be consulted, but in
few instances did Porter ask for advice. He kept his own counsel, turning infrequently to the Republican State Executive Committee, the governing council of the party. In two years the committee met on only
three occasions, all mandated by Texas election laws. Apart from in-
formal conferences with members of the party's financial elite, Porter
ran the party according to his own light.

Jack Porter thus continued R. B. Creager's pattern of strong party
control exercised by the national committeeman for several years. He
departed significantly from Creager's later leadership, however, with
regard not only to style but also to party direction. Secure in his leadership of the party, Porter was far more interested in winning elections
than Creager had been for the greater part of his tenure. Moreover,
Porter, unlike Creager, undertook a gradual accommodation of the new
activists; and he actively encouraged local party enthusiasts to seize
political opportunities and build their own organizations.

Thus, in 1954, when the possibility appeared of electing a Republican to Congress from Dallas, Porter made numerous trips from
Houston to aid in the recruitment of a candidate, and subsequently to
offer the county organization substantial support for Bruce Alger's campaign. In this instance, Porter's view of Texas Republican electoral
politics was plainly evident: selective challenges to the majority party
should be made, and the main effort of the state party ought to go into
candidate recruitment and fund-raising. Organizational details were best
left in the hands of the local party.[9] Porter's approach to party government and his belief in highly selective challenges to the Democrats

were generally respected but not unanimously accepted. Following the election of Bruce Alger, some Dallas Republicans, who gained new experience and confidence in the techniques of grass-roots politics, argued that the state organization ought to be staffed with additional skilled personnel who would aid local party groups in the formation of election organizations. Encouraged by Alger's victory, Dallas Republicans also claimed that they ought to have one of their number in one of the high state party positions, which, following Alvin Lane's resignation, were entirely in the hands of Porter's associates from Gulf Coast sections of the state. They received no satisfaction: Porter continued R. B. Creager's early policy of excluding rival factions from participation in party leadership. Creager's error in accommodating George Hopkins and the West Texans had not been forgotten.[10]

The cumulative effect of the intraparty rivalry and of the Eisenhower administration's fiat on cross-filing was a slackening of interest and energy in Republican ranks in 1956. On the floor of the state convention in May, 1956, the only manifestation of enthusiasm came when the Dallas County delegation staged a short but zesty demonstration in honor of their congressman, Bruce Alger. What else had Texas Republicans to be enthusiastic about in 1956? The national convention was equally sedate for the Texas delegation, which cast its votes for Eisenhower and Nixon dutifully but with no great relish. Accordingly, the campaign which followed the convention was no repetition of 1952 in terms of interest and high spirits. Conservative Democrats, led by Allan Shivers and Price Daniel, again endorsed Eisenhower and established a state Citizens for Eisenhower organization run by Weldon Hart, a prominent Texas journalist. The Citizens group staged an extensive publicity campaign, mustered some of the conservative Democratic vote, spent prodigally, and left the impression with the White House that it ran the entire Eisenhower campaign and was largely responsible for the President's landslide victory in Texas. This impression was worse than misleading: in fact, the Eisenhower vote in 1956 improved the most in those areas in which the Republican party had developed effective organization since 1952. For their part GOP leaders minimized the value of Eisenhower's coattails, though as Eisenhower carried ten urban counties by a total of two hundred thousand votes, he brought a substantial number of votes to several local candidates.[11]

Among the candidates who benefited from Eisenhower's strong victory was Congressman Bruce Alger. His opponent, Dallas County District Attorney Henry Wade, was a far more strenuous campaigner than Wallace Savage. More aggressive than Savage, and more conservative than Alger, Wade ran on a strict segregationist platform. Alger defended gradual integration. At some risk, he disavowed racial segregation and informed his constituents that "it would be foolhardy of any of us to think we can turn the clock back and deny rights to any of our citizens because of race." A mild enough statement, it still contrasted strongly with Henry Wade's opposition to "integration or mixing of the races on any basis." Perhaps in spite of his stand on this issue, Alger won reelection, but by a margin of only twenty thousand votes, while Eisenhower carried Dallas County by sixty thousand votes.[12]

Though under considerable pressure from the White House to do nothing to offend the conservative Democrats, the Texas Republicans planned to ride Eisenhower coattails in six congressional races and a greater number of contests for state legislature, principally in Dallas, Houston, and San Antonio. Despite vigorous campaigns in these cities, the Alger victory was their lone success. In Houston, Democrat Albert Thomas retained his congressional seat after a strong challenge from Republican Anthony C. Friloux. San Antonio Republican Jesse Oppenheimer ran a vigorous campaign for the state senate but lost to incumbent Henry B. Gonzalez by ten thousand votes.[13] More significant for the future of the Republican party than local victories and defeats, however, was the quarter-of-a-million-dollar debt it inherited from the Citizens for Eisenhower organization. Like the proverbial albatross, the debt weighed down the party, seriously impairing its ability to fund campaigns in 1957, 1958, and 1960, and absorbing attention and resources which were needed to expand the headquarters organization. When the debt was finally settled, largely as a result of several highly successful dinners at which Senator Barry Goldwater spoke, personal enthusiasms and political obligations were generated which became dominant in 1963 and 1964.[14]

As difficult as prospects for state development were after 1956, Porter and his friends could always hope that local opportunities like the Alger election in 1954 might recur or that the Democrats in Austin might incidentally provide a chance for Republican advancement. The first promising opportunity came in 1956, when United States Senator Price Daniel decided to retire from the Senate before his term expired in 1958 to seek the more politically powerful position of governor. Having turned back liberal Democratic opposition in the party's primary, in the regular course of Texas politics Daniel was as good as inaugurated. But considerable doubt remained as to who Daniel's successor would be and when he would be chosen. Few clues were given by Governor Shivers, empowered to set the date of the special election, who appointed William E. Blakely, a conservative Democrat widely respected in Dallas business circles, to succeed Daniel until a special election was held.

With the office filled, as the law said it must be, Governor Shivers delayed in designating a date for the election, for the conservative Democrats encountered difficulty in settling upon a candidate for the statewide contest. Blakely was generally acceptable to the conservatives, but they feared that he was not a sufficiently tough campaigner to stand up against the two opposing contenders for the post: Republican Thad Hutcheson, a forty-year-old Houston attorney—hard-working, personally appealing, and identified a year earlier as the man on the rise in the Texas GOP; and Ralph Yarborough, a folksy former county judge and the unsuccessful liberal candidate for the Democratic gubernatorial nomination in 1956. In Hutcheson the Republicans found a candidate they could all support. He was, moreover, not only personable but enthusiastic as well, the sort of candidate who could elicit the best efforts of supporters and volunteer workers.

The availability of such an attractive candidate was in itself enough to draw the GOP into the race. But the circumstances of the race made entry into the contest almost irresistible with a candidate like Hutcheson: having delivered their political wares in November, it was unlikely that courthouse gangs would be ambitious enough to marshal the vote for a conservative Democratic candidate. The predictable courthouse lethargy also favored Ralph Yarborough, himself a vigorous campaigner, who had succeeded in reviving the weak but persistent liberal faction in the state's majority party. Unlike regular elections, the special election would not be preceded by primaries, and the field of conservative Democratic candidates would probably be sufficiently large to give either a liberal Democrat or a Republican a good chance of being the front-runner. Under these uncertain circumstances, there was every reason for the conservative Democrats to stall until they could find a well-known, tough campaigner. But the party's proven vote-getters showed little interest in the contest. Texas congressmen, for example, were unwilling to surrender safe seats and valuable seniority to gamble for a more glamorous position. Only one of their number, Martin Dies, who had gained widespread recognition through his dogged harassment of alleged subversives as a member of the House Un-American Activities Committee, had ever run at-large in the state. Dies, for his own reasons, did not commit himself to the contest. Thus the search for an acceptable conservative Democrat went on through August and the remainder of the year, and Governor Shivers stalled for time.[15]

When Thad Hutcheson jumped into the contest, he believed that Ralph Yarborough would be the only well-known Democrat running against him. In this event, Hutcheson reasoned, defecting conservative Democrats would provide enough votes to put him into the Senate. Such a happy outcome became improbable as Shivers stalled. The longer the special election was postponed, the more likely it was that Hutcheson and Yarborough would be joined in the race by a powerful conservative Democratic candidate. Hutcheson accordingly tried to bring White House pressure on Shivers to call the election for November, 1956, and urged Sherman Adams to persuade Shivers to set the date. Adams, true to form, was unwilling to aid the Texas Republicans at the possible expense of the Shivercrats: he scrawled "no reply at present" on Hutcheson's telegram, and never answered it. In a press conference, when the subject of the election was raised, Eisenhower even joked about his own reluctance to invade the "sovereignty" of the State of Texas by conferring with Governor Shivers regarding the issue. Nor did Governor Shivers ever call the special election; he passed the responsibility to former Senator Price Daniel, his successor, who set the election for Tuesday, April 2. By that time, Martin Dies had been persuaded to enter the contest as the standard-bearer of the conservative Democrats, thus upsetting Hutcheson's calculations.[16]

For Hutcheson and other Republicans, the long wait had been annoying; the campaign was to be frustrating, exhausting, and punishing. With less than one-fifth of the funds he considered necessary for a strong race, Hutcheson set out to wage a two-front battle, supported by an army of amateur politicians, many of them suburban housewives. In San Antonio, Mrs. Florence Kampmann, attractive young wife of the late Marrs McLean's local attorney, effectively rallied upper-middle-class housewives of Alamo Heights, Olmos Park, and north San Antonio. The ladies became more than a match for the local courthouse gang; they rang doorbells, stuffed envelopes, dialed telephones, arranged meetings, and cheered tirelessly. Looking for a few votes in unlikely circles, among members of labor unions, one platoon of volunteers appeared at the local bus garages at five o'clock in the morning to ply drivers with coffee, doughnuts, and Republican pamphlets. When their candidate came to town, the ladies brought a large crowd of friends, neighbors, and husbands to greet him. With this support, the campaign went well for Hutcheson locally; borrowing more from the AFL-CIO Committee on Political Education's "How to Win" than from Emily Post, the ladies carried San Antonio.[17]

But Hutcheson lost the election. He was underfinanced. He was also the least known of the major candidates; and in the expanse of Texas, the necessary and highly expensive familiarity campaign by radio and television was beyond the party's means. Though enthusiastic volunteers promoted victorious campaigns in Midland and San Antonio, their counterparts in Dallas, Houston, and Fort Worth were less successful. In these cities, the Republicans found themselves thwarted by better-organized and more determined opposition. The power brokers of Dallas rallied solidly behind Martin Dies, making fund-raising difficult for Hutcheson and effective volunteer work hazardous for ambitious young business and professional men. For their part, Yarborough backers directed their fire against Dies, decorously ignoring Hutcheson, while he, Dies, and Searcy Bracewell of Houston fought for the state's dominant conservative vote. Yarborough carried a swelled liberal and labor vote to victory; Dies and Hutcheson split the smaller-than-anticipated conservative vote with Bracewell, with Dies running ahead of both Hutcheson and Bracewell.

Thad Hutcheson found some consolation in the election returns. He carried the so-called German counties along with Bexar and Midland counties. He also read a lesson from his defeat: localized party inertia and the lack of interest on the part of the electorate had produced a weak showing in Dallas and Harris counties, the two areas of decisive importance for Texas Republicans. If the party was to do better in the future, the state apparatus and the county groups would have to be made more potent during campaigns. Strongly reliant on volunteer labor, the party had to develop more effective ways of directing supporters in successful campaign work.[18]

Following his energetic but unsuccessful race for the Senate, Thad Hutcheson was named state chairman by the party's executive committee. Supported by able lieutenants, including Mrs. Florence Kampmann and John Tower, Hutcheson set out to build morale in the party; he looked ahead to the 1958 election, in which Ralph Yarborough would defend his newly won seat. Mrs. Kampmann, who became party co-chairman in 1958, turned her attention to increasing the party's state-wide effectiveness in canvassing and recruiting volunteer labor, while Tower worked on two newly established committees, on the legislature and on research and education. Both committees were created under Hutcheson's aegis and were added to the standing committees, head-quarters, finance, and convention. By 1959, the party had added three additional groups with responsibility for candidate recruitment, can-vassing, and young voters.[19]

The establishment of these new bodies stemmed from the intention of Hutcheson and many other young party members to improve the operational efficiency of the party and to increase the participation of rank and file members in party activities. Such a course was a marked departure from the views and practices of past years. R. B. Creager and his predecessors had adhered firmly to an elitist view of party gover-nance, and they presided over a party which was effectively controlled by a handful of notables. Jack Porter, the last of Texas's independently powerful national committeemen, generally shared Creager's view of party control, though he never adhered to Creager's opinion that control was more important than winning elections. But when circumstances prevented his performing his proper role, provider of sufficient funds in 1957 and 1958, Porter acceded to the diminution of his authority which was brought about by the proliferation of committees; and the party apparatus thus gradually outgrew the national committeeman's vest pocket.

An equally novel departure in fund-raising came with this change: Porter supported a "neighbor-to-neighbor" fund drive, an attempt to secure a large number of small donations from middle-class adherents of the party. With many large donors miffed at the Eisenhower natural gas policy and out of sorts with Porter, phone call finance, the kind of fund-raising campaign which could obtain one hundred thousand dollars from one hundred donors in ten days, no longer worked. In its place, Republicans hoped to develop a public campaign which might raise the same sum of money, though from thousands of donors, through door-to-door appeals. The door-to-door campaign was the technique of the United Fund; and the United Fund had given many younger Republicans their introduction to the techniques of fund-raising. Unfortunately, the door-to-door approach failed to raise sufficient capital for a serious cam-paign in 1958.[20]

With the prospect of another underfinanced effort, the party's brightest star, Thad Hutcheson, declined to run for the Senate; and party leaders were hard pressed to locate a likely candidate. They did not find one. So, taking the next best alternative, they found a man who was willing to pay his own way. Roy Whittenburg, a prosperous Amarillo newspaper publisher, largely unknown in both the party and the state, received the nomination. The selection of Whittenburg drew some highly indignant protests from those party members who looked to the Republicans to offer a formidable challenger to Ralph Yarborough, empty coffers or not. Thought to be right-wing even by conservative Texas standards, Whittenburg failed to build a broad base even in the GOP. In fact, he lost support by repeatedly calling for the election of all federal judges, a proposition which must have cost him the vote of nearly every conservative lawyer in the state, and by hammering away on the "Red menace" theme, which, following Senator Joseph McCarthy's political demise, was briefly out of style.

When the vote was in, Whittenburg and Edwin S. Mayer, the party's token opponent of Governor Price Daniel, had been soundly beaten. Whittenburg, running against a liberal incumbent, received only 24.1 percent of the major party vote, while Mayer's showing, 11.9 percent, was strongly reminiscent of the days of token opposition. The election was not, however, a total loss. Party leaders learned their lesson from Whittenburg's campaign; and after the election, the state executive committee established the new committee to recruit candidates.[21]

In local contests during 1958, Republicans managed to challenge the Democrats more convincingly. In Dallas, Bruce Alger defeated Harold "Barefoot" Sanders, a moderate-to-liberal Democratic state representative, by seven thousand votes. This campaign, like Alger's earlier races, was notable for the extent and effectiveness of Republican volunteer labor; it was managed by a wealthy young investor, Peter O'Donnell. Like Republican leaders across the country, he borrowed liberally from the printed literature of the Committee on Political Education of the AFL-CIO and applied his own talent for businesslike organization to COPE's practical suggestions. In short, O'Donnell engineered one of the most closely coordinated campaigns the area had seen.[22]

Party workers in other congressional campaigns had little reward for their labors. Republican T. E. Kennerly lost the congressional race with County Judge Bob Casey for the new seat in Houston, and E. A. Ross was easily defeated by Democrat John Dowdy in District Seven, in central East Texas, generally Democratic territory. State and local races were no more gratifying. Following a highly critical Republican report on the Texas legislature, released by Thad Hutcheson in 1957, twenty-nine urban Republicans, including Mrs. Beryl Milburn of Austin and Carlos Watson, Jr., of Houston, sought seats in the Texas House. Emboldened by Bruce Alger's victories in 1954 and 1956, Dallas County Republicans ran Robert B. Hamilton and Don Dossett for Commissioners Court. Not a single one of these contests, however, was successful for the GOP.[23]

Hard pressed for cash and candidates, the Republican party had nonetheless waged a number of spirited campaigns in 1958. But in the face of electoral defeats and a sizable party debt from the 1956 presidential campaign, opposition within the White House and the increasing vogue for "Modern Republicanism" in Washington, how long could operating funds be raised and volunteer spirit be maintained? These problems, pressing in 1958, had been major obstacles to the growth of the Republican party in Texas. Especially vexing to Texas leaders from 1952 through 1960, the Eisenhower administration showed only scant and sporadic interest in promoting its party in Texas. Though Eisenhower's candidacy had swelled the ranks of the presidential Republicans, he was not inclined to use patronage and other prerogatives in the interest of the party in Texas.

During the administrations of Harding, Coolidge, and Hoover, most GOP party members considered patronage and preferential treatment by the federal government to be the main advantages of political activity. Thus, R. B. Creager's ability to deliver these benefits sustained a manageable political machine. By 1953, after a twenty-year lacuna and an intraparty revolution, patronage and favors were still goals for party activists, but they were usually subordinated to the pursuit of more general programmatic and ideological goals. Conservative ideals led Jack Porter's enthusiastic backers to recruit strong candidates, create an effective state organization, and win elections. Their efforts were more often impeded than supported by the Eisenhower administration. Unlike Creager, Jack Porter had to disassociate the Texas GOP from the national party leadership and to overcome strong statewide disapproval of Eisenhower's patronage, petroleum, and racial policies. Despite the fillip provided by Eisenhower's election victories of 1952 and 1956, some of the policies of his administration were so detrimental to the Republican party in Texas that barely five years after he retired to his Gettysburg farm, the Eisenhower years were viewed with some justice as a part of the "dark age" of the party in Texas.

In 1965, VIM, a publication of the Republican party in Texas, carried a brief historical sketch by V. Lance Tarrance, an employee in the state headquarters office. Reflecting the general opinion of many newcomers to the party, Tarrance wrote:

Before 1960, the Texas Republican organization was virtually non-existent. The GOP in Texas conducted its first fully "Republican" effort for Richard Nixon. Although political scientists have singled out the year 1952 as the birthplace of "modern Texas Republicanism," the importance of 1960 is more revealing. The explanation is that *during the Eisenhower years*, the Texas GOP was more of a patronage organization than a political power, and the Democrats, for the most part, had run the campaigns of '52 and '56.

Not surprisingly, Tarrance received a sharp note from Jack Porter: "You will certainly find that what you wrote . . . was based upon conclusions and not on researched facts."[24] Though Porter, who had resigned as national committeeman six years earlier, did not spell out his own version of the facts, he did well to object. Tarrance had some of the elements of his interpretation quite reversed. The Texas GOP gradually developed a political organization, but it generally lacked patronage power. Several months after Dwight D. Eisenhower's election, it was clear that Texans would hold a number of leading positions in his administration. Robert Anderson served as secretary of the navy, Mrs. William P. Hobby as secretary of health, education, and welfare, and Dillon Anderson as consultant to the National Security Council. Unfortunately for Texas Republicans, all these appointees were Democrats. At lower administrative levels, Lawrence M. Lawson and William E. Wrather, both Truman appointees, were reappointed to their posts, respectively as commissioner of the International Boundary and Water Commission of the United States and Mexico and chief of the Geological Survey. Small wonder that Jack Porter soon wrote Eisenhower to protest: "Someone on your staff seems to have forgotten that it was the Republicans of Texas who helped secure your nomination and not the Democrats."[25]

Jack Porter and other party leaders knew that federal appointments at subcabinet levels were requisite to the development and cultivation of political talent. Out of office nationally for twenty years, the Republican party had a pressing need for a strong group of young candidates for state and congressional offices. Through judicious appointment to subcabinet posts, these candidates might receive both public exposure and politically useful experience in government, thus boosting their own careers and their party's prospects. The Texas Republican party, lacking a single statewide victory in nearly eighty years, was desperately in need of opportunities to groom new talent on the federal payroll. In this respect, Ben Guill, the only living Texas Republican to have served in Congress and the manager of the Eisenhower-Nixon campaign in Texas, was the party's brightest hope in 1952; the party leaders had contemplated ambitious plans for him. Guill himself planned to recapture his congressional seat by riding Eisenhower's coattails. He was dissuaded from this object by Jack Porter and Herbert Brownell, who prevailed on him to give up his candidacy to take on the management of the Eisenhower-Nixon campaign in Texas. An opportunity to return a Republican to Washington was thus passed up, presumably in consideration of a greater reward if Eisenhower were elected. But both Guill and Porter waited in vain for happy news of an appointment during the series of preinaugural announcements of cabinet and subcabinet appointments. By February, 1953, Guill had not been given a federal post, a situation which was "daily becoming more embarrassing" to Jack Porter. He had gone to market early for Eisenhower, but now it seemed that he could not deliver the goods.[26]

As one might expect, Porter's failure to obtain early patronage consideration delighted some members of the Republican old guard. John A. Donaldson, who served on the state committee from 1940 until the "Eisenhower Revolution" of 1952, wrote Daniel G. Gainey at the Republican National Committee: "Ike's batting average for the appointment of Democrats to office is now 999%. . . . The Republican slobs that got on Jack Porter's bandwagon are being well paid for their loyalty to their old friends, who paid all the bills during the lean years. May they starve to death." Gainey also heard from Porter's ally, Frank O'Brien, who reminded him that "there are plenty of competent Texas Republicans but not one has yet received a top appointment."

Eisenhower's patronage was indeed an increasing embarrassment to the new national committeeman. What was worse, though party loyalists from other states were subsequently appointed to federal posts, patronage never really improved much for the Texas GOP.[27] True, Porter's friends were not entirely forgotten: Ben Guill was finally made a special assistant to the postmaster general and later given an appointment to the Federal Maritime Board; Lamar Cecil was appointed federal district judge for the Eastern District of Texas; and Joe Ingraham was named to the Fifth Circuit Court. Some Republicans received lower level positions in the Justice and Post Office departments. But this was a small return for invested effort, and everyone knew it. For the next eight years, at state committee meetings, Texas Republicans complained bitterly of lack of consideration by the White House. How was it that Eisenhower ignored loyal supporters once he settled into the White House?

Herbert S. Parmet, author of a recent study of the Eisenhower administration, has pointed out that the extension and expansion of Civil Service coverage to federal employees under Franklin D. Roosevelt and Harry S. Truman severely limited the number of appointments at Eisenhower's disposal; by June, 1953, "Fewer than twenty-five hundred posts had been filled." The relative paucity of jobs tended to draw attention to both the political loyalties and the qualifications of the appointees, making it much harder for deserving Republicans to find a place on the payroll. Particularly annoying to Texas Republicans was the Eisenhower administration's strong preference for Texas Democrats, a situation which was partly accounted for by the influence of congressional Democrats and the strong endorsement of Eisenhower by Texas Governor Allan Shivers. White House aides tended to favor candidates from the ranks of the Citizens for Eisenhower over regular Republican applicants. Charles F. Willis, Jr., who superintended federal appointments, had been one of the founders of the Citizens movement along with Oveta Culp Hobby. Moreover, Sherman Adams, the *eminence gris* of the Oval Room, credited Eisenhower's victory in Texas to the efforts of Allan Shivers and the Citizens crowd. As a result, the Democrats from the Citizens connection entered the front door of the White House while Texas Republicans queued up for scraps at the Republican National Committee.

But the preferences of White House aides do not account fully for the neglect of deserving members of the Texas GOP. The nature and conduct of the Texas party, taken together with the unavoidable calculations of presidential and congressional politics, also influenced patronage. The White House made no determined effort to deprive Republicans of jobs within Texas. But unfortunately, on more than one occasion lack of agreement within Republican party ranks led to the appointment of Democrats for whom there was generally powerful congressional support.[28]

The power of the Texas congressional delegation, which included

Speaker of the House Sam Rayburn and Senate Majority Leader Lyndon
Johnson, was decisive in federal judicial appointments after the Democrats gained control of both houses of Congress in 1954. When, for
example, the death of Lamar Cecil in 1958 opened the post of federal
judge for the Eastern District of Texas, a dozen candidates came forward for the position, among them L. J. Benckenstein, onetime lawyer
for Marrs McLean; Enoch Fletcher, who pled the Taft case in Chicago;
and William Steger, Jr., all Republicans. None fared well during deliberations. Steger, a bright young Eisenhower Republican, was considered by White House aides to be too young for the post. Fletcher
and Benckenstein, both able members of the bar, were supported by
members of the Taft faction—including F. Trowbridge vom Bauer, who
had received a judicial post in the Defense Department—primarily because of their longtime party activity. Jack Porter, for his part, avoided
intraparty strife by routinely forwarding endorsements for Fletcher and
Benckenstein, hoping thereby to pull disaffected old guard Republicans
back into party activity. But Lyndon Johnson, who was in a position
to hold up action on the administration's Omnibus Judgeship Bill,
backed Joseph J. Fisher for the position. The White House temporized.

Finally, after a delay of more than a year and a half, Johnson had
his way, and Fisher was appointed. The administration advised Porter
that this move was the "only possible solution" to a tie-up in Senate
passage of the judgeship bill. Porter's reply to this cold comfort was
a complaint to the President: "Apparently the Attorney General wants
to sell the Republican Party of Texas down the river in this deal, in
order to secure confirmation of judges in other states. He used that
place and other judicial vacancies as pawns in a weird chess game in
an effort to get the omnibus judgeship passed this year." It was not an
inaccurate interpretation of what had happened.[29]

Even when congressional influences on judicial appointments were
muted, Texas Republicans were unsuccessful in securing the appointment of men from their ranks because they failed to agree on a single
candidate. In January, 1955, when the retirement of William H. Atwell,
a Republican appointee, created a vacant seat on the Federal Court for
the Northern District of Texas, fifteen candidates, including Senator
Price Daniel, were advanced. A. W. (Jess) Walker had the strong support of Sid W. Richardson, multimillionaire Fort Worth oilman and
good friend of the President, Sam Rayburn, and Lyndon Johnson. From
the beginning, the smart money was on Walker. In this instance, how-

ever, solid Republican opposition made the appointment untenable by March, 1955. Then the predictable hitch emerged: Texas Republicans agreed on their rejection of Walker, but they could not agree on a candidate of their own. Ralph Currie, long active in Dallas County Republican politics, had the solid support of Jack Porter and newly elected Republican Congressman Bruce Alger of Dallas. Unfortunately, the quality of Currie's legal training was questioned when Dallas newspapers disclosed that he had received his law degree from a reputable but then defunct law school. What looked worse, Alvin Lane, another prominent Dallas attorney and Republican state chairman until 1954, withheld his support from Currie. Caught between congressional pressure and Republican disunity, the Justice Department stalled, leaving the judicial post vacant for more than a year.

At last, in April, 1954, Currie withdrew from the race. With Currie out of consideration, Porter and Representative Bruce Alger endorsed a talented young Dallas attorney, M. Sims Davidson, who was given enthusiastic support by local party leaders. Davidson might well have been nominated but for his relative youth; the congressional Democrats effectively used the question of his age to block his appointment. Twice frustrated, Dallas Republicans ran out of willing candidates. In a final effort to fill the post and save face, a local Democrat, Joe E. Estes, was endorsed by the Dallas County Republican organization and seconded by Jack Porter. A choice fully to the liking of Rayburn and Johnson, Estes was confirmed without opposition.

The episode was both telling and significant. Even when political advantages were generally on their side, Texas Republicans were unable to promote a candidate whose qualifications were generally acceptable to the Justice Department and in their own ranks. In fact, Jack Porter had ill-advisedly told the White House in 1953 that attorneys were for the most part retained by corporations and that they were seldom eager for federal judicial offices, which were frequently less remunerative than their private practices: Porter mistakenly counseled the President that judicial appointments would probably have to be made from the ranks of the Eisenhower Democrats.[30]

Appropriate candidates or no, the party's failure to produce the heavy loaves and big fishes of patronage rapidly demoralized party members. How could so little come to them with their party's man, Eisenhower, in the White House? They and their leaders protested to the White House with considerable frequency but to no avail that the appointment of Democrats worked contrary to their attempt to build the Republicans in Texas into a powerful competitive party organization. In late 1953, Jack Porter wrote: "We cannot build a Republican party in Texas by naming Democrats to jobs in Washington." The White House turned a deaf ear to this complaint. Eisenhower and his aides were, after all, far more interested in getting business done in Congress than in promoting party growth in Texas. Sam Rayburn and Lyndon Johnson loomed far larger in their calculations than Jack Porter and his friends. Moreover, the politics of presidential reelection brought the White House to court Democratic votes in Texas by maintaining friendly and accommodating relations with Governor Shivers, necessarily at the expense of the Texas Republican party.[31]

Protests to the White House having gone unheard, most members of the Texas GOP were obliged to subside in sore resignation. After eight years of disappointment, only relative outsiders like George Atkinson bothered to complain about patronage.[32] But the political consequences of the inability of Porter and the Texas Republicans to control patronage went beyond the denial of places to party faithful and the attendant failure to groom strong candidates for state and congressional offices. Equally significant was the fact that Jack Porter and other party leaders could not demonstrate to influential state conservatives that the Republican party in Texas was to be taken seriously. How could it be seen as a likely political alternative to the Democratic party when appointments and favors were more reliably secured by Texas Democrats? It was cold comfort indeed to know that White House patronage policy, heedless of plans by national party leaders to develop Republican strength in the South, created the same sort of problem for Republican leaders in other southern states.

Within Texas politics, though patronage was lost, the state's strongly dominant economic interest group, petroleum, might still be courted by the Republican party. Winning the oil interest solidly for the Texas GOP, however, depended on national rather than state action; within Texas, the industry effectively controlled the Texas Railroad Commission, the regulatory body with intrastate jurisdiction. Only if the national party, in Congress and the White House, followed petroleum resource and tax policies which suited Texas oil and gas interests could oil be wooed and won; but, in the relative scale of political advantage, service to the petroleum industry offered far greater opportunities for party growth than the dispensation of patronage. Though jobs might attract some able party workers and candidates, cash would do better in developing candidates and running campaigns. With oil interests on their side, the Republicans could produce their own John Nance Garners, Sam Rayburns, and Lyndon Johnsons. Such was the prospect in 1953. But achieving the goal, bringing petroleum interests around to support the party in a major way, required a long and strenuous campaign which was marked by as many reverses as gains.

Opportunity for the Republican party of Texas emerged in the general falling out of conservative Texas oilmen and the national Democratic party over federal petroleum policies. After World War II, the petroleum industry hoped for a rapid end of wartime price controls over their principal product. It was consistently disappointed during Harry Truman's administration. Admittedly beyond Truman's immediate control, the Supreme Court decided in U.S. *v.* California that jurisdiction over the tidelands rested with the federal government; and the court left the definite issue of tidelands ownership unresolved. Congress then passed legislation which recognized state claims, an action which would have left control over production strictly in the hands of state regulatory agencies, which were generally friendly to petroleum interests, and would effectively have rescinded price controls over petroleum products. The legislation was opposed by much of the eastern press, most notably the influential *Washington Post*, and by liberal Democratic representatives and senators from oil and gas consuming states. When the bill reached the White House, Harry Truman cast his lot with these groups and vetoed the measure.[33]

Natural gas legislation fared no better than the Tidelands bill. At the behest of producers, Senators Robert S. Kerr of Oklahoma, Russell Long of Louisiana, and Lyndon B. Johnson of Texas introduced legislation which would have removed gas production from the jurisdiction of the liberal-dominated Federal Power Commission by ceding regulatory power to state agencies. The Kerr Bill, though opposed in the Senate by Wayne Morse of Oregon and Paul Douglas of Illinois, passed easily in that body but slipped through the House by a scant two-vote margin, with many members avoiding commitment by not voting. Once the Kerr Bill was in his hands, Harry Truman vetoed it, despite the urging of congressional leaders and Democratic Governor Allan Shivers of Texas. Truman correctly assumed that his veto would not be overridden in the House. In a more threatening move, Truman took on petroleum interests in a vital area, taxation. In his budget message of

1950, Truman proposed both lowering the oil depletion allowance from 27.5 percent to 15 percent and abolishing tax credit for drilling. These proposals came to nothing when Sam Rayburn and Lyndon Johnson blocked consideration of them. However, the issue of the oil depletion allowance was raised again during the following year by Senator Hubert Humphrey, openly supported by Harry Truman. Once again, Lyndon Johnson succeeded in quashing the measure; but Harry Truman was clearly no friend of the oilman.[34]

The battles over the oil depletion allowance, natural gas controls, and the tidelands convinced Texas oilmen that the national Democratic party would do little to serve their interests. In a field of narrow options, the Republican party was regarded with new favor. For his part, General Dwight D. Eisenhower courted this favor. Through extensive and amicable contacts with Sid W. Richardson of Fort Worth—who was sufficiently powerful to summon both Lyndon Johnson and Sam Rayburn to his vacation home on St. Joseph Island for occasional conferences—Eisenhower pledged himself to support the states' claims of ownership of offshore petroleum deposits. For his part, Richardson promised to raise several million dollars in campaign funds for the general. Publicly, Eisenhower offered the assurance of his support of the petroleum industry through Jack Porter, in a letter dated March 28, 1952: "I agree with the principle that federal ownership in this case as in others is calculated to bring about steady progress toward centralized ownership and control, a trend which I have bitterly opposed." In the heat of his campaign for the Republican nomination, Eisenhower let Porter release a statement which seemed to cover both the issue of the tidelands and that of controls over natural gas: "To the extent constitutional [I] prefer legislation by the Congress to vest control in the states to the three-mile or league-limit as appropriate. I believe in decentralizing government and bringing its responsibilities, control, and services as close to the people as possible." Though closemouthed to Porter about his stand on other issues, the General was not afraid to commit himself on oil.[35]

With these assurances, Texas oil interests quite understandably expected to receive consideration when Dwight Eisenhower was in the White House. And, true to his promise, he supported the Outer Continental Shelf Act, which passed the same year, thus making good a substantial part of his campaign commitments. Ike also held firmly against the lowering of the depletion allowance, and he authorized Secretary of the Treasury George Humphrey to oppose Senator Hubert Humphrey's bill in 1954, when it was reintroduced. Subsequent efforts by U.S. Senators Williams, Douglass, and Proxmire to scale down the depletion allowance met with little more success during Eisenhower's second term.[36]

With a friend in the White House and a perfect legislative record by 1956, national oil interests moved to remove federal controls over the price of natural gas. The old Kerr bill was reintroduced in the House by Representative Oren Harris of Oklahoma and in the Senate by William Fulbright of Arkansas. The legislative campaign moved smoothly under the efficient administrations of Rayburn and Johnson; operations were assisted by the well-financed lobby and publicity campaign of the "Natural Gas and Oil Resources Committee," headed by Leonard F. McCollum, president of the Continental Oil Company in Houston. According to the anti-oil *Washington Post*, McCollum's committee spent at least $1,750,000 in support of the Harris-Fulbright Bill between October, 1954, and March, 1956.

The liberal opponents of the measure countered with effective use of the issue of widespread and splashy spending of oil money to influence congressmen. They were given their most effective ammunition by a supposed supporter of the bill, Senator Francis Case of South Dakota. Case announced that John M. Neff, a Nebraska lawyer and lobbyist, a representative of the Superior Oil Company of Austin, Texas, had offered him $2,500 to clinch his vote for the bill. The *Washington Post* gave great play to Case's claim and a furor ensued in the liberal eastern press.

Apprehensive that the Harris-Fulbright bill would be turned into an effective campaign issue by the Democrats, President Eisenhower vetoed the measure when it reached his desk. Taking the issue away from the opposition, Eisenhower denounced "arrogant lobbying" for the measure and claimed that the tactics which had been used to secure its passage in Congress were "so much in defiance of acceptable standards of propriety as to risk creating doubt . . . concerning the integrity of the governmental processes." This deft political move by the President made it difficult for liberal Democrats to claim that his administration and the Republican party had sold out to the oil lobby, but Eisenhower's action also posed formidable problems for Republican leaders, especially in oil-producing states, who had been expected to "deliver" by the oil interests.[37]

In Texas, Jack Porter, who had headed the Texas Independent Producers and Royalty Owners before he became national committeeman, knew that he was in political trouble with local oilmen as the result of Eisenhower's veto. He told Eisenhower that he needed to discuss the problem of gas legislation during the next session of Congress: "I need to do this before I can go to a convention of independent oil and gas producers in Dallas on the 15th and 17th of April." White House aide Bernard Shanley replied by urging Porter to take the matter up with Presidential Assistant Sherman Adams, a suggestion which Porter turned down with some tact. It was more than unlikely that he would get any sympathy from Adams. After a number of fruitless exchanges, Porter was left to placate angry oilmen by his own devices.[38]

If Eisenhower had become aloof, especially once secure in office for his second term, not all Republicans of national influence would follow his example. A longtime ally of Texas oilmen's efforts to secure favorable legislation was the erstwhile speaker of the House, Representative Joseph W. Martin of Massachusetts. Jack Porter met Martin in 1947 when he and Hugh Roy Cullen traveled to Washington to promote favorable action on gas legislation. In 1948, at Cullen's behest, Porter organized a small dark-horse movement on Martin's behalf at the Republican National Convention. This had of course no political result, but it was highly agreeable flattery. Joe Martin could be counted on.

Once he was national committeeman, Jack Porter made good use of Martin's loyalty. In February, 1955, Porter held a fund-raising dinner at the Adolphus Hotel in Dallas, with Martin as honored guest; more than one thousand tickets were sold at one hundred dollars each. As one might expect, fund-raising dinners were not particularly newsworthy; and the affair received scant notice in the Texas press. Three years later, however, a similar affair brought down the house on Jack Porter and adversely affected pending natural gas legislation, through which congressmen from gas and oil producing states sought to revive the Harris-Fulbright Bill of 1956.[39] In January, 1958, Jack Porter sent several hundred letters under the letterhead of the Republican National Committee to oil and gas men, whom he correctly reminded:

Joe Martin . . . has always been a friend of Texas, especially of the oil and gas producing industries. He mustered two-thirds of the Republican vote in the House each time the gas bill passed. As Speaker of the 83rd Congress he led the fight for adoption of the tidelands ownership bill. It will be up to Joe Martin to muster at least 65 percent of the Republican votes to pass the gas bill this year. He has to put Republican members from the North and East consuming areas on the spot politically because the bill is not popular due to the distortion of facts by newspaper columnists and others. The dinner must raise substantial amounts of money for the Republican Party as part of these will go towards the election of Republican Congressmen and Senators.[40]

This astoundingly frank and widely circulated letter found its way to the *Washington Post*, which was again leading a newspaper crusade against the gas bill. On the scent of a *cause célèbre*, Edward T. Folliard was dispatched to Houston to cover the dinner. In the February 11, 1958, issue of the *Post*, the story of the "natural gas bandits" broke open. Folliard reported that Porter had sold at least one thousand tickets at one hundred dollars each and that several well-heeled oilmen purchased blocks of twenty to thirty tickets. Folliard knew, of course, that large-scale fund-raising in Texas was not in itself much news. "The extraordinary thing about the dinner here tonight, however," he wrote,

was the promise held out to those asked to attend. It was a promise that Martin would again throw his power and influence behind legislation that would help the Lone Star State in general and its well-heeled gas producers in particular. In turn, the diners were asked to contribute to the Republican Party treasury and so help elect Republicans to the Senate and House this year. . . . The stakes are high, since an increase in the wellhead price [of natural gas] from ten to fifteen cents per thousand cubic feet would boost the value of existing reserves from about $24 billion to $36 billion. . . . Half the natural gas reserves are in Texas.[41]

The *Post*'s exposé brought volumes of self-serving criticism down upon Porter. Richard M. Simpson, chairman of the Republican Congressional Campaign Committee, called Porter's letter "crude and inexcusable"; he was, however, still willing to accept funds from the proceeds of the dinner. More seriously, the chairman of the Republican National Committee, Meade Alcorn, announced that "acting with President Eisenhower's personal approval," the committee "will not accept any funds from the proceeds of the dinner." Several days after this announcement, Eisenhower reiterated his disapproval of Porter's letter. With this incident, relations between Eisenhower and Porter effectively ceased; in June, Porter was still trying to see the President to present his side of the story.[42] His standing with fellow oilmen in Texas, always an important element of Porter's fund-raising prowess, the basis of his political power, was for a while not much higher than his standing at the White House. The *Washington Post,* in an editorial entitled "Of Gas and Arrogance," demanded a full-scale congressional investigation, a suggestion that was unwelcome to politicians and oilmen alike. Even more disastrous, congressional leaders, including Joe Martin and Sam Rayburn, agreed that the gas bill was dead and that Jack Porter had effected its demise. Rayburn seized on the occasion to embarrass Porter by claiming, "If he had wanted to kill the bill, Porter couldn't have been more effective in defeating it by sending out a letter like that." Democratic Congressman Frank Ikard of Wichita Falls, a supporter of the bill, added: "He made it impossible for anybody outside the producing states to support it." The *Dallas Morning News,* which agreed that the disclosure of Porter's letter doomed the bill, added worse news: Senator George Aiken of Vermont was now using the issue to support his campaign to end the 27.5 percent oil depletion allowance![43]

Not surprisingly, White House officials feared that Porter's letter would be used against Republican congressional candidates in November. Thus, the *Washington Post* reported White House pressure on Porter to resign from the Republican National Committee. Porter refused. Within Texas, the widespread belief that Porter's letter had cost the oil industry several billion dollars undermined his once great popularity with fellow oilmen. Dallas producers, already somewhat unhappy with the near-monopoly of party positions by Porter's Houston group, added their voices to the demands for Porter's resignation. Again, Porter refused. In resisting these pressures, Porter knew that there was little the White House could deny him that it had not already refused to provide and that Texas oilmen would continue to finance Republican presidential candidates for their own reasons. He was largely correct on both counts. Moreover, Porter's long and strenuous service in the party had earned him more than a few friends; and some Texas Republicans were much more upset by the rough treatment of Porter by the White House than by Porter's indiscreet promotion of the Martin dinner.[44]

Given all the difficulties facing Jack Porter, one might wonder how he kept his place. Though there was never a likely prospect of a party revolt in Texas—a repetition of the events of May, 1952—unmistakable evidence of growing disaffection between Texas Republicans and the Eisenhower administration posed serious problems for him. Porter was often hard pressed to defend certain policies of the national government within the Republican party. At the state convention held in Houston in May, 1956, the Resolutions Committee engaged in lengthy and heated debates over states' rights, desegregation, and the Harris-Fulbright Natural Gas Bill. Only the tactful intervention of the committee chairman, Thad Hutcheson, brought the committee to produce a state party platform which was not strongly condemnatory of the Eisenhower administration. On the natural gas resolution, Jack Porter himself was forced to appear to dissuade the committee from direct criticism of Eisenhower's veto of the gas bill.[45]

Porter's problems aside, a contretemps between Eisenhower and the conservative wing of his party had been in the making for some time. Accommodating the eastern progressive wing of the GOP, beginning in 1955 Eisenhower supported progressive programs in health, education, and civil rights. In the process, he moved nearer liberal positions which party conservatives, including the anti-New Deal Republicans of Texas, opposed. Suspicions of Eisenhower's future plans were heightened several weeks before the presidential election when Paul G. Hoffman, an "insider" in eastern Republican circles, wrote a highly controversial article, "How Eisenhower Saved the Republican Party," for *Collier's*. Hoffman told his readers of Ike's firm commitment to moderate reforms and singled out a number of senators, including Barry Goldwater, for criticism because they threatened to obstruct the President's forward-looking program. Not surprisingly, Goldwater protested to the White House:

I would like to know if the President feels that I am possessed of "dangerous thinking and reckless conduct." I want to know if the President feels that I am one of those "people you cannot afford to have as friends." I want to know if the President now feels that the United States Congress should be made up entirely of "Yes" men.

Goldwater received little satisfaction from Sherman Adams, who tactlessly sent a highly patronizing reply, but Eisenhower's subsequent disavowal of the Hoffman article might have taken some of the sting out of the controversy.[46]

Eisenhower's remarks at his press conference on November 15, 1956, about one week after his reelection, served, however, to revive the controversy over "modern Republicanism." In a conference which was largely given over to comments on international affairs, Eisenhower briefly explained his earlier reference to "modern Republicanism":

It is a type of political philosophy that recognizes clearly the responsibility of the Federal Government to take the lead in making certain that the productivity of our great economic machine is distributed so that no one will suffer disaster, privation, through no fault of his own. Now, this covers the wide field of education and health, and so on.

It is not surprising that party conservatives, including Texas Republicans, more comfortable with the views of the late Robert A. Taft than with those of Paul G. Hoffman, suspected that the whole panoply of New Deal socialism was hidden in Eisenhower's "and so on," particularly because national newspapers such as the *New York Times* and regional papers such as the *Dallas Morning News* did not generally report the remarks which followed immediately after the above statement:

We believe likewise in the free enterprise system. We believe that it is free enterprise that has brought these blessings to America.

Therefore, we are going to try our best to preserve that free enterprise, and put all of these problems in the hands of localities and the private enterprise of States wherever we can. It happens that the great difference, as I see it, between myself and people of a philosophy that believes in centralized governments, is that I believe to have this free enterprise healthy, you must have, first integrity in your fiscal operations of the Government; second, you must preserve a sound dollar or all of our plans for social security and pensions for the aged fall by the wayside, they are no good; and thirdly, in this dispersion of power.

Now that, at home, as I see it, represents Modern Republicanism.[47]

However moderate Eisenhower's remarks might seem in the total context of his statement, the abbreviated form in which they were reported simply served to deepen doubts of Eisenhower's conservatism in the ranks of conservative party members. And in Texas, at least, ideology was more important than jobs after 1956, especially to rank-and-file party members. When the 1960 Census was taken, for example, a large number of temporary jobs were available to Republicans. There were few takers in either Dallas or Houston. In Dallas, housewives who had worked in Bruce Alger's campaigns had to be persuaded that they ought to take the census jobs in the interest of getting the job done.[48] Issues were also more important than jobs in deepening the split between the Eisenhower administration and the Texas Republicans during the President's second term.

For a time, Jack Porter discouraged the expression of plainspoken anger in Goldwater's style. Even after numerous and frustrating reversals, Porter was aware of the need for getting along with the White House, come what may. Thus he had persuaded the Texas party not to make a strong objection to the veto of the gas bill in 1956. Later, on a more volatile issue, Porter contended before the state committee that the sending of federal troops to Little Rock "resulted from the activities of extremists on both sides." Though not wholly of this persuasion—Thomas Anderson, committee member for Houston, resigned in protest of the Little Rock incident—the Texas party alone in the South did not go on record in strong condemnation of Eisenhower's actions; nonetheless, few of its members approved of federally enforced integration.[49] Despite Porter's efforts to stifle direct criticism of the Eisenhower administration, occasional party statements made clear the increasing dissatisfaction of a large number of Texas Republicans with national policy. Beginning in 1956, the conservatives found their spokesman in Professor John G. Tower, a Taft supporter in 1952, who was both more articulate and better informed than other members of the state committee. Tower wrote the larger part of the 1956 party platform, which included a plank broadly critical of "centralization of power in Washington." One year later, the state committee publicly condemned "Modern Republicanism" and passed one of John Tower's resolutions: "We feel the present administration is now deviating from the principles upon which we originally supported the candidacy of Dwight D. Eisenhower." In 1958, in a "Statement of Principles," the committee went so far as to declare that "the drift toward socialism in the U.S. is astounding and alarming to all conservatives." Clearly the Texans, along with the increasingly numerous and vocal conservative Republicans, rejected the centrist politics of their national party leaders.[50]

By June, 1960, the ideological split between the White House and the conservative Texas Republicans was complete; the state party's platform represented a repudiation of "Modern Republicanism" and hence of both the Eisenhower administration and the eastern leadership of the party. The Texans declared themselves against "federal aid to education, federal health insurance schemes, federal welfare programs, federal economic controls, the discontinuation of nuclear testing, and federal encroachment on the remaining rights of the states." Bruce Alger was right on the mark ideologically when he told the September, 1960, party convention:

For us Republicans the issue is clear. For the future of our great nation will it be government determination or self-determination that determines an individual's life. Will it be regimentation by bureaucratic planning, spending and control or will we decide to stay within the constitutional Republic in a democracy that limits the Federal Government and preserves individual freedom.

Politically, modern Texas Republicans had been pragmatic enough to follow Dwight D. Eisenhower; ideologically, they never abandoned Robert A. Taft.[51]

Apart from ideology, Texas Republican leaders had an additional motive for disagreeing with the policies of the administration: "Modern Republicanism" was not a salable political commodity in Texas. It not only hindered the party's persistent attempts to woo conservative Democrats, to whom they issued numerous private and public invitations to join the Republican party, but also made it difficult for GOP leaders to retain their own members. In Texas and the rest of the South, I. Lee Potter, head of the national committee's Operation Dixie, found that Eisenhower's action at Little Rock brought a sharp drop in volunteer activity among southern Republicans. The ladies, for example, were dropping out of Republican politics. In a letter to National Chairman Meade Alcorn, Mrs. Richard Elam, president of the Texas Federation of Republican Women, objected to oil imports, to Alcorn's critical statements about Jack Porter's dinner for Joe Martin, and, most of all, to "the Little Rock Situation." The latter issue was especially urgent; it had caused Republican Women's Club membership to drop by two-thirds in some parts of the state. Mrs. Elam observed: "The National Republican policy seems to be to snap its fingers in our faces and take an 'we don't care whether you like it or not' attitude. And that is the way the situation looks to most people."[52]

Apprehension and even open hostility toward the Eisenhower administration were not allayed by the national party's occasional attempts to aid the state organizations in the South. In pursuit of the chimera of a Republican South, widely written about as an emerging possibility during the late 1940s and early 1950s and mulled over by Herbert Brownell and White House political aides, the Republican National Committee established in January, 1957, a special division to promote its "Operation Dixie." Jack Porter volunteered to ramrod the project, but he was passed over in favor of a less controversial figure, I. Lee Potter of Virginia, who had been on the party's national staff for two years. Thus snubbed, Porter declined to participate in the project. "I thought that when they selected a man from one of those small states," he explained, "they had the tail wagging the dog."[53]

It is difficult to assess the actual effect, if any, of Operation Dixie on the Texas Republican party. The project produced "how-to-do-it" booklets relating to the organizing of fund-raising dinners, information which the Texans had drawn from their own experiences years before; the establishing of booster fund-raising programs; and the formalizing of state party offices and managerial structures. Less concerned in the mid-fifties with managerial problems, the Texans tended to ignore the last of these three subjects. Among state party leaders, the greatest interest in the project was shown by State Chairman Thad Hutcheson; but Hutcheson was enthusiastic by temperament. Porter dismissed Operation Dixie as more of the same talk about attracting conservative Democrats that had been common in the party for decades. And it was. Moreover, Lee Potter's promising initiatives were abandoned when the White House turned him into a troubleshooter for the Eisenhower administration. After working to great effect in Florida, Virginia, and the Carolinas, Lee Potter finally found himself relegated to the unwelcome role of front office apologist for the White House; he was dispatched to Little Rock during the federal intervention in 1957 and to Texas in 1958 to read a prepared statement regarding the Martin Dinner.[54] Operation Dixie, optimistically begun as a vehicle by which the national party would foster Republican development in the South, petered out as the Eisenhower administration turned the program to its own purposes and as the southerners fell out with the Eisenhower administration.

Generally speaking, the Eisenhower administration worked at cross-purposes with party leaders. Though the General's successful campaigns generally boosted support of the GOP by the party-in-the-electorate, the continual accommodation of Democratic leaders in patronage matters, the inconsiderate handling of state leaders, and the pursuit of measures and ideas pervasively unpopular with party activists hampered the growth of the GOP in Texas. It was all uphill running for Republicans in Texas; the added drag of the Eisenhower administration simply wore out the party's captain. Weighed down by these problems and by chronic ill health, the party's most dynamic fighter, Jack Porter, retired as national committeeman in 1960. What had he accomplished? A fair answer is clearly implied by his unofficial title, "Mr. Republican," respectfully accorded him by Republicans and Democrats alike. More than anyone else, Jack Porter had brought the Texas GOP into competitive electoral politics.[55]

7

"The Day of the Republicans Dawned Tuesday"

WHEN ALBERT B. FAY, a Houston oilman and a successful fund-raiser, succeeded Jack Porter, the immediate political prospects for the Republican party in Texas were not encouraging. In the face of defeats and of mounting disenchantment with the Eisenhower administration, the likelihood that Texas could be carried for the Republican presidential nominee in 1960 was slim, especially if the candidate were to associate himself with Eisenhower's unpopular welfare, petroleum, and integration policies.

Dissatisfaction with Eisenhower was transferable to other prominent members of his administration: as early as November, 1957, the *Dallas Times Herald* observed of Richard Nixon that "the Republican fair-haired boy of six months ago had been a lonely and forlorn figure."[1] To preserve his chance at the presidential nomination in 1960, Nixon gave great attention to the construction of political contacts independent of the White House. In Texas, he had an extensive pen-pal correspondence with Dallas County GOP Chairman Maurice I. Carlson, a live-wire insurance executive: from 1958 to 1960 at least fifty items of specialized correspondence were exchanged between Nixon or members of his staff and Carlson. But when Carlson lost his post to Peter O'Donnell in 1959, Nixon prudently transferred his attention to the new officeholder.[2] By

170

1960, through persistent cultivation, Nixon had momentarily persuaded most southern Republican leaders that he was not seriously contaminated with "Modern Republicanism."[3]

But persuasion was a far cry from wholehearted conviction. The Texas party convention sent a Nixon delegation to the Republican National Convention, but one-third of the group leaned strongly to the local favorite, Barry Goldwater. Their sentiments became obvious after Richard Nixon, moving to guarantee party unity, met with New York Governor Nelson Rockefeller in July, 1960, and subsequently issued a statement of agreement, the so-called "Treaty of Fifth Avenue," which some Texas Republicans thought signaled the vice-president's surrender to the "New Deal Republicans" of the East. Conservative resentment mounted on the national convention floor in response to a rumor that Nixon was still bargaining with Rockefeller as the Platform Committee met. And so Texans protested: they joined the short-lived "Stop Nixon" movement at the convention, and about one-third of the Texas delegates disregarded the instruction of their state convention by voting for Barry Goldwater. National Committeeman Fay and State Chairman Tad Smith of El Paso, Thad Hutcheson's successor, did not support the revolt; but they were unable to prevent it. Sore feelings about the Republican party's eastern leadership had been developing for nearly four years; the stop-Nixon movement was merely one of the occasions on which conservative resentment was expressed in political action.

Following the convention, Texas GOP leaders found that rank and file members harbored the same ill feelings toward Nixon and the "Treaty of Fifth Avenue" as did the rebellious convention delegates. Volunteer work began slowly. It lagged considerably behind the efforts made for Eisenhower, though some influential conservative Democrats, including Allan Shivers and Carr Collins, actively supported Nixon against Kennedy and "Landslide Lyndon"; Lyndon Johnson attracted considerable hostility from Dallas, Collins's hometown. Animosity was, in fact, the outstanding characteristic of the political encounters in the 1960 campaign.[4]

But why should feeling against Lyndon Johnson among conservative Democrats in Dallas have been so pronounced? The explanation of this sentiment must refer back to Johnson's campaign against Coke Stevenson in the 1948 Democratic party primary election. He had defeated the conservative Stevenson in a markedly close and bitter contest. The ill will generated by Johnson's triumph was revived in 1960 by a fraudulent

campaign advertisement in the *Dallas Times Herald*. Shortly before
Johnson's visit to Dallas in November, that newspaper carried a full-
page advertisement which listed thirty-five hundred prominent local residents as Johnson supporters. Surprisingly, even the new GOP county
chairman, Paul O'Rourke, was listed. In response to the advertisement,
the newspaper was flooded by complaints from indignant Dallasites
who claimed that their names had been used without their knowledge;
and, indeed a spot check of several hundred alleged signers disclosed
that a large proportion of them had not consented to the use of their
names. In the opinion of indignant Republicans and some conservative
Democrats, "Landslide Lyndon," the master of the slow count and the
rigger of elections, was up to his old tricks; and some sort of effective
protest had to be made.[5] Johnson's midday appearance at the Adolphus
Hotel seemed a convenient occasion. Active as ever, Republican women
organized a protest demonstration, painted signs, and appeared at the
hotel to make their point. As Johnson arrived, several hundred ladies
crowded the sidewalk of the Adolphus and packed the spacious lobby
inside. Congressman Bruce Alger, who had just left a meeting with his
campaign volunteers at the Baker Hotel, directly across the street, un-
wisely joined the ladies and was photographed holding a sign which
read, "LBJ Sold Out to Yankee Socialists." Johnson, his wife, and their
entourage brushed past Alger and the sidewalk demonstrators without
a word and pushed into the crowded lobby, where nervous security aides
muscled their way through the pack of ladies, bruising shins and setting
up a shoving contest; the ladies pushed back, and during the melee
Lady Bird Johnson was buffeted roughly by the crowd. After a few
minutes, the Johnson party made its way across the hotel lobby and
escaped up a flight of stairs, ignoring John Tower, Johnson's Republican opponent in the forthcoming senatorial election, who waited in
the hope of egging Johnson into a spontaneous public debate. Johnson
smiled smugly at Tower and turned away.[6]

Lyndon Johnson ignored Tower, but he did not overlook the political value of the highly publicized incident at the Adolphus Hotel.
Stirring up sympathy votes, he told a Houston audience: "It was sad
in Dallas—you wouldn't have believed you were in Texas." On election
eve, Johnson made repeated use of the anti-Dallas theme, saying, "God
forgive them for they know not what they do." Johnson's skillful use
of this issue probably gained him support in what proved to be a close
presidential race, which was finally decided by a handful of votes in

Illinois and Texas. At any rate, Johnson thoroughly diverted public attention from the potentially damaging fraudulent advertisement.[7] John F. Kennedy and Lyndon B. Johnson carried Texas by forty-six thousand votes out of more than two million cast. They lost Amarillo, Lubbock, Midland, Odessa, Dallas, Houston, and much of East Texas; but they carried Fort Worth, Beaumont, and Galveston, where labor unions mustered support, and southwestern Texas, where Johnson had always been strong. Indeed, in 1960, Johnson ran uniquely well in that he was re-elected United States senator and received the Texas vice-presidential vote at the same time. This adroit accomplishment was made possible when, in 1959, the Democratic-controlled legislature obligingly passed the so-called Johnson Act, which permitted the listing of a candidate on the ballot for U.S. Senate at the same time his name appeared for president or vice-president. Johnson won reelection to the Senate handily, by nearly four hundred thousand votes. He had, however, encountered his most serious challenge for the seat, a development which came as something of a surprise to Republicans and Democrats alike.[8]

Earlier in the year, Republican leaders had been generally pessimistic regarding the success of a challenge to Senator Johnson. As usual, there was the grave problem of finding a likely candidate. Ben Guill was inclined to remain in Washington. Thad Hutcheson, still the party favorite, who had been kept more or less in the public eye as state chairman, decided to wait for a more promising contest in the future. In 1960, moreover, with the debt from the 1956 presidential campaign still unpaid, the party could offer only meager financial backing for its candidate; available funds were committed to the more pressing presidential election campaign. Clearly, the senatorial contest would be an uphill battle. After better-known and wealthier party members declined to make the race, John Tower, impecunious but articulate spokesman of the state party's dominant conservatism, came forward and received the Republican nomination.[9]

Tower launched a vigorous campaign. The son of a Methodist minister who had served churches in East Texas and Houston, Tower returned to Texas after he was discharged from the Navy at the end of World War II. He worked as a radio announcer and as a salesman in North Texas before taking graduate study at the London School of Economics and Southern Methodist University. He married Lou Bullington, cousin of Republican leader Orville Bullington, and settled down in Wichita Falls to teach politics and government at Midwestern State College.

Following his own interests, which were shared by Orville Bulling-ton, Tower became prominent in local Republican affairs and ran un-successfully for the Texas House of Representatives in 1954. He gained a seat on the Republican state committee, managed Thad Hutcheson's campaign in the Wichita Falls area in 1957, and served as a delegate to the Republican National Convention in 1960. Like Thad Hutcheson before him, Tower ran an energetic if underfinanced campaign; he solicited support even in the strongly Democratic sections of East Texas, where his father's earlier services brought him a considerable friends-and-neighbors vote. With less than two hundred thousand dollars to sustain his efforts, Tower cut corners where he could. He stayed with party workers to cut down on hotel bills and recorded his own political announcements for broadcasting media. As with the earlier Hutcheson campaign, volunteer workers provided by far the greatest measure of campaign support, particularly in the cities of San Antonio, Houston, and Dallas.

The reward for Tower's risk and his workers' exertions came with the election results: Tower lost, but he took 41.5 percent of the major party vote. By contrast, Carlos Watson had received only 15 percent of the vote when he opposed Johnson six years earlier. The returns from the cities were especially favorable. Midland gave Tower 58 per-cent of the vote, Dallas 57 percent, Tyler 51 percent, Houston 49 per-cent, Odessa slightly more than 50 percent, Lubbock 46 percent, Ama-rillo 49 percent, and Fort Worth 44 percent. In rural East Texas Tower carried a number of counties, including Rusk, where he won more than 55 percent of the vote. Among the state's urban areas, only strong union cities, Galveston and Beaumont, which Nixon also lost on the presidential ballot, gave Tower a showing below his statewide average. Tower had campaigned industriously, had become widely known as a result of his campaign, and had stood up unprecedentedly well against Johnson; after the 1960 election he was beyond any doubt the best-known potential candidate in the Texas Republican party. For this reason, he had little difficulty in securing the party's endorsement in 1961, when Lyndon Johnson's election as vice-president necessitated a special election to fill the senatorial office.[10]

In spite of the growth of the party organization, Tower faced a problem which had not confronted Thad Hutcheson; in 1957 a special election for U.S. senator had been won by liberal Democrat Ralph Yarborough by a simple plurality of the vote. The possibility of either another liberal Democratic or a Republican plurality victory was fore-stalled by the conservative leadership of the Democratic party, who had firm control of the legislature, by changing the law; they required the winner to have at least half of the vote and provided for the holding of a runoff contest between the two front-runners if no candidate secured the required majority in the first contest. Following a frequent pattern of Democratic primary elections, there were scores of candidates and five major contenders: the party's liberal faction, represented by Con-gressman Jim Wright of Fort Worth, State Senator Henry Gonzalez of San Antonio, and former State Representative Maury Maverick, Jr., car-ried their respective followings; but they lost to conservative Democrat William Blakely, the interim appointee to the vacant Johnson seat, and Tower, the only Republican candidate.[11]

Conservative Democrat was thus matched against conservative Re-publican. Setting his sights on Blakely in the runoff, Tower effectively trapped the old conservative through persistent criticism of his absence from the Senate during the campaign. In order to refute Tower's charge, Blakely kept doggedly at his job in Washington, losing valuable cam-paign time, while Tower flew one hundred thousand miles and made eighty-nine major engagements in thirty-six days. When Blakely be-latedly opened his campaign with a dinner at Waco on May 25, his audience was thin and lethargic. One disillusioned Democrat reported: "There was enough food left over to run the whole Food for Peace Program; right good food, too." Worse yet, in the opinions of Demo-cratic congressmen, Blakely used the dinner at Waco, in the central Texas farm belt, as an opportunity to attack the locally popular Kennedy farm program. He further dismayed Democratic leaders by giving over the main portion of his address to a dry discourse on constitutional gov-ernment. One state legislator wryly commented: "People only want to hear about the Constitution on the Fourth of July."[12]

While Blakely inadvertently assisted him with blunders, Tower worked to win over conservative Democrats, particularly in urban re-gions. In this effort he was aided by Blakely's tepid campaigning, the continued support of Republican volunteers, a series of speeches by Senator Barry Goldwater, the favorite of many Texas conservatives, and an enthusiastic endorsement from former President Eisenhower. Accord-ingly, money was somewhat easier to come by than it had been a year before: Tower was thought to have a good chance of winning. Even so, fund-raisers, including National Committeeman Albert Fay, worked under the hammer as a consequence of the 1956 debt; and the quarter-of-a-million-dollar campaign fund supported a bare-bones campaign. Relative to the expense of subsequent Texas campaigns, in 1961 Tower was, in Fay's words, a "bargain Senator." A "bargain Senator" or not, when the votes were in, Tower was an elected member of the United States Senate, the first Texas Republican to hold that post since Reconstruction.[13]

The Republican party came through John Tower's successful senatorial campaign with the exuberance which only victory brings in electoral politics and with an organization which had stood the test, particularly in the major population centers of Texas. During the decade which followed, the GOP became increasingly effective in fundraising, candidate recruitment, turning out supporters, and other elements of party management. For the most part, these efforts were directed at securing additional elective offices for party candidates. Political energies were generally applied to useful ends, though the persistent intraparty factionalism which tended to hamper party operations before Jack Porter's term as party leader reemerged during the party's decade of major growth.

The first opportunity to follow up on Tower's triumph was provided late in 1961 when President John F. Kennedy appointed Democratic Congressman Paul J. Kilday of San Antonio to the Military Court of Appeals. Kilday's resignation from the United States House of Representatives gave Bexar County Republicans an exceptional opportunity to regain Harry Wurzbach's seat in the ensuing special congressional election. As the contests fought by Ben Guill and John Tower seemed to demonstrate, GOP organizers were more successful than the Democrats at turning out supporters for infrequent single office contests.

But the want of a visible and seasoned Republican candidate blocked easy realization of victory in San Antonio. From a relatively weak position, the Republicans made their strongest move by nominating John Goode, a personable attorney who was Republican county chairman. As local party chief, Goode had achieved at least a measure of public recognition. After a decade of service in the Bexar County organization, he could count on the loyal support of party workers. In the forthcoming contest, however, Henry B. Gonzalez, Goode's Democratic opponent, enjoyed a number of important advantages. Gonzalez, son of Mexican immigrants, had established his popularity with Latin voters as San Antonio city councilman from 1953 to 1956 and, since 1956, as state senator

from San Antonio. In 1958 he campaigned as a liberal for the gubernatorial nomination of the Democratic party.

Not surprisingly, in 1961 Gonzalez received considerable encouragement and support from the liberal and moderate leaders of his party.
Endorsements from President Kennedy, Vice-President Lyndon B. Johnson, Governor Price Daniel, and U.S. Senator Ralph Yarborough provided at least the appearance of exceptional Democratic unity behind
Gonzalez's candidacy. Like Goode, however, Gonzalez faced one major
problem: the possibility of a weak voter turnout. Failure of the Latin
bloc vote to turn out might well throw the contest to Goode. Both
Gonzalez and Goode thus reasoned that victory depended on widespread
publicity. Goode sought recognition from conservative voters; Gonzalez
needed a sizable Latin voter turnout.[14]

Despite the candidates' desire for exposure, campaign exchanges
between Goode and Gonzalez generated little public interest. Goode, a
political moderate, pitched his appeal to the political right by making
a major issue of Gonzalez's honorary directorship of the Americans for
Democratic Action. Speaking at a rally for Goode on October 4, John
Tower added spicy campaign rhetoric as he denounced Gonzalez as a
"red-eyed radical." Gonzalez, in turn, made capital of the backing which
Goode received from the members of the John Birch Society, following
publicity given the campaign in *Human Events*. The right-wing label
was an effective fabrication: Goode's campaign slogan, repeated on
radio, television, and billboards, identified him as a "militant conservative," even though Goode expressed support for medical care for the
aged and for the United Nations. To offset Gonzalez's damaging charge,
Goode was forced to disavow rightist support late in the campaign, a
move which cost financial backing and votes. Yet, even with the exchanged charges of radicalism, the candidates failed to generate interest
in the contest. By mid-October the special election campaign was still
a conventional, generally unheeded battle—a situation which both candidates sought to overcome.[15]

In their effort to overcome voter apathy, both candidates sought
and received considerable help from state and national organizations.
Goode's campaign was engineered by a three-man group of professional
campaign organizers with Mickey Ledrick, executive director of the
Texas GOP, in charge. Gonzalez's campaign organization included members of Vice-President Johnson's staff, an organizer from the Committee
on Political Education of the AFL-CIO, and Charles Roach, deputy chair-

man of the Democratic National Committee. Clearly, state and national leaders had decided to stake much more on this special election than was customary in congressional races. Goode received impressive backing from major Republican leaders. Former President Dwight D. Eisenhower issued a strong endorsement of Goode and flew to San Antonio for an extended campaign appearance at the end of October. The former President electioneered with retired soldiers and old friends, lunched with precinct workers, and spoke at a rally for Goode in Alamo Plaza, where Eisenhower had received a tumultuous welcome in 1952. Ominously for Goode, the crowd, estimated at only nine thousand by the *San Antonio Express*, was a small fraction of the number of residents who had cheered the military hero nine years earlier. The effect of Eisenhower's efforts on the powerful conservative establishment in San Antonio was more encouraging: Goode thereafter received significant financial support from conservative Democrats. For his part, Henry Gonzalez publicized a glowing endorsement from President Kennedy, who was highly popular with Catholic voters, and received invaluable aid from Vice-President Johnson, who appeared with him on November 2 at a rally at La Villita, the restored "old town" section of San Antonio. Johnson, the veteran Texas politician, worked the beer and tamale circuit and roused Gonzalez's campaign workers with short pep talks.

Noting the exceptional involvement of national party leaders in the lone congressional contest, national news commentators described it as the first political test of the "new frontier," thereby heightening general and local interest in the special election. As if to make this piece of journalistic hyperbole into fact, Vice-President Johnson told Bexar County voters that the nation would view Goode's election as a repudiation of the Kennedy administration. Underscoring the importance of these remarks, Johnson and Cantinflas, the popular Mexican cinematic comedian, spent much of election day riding through the Latin neighborhoods, "pressing flesh" and leading crowds of Gonzalez supporters to polling places. When the polls closed, both parties had expended all of their resources; they had tried all known gambits.[16]

In the end, LBJ, Cantinflas, and the stronger candidate were victorious. Possibility of victory for Texas Republicans had rested as always on their ability to get out a disproportionately large segment of their vote to offset the Democratic advantage in the number of registered voters. But this seasoned strategy failed in San Antonio in November, 1961. Apart from Gonzalez's considerable advantages of visibility, bloc support, and massive publicity and Goode's waffling of the issue of radicalism, San Antonio Republicans contended unsuccessfully with the new problem of fatigue in their own organization. It had conducted effective and exhausting campaigns for Richard Nixon and John Tower in 1960 and again for Tower early in 1961. By November, as one party leader expressed it, "Most of our workers were just plain burned out." The effect of worker fatigue is clearly reflected in the election returns. Goode failed to raise enough of a vote in the strongly conservative areas, principally the northeastern section of San Antonio, Olmos Park and Alamo Heights, to offset the strong Latin vote for Gonzalez. The predominantly Latin West Side returned nearly twelve votes for Gonzalez for every vote for Goode; Latin and black precincts on the East Side went for the liberal Democrat by a six-to-one ratio. Prosperous Anglo precincts, such as Olmos Park, supported Goode four to one over Gonzalez; but the Republican margin among middle-class Anglos was a disappointing 60 percent of the whole vote, and the turnout of Republicans in this sector—highly important to Republican candidates—was low. In short, Gonzalez mustered his supporters, and Goode did not. The New Frontier had passed its first test; the first opportunity for Texas Republicans to follow up on the Tower victory was lost.[17]

In spite of the discouraging defeat in San Antonio, statewide prospects for Republicans were encouraging in 1962, for, a full year before the general election, a potentially strong Republican gubernatorial candidate—the first since 1932—had appeared on the scene. On November 2, 1961, Jack Cox, onetime Democratic member of the state legislature, announced that he would seek the GOP nomination in the 1962 Republican primary. Cox, one of a growing number of conservative Democrats who switched to the Republican party, was the only living Republican who had sat in the state senate. More important, as an officeholder and as the principal conservative Democratic challenger to Governor Price Daniel in the 1960 Democratic primary election, Cox had attracted considerable public attention and financial support from conservatives. Operating as an oil well drilling contractor, Cox had also accumulated a modest personal fortune which he threw into the campaign. With public visibility and adequate financial backing, along with the support of influential Republican leaders including State Chairman Peter O'Donnell of Dallas, Jack Cox was the GOP's ready-made candidate. After an unexciting primary race against Amarillo publisher Roy Whittenburg, Cox turned his attention to his Democratic opponent.[18]

The Democrats suffered from no shortage of likely candidates; quite to the contrary, the first Democratic primary election was a "horserace," as both politicians and journalists saw it. Incumbent Governor Price Daniel faced a large field of strong opponents which included Attorney General Will Wilson of Dallas; Marshall Formby, an influential legislator from East Texas; retired former Army General Edwin A. Walker; Houston attorney Don Yarborough, who was tied by liberal politics but not blood relationship to Senator Ralph Yarborough; and Secretary of the Navy John Connally. By virtue of strong political ties to Democratic loyalists through Sam Rayburn, and on the strength of support from some conservative elements of the business community stemming from his service as attorney to Sid Richardson, wealthy and influential Fort Worth oilman, and to the Richardson Foundation, Connally was generally viewed as the front-runner, though some observers doubted that he could form a majority coalition in the disunited party. With a large field of candidates, it was likely that Connally would face a runoff contest against either Daniel, Wilson, or Yarborough.[19]

The Texas Democratic primary resembled nothing so much as a family feud; the fighting was bitter, and no victor emerged. Connally did not secure the nomination. As front-runner with 30 percent of the whole vote, he was trailed by Yarborough, Daniel, and the other candidates. Having eliminated Governor Daniel from the competition, Connally, "the boardroom lackey," faced Yarborough, "the labor stooge," in a bare-knuckles political fight before the June runoff primary election. After a brief but intense campaign, Connally emerged with the Democratic nomination by an uncomfortably slim margin, 51 percent of the vote. More important to his prospects in the general election, Connally was faced with the burden of intraparty antagonisms which had been sparked during the heated Democratic primary campaigns. In John Connally's problems the Republicans found cause for optimism.[20]

As November approached, Republicans and Democrats alike scented victory in the political wind. Both parties labored with unprecedented industry and efficiency. Cox mounted the most strenuous GOP campaign for governor in Texas history. Under the industrious and methodical management of Peter O'Donnell, Texas Republicans carried on a lengthy, expensive, and effective drive for Cox. Unlike so many of his predecessors, Cox was no token candidate. He campaigned for three months before the November election; flew to all of the population centers of the state; toured East Texas in a bus, along with a country and western band; spoke at fully one hundred party rallies; and appeared on scores of television programs.[21]

The efforts of Cox and his supporters were sustained by a number of encouraging signs. One month before the election, Cox occasionally outdrew Connally. On October 3, for example, while Cox appeared before a thousand voters at a neighborhood jamboree in San Antonio, one of a dozen appearances in the Alamo City, John Connally was addressing a polite but meager gathering of three hundred West Texas Democrats at a luncheon in the Crystal Ballroom of the Scharbauer Hotel in Midland. Even the press, securely in the hands of conservative Democratic publishers, bestowed unprecedented coverage on the Republican challenger, by virtue of his novelty as a strong Republican contender. When Jack Cox appeared in the state's major cities, he frequently received front-page treatment, whereas earlier GOP candidates had usually been buried near the obituary columns. Though his candidacy was not without its problems, principally of finance and publicity, Jack Cox was a formidably lively campaigner.[22]

John Connally, well financed, widely known as John F. Kennedy's photogenic and charming navy secretary, and the apparent choice of both Sam Rayburn and Lyndon B. Johnson, meanwhile faced the persistent problem of Democratic gubernatorial candidates: reuniting his party, which had been seriously split by the primary elections. Party regulars worked to keep the conservative, moderate, and ethnic blocs in line. Congressman Henry Gonzalez appeared with Connally in San Antonio and reminded fellow Latins and liberals that "there ain't no such thing as a neutral." The rural connections of Price Daniel and Sam Rayburn rallied to shore up sagging support for Connally in East Texas; and with the help of Lyndon Johnson, Connally wooed the labor vote in Fort Worth and in the Gulf Coast cities. But this effort brought no real return. Nursing a grudge from Connally's runoff victory over Don Yarborough and suspicious of Connally's close ties to the state's dominant corporate interests, labor yielded an embarrassingly unenthusiastic endorsement of Connally, even after Ralph Yarborough, titular leader of the liberal-labor faction, intervened on Connally's behalf. Yet, even with little labor support, Connally could be assured of victory if he maintained the commitment of the conservative Democrats in Texas. This task was undertaken and mastered with no great difficulty in the two hundred rural counties, where the traditional electioneering organization, county officials and local party chairmen, turned out to vote for Connally, just as they had for previous Democratic candidates. Conservative voters in Texas cities were less easily reached. The urban Democratic organizations, still in the hands of courthouse crowds, enjoyed the support of the downtown connection but lacked effective precinct-level organizations. The majority of urban conservatives were thus beyond the effective control of the local Democratic leaders, while urban liberals were indifferent, at best, to Connally's candidacy.[23]

Connally's effort to unite Texas Democrats behind him failed most conspicuously with the liberal segment of his party. In response to grudges acquired during the hard-fought runoff campaign and numerous rumors of serious election irregularities in South Texas, where both Lyndon Johnson and John Connally enjoyed considerable support, former supporters of Don Yarborough withheld support from Connally; in some instances, they actually endorsed Jack Cox. Thus, David Copeland, who had served as campaign coordinator for Don Yarborough, formed Texans for a Two-Party Texas and endorsed Cox; he declared that he intended to vote for "a Republican who admits that he is a Republican," rather than for John Connally, whom Copeland characterized as a crypto-Republican.[24]

Jack Cox ignored such token support from disgruntled liberal Democrats and aimed directly at the more glaring gaps in Connally's campaign armor. Day after day, before large rally audiences, on television, and in the newspapers, Cox admonished voters to "keep Texas free from Washington control" by rejecting Connally, John F. Kennedy's candidate. Acting to fuse anti-Kennedy, anti-Johnson, and anti-Connally sentiment, Cox identified his own candidacy squarely with conservative positions on such issues as the power of the United States Supreme Court and federal regulation of the oil industry.

The strategy of Cox's managers to identify him as the most reliably conservative candidate was applied persistently in the population centers of Texas, and with considerable effect. As the campaign progressed, political observers could see that the gubernatorial election would be close and that Cox gained votes while Connally worked to hold his splintered forces together. Three weeks before the election, Eugene Locke, Connally's campaign manager, observed that Cox was "in better shape than any Republican running against a Democrat in a hotly contested race in the last ten years." Cox's managers, including state chairman Tad Smith of El Paso, agreed and pointed to strong Republican efforts in Dallas, Houston, San Antonio, and West Texas. Locke insisted that the outcome would be decided by the level of voter turnout, with a high level of participation insuring a Connally victory while a low turnout, marked by a large GOP vote in the cities, might well throw the election to Cox.[25]

Both parties shared Locke's view of the contest. Consequently, both candidates campaigned longer and harder. Toward the close of the campaign Cox made ten or more public appearances on some days, a practice which occasionally took its toll; at one point during his campaign in Dallas, he found himself voiceless, whispered a brief talk to the League of Women Voters, and was forced to cancel an important television appearance. In response to Cox's energy, Connally abandoned the campaign style of previous Democratic gubernatorial candidates; he accelerated the pace of his efforts in the closing days of the campaign by scheduling a thirty-one-stop flying tour, billed as a "campaignathon," for the forty-eight hours which preceded the opening of the polls. Moving no less rapidly, Cox observed that Connally was "not just pushing the panic button now. He is so scared that he is jumping up and down on it."[26]

With an accelerated pace came the kind of heated campaign crossfire Cox's remark typified. Cox branded Connally a crypto–New Dealer and a "cheap lobbyist," claiming that Connally had been paid "a fantastic salary" to lobby on behalf of major oil companies for the Harris Bill in 1957. Not to be outdone, Connally denounced Cox as a party-switcher, described him as "a Boy Scout," and added: "He doesn't have any qualities that would qualify him for the governorship." As he appealed to party conservatives, Connally played on deep-seated anti-Republican prejudices, reminding them that "the last time a Republican governor was elected in Texas, it was under Federal supervision and at the point of federal bayonets." Among liberal Democrats, Connally labored to discredit Cox by connecting the Republican candidate with the radical right. He charged that Cox was "a former agent for a dangerous secret society"; he warned liberals that his opponent's camp "talks about principles, but they preach prejudice." Without resort to hyperbole, therefore, journalists described the 1962 gubernatorial campaign as the most spirited contest in decades.[27]

Contrary to Republican hopes and Democratic fears, the exertions of Cox and Connally brought a record off-year voter turnout. It favored Connally, as most political observers had predicted. The total number of ballots, 1,569,181, was down only one-third from the number which were cast in the 1960 general election. With 46 percent of the major party vote, Cox ran well in most of the major cities, carrying Dallas, Houston (narrowly), Lubbock, Amarillo, San Angelo, Tyler, Midland, and Odessa, along with a scattering of rural counties in the Panhandle, West Texas, and the Hill Country. He lost Fort Worth, officially Connally's hometown, by less than 600 votes. Cox ran well, but he failed to counter Connally's strength in South Texas, Austin, Waco, and the industrial Gulf Coast cities. John Connally's victory was built on the traditional rural bulwark of the Democratic party and on the Latin counties; the latter provided half his margin, 130,000 votes. He won Corpus Christi, El Paso, San Antonio, and Laredo, along with Cameron, Hidalgo, Duval, and Gonzalez counties, with comfortable margins; carried about thirty non-Latin rural counties with margins of 1,000 to 3,000 votes; and held the Democratic cities of Austin, Beaumont, Port Arthur, Galveston, and Wichita Falls safely. In Harris County, he held Cox's margin to a mere 3,000 votes, substantially less than John Tower had received in both 1960 and 1961. Thus, though John Connally had lost support on both fringes of the Democratic party, he managed to hold on to enough of the traditional Democratic vote to turn back Cox's challenge.[28]

Though the defeated candidate, Cox had nonetheless served the Republican party well. More than seven hundred thousand voters were attracted to the Republican column in support of Cox. The large increase in the number of Republican voters, moreover, was tangible evidence of the effectiveness of intensive organizational work of the party apparatus, which mustered more than half a million voters for the party's candidate. With a strong candidate at the head of the ticket and a full head of steam, the Republican party had made its strongest showing at the polls to date. Nor was their energy limited to Cox's campaign.

In addition to their challenge to Democratic control of the governor's office, Texas Republicans contested seats in the state legislature and in Congress. In this initial widespread challenge to the majority party, Texas Republicans offered candidates for seventeen seats in the U.S. House of Representatives. Though the party lacked the candidates and financial resources to make good all of these challenges, three races were especially encouraging. Bruce Alger was reelected in Dallas, though by a less generous margin than in 1960. In East Texas, William Steger of Tyler came within 4 percent of the vote of defeating Democratic incumbent Congressman Lindley Beckworth. But most encouraging was the gain of the house seat in the sprawling Sixteenth Congressional District in West Texas, where thirty-year-old political novice Ed Foreman defeated the five-term Democratic incumbent, J. T. "Slick" Rutherford of Odessa.

Rutherford was connected in the public eye with the scandals which surrounded West Texas entrepreneur Billie Sol Estes, from whom he had accepted a $1,500 campaign contribution. Seizing the advantage in this situation, Foreman's manager, Rudy Juedeman of Odessa, built an old-fashioned "clean government campaign" which Rutherford's backers never countered effectively. More to the point, Rutherford's managers failed to take Foreman's challenge seriously—a safe tactic with past Republican challengers in Texas, but broadly out of step with the new political realities of a revived and aggressive political party. Having survived serious challengers in the Democratic primary election, Rutherford rested during most of the campaign. While Rutherford relaxed, the Foreman group developed a highly effective appeal to the conservative elements of both parties. Foreman's strong objections to federal aid to education and forced integration won him numerous friends—enough, as it turned out, to win the election. As in other parts of the state, the urban Republicans in West Texas simply outorganized their opposition. Juedeman, onetime speaker of the Montana House of Representatives, and Nadine Francis, an Odessa housewife, turned out a door-to-door effort in Odessa, of a sort which none of the West Texas towns other than Midland had experienced before. Though Rutherford's managers failed to perceive it before election day, the advantage rested with Foreman. The combination of a scandal-tainted opponent, unimaginative Democratic opposition management, an appealing candidate of their own, and effective organizational work won the day for West Texas Republicans.[29]

Victories in state legislative and local contests further brightened Republican hopes. Dallas Republicans contested six seats in the Texas House and won them all by engineering a highly effective voter turnout campaign in North Dallas; their strategy was organized around the candidacies of Bruce Alger and Jack Cox. The *Dallas Morning News*, which endorsed Alger's opponent, credited the Republican gains to Cox and assessed the consequences of the Republican victories: "Cox gave the GOP ticket the momentum it needed in Dallas County—now the bulwark of Barry Goldwater–John Tower Republicanism in Texas and maybe in the nation."[30] These were strong words from a newspaper which supported conservative Democratic candidates with predictable regularity. There was indeed cause for celebration in Dallas.

Republicans in other Texas cities were equally jubilant. In Midland, nearly five hundred party workers mustered a record off-year vote, thereby bringing Cox about two-thirds of the total vote and carrying nine of thirteen precincts for Ed Foreman. Even more encouraging for local Republicans were the victories of Bill Davis, their candidate for the Texas House of Representatives, and Barbara Culver, candidate for county judge. At her election, Mrs. Culver was the only woman and the only Republican to hold that office in Texas. The *Midland Reporter-Telegram* observed: "The day of the Republicans dawned Tuesday in Midland County." Indeed, it had dawned throughout Texas. With another attractive lead-ticket candidate, hard organizational work, and an appealing party line, the new day might well become a new era."[31]

Behind the organizational energy which achieved GOP victories in 1962 was ideology: it was the mainspring of the Republican revival. Many of the party's workers were attracted by the antiliberal banner it paraded; candidates such as Congressman Alger and Ed Foreman carried the antiliberal cause with great success. Though the "new Republicanism" of the late fifties and early sixties was usually described as a novel feature of political life, in Texas strong conservatism was a historically continuous aspect of the party. Since 1936, biennial party conventions of the Texas GOP had passed, with predictable regularity, resolutions condemnatory of New Deal liberalism and the welfare state. After World War II, the Republicans extended their attack to include federal regulation of the oil industry and the Democratic administration's "soft" attitude toward Communists and fellow travelers. The Texans, supporters of Senator Robert A. Taft from 1940 through 1948 and of Taft's opinions, albeit not of his candidacy, in 1952, never subscribed to the "one world" view of eastern party leaders. Like middle western conservatives, they rejected the acceptance of some aspects of the New Deal which marked the eastern wing of the party. In Texas, consistent conservatism was also practical politics. Since 1935, party leaders had believed that future growth of the Republican party depended on its ability to lead the attack on the policies of the Roosevelt and Truman administrations. Thereafter, Texans and other conservative Republicans found themselves at odds with members of the Eisenhower administration on various general issues.

Texan and other conservative Republicans saw little good in "modern Republicanism," of the variety represented by Arthur Larson's *A Republican Looks at His Party*. They greeted Larson's limited accommodation of New Deal liberalism with scorn. The *National Review* rejected it out of hand as a testament of "me-too-ism." Joining the swelling chorus of conservative dissent at their March, 1958, meeting, the Texas Republican State Executive Committee adopted a statement of principles which was drafted by John Tower. The statement condemned the "drift toward socialism," which had presumably continued through the Eisenhower administration. The United States Supreme Court, government competition with private business, federal regulation of natural gas, federal aid to education and agriculture, and inadequate attention to defense preparedness were denounced in the bill of particulars. With few substantive changes, Tower's statement was given unanimous endorsement by the Republican state convention in September. Thus, in Texas, as in most states outside the Northeast, Republican conservatism was a long-lived persuasion.[32]

In December, 1962, conservative Republicans thought they saw a prospect of electoral success of great magnitude if only the party could find a suitably conservative champion at the polls. The champion was waiting in the wings. Barry Goldwater had long been building his reputation as the principal spokesman for the conservative wing of the GOP, a place left vacant at the death of Robert A. Taft in 1953. As chairman of the Republican Senatorial Campaign Committee from 1956, Goldwater stumped the nation in support of candidates and in aid of party fund-raising efforts, thereby developing a widespread network of connections and obligations with Republican leaders across the country. In Texas, Goldwater was a powerful unifying personality for Republican efforts. Tremendously popular among conservative businessmen, he both stirred interest in his party in Texas and helped keep it financially afloat by speaking at fund-raising dinners. Texas Republicans were obligated to Goldwater, an obligation they were willing, eager, and able to pay.

The ties to Goldwater were cinched when he campaigned for John Tower in 1960 and 1961. Goldwater's highly valuable support and the near-total agreement of the two men on current issues placed Tower in the position of promising protégé, an identity which he relished in 1961. During the next year, after the appearance of Goldwater's *The Conscience of a Conservative*, Tower issued *A Program for Conservatives*. The two volumes seem more like two drafts of the same manuscript than like two separate works. Agreement on principal issues in foreign and domestic politics is complete; they share the popular phrases—such as "victory over communism"—of the emerging Right. The principal differences between the two works lie in style and tone. Goldwater's ideas are couched in the snappy language of the popular luncheon speaker, Tower's in the more sophisticated vocabulary of the lecture hall. Goldwater, so to speak, wrote copy for the *Reader's Digest*, Tower for the *National Review*.[33]

The Texas GOP state executive committee publicly urged Goldwater to seek the Republican presidential nomination and commended Goldwater's book as "an affirmative philosophy and program for political action."[34] The proposal was brought to the body by its newly elected chairman, Peter O'Donnell of Dallas, who had helped organize John Tower's Washington office and who had headed Jack Cox's campaign organization until he resigned to accept the state chairmanship. By the fall of 1962, most Texas party leaders were firmly committed to Goldwater's candidacy. Not only did they agree with his opinions, but they also saw a Goldwater presidential campaign as the most promising vehicle to attract conservative Democrats into the Republican fold.

Tower's victory and Goldwater's grass-roots appeal acted as strong lures to disgruntled Democrats; at "resignation rallies," the political counterpart of religious revivals, impressive numbers of old-line Democrats foreswore their old allegiances and attested loyalty to the GOP. Staged for maximum media effect, the rallies paraded new Republicans, whose ranks included scores of former Democratic precinct leaders, before the public. The most notable show was staged in the lower Rio Grande Valley at Harlingen, where nearly one thousand former Democrats announced their "conversion" to the Republican cause. A Houston rally excited considerable attention in the press when a rumor surfaced that former Governor Allan Shivers was about to join the GOP. Goldwater thus was personally appealing, ideologically acceptable, and politically useful to Texas Republican leaders.[35]

There was more than candidate appeal in Goldwater's growing strength in Texas. In considerable measure, the Goldwater movement in Texas grew out of the Dallas County Republican party, led by Peter O'Donnell; Harry Bass, a Dallas oilman and an important Republican fund-raiser; Mrs. Richard Bass, an influential Dallas socialite; and Mrs. J. C. Mann, housewife and party organizer. Like their counterparts in other Texas cities, the Dallas party chiefs were both "new conservative" and established leaders in local affairs. Rita Bass and Joanne Mann had both been initiated into organizational work during the 1952 presidential election, while Harry Bass had been active occasionally in local Republican politics since 1948. O'Donnell began political work as president of the Dallas County Young Republicans in 1950, served as precinct chairman in wealthy Highland Park, became county chairman, and held high positions in the campaign organizations of Bruce Alger and John Tower before he became state chairman. In short, the Goldwater movement in Texas was led by seasoned party leaders: it was not the work of a conspiratorial clique of newly arrived political extremists, as various writers alleged of the movement across the country. Peter O'Donnell quickly took control of Goldwater forces in Texas as state chairman; and with Senator Tower's backing, he effectively rallied support for Goldwater, leaving little doubt, even in 1962, that Texas's votes at the 1964 National Convention would be safely in Goldwater's column if the senator were a declared candidate.[36]

Following earlier moves by Tad Smith, his predecessor as state chairman, O'Donnell became involved in the behind-the-scenes efforts which were made to promote Goldwater's national candidacy. After the December, 1962, meeting of the then unpublicized Draft Goldwater Committee, O'Donnell became chairman of that group; and with F. Clifton White, former college professor and Young Republicans organizer, he set off on a hunt for delegates. In league with John Grenier, Republican national committeeman from Georgia, O'Donnell cornered the southern votes, which, together with the California delegation, served as the foundation for Goldwater's convention victory. O'Donnell and White together then launched the Draft Goldwater movement and generated widespread publicity, a development to which Senator Goldwater's response has been described as "furious" and "acutely negative." Goldwater denied encouragement to White and O'Donnell when they brought the draft organization into the open in 1963 and refused direct communication with them; John Tower was their only link to Goldwater, and even Tower could not keep Goldwater from refusal to express interest in the draft movement when he was contacted.

O'Donnell would not be dismayed at Goldwater's obduracy. In characteristically aggressive fashion, he worked to pressure Goldwater into both recognizing the draft movement and declaring his candidacy in 1963. Both steps were necessary to permit the widespread fund-raising and the organization of a citizen's organization, which in turn would be required by an effective campaign for the nomination. O'Donnell hoped to force Goldwater's hand. According to Stephen Shadegg, a Goldwater campaign lieutenant, O'Donnell declared: "If Goldwater doesn't want to make up his mind, we will draft him. And because he might say 'No,' we'll tell him what we're going to do. We won't ask his permission to do it!"[37] While O'Donnell's forcefulness presented a strong contrast to Goldwater's easy manner and public air of diffidence, the senator was not about to be pushed into an early declaration of his candidacy. His negative feelings about the draft movement appeared to extend to include its chief proponent, O'Donnell. In January, 1964, when the senator officially threw his hat into the ring, both O'Donnell and Clifton White were excluded from prominent positions in his campaign organization. Despite John Grenier's urging, Goldwater blocked O'Donnell's appointment as director of political operations at his national headquarters, and the Texan was largely limited to a lesser role in southern and Texas work.[38]

By the time of Goldwater's official declaration of candidacy, the course of national politics had been altered radically by the assassination of John F. Kennedy in November, 1963. Goldwater's electoral strategy—and a large part of the hidden vote theory—had been predicated on the assumption that Kennedy would again be the Democratic candidate and on the recurrent rumor that Kennedy would drop Lyndon Johnson as his running mate. With Kennedy's death, the political world turned upside down. Texas Republicans were faced with the bleak prospect of opposing a native son, incumbent in the White House. Influential allies deserted the Texas GOP. Oveta Culp Hobby and Robert B. Anderson, cabinet members of the Eisenhower administration, both endorsed Johnson, as did former Governor Allan Shivers, who retained widespread political contacts in Texas business circles and in rural counties in the southwestern part of the state. Within the party, former GOP notables—including Maurice Carlson and Edward T. Dicker of Dallas—were identified as "Republicans for Johnson."[39]

As the handful of moderate Republicans dissented and the Goldwater campaign mired in misspeaking, it was clear that the promotional work of the Eisenhower years and the organizational labors which followed were enlisted in support of an increasingly untenable candidate. Prospects grew even bleaker during the mismanaged Goldwater campaign. Long on misconceived image-building and short of political sense, the effort generated a picture of Goldwater as a granite-jawed, bomb-throwing extremist, bent on overturning the conventional political order. An unfriendly working press did inestimable damage to Goldwater by giving national currency to the pronouncements he intended for strictly local consumption. Thus, the luncheon speaker's strategy of making strong remarks to specific audiences proved impracticable when the audience was composed of the nation's evening news viewers rather than the chambers of commerce of Alexandria, Virginia; Atlanta, Georgia; or Dallas, Texas. Goldwater's campaign progress, punctuated by political disasters, was a sorry disillusionment to Texas Republican leaders. Indeed, in response to Goldwater's apparent stand on one campaign issue, Peter O'Donnell observed that Goldwater had an "atomic thorn in his heel."[40]

Unfortunately for Texas Republicans, the Democrats in Texas were both clever—not uncommon—and united, considerably more than unusual. They exploited the assorted mishaps of Goldwater's campaign with telling effect in the Senate races between Ralph Yarborough and George Bush. A moderate Republican by national standards, Bush, son of U.S. Senator Prescott Bush of Connecticut, had moved to Texas during the 1950s. Operating as an oil service salesman from Midland, George Bush successfully rode the Permian Basin oil boom and accumulated sufficient capital to become an independent oil operator. At the end of the decade he moved to Houston, where he operated the Zapata Oil Company; he ventured into offshore exploration and built a modest personal fortune. Taking active part in local politics, Bush rose through the Harris County GOP to become county chairman. In 1963, before the assassination of John F. Kennedy, Bush committed himself to the U.S. Senate race. Bush embarked on opposition to the liberal Democratic incumbent with the realistic expectation that Yarborough would face a bitter primary challenge. Win or lose, Yarborough's candidacy could be expected to send legions of disappointed Democrats to the Bush camp.

As with all other Republican calculations, the death of Kennedy and the consequent candidacy of Lyndon B. Johnson upset all plans of the Bush campaign organization. Johnson, in pursuit of a sizable Democratic majority, imposed effective party unity, discouraged primary election opposition to Yarborough, and eliminated significant defections to Bush. Worse yet, Yarborough, an effective campaigner himself, took the Bush campaign seriously and mounted a spirited defense of his Senate seat. He was no William Blakely. Nor was George Bush a John Tower. Tower's campaigns, though thinly financed, were well organized, while

Bush's campaign organization was forced to undergo a major restructuring in mid-race. While Tower had no rivals for the nominations in 1960 and 1961, George Bush was challenged in the 1964 Republican primary by Jack Cox, who was well known and highly regarded as the party's gubernatorial nominee in 1962. As tough a campaigner as ever, Cox lost out in the primary; but the contest cost Bush scarce financial resources and limited organizational energy. The unusual conjunction of Democratic unity and Republican disunity, along with disciplined Democratic organization and organizational confusion in the Bush campaign, weakened the GOP candidate.

With all these difficulties, George Bush also faced the liabilities of Goldwater's foundering national campaign. Ralph Yarborough picked up Lyndon Johnson's description of Barry Goldwater as a dangerous extremist and applied the label to Bush, whom he inaccurately and unfairly characterized as "the Darling of the John Birch Society." Dallas Mayor Earle Cabell, opposing Congressman Alger, used the same tactic, alleging that Alger was "outside the basic beliefs of his own party." The wild-eyed extremist label which was successfully pinned on Goldwater stuck to other Republican candidates in Texas.

The GOP contenders did what they could to belie the extremist tag. Thus, while Bruce Alger's Democratic opponents had been strictly racist in some campaigns, he, like Ed Foreman of Odessa, avoided direct appeals to racial prejudice. Similarly, George Bush refused to exploit the volatile racial issue in the general election; he won about 15 percent of the black vote. While their party's presidential candidate used code issues such as "crime in the streets" and the limitation of the power of the Supreme Court to win over white audiences, particularly in the South, the Texans rejected racist strategy, as they had done since 1920. According to one Goldwater campaign insider, Peter O'Donnell was alone among southern state chairmen in not being an avowed racist.

Regardless of the injustice of the Democratic depictions of the lot of Republican candidates as right-wing extremists, the charge stuck with a sufficient number of voters to cost Bush, Alger, and Foreman their contests and to deprive nearly all Texas Republicans of their offices. The only survivor of the Democratic sweep of the legislature was State Representative Frank Cahoon of Midland. In Dallas County, only Frank Crowley, a county commissioner for North Dallas, bucked the anti-GOP tide.[41]

The Bush-Yarborough race, which had looked like a "photo finish" to many observers, including veteran journalist Allan Duckworth of the *Dallas Morning News*, was safely won by the incumbent, though Bush ran more than 175,000 votes ahead of the national ticket and carried the principal Republican counties. Yarborough kept a majority of the racial and ethnic minority vote behind his candidacy. Alone among southern senators, he had voted for the 1964 Civil Rights Act, an act which insured the continued loyalty of a strong majority of the black electorate. Yarborough ran well in the Latin counties, where the strong influence of Lyndon Johnson and John Connally kept voters in the Democratic fold. Bush lost his first campaign for a major elective office, but he had established his identity as the party's most available and appealing candidate. He ran again, twice successfully for the U.S. House of Representatives in 1966 and 1968, and once more, unsuccessfully, for the United States Senate in 1970.[42]

Goldwater's defeat was followed by a major struggle for position and power in the national committee. His handpicked national committee chairman, Dean Burch, was ousted after Lyndon Johnson's lopsided election victory. Ray Bliss, veteran state chairman of the Republican party in Ohio, succeeded Burch, with instructions to piece the party together and to prepare for the 1966 elections. In Texas, defeat brought strong criticism of Peter O'Donnell's heavy involvement with the Goldwater campaign, allegedly at the expense of Texas candidates such as George Bush. Former GOP senatorial candidate Thad Hutcheson, with other GOP leaders in Houston and former Dallas County GOP chairman Maurice Carlson, demanded the resignation of state party leaders, a demand which Senator John Tower dismissed as a tempest in a teapot and which both O'Donnell and national committeeman Albert B. Fay of Houston ignored. Tower, O'Donnell, and Fay could afford to pay no heed to the demands. In spite of sizable losses, the Goldwater campaign strengthened the position of O'Donnell and other party leaders. The explanation for so paradoxical a situation is easily found; not only was Goldwater the overwhelming choice of party activists, from precinct chairmen through national committeeman, but also, even after the events of November, 1963, Goldwater's candidacy had brought large numbers of first-time volunteer workers into party ranks and sizable contributions into party coffers.[43]

For party leaders, these assets offset electoral liabilities. During the Goldwater campaign in all of the major cities of Texas, conservative Republicans, some of whom were former supporters of the late Robert

A. Taft, signed up for canvassing duty and opened their billfolds and pocketbooks in unprecedented numbers. In Dallas, Houston, Midland, Odessa, and other cities, new recruits came from the ranks of previously inactive Republicans, from a sizable segment of disgruntled conservative Democrats, and from ultraconservative organizations such as the John Birch Society. County chairmen welcomed all hands, but in the case of Birch Society members, GOP leaders felt obliged to take precautionary measures. As Larry Goodwyn, writing in the liberal biweekly *Texas Observer*, commented: "This is a delicate matter, for the Birchers and related kinds of people are dedicated precinct workers in the party and their political value far exceeds their numerical strength."[44] Within the Texas Republican party, as within the national party, organization Republicans were apprehensive lest the secret society take effective control of GOP organization. Convinced that the society would exploit the party for the realization of narrowly sectarian aims, thereby damning the Republican party to splinter-group status and diminishing its national political base, Texas county chairmen rallied non-Birch precinct leaders, who turned out large numbers of party regulars for conventions, thereby insuring continued control of the party organization by party regulars.

If the Birch Society attempted to seize the party—and little supporting evidence for this contention has come to light—party leaders easily turned back the challenge in all but a handful of precincts in Harris and other urban counties. Contrary to the expectations of Republican leaders, moreover, John Birch Society members often lost interest in the society as a direct result of Republican party activity. The new party activists in Midland, Houston, and other cities tended to throw over the Welch organization for the more purposeful activities of a major political party. Once bitten by the political bug, onetime Birchers would become strongly committed either to the Republican party or to George Wallace's American party. The apparent triumph of ultraconservatives, in Goldwater's nomination, ironically led to the diminution of interest in splinter-group politics.[45]

With election results in hand, GOP leaders could also find some comfort in the fact that Lyndon B. Johnson ran no better in Texas than in the United States as a whole. Despite his acknowledged advantage as a native son, the first President from Texas, Johnson's part of the presidential ballots in Texas was barely 2 percent above the national figure of 61.5 percent. Moreover, excepting the elections of 1952, 1956, and

1960, Johnson's support was no better than the normal level for Democratic presidential candidates in Texas.[46] If consolation could be found in defeat, for Texas Republicans it rested in the fact that Goldwater's loss in the Lone Star State was not an exceptional calamity. Still, the apparent truth of the situation was described by *Dallas Times Herald* reporter Bill Hollingsworth: "Texas Republicanism stood almost precisely where it stood on the eve of the 1952 election, with organization" . . . but little else.[47]

Hollingsworth's grim assessment of the GOP's prospects was widely shared by veteran political observers in the nation and in Texas. Journalists writing for the major news magazines, nationally circulated newspapers, and state journals all agreed that the Republican party was going the way of the mastodon and that the Democratic party would have little competition from its once lively opponent. Many of these gloomy predictions were based on flimsy reasoning and an injudicious reading of the evidence, but more disciplined studies supported similar conclusions. In Texas, for example, Joseph L. Bernd, a political science professor at Southern Methodist University, observed a serious erosion of Republican strength in metropolitan areas as the major cities returned strong Democratic margins, as they had generally done before 1952. In Bernd's view, the trend toward Republicanism had been reversed; and the state's traditional adherence to the Democratic party was reestablished.

Had Bernd's observation been correct, had Hollingsworth's estimation of the value of the surviving Republican organization been accurate, the sun would have set on the party in Texas. But the calculations of both writers were seriously inaccurate. Both responded too strongly to the apparent calamity of 1964. In fact, as the party's history demonstrated, the GOP already had deep roots in Texas; and its organization was too well established to be blown away by the first hot political wind.[48]

In John Tower's victory in 1961, the party had proved its ability to win. True to the pattern of previous Republican candidates, Tower ran well in urban areas, carrying all of the major cities except Austin and Beaumont; but he showed less strength in rural areas, East Texas excepted. Tower was clearly an urban senator. This development, the rising of Republican strength in southern cities, had been foreseen by V. O. Key, Jr., among other political scientists. Among "the Portents of Change" Key anticipated in 1949 were the "extraordinary growth of industry in Texas" and the consequent expansion of the urban middle class. Key observed of both Florida and Texas, "If Republican leaders had either incentive or ability, they might over the long run build a Republican party of the midwestern variety by using the pulling power of the presidential campaign." Writing twenty years after Key, Kevin P. Phillips further developed the notion that urbanization and the pulling power of Republican presidential candidates would ultimately produce "The Emerging Republican Majority." Both Key and Phillips after him were essentially correct in the broad outlines of their argument. A more detailed analysis of the growth of the Texas cities and of the Republican vote, however, permits elaborations and requires modification of these notions.[49]

John Tower's victory in 1961 was actually achieved in areas of traditional Republican strength. Despite Key's and Phillips's preoccupation with the presumably shifting geographical patterns of voting, in Texas the Republican vote moved scarcely at all. George Butte, the party's gubernatorial candidate in 1924, ran a hard-fought campaign and received more than one-third of his vote in ten counties, most of them urban. Running for the U.S. Senate thirty-seven years later, John Tower received more than half of his vote in these same counties. Texas cities, and a handful of rural counties, have long been the repository of the Republican vote in Texas. Both Butte and Tower won in urban areas, including Dallas, Houston, Fort Worth, El Paso, Brownsville, and Tyler, while Tower added Amarillo, Lubbock, San Angelo, Midland, Odessa, and San Antonio to the Republican column. In both contests, the German counties and conservative Panhandle and West Texas counties gave a majority of their votes to the Republican candidates.[50] Presidential Republicanism, as both Key and Phillips understood it, did not entirely account for the upward trend in the Republican vote. In 1948, for example, H. J. Porter, the GOP candidate for United States Senate, drew votes substantially better than Thomas E. Dewey, the party's presidential candidate, in Dallas and Houston, the principal cities of the state, and in Midland and Smith Counties, oil-rich and fast-growing.

The presidential Republican thesis does not fit all of the facts. It does go a long way, however, in describing the long-term political development of many of the principal urban counties in Texas. The principal gains of the Texas GOP have been made since 1952, frequently on the impetus of presidential elections. With only two exceptions, in

1961 Tower carried the same counties that Eisenhower won in 1956. A comparison of Nixon's showing in 1960 and Tower's in 1961, however, indicates that the senator won four more counties—principally either labor or Latin and Roman Catholic counties—than Nixon and trailed the earlier Nixon performance in Protestant Abilene, in Taylor County. Thus, though some voters transferred loyalties from Republican presidential candidates to GOP candidates for Congress and state office, the actual pattern is more complicated than the theory; on some occasions state-level candidates have done significantly better than presidential candidates.

Between 1952 and 1972, the Texas Republicans found it increasingly easy to muster a majority of the voters in Dallas, Harris, Ector, Gregg, Midland, Potter, Randall, and Smith counties. As a group, these counties contained more than one-third of the state's population in 1970. Republican candidates were at least strongly competitive in seven other urban counties: Bexar, Cameron, El Paso, Galveston, Lubbock, Tarrant, and Taylor. A third group of urban counties—Grayson, Hidalgo, Jefferson, McLennan, Nueces, Travis, Webb, and Wichita—usually returned reliably Democratic majorities. Of these three groups, the Republican counties have generally been areas of rapid growth. Harris County, for example, added half a million new inhabitants between 1960 and 1970. With the exception of Bexar County, the swing counties had either experienced slow population growth, like El Paso and Lubbock, or, like Cameron County, had actually lost inhabitants. Most of the consistently Democratic counties showed slow growth patterns, while Wichita and McLennan counties lost population. Only Travis County, the seat of both the state government and the state's principal university, sustained growth. Economic growth in the major cities brought new industries and with them members of the technical and professional middle class, at least good prospective Republicans in Texas and often self-identified conservatives before their arrival. By 1961, the numerical growth of the urban middle class made Republican victories increasingly probable.[51]

The urban character of Texas Republicanism corresponds with a general development throughout the southern states. Beginning in 1952, middle income whites have been attracted to the GOP throughout the South. In Alabama, as in Texas, the Eisenhower movement led to a revitalization of the party and to the creation of a state GOP organization. In Arkansas, 1964 support for Barry Goldwater and the GOP gubernatorial candidate, Winthrop A. Rockefeller, was distinctly urban.

TABLE 2
GROWTH OF THE PRINCIPAL URBAN COUNTIES IN TEXAS, 1920-1970

County	1920	1930	1940	1950	1960	1970
Bexar	202,096	292,533	338,176	500,460	697,151	830,460
Bowie	39,472	48,563	50,208	61,966	59,971	67,813
Cameron	36,662	77,540	83,202	125,170	151,098	140,368
Dallas	210,551	325,691	398,654	614,799	951,527	1,327,321
Ector	760	3,958	15,051	42,102	90,995	91,805
El Paso	101,877	131,597	131,067	194,968	314,070	359,299
Galveston	53,150	64,401	81,173	113,066	140,364	169,812
Grayson	74,165	65,843	69,499	70,467	73,043	83,225
Gregg	16,767	15,778	58,027	61,258	69,436	75,929
Harris	186,667	359,328	528,961	806,701	1,243,158	1,741,912
Hidalgo	38,110	77,004	106,059	160,446	180,904	181,535
Jefferson	73,120	133,391	145,329	195,083	245,659	244,773
Lubbock	11,096	39,104	51,782	101,048	156,271	179,295
McLennan	82,921	98,682	101,898	130,194	150,091	147,553
Midland	2,449	8,005	11,721	25,785	67,717	65,433
Nueces	22,807	51,779	92,661	165,471	221,573	237,544
Potter	16,710	46,080	54,265	73,366	115,580	90,511
Randall	3,675	7,071	7,185	13,774	33,913	53,885
Smith	46,769	53,123	69,090	74,701	86,350	97,096
Tarrant	152,800	197,553	225,521	361,253	538,495	716,317
Taylor	24,081	41,023	44,147	63,307	101,078	97,853
Tom Green	15,210	36,033	39,302	58,929	64,630	71,047
Travis	57,616	77,777	111,053	160,980	212,136	295,516
Webb	29,152	42,128	45,916	56,141	64,791	72,859
Wichita	72,911	74,416	73,604	98,493	123,528	121,862

SOURCE: *Texas Almanac, 1972-1973* (Dallas: A. H. Belo Corporation, 1971), pp. 157-60.

In Georgia, "higher income suburbanites" supported Goldwater in 1964, Nixon in 1968, and Howard H. ("Bo") Calloway for governor in 1966. In Louisiana, political scientist Perry Howard found that support for Nixon "varied directly with urbanization." In North Carolina, Preston W. Edsall and J. Oliver Williams discovered, "The rise of presidential and gubernatorial Republicanism can be attributed largely to the ability of the party's candidates to attract the support of the urban middle class voters." The economic development of the South, including Texas, promoted social and political change, most notably the enhancement of the electoral fortunes of the Republican party, with the support of the urban white middle class.[52]

The urban white members of the middle class who tended to vote for southern Republicans came, in significant numbers, from other parts of the country, particularly the East and the Middle West. Republican primary election returns for Dallas for 1926 indicate that fully one-quarter of the Republican electorate in that year had lived in Texas less than ten years. A similar pattern holds into the present era, as 1960 census figures reveal that nearly one-third of the citizens of both Dallas and Houston had moved into Texas since 1950, a development which compares with the development of strongly Republican cities in Virginia.[53] A recent study of Democratic and Republican county chairmen relates directly to the migration of Republicans to the state. Charles R. Elliot has found that almost half of the Republican county chairmen he studied had lived in Texas less than twenty years, whereas 97 percent of the Democratic party chairmen had lived in Texas for at least twenty years. Many Republicans are relative newcomers, most of whom moved to Texas cities to work.[54]

The rise of the Republican vote in the metropolitan centers of Texas was the result of a number of economic conditions, most notably the growth of light industry, which brought an influx of technical and managerial personnel to Dallas and Houston. Texas growth industries, like those of Florida, another Republican boom area in the South, provided a large number of white collar jobs and relatively few of the blue collar jobs that might have attracted liberal-Democratic voting labor union members. According to figures current in 1967, only 6.1 percent of the total number of employees in Texas were engaged in manufacturing, whereas comparable figures for other states include: Pennsylvania and Ohio, both 13.4 percent; Michigan and Massachusetts, both 12.9 percent; New Jersey, 12.5 percent; and Illinois, 12.8 percent. Within Texas, the rapid expansion of the electronic and service industries provided disproportionately large numbers of white collar jobs which attracted employees who identified with the Republican party.[55]

Within Texas cities, the relative scarcity of blue collar labor is evident. Strongly Republican towns, Amarillo, Lubbock, and Midland, had 11.9, 10.6, and 5.0 respectively, of their labor forces engaged in manufacturing. These figures contrast sharply with those of Democratic cities in the North and Middle West: Cleveland (40.8 percent), Detroit (37.4 percent), and Chicago (33.5 percent). Outside of the oil refining and petrochemical producing areas, such as Galveston, Beaumont, and Port Arthur, where about 60 percent of the workers are employed in either manufacturing or transportation, the expansion of the state's economy has tended to boost the number of salaried managerial or technical employees. Summing up postwar industrial development to 1964, James R. Soukup, Clifton McClesky, and Harry Holloway, authors of *Party and Factional Division in Texas*, concluded:

Industrialization in Texas has not been a story of mass-production industries employing large percentages of unskilled, immigrant labor; rather it has been distinguished by its relatively high ratio of skilled to unskilled, white collar to blue collar, native-born white to nonnative nonwhite personnel. Plants are smaller, managerial and professional personnel more numerous, automation much more practiced and practical.[56]

The practical economic effect of this pattern of industrial growth is reflected in the per capita income levels of the major urban counties. Of twenty-two counties which can be classified politically on the basis of Table 2, seven are Republican, six are marginal, and eight are Democratic. The Republican counties have per capita income levels which range from $3,147 to $4,508, with an average of $3,611. In the Democratic counties, the average per capita income is $3,063, and the range is $2,214 to $3,817. The Republican counties, in this comparison, show higher income levels, reflecting the concentration of white collar workers. Unfortunately, the work of comparison breaks down because regional and ethnic variations in income become significant in any comparison of either the Democratic or Republican counties and the marginal counties, where the average income was $2,763 and the range from $1,777 to $3,570; these counties contain large numbers of Mexican-American agricultural laborers in the relatively poor Rio Grande counties of Cameron, Hidalgo, and El Paso. The significance of these data, viewed from the common perspective of Key, Phillips, Soukup, McClesky, and Holloway, is that the Republican party in Texas, as in Virginia, Florida, Georgia, North Carolina, and Arkansas, has appealed more successfully than the Democratic party for the allegiance of the white middle class. The Republican party in Texas and the South rode the major currents of social and economic change.[57]

Since Sam Rayburn entered Congress and C. Bascomb Slemp sat in the House for the Valley of Virginia, Texas and most of the rest of the South have changed socially, economically, and politically. Sam Rayburn's Texas still votes Democratic, "early and often." In the eighty-two most rural counties, nonpresidential candidates of the Republican party in Texas rarely receive as much as one-third of the vote. And so it would still be over most of the state if Texas had not changed between 1920 and 1961 and if these changes had not worked to the advantage of the Republican party. The growing Republicanism of Texas cities rested on a number of political conditions. Urban low income groups, blacks, whites, and Mexican-Americans, tended to show low levels of voter turnout, even after the repeal of the poll tax in 1966. The Negro machines of rural East Texas and the Mexican-American organizations of rural South Texas had no effective counterpart in many cities, though lower Rio Grande Valley towns and San Antonio have had Latin machines of long standing. By contrast, the Anglo-American middle class which settled in the cities was more likely both to vote and to participate in active party work. It was simply easier to turn out the growing Republican vote through formal organizational work than it was to manage the ethnic and racial minority vote in Texas cities.[58]

Democratic efforts to muster supporters among minority group ranks were seriously handicapped by the lack of substantial urban patronage. During the 1920s and 1930s, scores of Texas towns and cities, including San Antonio, Dallas, and Fort Worth, adopted versions of "nonpartisan" Council–City Manager forms of municipal government and placed city elections and posts on competitive bases which did not correspond to Democratic-Republican divisions. Thus, in San Antonio the long-dominant Taxpayers' Association was led by conservative Democrats, such as Robert McMillan, and Republicans such as Joe Sheldon. Though county patronage could greatly aid the Democratic party, as has been true in San Antonio, the increasingly large city payrolls of San Antonio, Dallas, Fort Worth, and other cities have not supported the development of urban Democratic machines.[59]

The concentration and activity of Republicans—particularly of Republican Women's Clubs—in areas like North Dallas has also tended to attract new adherents to the party. Newcomers who seek opportunities for political activity are more likely to find accommodation with the Republicans than with the less organizationally oriented Democrats. Moreover, potential voters who have identified themselves as "independents" in other locales are frequently recruited for the GOP by their neighbors. Not surprisingly, newcomers locating in North Dallas or in such suburbs as Richardson and the Park Cities tend to identify with the locally dominant political party; political scientists have found this tendency toward political conformity among newcomers in other American cities.[60] This kind of political adaptation is more closely analogous to the "halfway covenant" than it is to a conversion, for Republican parties in most metropolitan counties tend to bid most strongly in support of presidential, congressional, and gubernatorial candidates and less strenuously for local positions. The control of Democrats over the courthouses in the cities has only recently been challenged by urban Republicans, in part because Republican leaders in Texas, as in Virginia, hoped to keep voter turnout low in strongly Democratic precincts and to avoid bringing some of their voters to make the straight ballot decisions necessary to challenge locally influential sheriffs and judges. Thus, even if an urban Republican were a lapsed Democrat, the transformation would not necessarily be complete; and his vote could occasionally be sought and won.[61]

From the perspective of social, economic, and demographic change, the Republican party's growth would appear irresistible: let the city population grow and with it would naturally grow the Republican vote. However, only the blindest faith in simple statistics could sustain the belief in inevitable long-term trends of this kind of politics. Victories and party growth are more often the result of purposeful activity. Thus, in Texas the demographic factors which underlay party growth were perhaps less important than the organizational skill with which Republicans recruited and activated the white-collar, middle-class vote in San Antonio, Houston, Dallas, Midland, Amarillo, Tyler, and other Texas cities.

National and state party leaders cooperated with local Republicans to build a more effective party organization. Tad Smith, state chairman, began in 1959 to promote precinct and block level organization for effective canvassing. By the time of the presidential election in 1960, about twenty targeted urban counties were fully covered by Republicans. During the next six months, GOP grass roots organizations were developed in more than fifty additional counties, in time for the special election for the U.S. Senate. In 1962, the measure of the growth of the formal party was indicated when GOP primary elections were held in 218 (of 254) counties. Four years earlier, Republican primary elections were conducted in only 68 counties.[62]

Auxiliary groups, such as the Republican Women's Clubs, had grown rapidly. From less than a dozen active clubs in July, 1952, the number of women's groups had grown to twenty-seven in 1961 and to about one hundred by the end of 1963. Every new club and every expanding unit brought new volunteer workers into the party, boosting the organizational activities of the GOP.[63]

An effort was made after the special election in 1961 to propagate vote-getting techniques outside of Dallas, Houston, San Antonio, and the other urban areas which had been targeted earlier for organizational development. Relying in part on educational programs which were developed by the Republican National Committee, Mickey Ledrick, executive director of the Texas GOP, and two full-time field men organized a series of regional workshops, which were held during September. Local Republican leaders were taught how to organize precincts and counties, how to recruit candidates, and how to raise money.[64]

Beginning in 1962, the state headquarters operation was upgraded by the collaboration of Mickey Ledrick and Peter O'Donnell, who succeeded Tad Smith as state chairman. The operating efficiency of the state party was increased through improved liaison and communication with local party organizations. Six paid employees were added to the state headquarters to supervise research, media, and liaison operations. The state committee itself was reorganized in 1963 with thirteen task-related subcommittees. At the same time, GOP county organizations also expanded their year-round operations and staffs, principally in Dallas, Houston, and San Antonio.[65]

State party leaders, recognizing that there would be no more "bargain senators," enhanced the fund-raising capabilities of the GOP. Two professional fund-raisers were hired to work with National Committeeman Albert B. Fay in Houston. Novel fund-raising techniques, including the highly successful publication of an almanac, were undertaken. Direct solicitation techniques were improved in 1964 with the creation of new donor categories, including that of "Charter Key Republican," awarded to party members who gave or raised $5,000 for the party. By May, nine members had received the honor; and more donors were similarly recognized during the following months.[66]

All of the new activities and new employees were tightly coordinated as Peter O'Donnell applied standard business practices and accepted advice on organization from national party headquarters. Extensive job descriptions were written, terms of responsibility and accountability were clearly defined, and other management controls were instituted. As with fund-raising and canvassing, improved party management both demonstrated and supported the increasing strength of the Republican party in Texas, while the increase in the party-in-the-electorate made success at the polls increasingly probable.[67]

Organizational skills were often tightly keyed to analysis by Republicans of those same demographic factors to which political scientists credit the Republican growth. To take Dallas as an example, beginning with Bruce Alger's first congressional campaign, precinct and block work, extensive canvassing, and all of the techniques which the Committee on Political Education had codified earlier were adopted by Republican party workers. Through successive campaigns, veteran workers such as Mesdames Richard Bass, James F. Biggart, Jr., and Ben Kanowsky worked with campaign managers Frank Crowley and Peter O'Donnell to identify and turn out the Republican voters, most of whom lived north of Fitzhugh Street, substantially north of downtown Dallas.[68] The special election in which John Tower was chosen U.S. senator gives ample evidence of the success of their sustained efforts. The North-of-Fitzhugh area provided Tower's winning margin in Dallas County; of forty-five precincts in this area, Tower carried forty-one. Equally significant, voter turnout was markedly high in the region; in Dallas County as a whole only 46 percent of the eligible voters turned out; the percentage was higher in thirty-four precincts, and Tower carried thirty of this number. To evaluate the work of party volunteers from a different perspective, the North-of-Fitzhugh area contained only 31 percent of the registered voters in Dallas County; but John Tower received more than 53 percent of his Dallas County votes in this area.[69] Precinct 122 in University Park had .32 percent of the registered voters in the county, but it contributed .62 percent of Tower's vote in the county.[70]

The social, racial, and economic characteristics of the North-of-Fitzhugh vote match those of Soukup, McClesky, and Holloway's "Republican Voter," and indicate that in this limited area, as in other southern cities, Republicans made their greatest gains in the ranks of the white middle class. In Dallas, the North-of-Fitzhugh area housed doctors, lawyers, and employees of the vast financial institutions and of the large electronic corporations which grew during the 1950s. The area would almost surely have voted Republican had it been located in any city in the nation. It was 90 percent white. It was also wealthy. Of forty-five census tracts in the area, only four were below the median Dallas County income of $6,188 per household in 1960. Nine tracts doubled the county median, and two tracts tripled it. Tract Ninety-nine, the only predominantly black precinct in the area and the strongest Democratic precinct in the area, was lowest in median income with an average household income of $4,677 in 1960.[71] Simply put, the white, middle class urban voters preferred Republican candidates. Dallas Republicans knew they did and knew where to find their supporters.

All these figures suggest that though a wide variety of nonpolitical factors supported the growth of the GOP in Texas cities, a considerable amount of effective political organizational effort accounts for the ability of Republicans to take advantage of demographic, sociological, and economic factors which would work to the long-term advantage of their party. As any working politician knows, in politics nothing just happens: good managers make them happen, and good organization is often their best instrument. Basic trends in growth were not reversed by Goldwater's defeat. Carefully built and ably managed party organizations were not destroyed by the deep gloom which followed the disasters of 1964.

8

"The Political Tides Change"

AS BLEAK as GOP prospects seemed on November 8, 1964, the Texas Republican party was not incapacitated by defeat. Though the Johnson landslide temporarily demoralized party leaders, who fell out briefly among themselves, it did not wipe out the organizational advances which had been made since 1952. State and local parties survived, auxiliary organizations continued to grow, and two years later volunteer workers turned out in large numbers to man the Tower campaign. With the uncertain prospects of the general election of 1966, the Republican party needed all help and all hands. Not only would John Tower's U.S. Senate position be defended, but Republicans would make a major effort to regain some of the offices which had been lost in 1964.

Enjoying widespread name recognition as an incumbent and guaranteed the strong support of his party, John Tower seemed to hold considerable advantages at the beginning of the year. After five years in the Senate, Tower's strongly conservative record both solidified Republican support and promised to attract the votes of conservative Democrats. Most of this potential advantage, however, was lost when Waggoner Carr, the incumbent attorney general and a veteran conservative Democratic leader, declared for the post. Carr's candidacy tied the conservative Democrats to the party, threatening to block Tower's most promising avenue to victory. Early in the campaign, observers agreed that Carr would probably hold together enough of the Democratic coalition of Anglo conservatives, Latins, blacks, labor, and Anglo liberals to win handily.[1]

Democratic party leaders mistrusted these comfortable assumptions; President Lyndon B. Johnson and Governor John Connally worked assiduously to hold regular Democrats in line behind Carr. Texas Democrats in Congress and in state posts appeared with Carr and, with few exceptions, gave him their support. Representative George Mahon campaigned for his fellow conservative in West Texas and in the Panhandle; Jack Brooks stumped the Gulf Coast region with Carr; while Henry Gonzalez appealed to Latin voters on his behalf. Only labor-liberal Congressman Robert Eckhardt of Houston withheld support. Among state officials, there were no holdouts. Governor John Connally, Lieutenant Governor Preston Smith, House Speaker Ben Barnes, Agriculture Commissioner John C. White, Attorney General candidate Crawford Martin, and the Democratic members of the Senate and House endorsed Carr; and many of these officeholders made campaign appearances with him. Natural loyalty combined with persistent political arm-twisting by Johnson and Connally produced an unprecedented show of party unity early in the campaign.

John Connally, not content merely to let his support of Carr be known, entered Carr's campaign with a full measure of aggressive energy. He made public endorsements and campaign appearances. In October Connally assumed effective control of Carr's campaign effort, which the *Houston Post* described as "in considerable disarray," by placing his own political lieutenants in its management. The governor's strenuous exertion on Carr's behalf, taken with the backing of President Johnson, soon offset Tower's initial advantages; indeed, his reelection began to seem doubtful. Carr had no dearth of influence behind him, nor did he lack campaign funding: Edward Clark, leading Democratic fund-raiser, effectively drew contributions from regular donors, as he had done for Ralph Yarborough two years earlier.[2]

Heightened voter interest in the contest made Tower's chance for reelection increasingly slim. As the candidate of the permanent minority party, Tower's best chance for success rested in generally low voter turnout; the relatively efficient urban organizations of the Republican party could be relied upon to turn out a higher proportion of their adherents than the Democrats could muster outside heated primary election contests. As voter interest in the Tower-Carr contest seemed to climb, Tower fell behind in the polls. The Belden Poll, most prestigious in the state, reported that Tower was trailing Carr by ten percent on the eve of the election, while Republican polls showed Tower behind but closing on Carr as the campaign went into its final weeks. With some apprehension, just short of pessimism, Republican leaders activated their organization, identified the vote for Tower, and labored to turn it out.[3]

But Carr was in not as comfortable a position of leadership as might have been presumed from his base of political support. He was less popular with voters than with Democratic leaders. On campaign, Carr received polite but unenthusiastic applause from embarrassingly small crowds. When he kicked off his campaign in Lubbock, his hometown, only two thousand people appeared; ten thousand had been expected. By contrast, Tower's first major rally, at Dallas's State Fair Music Hall, drew more than five thousand enthusiastic supporters. Worse yet for Carr, thirty minutes of his Lubbock rally were carried by a network of West Texas television stations; and viewers noted that applause was thin, even when promoters held up "Cheer" signs. News of the fiasco appeared even in sympathetic newspapers. The *San Antonio Express* covered the failure in greater and more colorful detail than Carr's speech, which amounted to an attack on Tower's weakness at the pork barrel during the Democratic administration and Carr's promise to secure the distribution of National Science Foundation research funds to states on a per capita basis. Newspaper accounts of the rally report no particular response to the latter proposal.[4]

Carr's proposals were far less exciting than the campaign contest. As campaigning grew hotter, Carr lashed out at Tower. In an appearance at Amarillo, he both attested to his own opposition to organized labor and ridiculed John Tower: "I was fighting for the right-to-work law when he was still teaching school in Midwestern University and didn't know what 14B was, unless it was a number on a hotel room." After another Carr attack, alleging Tower's receipt of large out-of-state donations as a part of an alleged political deal, Tower snapped back: "How true to character it is, that Waggoner Carr should cry 'Deal.' His own career as a politician has been built on deals." Such exchanges prompted the *Houston Post*, which endorsed Carr as "uniquely qualified," to describe the Tower-Carr contest as "the hottest political race in Texas."[5]

As election day drew near, Carr predicted that 2.1 million of 3 million eligible voters would cast ballots. Tower foresaw a lower figure, 1.8 million, which Democrats conceded would spell trouble for Carr. On the eve of the election, the unofficial Texas Election Bureau forecast a turnout of only 1.7 million votes, a discouraging estimate for Carr forces. In the end, all of the polls had overshot the mark, as only 1.5 million voters cast ballots in the contest; and 56.7 percent of this number went to the incumbent Republican. Tower's preelection claim of 890,000 firm votes came up less than 50,000 short. Low voter participation, down 6.5 percent from the 1962 gubernatorial election and the lowest in a decade, was uneven in its effects. The decline was less marked in pro-Tower strongholds such as Dallas, Midland, Lubbock, and Tyler than in Carr's territory—San Antonio, El Paso, Fort Worth, Laredo, Corpus Christi, Galveston, and the Rio Grande Valley. Despite the general support of Carr by party leaders, Democrats in important areas were indifferent to his candidacy, and he made the worst showing of any Democratic candidate for statewide office in the twentieth century.[6] Carr's defeat and the magnitude of Tower's victory startled journalists and Democratic leaders, most of whom had failed to assess the consequences of Carr's failure to hold the Democratic coalition together.

To explain John Tower's victory, it is necessary to explain how Waggoner Carr courted defeat. Beginning with his write-off of organized labor and ending with the alienation of a significant number of Latinos, Carr undermined his own candidacy as the campaign progressed. Members of the labor-liberal factions nursed old grievances against Carr and the conservative Democrats. Faction leaders, such as Texas AFL-CIO Secretary-Treasurer Roy Evans, resented Governor Connally's successful pressuring of prolabor Congressman Jim Wright of Fort Worth out of contention for the Democratic nomination for the U.S. Senate. Carr was not an acceptable substitute. Evans predicted that labor would "take a walk again," as they had in 1961 in objection to William Blakeley. Liberal Senator Ralph Yarborough, continuing his long-standing feud with the conservative Democrats, dropped broad hints to the effect he would prefer Tower to Carr as a colleague. Tower, for his part, returned the muted compliment by praising Yarborough for his work on the G.I. Bill.

While liberal and labor votes escaped Carr's grasp, in South Texas the traditional Democratic monopoly of what was called "the Latin vote" fell apart in the face of factional rivalries and a major Republican effort to attract Mexicano votes. Celso Moreno, hired in 1965 as director

of the Latin-American program committee by the Texas GOP, success-
fully exploited divisions among Democrats and rivalries among *jefes.*
In Corpus Christi, for example, William Bonilla as well as members
of the influential Yturria family endorsed Tower. In San Antonio,
Albert Fuentes, former president of the Political Association of Spanish-
Speaking Organizations, endorsed Tower, as did Albert Peña, a Bexar
County commissioner and a leader among liberal Democrats. Peña
claimed that most Texas liberals "would as soon have Senator John
Tower as a Democrat who votes like Tower. At least Tower is honest."
The disaffection of other liberal and moderate Latinos was demonstrated
when both PASO and the G.I. Forum, the principal ethnic political
groups in Texas, refused to endorse Waggoner Carr.[7]

Aware of Carr's opposition within ethnic political groups, in the
closing months of the campaign Tower intensified his appeals to Latinos
through campaign appearances, Spanish-language advertising on radio
and television, and personal cultivation of Latino leaders. More general
appeals for public support were not encumbered by misplaced sophistication: billboards in South Texas promised "*Mas pan con Juan.*" Tower
and his supporters worked for the Latino vote; but their efforts were,
perhaps, less effective than a monumental blunder on Carr's part.[8] In
August, 1966, Mexican-American farm workers from the lower Rio
Grande Valley staged a march from the Valley to Austin to dramatize
their efforts to unionize field labor. With thousands of workers on U.S.
Highway 10, on their way to Austin, "La Marcha" received widespread
attention in both state and national news media, particularly after
Governor Connally, responding to pressure from growers, called out the
Texas Highway Patrol and the Texas Rangers—the latter known among
Mexican-Americans for their virulent prejudice against minority groups
—to disperse the marchers. Connally claimed that the marchers were
interfering with the movement of vehicular traffic. The confrontation,
which liberal Mexican-Americans referred to as their "Selma," became
a melee; it generated heated charges of brutality on the part of the police,
particularly the Rangers.

With the dispersal of the march, union organizing efforts received
a setback; but the damage to Carr's campaign was profound. Connally
and Attorney General Carr suffered a sharp loss of prestige within
Mexican-American communities. Mexican-Americans, organized labor,
and white-collar liberals, moreover, were united in their heightened
hostility to the labor-busting governor and the attorney general who rode

shotgun for him. Writing in the liberal and influential *Texas Observer*, publisher Ronnie Dugger and Larry L. King turned from rejection of Carr to grudging support of Tower, much as *Observer* editor Willie Morris had chosen Tower over Blakeley in 1961. Not surprisingly, the liberal journalists identified Tower as the lesser evil in both instances. King described Carr as "so much a willing eager part of the Texas establishment that he should wear a nose ring." King concluded his statement with an agonized endorsement of the conservative Republican: "Long Live (Ugh! Choke! Sigh!) John Tower."[9]

Such sentiments produced few votes for Tower, but they seem to have undercut Carr. While the Republican vote was high, enabling Tower to carry almost all Texas cities with populations over one hundred thousand, turnout in Latino, labor, Negro, and liberal areas was low. Thus, Tower won the Gulf Coast labor areas, where union members followed the advice of their leaders and "went fishing" on election day. There was also a significant liberal vengeance vote in some areas. In Austin, voter turnout was higher than in the state as a whole; and 62 percent of it was cast for John Tower. In San Antonio Latino cross-over voters produced startling results: Tower received 53.5 percent of the vote, while 69.4 percent of the voters supported John Connally for re-election. Statewide, John Tower won handsomely with 57 percent of the major party vote. Waggoner Carr had received an unpleasant lesson in Democratic politics.[10]

The Tower campaign was the GOP's major electoral effort. It was carried out through the established party organization, and the lion's share of party funds was spent on the Tower campaign. The campaign for Tower, the principal Texas Republican officeholder and party leader, thus received priority over other statewide contests. The *Houston Post* observed that "Republicans concentrated their time and money on sending Tower back to Washington and almost ignored the scattering of other state-wide GOP races." Gubernatorial candidate T. E. Kennerley, therefore, ran an undermanned and underfinanced campaign against two-term incumbent John Connally. Kennerley received about one-quarter of the major party vote, the weakest Republican showing for the decade.

Localized contests for Congress and state legislature, however, brought some victories for the Republican party. Bob Price regained the Panhandle congressional seat, while George Bush successfully opposed Harris County District Attorney Frank Briscoe for the newly created U.S. House District Three seat in Houston. Bush succeeded in putting

1964 behind him by continuing to disassociate himself from reactionary conservatism. He told a Houston audience: "I want conservatism to be sensitive and dynamic, not scared and reactionary." According to the *Texas Observer*, Bush, a moderate conservative, was favored over Briscoe, "a right-wing conservative," because Bush was "civilized in race relations." Black voters seem to have gotten the message: they gave 35.3 percent of the ballots in predominantly black precincts to Bush, who won with 50 percent of the vote in the whole district. Bush's unusual ability to cut into the Democratic coalition was further demonstrated in the rural areas of the congressional district, where he received 44 percent of the vote. Houston also sent Henry Grover, a former Democratic member of the Texas house, to the State Senate, the first Republican to sit in that body since Julius Real represented rural Kerrville in 1927. National committeeman Albert B. Fay of Houston, who waged an unsuccessful campaign for land commissioner, had been accorded by the local press a "good chance" of defeating the colorful incumbent, Jerry Sadler. The victories of Bush and Grover, along with Fay's strenuous campaign, were signs of renewed vitality in the Harris County Republican party.[11]

Elsewhere in Texas, the GOP made encouraging gains. The lone Republican in the Texas House of Representatives, Frank Cahoon of Midland, was reelected; he was joined by Malouf Abraham from the Panhandle town of Canadian and former Representative Charles R. Scoggins of Corpus Christi, who had been unseated in 1964. Some Republican candidates for local office were successful in Dallas, Houston, Midland, and other cities. These victories and the successful Tower campaign demonstrated the capacity of the party to bounce back, in this case from the debacle of 1964.[12]

The Republican party, which often took advantage of divisions in the Democratic party, had factional problems of its own by 1968. The most serious factional division in the party since the Porter-Zweifel battle of 1952 surfaced in the spring of that year. As in 1952, the dispute ostensibly involved rival candidates for the Republican nomination for President; and, in part, it did. West Texas and Houston Republicans, led by Nancy Palm and represented publicly by National Committeeman Albert Fay, supported Governor Ronald Reagan; Dallas, Fort Worth, and San Antonio followed Senator Tower, represented by Peter O'Donnell, into the camp of Richard Nixon. Though both factions had convincing reasons for adherence to their candidates, the real struggle was for control of the party, which the Houston faction had lost in 1962 with the election of Peter O'Donnell to the state chairmanship.[13]

Open contention surfaced in the state convention in June when O'Donnell let it be known that he intended to challenge Fay for the national committee post. In the event of his victory, O'Donnell's successor as state chairman would also come from Dallas; Representative Fred Agnich was most often mentioned. No serious thought was given to an accommodation for the Houston faction, though Senator Tower warned O'Donnell against deepening existing divisions through hasty action. As a result of Tower's warning, O'Donnell's drive was slowed, but it was not stopped. At the June convention, Nixon forces won handily, with nearly three-quarters of the body following O'Donnell and Tower. O'Donnell might well have seized the occasion to displace Fay, had Tower failed to intervene. Largely at the senator's behest, Fay was selected as national committeeman with the tacit understanding that he would resign and make way for O'Donnell if an acceptable federal appointment came his way. For the time being, truce was declared.[14]

By the time of the September convention, however, ill feeling had bubbled up again, this time over O'Donnell's apparent decisions to shut county organizations out of the Nixon campaign and to curtail funding of all other candidates in order to direct funds to Nixon's organization. In reality, Nixon's national campaign leaders had chosen to wage the campaign through various citizens' groups, controlled by national campaign manager John Mitchell; and O'Donnell was simply the local implementer of the plan. The dispute over the funding of candidates reflected more general disagreement over party growth strategy. The GOP in Houston, Midland, and the Panhandle had enjoyed considerable success in congressional, legislative, and local contests. Success had boosted organizational effectiveness which, in turn, brought additional electoral success. Experience demonstrated to this faction that the party could be built from the local level upward if the bigger campaigns—for President, U.S. senator, and governor—did not dry up funds for local contests.[15] But party leaders in other areas argued that it was more important for the Texas party to elect Richard Nixon President than it was to send a few more state representatives to Austin: if there were to be a choice between electing a U.S. senator or a handful of county judges, a choice would be easy. Without control of the executive branch of the federal government, the Republican party in Texas and elsewhere would be denied the prerequisites of appointive office and favors which would encourage party adherents. Without John Tower in the Senate, the party would hold no statewide elective office; it would not be a credible political power in more than a handful of urban counties.

In short, the factional dispute grew out of conflicting theories of party development, adherence to rivals for the presidential nomination, and personal animosities; it took shape through geographically based factions, much as it had in the days of the Wurzbach-Creager battles. In 1968, however, party leaders agreed to something of a ceasefire—but it was no more than that. In the next few years, the dissident faction continued to challenge the Tower group, led variously by Peter O'Donnell, Fred Agnich, and Ray Hutchison, all of Dallas.[16]

Despite internal divisions, the Texas GOP mounted an unprecedentedly ambitious electoral program for 1968 with the intention of capitalizing on the drawing power of the presidential election. Most congressional seats, many local posts, and all state executive offices were contested by a large field of GOP candidates. If even moderately successful, this widespread challenge to the nearly permanent majority party would have stabilized the painstakingly constructed party organization and brought the party to a prominence it had not enjoyed in ninety years. So rosy a prospect, beguiling in its own right, was given considerable credibility by the disunity of the Democratic party after its violence-marred convention in Chicago, by the presidential campaign of Alabama Governor George Wallace, and by the apparently enhanced popularity of the Republican candidate, Richard Nixon, who was nominated at the generally harmonious Republican National Convention.

After the nomination of Vice-President Hubert Horatio Humphrey for the presidency on their ticket, Democratic leaders worked feverishly to heal the political wounds which were inflicted in Chicago. President Lyndon Johnson and Governor John Connally labored to pull the Texas party together behind Humphrey. They hoped to minimize presidential Republican defections and to offset the appeal of the American party candidate, George Wallace, whose popularity was unmeasured—and all the more feared for that reason. In such Democratic problems might lie Republican victories.[17]

Following a pattern familiar for forty years, some conservative Democrats openly supported the Republican candidate, despite the efforts of Lyndon Johnson. The Democrats for Nixon were headed by former Governor Allan Shivers, who had supported Dwight D. Eisenhower in 1952 and 1956. This time he was joined by former Governor Coke

Stevenson, LBJ's primary election opponent in 1948; Mrs. Dan Moody, wife of the late governor; long-term Congressman Martin Dies; Attorney General Will Wilson; and Claude Wilson, former speaker of the Texas house. Though its members were important as symbols of Democratic support for Richard Nixon, the Democrats for Nixon organization was kept subordinate to the Republican state party. National Committeeman Albert B. Fay of Houston and State Chairman Peter O'Donnell of Dallas had learned from Jack Porter's experience. They did not let the citizens' organization become a power in its own right as it had been in 1952 and 1956: Allan Shivers and the other Democratic defectors would not stand between Texas Republicans and the door to the Oval Office another time. Nor would the Democratic defectors be able to get out their vote for Nixon as effectively as they had for Eisenhower sixteen years earlier, for the presence of the third major candidate made earlier political calculations obsolete. Governor Wallace appealed strongly to many Shivercrats as well as to rural Democratic loyalists. The frequently disunited Texas Democratic party was thus divided in still another way. Surveying the confusion in the Democratic party, John Tower wryly quipped, "It's a difficult beast to pull together."[18]

Republicans were much more nearly united behind Richard Nixon and the flood of state and local candidates who hoped to ride his coattails into office. The state ticket was headed by Paul Eggers, a tax attorney and GOP leader in Wichita Falls. Though campaigning on a highly restricted budget of about $500,000—the Nixon campaign had funding priority in Texas—Eggers made selective and effective use of electronic media, especially of a twenty-second television spot commercial which sustained an image of dash, firmness, and imagination—a "Marlboro man" image, according to some observers. But radio and television time was costly. Eggers hoped to reach potential supporters through the news columns and at traditional political rallies.[19]

Eggers campaigned hard and aggressively. He made more than two hundred campaign appearances, campaigning six and seven days a week, in the company of Republican notables like Richard Nixon, John Tower, and George Bush. He took fair measure of his opponent, Lieutenant Governor Preston Smith, a Lubbock theater owner, by developing moderately progressive stands on education and racial issues. He advocated a sizable boost in pay for Texas teachers and took his campaign to the campuses of Rice University, the University of Texas, the University of Houston, St. Mary's University, Stephen F. Austin University, Southern

Methodist University, and numerous other colleges, universities, and community colleges.

The Republican candidate met with black political leaders, with labor union officials in East Texas and Gulf Coast areas, and with influential Mexican-Americans in South Texas. In the Rio Grande Valley, Eggers promised field workers rapid action to alleviate the pervasive poverty, which he described as "a cancerous tragedy." At the risk of losing scattered support among growers in the Valley, Eggers endorsed the demands of labor leaders for a "reasonable minimum wage" for agricultural workers. In return, several labor leaders endorsed Eggers, and Clemente Garcia drummed up support through the Amigos for Eggers. All of these events were unusual and newsworthy, and Eggers's progressive stands also brought the reward of widespread newspaper coverage of his campaign. The *Texas Observer*, which endorsed Eggers, claimed that his campaign "could herald the beginning of a new, progressive era of Texas politics."[20]

Additional media attention was drawn to Eggers by strongly worded attacks on his Democratic opponent. Taking full advantage of Smith's conservative "ol' boy" public image, Eggers denounced him as "lobby controlled, an obstructionist of much worthwhile legislation and an impediment to progress." Capitalizing on the traditional—if not well-founded—belief of Texans in the existence of widespread corruption in Austin, Eggers promised to end what he described as the "clubhouse approach to government." He told supporters in Dallas: "We cannot afford to have political hangers on, the political hacks, appointed to important state boards and commissions." The newspapers, not surprisingly, found that Eggers made good copy; and they gave widespread coverage to well-turned insults. Near the end of the campaign, Eggers made the front page of the *Houston Post* with one of his sharper attacks: "If Mr. Smith wins, the thing he will need more than anything else in this state is fervent prayer." By the time of the election, Eggers was well known, an honor he shared with only Orville Bullington and Jack Cox among twentieth-century GOP gubernatorial candidates in Texas.[21]

Eggers's vigorous campaign, taken with their limited successes since 1966 and the potential coattails of Richard Nixon, prompted local Republican leaders to make a record number of challenges. In Houston, for example, the reorganized county party, led energetically by Mrs. Nancy Palm, contested thirteen of nineteen seats in the Texas House, two seats in the county commissioners' court, and two judicial posts. In Dallas, the party offered a fifteen-man slate for the Texas House. In all, Texas Republicans contested 69 of 150 seats in the Texas House of Representatives. All nonjudicial posts in the state government were contested, including the usually safe berth of Jesse James, the state treasurer.[22] Attempting to strengthen its ties to Mexican-American voters, the GOP nominated Manuel A. Sanchez III of Brownsville to oppose James. Sanchez, owner and operator of a fleet of shrimp trawlers in Brownsville and a graduate of the Wharton School of the University of Pennsylvania, campaigned hard to cut into Democratic control of the Latino vote. His attempts and other Republican efforts to win 40 percent of this vote bloc for Nixon and Eggers alarmed Democratic party leaders like Preston Smith and John Connally into taking "precautions," according to one veteran reporter, Richard M. Morehead, chief of the Austin Bureau of the *Dallas Morning News.*

Presumably "precautions" included recourse to the time-honored techniques of reward and threat, described in the Valley as the *pan o palo* ("bread or stick") method of party discipline.[23] But Republicans were convinced that the Democratic plan also included provision for election fraud, much like that which they believed had carried Texas for the Kennedy-Johnson ticket in 1960. This time, the GOP intensified its ballot security program by recruiting and training poll watchers throughout the state. John M. Stokes, executive director of the Texas Republican party, claimed that "a poll watcher in a Democratic precinct is worth 100 votes to the Republicans, on an average." Party leaders also threatened to have photographers all over the state in an attempt to obtain photographic evidence of attempts of Democratic party officials to bribe voters. The ballot security program, partially implemented as early as 1960, was promoted with relative vigor in 1968.[24]

Republican campaign workers found considerable encouragement in the victory of James M. Collins in a special election in the Third District. Following the death of Joe Pool, who had won election to a new seat, Dallas Republicans made a spirited attempt to gain that seat. Collins, a prominent Dallas businessman and civic leader, won out over the widow of the late congressman and was reelected to the 91st, 92nd, 93rd, 94th, and 95th Congresses. Coming little more than two months before the general election, Collins's initial victory, as an augury of things to come, moved party workers to greater exertions on behalf of Nixon, Eggers, and local candidates.[25]

All of the GOP efforts produced a few victories and a record number of narrow defeats. Richard Nixon trailed Hubert Humphrey by less than 40,000 of the 3,079,190 votes cast. Hubert Humphrey ran well in the cities, with a clear majority of the votes in Corpus Christi and San Antonio; his best showing came in rural regions, especially in South Texas where Jim Wells, Duval, Zapata, and Starr counties gave lopsided majorities to the Democratic candidate. By contrast, Richard Nixon ran well in suburban areas, with 41.9 percent of the vote. George Wallace made his best showings in the strongly Democratic areas of East Texas, particularly in the first and second congressional districts; he carried the latter. Paul Eggers won about 43 percent of the vote for governor, receiving some 26,000 votes more than the party's presidential candidate. In general, Republican candidates on the statewide ballot received uniform support, as Democratic party leaders effectively discouraged ticket-splitting on state and local offices. In Corpus Christi, for example, there was not one thousand votes difference in the total ballots cast for party candidates from the top to the bottom of the ticket. The consequence, statewide, was that the gains which Republican leaders had anticipated simply did not appear. To return to the Corpus Christi example, the GOP lost its seat in the Corpus Christi delegation to the Texas legislature when incumbent Representative Charles Scoggins was defeated by Frances ("Sissy") Farenthold, a strong-minded lawyer and liberal Democratic leader.[26]

In other parts of the state, the picture was brighter. U.S. Representatives Price and Collins were reelected handily, as was Representative George Bush of Houston. Six of the seven Texas House seats which corresponded to Bush's district were won by Republicans, as were seats in Midland and in the Panhandle. In the State Senate, Henry Grover sat for District 15 (Houston), and O. H. "Ike" Harris was elected from District 6 in Dallas. Generally, candidates for local offices were not successful. But the election was over; the party had won the presidency; and there were enough local victories to sustain the morale of party workers—and to keep factions in the party alive.[27]

In 1969 Albert B. Fay resigned as national committeeman, and Peter O'Donnell succeeded him. Fay, who had turned down various diplomatic and executive posts, declined to make way for O'Donnell until he was strongly urged by John Tower and Richard Nixon to do so. Even then, O'Donnell rushed events by publishing the acceptance of Fay's resignation on the agenda of the State Executive Committee meeting before Fay announced his intention publicly. Ignoring this affront, Fay resigned; and O'Donnell assumed his post. Factional struggling was thus settled, for the moment, and planning was initiated for the elections of the next year.[28]

The 1970 elections brought hundreds of Republican candidates into the field. The GOP contested eleven of twenty-three U.S. House seats, five major state posts, five State Senate seats, fifty-nine seats in the Texas House of Representatives, and numerous posts in county government. But, once again, though the party mounted one of its most widespread challenges to the Democrats in its history, victories were scattered, and few gains were realized. Congressman Collins retained his seat in Dallas, and former state representative W. A. Archer succeeded to George Bush's seat; but no new congressional posts were won, though Frank Crowley, once former Congressman Bruce Alger's chief aide, ran well against incumbent Congressman Earle Cabell in the Fifth District. The story was much the same in the State Senate, where the Dallas and Houston "safe" seats were retained, but no new Republican senators were elected. Several narrow defeats, of Malouf Abraham in the Panhandle and Jim Nowlin in San Antonio, were disappointing to local party workers who had expected narrow victories. The Houston GOP produced the most impressive gains in the state legislature. The seven Harris County districts which were coterminous with Bush's congressional district elected six Republicans to the lower house. Revival of Dallas County's GOP delegation was marked by the election of a lone representative, Fred Agnich. The Dallas party had offered candidates in twelve of fifteen districts; but Agnich, a wealthy investor, alone ran an adequately financed campaign. He joined Maurice Angly, Jr., of Austin, Tom Christian of Claude, and Tom Craddick of Midland, who were reelected.[29]

The principal prizes at stake in 1970 were a seat in the United States Senate, held by Ralph Yarborough since 1957, and the governorship. The Republican party offered its brightest political prospect, U.S. Representative George Bush, for the former office, and its popular 1968 gubernatorial candidate, Paul Eggers, for the latter. Both contests were presumed to be rematches. Bush had run well under adverse circumstances against Yarborough in 1964. By appealing to the conservative sentiments of the majority of Texas voters, Bush would surely wrest the second Senate seat away from the liberal Democrat and join John Tower in Washington. Paul Eggers expected to reap the fruits of dissatisfaction with Preston Smith. Never popular with liberal Democrats, Smith now faced a rising tide of dissatisfaction with his administration, which critics continued to describe as "weak without moderation and indecisive without caution." Before the May primaries, when Bush and Eggers decided to challenge Yarborough and Smith, their chances were highly promising.[30]

Bush's calculations were upset, however, when former Congressman Lloyd Bentsen, Jr. challenged and defeated Yarborough after an acrimonious, no-holds-barred primary election campaign. Bentsen's candidacy, for the so-called Connally faction, surprised the Texas GOP. His victory, with about 52 percent of the vote, was a stunning blow to Republican plans. A conservative Houston banker, Bentsen did not share Yarborough's vulnerability on the conservative side of his party. From the beginning of their postprimary campaigns, Bentsen and Bush encountered difficulty in building distinctive political images with the majority in the electorate. With a large measure of truth, the Bush–Bentsen contest was viewed by the Texas press as a Tweedle Dum–Tweedle Dee choice. Both candidates were relatively young. Both men had established conservative records in the U.S. House of Representatives, Bentsen sitting for Southwest Texas for six years and Bush for the prosperous South Houston seat since 1966. At the time of the contest, both candidates lived in Houston.

Outside talent was brought into both camps. Harry Treleaven, a media supervisor for Richard Nixon in 1968, performed the same service for George Bush, while George Christian, former LBJ aide, served as a campaign adviser for Lloyd Bentsen. Both candidates were relatively familiar to the public, Bush through his senatorial campaign in 1964 and subsequent election to the House, Bentsen largely through the primary election campaign. Bentsen, the majority party candidate, held the apparent advantage of greater name identification.[31]

Bentsen was in fact better known than Bush, but this advantage brought with it a great weakness. Many of the voters who remembered him best were bitter labor-liberal backers of Ralph Yarborough, losers in the closest thing to a "holy war" in Texas since the Homer Rainey–Coke Stevenson gubernatorial contest in 1944. In sensational television spots, Bentsen had implied that Yarborough was to blame for student riots and most other unsettling aspects of life in the 1960s. These tactics were denounced as unfair and unethical, even by the canons of Texas politics, by Yarborough and his liberal supporters. Worse yet, from their perspective, the liberals were defeated by these cunning appeals to fear and prejudice.

The liberals neither forgave nor forgot the events of the primary campaign. With the irreconcilability of post-Civil War Confederates, they prosecuted their recently lost cause by throwing support to George Bush. Labor also favored Bush. The Teamsters Union openly endorsed him and contributed to his campaign. More cautiously, the AFL-CIO withheld an endorsement of Bentsen, while labor leaders passed word unofficially that labor would be at no disadvantage if Bush were elected to the Senate. Splinter groups of disgruntled liberals campaigned for Bush. Country editor Archer Fullingim of Kountze, who headed the Democratic Rebuilding Committee, raised potentially significant charges of fund-raising irregularities in Bentsen's primary campaign and denounced Bentsen as "a contemptible opportunist and bigot." Showing old wounds, Fullingim reminded liberals that Bentsen's campaign against Yarborough had been "the most evil campaign in Texas political history." Bentsen, baited into a fight, denounced the Rebuilding Committee as a "little pack of jackals." In traditional form, Texas Democrats were expending great energy in intraparty battle.[32]

George Bush received highly visible support from Washington during his campaign. He tied prospect of victory to the popularity of the Nixon administration. As Dick West, editorial director of the *Dallas Morning News*, observed: "The political tides change. You rarely hear a Texas Republican urge a vote for Bush in the interests of conservatism. The plea is that 'he can do more' or help Nixon." Bush reminded voters that he voted with the administration 64 percent of the time and that he supported even controversial White House proposals, such as the "welfare reform" scheme which failed of adoption.

For its part, the Nixon administration attempted to boost Bush's political stock through endorsements and personal appearances. Thus Treasury Secretary David M. Kennedy campaigned for Bush in the Dallas financial community. Interior Secretary Walter Hickel visited the Big Thicket to rally conservationist support and addressed Bush backers at a Houston dinner, which was also attended by Senator Howard Baker and Representative Dan Kuykendall, both of Tennessee, by astronaut Walter M. Schirra, Jr., and by athletes from the Houston Astros and the Houston Oilers. President Nixon and Vice-President Agnew both campaigned with Bush in Texas—Nixon in Dallas and Longview, Agnew in Dallas, Amarillo, and Lubbock. Bush's public identification with the Nixon administration could not have been more complete.[33]

Lloyd Bentsen, mounting a hard-hitting campaign against Bush, worked to turn Bush's Washington support to his own advantage. He criticized the inability of the administration to control inflation and unemployment, making strong protests over the layoff of nine hundred space workers in Houston and criticizing Nixon's welfare proposal and Bush's support of gun-control legislation. Bentsen skillfully revised old historical myths, describing Agnew as a carpetbagger: "A Maryland politician trying to get a fellow from Connecticut [Bush] elected Senator and one from Indiana [Paul Eggers] elected Governor." According to Bentsen, the heavy intervention by Nixon and Agnew transformed the Texas senatorial contest into an open power play by Washington politicians—never a popular group with Texas voters, as Bentsen knew. Bush countered that Bentsen himself, with the backing of LBJ, represented the "old machine—the old-style backroom, deal-making politician."[34]

Despite such exchanges, which generally found Bentsen attacking and Bush defending, the campaign was considerably less lively than the Democratic primary contest between Bentsen and Yarborough. In large measure, the candidates remained at arm's length, resorting less to running controversy than to intensive image-building through broadcasting media. Bush's efforts were persistent and sophisticated, perhaps more appropriate for New York than for Texas. George Bush was described as youthful and vigorous through one-minute television spot commercials which showed him jogging, trotting, bounding up the steps of the Capitol, and playing touch football. Exploiting Bush's apparently strong ties to the White House, Harry Treleaven's creations told listeners and viewers that "George Bush can do more for Texas." One particularly effective television spot showed the naturally affable Bush in shirt sleeves shaking hands and talking casually with Texas farmers. The *Texas Observer* commented ironically that the candidate "once just wipes the sweat off his face like Real People." Clearly concerned about the possible effect of Treleaven's clever packaging of candidate Bush, Lloyd Bentsen charged that the city slickers were trying to sell Bush "like a bar of soap," an accurate and perhaps a damaging appraisal.[35]

Despite intensive media advertisement and news coverage, Texas politicians in both parties were convinced that the candidates had failed to stir voter interest. Democratic leaders, in fact, met hurriedly and secretly in Austin during September in an attempt to devise means to raise the level of voter turnout in November. Like their Republican counterparts, they realized that low turnout enhanced the likelihood of

Republican success. Apprehension was heightened in October when polls showed the races for both senator and governor to be close, with Bush favored by 48-49 percent of the eligible voters and Paul Eggers chosen by 46-48 percent of the potential electorate. Alarming to Democrats and comforting to Republicans was the knowledge that the GOP was generally more effective in turning out adherents. Thus, a rough projection of the polls in October to election returns in November suggested to both candidates that Bush would perhaps win by a narrow margin. The only Democratic remedy was a greater turnout of voters; and, with the election less than one month away, the Bentsen and Smith camps had still found no effective means to achieve this end. The *Dallas Morning News*, which endorsed Bentsen, lamented editorially, "There is the distinct possibility Texas may elect a second Republican United States Senator."[36]

What Bentsen could not do for himself, however, Nixon, Agnew, and Demon Rum brought to pass. During late October, contending forces mounted widespread, attention-getting campaigns around the referendum on "liquor by the drink." Religious and other temperance groups stirred the interest of rural Democrats while the proliquor faction roused voters in urban areas, especially in the Latin counties. Off to the polls to settle this long-standing issue, Democratic voters would presumably support Bentsen and Smith at the same time. The influx of Republican celebrities, especially Nixon and Agnew, also generated additional interest in the November election. Bentsen jubilantly claimed that each visit by a Republican celebrity would turn out 100,000 more voters. Though Bentsen could not foresee it when he made this prediction, serious miscalculations by Nixon and Agnew would give him further advantages. Agnew, speaking in Amarillo, leveled vituperative remarks at youthful dissenters, seriously undermining Bush's and Eggers's careful cultivation of young voters on the state's campuses. Appearing in Longview, Nixon spoke in opposition to bussing students to achieve racial integration, reopening a sore issue which responsible community leaders worked to close. Moreover, Nixon's remark came only two days after two men had been convicted on charges of bombing Longview's fleet of school buses. Careful Republican plans to win over black supporters of Ralph Yarborough were set back sharply by the President's remarks. Bush, locally countering charges by GOP leaders that Nixon and Agnew were torpedoing his campaign barge, defended the visitors but avoided even the appearance of endorsing their remarks. Nonetheless, the dam-

age was done. By November the elections interested more voters than the
GOP had expected.[37]

In some measure, larger than expected voter turnout was also encouraged by an apparently close contest between Paul Eggers and Governor Preston Smith. Eggers, a game candidate in 1968, was even
stronger in 1970. Since his earlier loss to Smith, Eggers had been
groomed by the Nixon administration as general counsel of the United
States Treasury. He had thus promoted his own career as a tax attorney
and acquired valuable political experience. In the meantime, Governor
Smith had spent two frustrating years as titular head of the faction-ridden
Democratic party, acquiring experience and opposition in unequal quanti-
ties. Both gubernatorial candidates waged long campaigns with adequate
resources, though the senatorial contest diminished the coffers of both
aspirants. Eggers raised nearly one million dollars, while Smith came
by a somewhat larger sum.[38]

Contests for lesser offices also stimulated more interest than is common in off-year elections. Lieutenant Governor Ben Barnes of Brown-
wood, "the wonderboy of the Texas Democratic party" and thought to
be the man on his way up, was challenged by University of Texas law
professor Byron Fullerton, who waged an extensive effort which was
unprecedented for Republican candidates for the state's second highest
post. Fullerton traveled widely, appearing with Senator Barry Goldwater,
Desi Arnaz, and Dorothy Malone in El Paso and with state and national
leaders on numerous platforms. Edward Yturri, GOP candidate for
attorney general, worked Mexican-American neighborhoods intensively,
attracting considerable notice as the Mexican-American nominee for
statewide judicial office. Yturri reminded fellow Mexicanos: "I'm a
Mexican-American and I'm a statewide candidate for attorney general
of Texas. That's one statement no Democrat has ever made. Why it
has never been said is vitally important." His appeal was locally successful—he ran ahead of the ticket by nearly three thousand votes in
Corpus Christi, while he trailed it statewide. The lesson was there to be
read: Mexicanos would support *los hermanos* as friends and neighbors,
but other voters would not. Thereafter, young Mexicanos looked to the
nascent La Raza Unida party, which made its first appearance in 1970
and entered Republican party calculations in subsequent elections, as
party leaders expected the new party to attract Democratic voters. During the gubernatorial contest of 1970, liberal Democrat Albert Peña,
a commissioner of Bexar County, shifted to La Raza Unida and declined

to endorse either Smith or Eggers. Peña did claim, however, that a Republican governor would be no worse than Governor Smith for Mexicanos: "When you're sleeping on the floor, you can't fall off the bed." Eggers, Fullerton, and Yturri each reached pockets of voters who might not otherwise have turned out for the general election.[39]

The consequence of enhanced voter interest was the appearance of 300,000 more voters than had been expected when forecasts were made one month before the election. In fact, 53.8 percent of the registered voters went to the polls, while only 47.1 percent had done so during the preceding off-year contest in 1966. Increases were striking in some Democratic strongholds. In San Antonio, where John Tower had carried 54.1 percent of the vote when only 37.8 percent of the registered voters cast ballots, George Bush won only 41 percent of the total in 1970, when 53.7 percent of the registered voters went to the polls. Even in areas of Republican strength, the enhanced turnout tended to favor Bentsen. In Dallas County, for example, turnout increased from 43.9 percent to 50 percent, with sharp increases in Democratic precincts. Lloyd Bentsen, riding on a wave of new interest and support, won by a comfortable margin of 150,000 votes, with Preston Smith securing roughly the same vote for governor. The very effort Republicans put into the 1970 campaign may have helped to bring about defeat.[40]

By November, 1970, it was clear that the Republican party in Texas was no longer token opposition to the Democratic party. The GOP had become an effective challenger—the minority party in a two-party state. Electoral disasters, primarily those of 1964, had only limited effects on political vitality and organization. The crippling defeat of Herbert Hoover and the long period of nominal opposition which followed had no parallel after 1961. Party organization also changed significantly. No longer was organization a matter of pins on the map, as it had been during R. B. Creager's long domination of party affairs. As early as 1947, conservative businessmen had worked to transform the party into a serious contender for loyalty and victory—an effort which was advanced greatly during H. J. Porter's tenure as national committeeman. Subsequent activity by scores of party leaders including Peter O'Donnell, Anne Armstrong, Nancy Palm, and Rita Clements and aggressive campaigns by John G. Tower, George Bush, Bruce Alger, Ed Foreman, Paul Eggers, Henry Grover, and other candidates established the Texas GOP as a significant force in the state's political life.

Yet, even in 1970, the party continued to wrestle with many of the problems which had perplexed leaders during previous decades. Endemic factionalism, based on geography rather than on ideology, continued to distract effort and attention from the main goal, winning. As Creager was battered by intraparty rivals in Dallas and San Antonio, John Tower and Peter O'Donnell had to contend with high-powered opponents from Houston and West Texas. Division within the Republican party continued to undermine its effectiveness in Tower's day as in Creager's; divisions within the Democratic party offered Republicans their main chance in 1961, 1966, and 1972, just as they had in 1922, 1924, and 1932. The volatile coalition of conservatives, labor moderates, liberals, blacks, and Mexican-Americans proved to be even harder to hold together in the Democratic party during the 1960s than the major factions had been during the 1920s.

Demographic and economic trends which were already established by 1920 continued to provide an expanding base for Republican activity. Growth of the principal cities, the expansion of the salaried middle class, and the influx of Republicans from the Middle West and East provided a foundation for the increasingly effective organizational work of party leaders. Continued opposition to the growing encroachment of the federal government on the exercise of individual liberty and the operation of private enterprise tended to provide the party with an identifiable ideological cast in 1970 just as it had thirty years earlier. A strongly conservative position on state and national issues continued to attract Democrats to Republican candidates and Independents and some Democrats into GOP ranks. By 1970 it was clear that this process, taken with effective leadership, had brought the GOP far beyond its early preoccupation with federal patronage. It remained to be seen if organizational skill, demographic and economic trends, and militant conservatism would enable the Republican party to gain the Democratic party's place in the sun. The world had not been turned upside down, nor was it clear that it would be.

9

"The Lord Smiled on Tuesday!"

THE REPUBLICAN PARTY in Texas had come a long way since the "Eisenhower revolution." Since 1952, the party had passed through a long period of organizational maturation. It had mastered the constant and manageable aspects of politics. Its grass roots organization had repeatedly proved its ability to turn out exceptional proportions of the Republican vote. It had reduced door-to-door canvassing, direct mail contacts, and the operation of telephone banks to smooth routines in Dallas, Houston, Midland, Amarillo, and other Republican strongholds. In the process, large numbers of party members had acquired experience in volunteer capacities. Party leaders had refined fund-raising techniques and had developed considerable sophistication in the employment of polling organizations and media consultants. By 1970, Texas Republicans had learned the ropes.

It was still open to question, however, how much the GOP had broadened its base of support in the whole Texas electorate. On the eve of the general election in 1972, a poll taken for the Tower organization found that only 19 percent of the registered voters actually identified themselves as Republicans; 52 percent said they were Democrats, 28 percent were independent, and 1 percent did not give classifiable responses. With less than one-fifth of the electorate committed to it, the Republican party could expect few victories outside a handful of urban counties. The poll, generally accepted as reliable, seemed to indicate that with the expansion of known Republicans from about 10 percent in 1952 to nearly 20 percent in 1972, the party had realized its maximum potential and that further gains of this magnitude were unlikely. Party leaders could find some encouragement, however, in the tendency of independent voters to split their ballots to support Republican presidential candidates, John Tower, and some Republican candidates for congressional and state-level posts, while they continued to vote for Democratic candidates for most local offices.[1]

The same poll contained additional information which party leaders found reassuring: only 23 percent of the respondents called themselves liberals, while 35 percent said they were conservatives; and the largest number, 42 percent, identified themselves as moderate in the context of Texas politics. This breakdown confirmed the long-standing strategy of working into factional divisions within Democratic ranks by appealing to conservatives and moderates to support Republican candidates for local, state, and national offices. With its organization in place and working efficiently, the GOP waited for opportunities to exploit.[2]

The first promising avenue opened in 1971, with the collapse of the insurance and banking ventures of Frank W. Sharp, a Houston developer. In the fallout, federal grand jury investigations brought the names of Gus Mutscher, Jr., the speaker of the Texas House, Governor Preston Smith, Lieutenant Governor Ben Barnes, Waggoner Carr, and other prominent Democrats into the headlines, linking them in various ways with Sharp's operations and damaging their reputations. Barnes, in particular, was compromised when it was disclosed that he borrowed $60,000 from the Sharpstown Bank without collateral. Until the scandal emerging from Sharp's dealings muddied his reputation, Barnes had been the Democrats' rising sun, a man whose ascent to the governorship was generally taken for granted by most students of Texas politics. But the "Shadow on the Alamo," as one writer described the investigations, eclipsed Barnes, and, by compromising the state's most prominent Democratic leaders, disoriented the Texas Democratic party for nearly a decade. The Sharpstown debacle forced a sudden and unforeseen diversion in the smooth-worn channels of Democratic politics.[3]

The most impressive political consequences of Sharpstown were manifest in the Democratic primary of 1972, when both Governor Preston Smith and Ben Barnes lost out in the contest for the gubernatorial nomination to Dolph Briscoe, a wealthy West Texas rancher-banker and former legislator who had run unsuccessfully for the nomination four years before. Frances "Sissy" Farenthold, a member of the "Dirty Thirty" reform group in the Texas House, ran second with strong liberal, black, and Mexican-American support. Both Briscoe, who won the nomination in a runoff election with Farenthold, and "Sissy" were out of the main line of Texas politics. What their showing in the primary meant for the Democrats in November was hard to predict. All signs indicated that the divisions of the primaries would not be healed by November.

Political forecasting became even more complex with the appearance of a strong third party candidate, Ramsey Muniz, gubernatorial candidate of La Raza Unida party, who made his first try for statewide office. La Raza Unida was little known outside of Crystal City, Muniz's vote-getting potential was untested, and the extent to which he would cut into the Mexican-American and liberal Anglo vote was hard to gauge. Without a doubt, however, Muniz's candidacy would siphon votes from Briscoe and thus enhance the showing of a strong Republican candidate —if the Republicans could find one.[4]

By May, 1972, however, no likely Republican champion had come forward. Only 113,716 voters participated in the Republican primary, in which six gubernatorial candidates ran. The front-runner, State Senator Henry C. Grover of Houston, who received 39 percent of the vote, faced Albert B. Fay, runner-up, in the runoff election. Fay came from the so-called country club wing of the party; he would be a respectable candidate who could be counted on to wage a low-keyed and gentlemanly campaign. Grover came from the "Lions Club" wing of the party; during twelve years in the Texas legislature he had been brashly forceful, a favorite of grass roots party workers, particularly those who supported the presidential aspirations of Ronald Reagan. Contrary to the expectations of top party leaders, Grover won the nomination with two-thirds of the vote, and he was determined to make a real race of it.[5]

GOP chiefs now had Grover's statewide race to contend with, in addition to those of Richard Nixon and John Tower. Where would the money for three races come from? Would an aggressive challenge to Briscoe work against the tendency of conservative Democrats to split their tickets to vote for Nixon and Tower? The shortage of money was an unending worry in Grover's camp for the duration of his campaign, as Nixon and Tower had prior and stronger claim upon contributors.

As his campaign progressed, the reaction of Democratic voters to Grover was, in turn, a matter of concern for party leaders in Dallas, in part because of Grover's acerbic campaign style. Hard-hitting, outspoken, and articulate, Grover tore into Briscoe with a constant barrage of charges, including the unsupported allegation that most of his work had "been spent supervising wetback laborers on his gigantic ranch." Grover appealed strongly to Wallaceites who resented Briscoe's *pro forma* vote for George McGovern on the final ballot at the Democratic National Convention, an action which had cost Briscoe conservative support without gaining liberal backing in Texas. But Briscoe appeared unperturbed by Grover's barbs. Rather than spend time on either his opposition or the press, Briscoe cultivated the Democratic courthouse regulars whom he needed to turn out the vote. Briscoe moved calmly and cautiously, leading Grover to satirize him as "the quiet man" and Muniz to brand him "La Vaca," the cow.[6]

While he found it easy to fire off a broadside of challenges and insults, Henry Grover had a far harder task in developing a positive base of support throughout the state. To build strength in the principal urban areas, from which he could hope for the greatest proportion of his vote, Grover planned extensive radio and television exposure to overcome his problem of inadequate name identification. But though he enlisted the help of Phil Nicolaides of the Agora Group, high-powered specialists in political media work, inadequate funds cut short planned exposure. A final election week television blitz, for example, never came off, for lack of fifty thousand dollars.

Grover never solved the problem of name identification. The frustrated candidate came to blame his funding problem on John Tower; he believed that Tower had deliberately dried up financial support in order to insure his defeat and Tower's own continued preeminence in the party. As his campaign approached its end, Grover seemed to be as eager to do battle with Tower as with Briscoe, and, as a result, he drove away would-be contributors, particularly after he tried to oust the Tower group from leadership positions at the party's postprimary convention. Henry Grover was a great scrapper, too great a scrapper to limit himself to one opponent at a time. By November it was clear that he had not concentrated his full effort against Dolph Briscoe because he insisted on sparring with John Tower.[7]

Though Tower was more than able to fend off Henry Grover within the Republican party, meeting the challenge of the Democratic contender for his Senate seat was more demanding business. Tower's most able opponent up to that time, Harold "Barefoot" Sanders, was a former state legislator, a former opponent of Bruce Alger, and, most recently, an assistant attorney general in the Justice Department during the Johnson administration. But though Sanders was both able and the candidate of the majority party, he was not without serious handicaps. The most obvious was his lack of name identification. Few Texas voters knew who Barefoot Sanders was before he won his party's nomination, in part because Sanders had never held statewide office. His greatest liability, however, was George McGovern, the liberal presidential nominee of the Democratic party. From the day he was nominated, Texas Democrats were convinced that the antiwar Democrat would have "reverse coattails"—that he would drive Texas Democrats into the Republican column on the ballot. Sanders and Briscoe alike avoided appearing with McGovern when the presidential candidate campaigned in Texas. Both Sanders and Briscoe extolled the virtues of ticket splitting in the general election. While Sanders thus put some distance between himself and his party's presidential candidate, John Tower repeatedly reminded voters that Sanders and McGovern were on the same ticket; Tower happily made the most of his own association with Richard Nixon, making campaign appearances with the President and emphasizing his apparent influence with the administration in television spots.

Yet a third difficulty Sanders encountered was that of choosing a position from which he could attack Tower while rallying the various and divided elements in state Democratic ranks. Sanders's decision to challenge Tower's voting record was calculated to attract liberal, black, and Mexican-American support; Sanders made a great point of the senator's negative voting record in general and his diehard opposition to the 1965 Voting Rights Act in particular. Sanders's wooing of minority voters, however, gave Tower an opening against him, for Tower channeled debate into the bussing issue, on which the Democrats were painfully divided. Backed into a corner, Sanders came out against bussing, thus undoing what he tried to accomplish among the state's minorities by campaigning on civil rights. Tower's greatest campaign assets in 1972 were undoubtedly money and national politics. With adequate financing and with organizational support from both the Republican party and the Committee to Re-Elect the President, Tower's situation provided a sharp contrast to that of Barefoot Sanders, who coped with scanty funds and a divided party.

The consequences of the division were apparent when election returns were tallied. Richard M. Nixon won a crushing victory over George McGovern, with two-thirds of the major party vote in Texas. Nixon actually surpassed Lyndon Johnson's 1964 high mark by nearly 3 percent. There was no doubt in the minds of careful observers that Theodore H. White's summation of national politics fit Texas: "The election was decided the day McGovern was nominated. The question after that was only how much. McGovern did to his party what Goldwater had." In Texas, it was even more so. He could hardly have been more out of step. In the opinion of a sympathetic foreign journalist, George McGovern was closer to the mainstream of the Social Democratic politics of Norway than to that of America. But Oslo was ideologically far removed from Dallas and Houston, and George McGovern cost the Texas Democrats a United States Senate seat. He nearly cost them the governorship as well.[8]

The Nixon tide thus carried John Tower to a third term in the Senate. With 53.4 percent of the vote, Tower had a solid victory, but he trailed Nixon by nearly 13 percent of the vote, more than double his preelection estimate, and he ran ahead of Nixon in only two rural counties, Jim Hogg and Maverick. There were ominous signs of soft spots in Tower's victory: he had run better in 1966, without the benefits of presidential coattails, and in 1972 he even trailed the GOP gubernatorial candidate in Galveston and Harris counties, carrying the latter by less than 2 percent. The dissident Harris County faction had backed Grover, one of its own, but Tower lost important precinct-level support from Republicans in Houston, who both resented his opposition to the stillborn presidential candidacy of Ronald Reagan and believed Grover's allegations of sabotage.[9]

Grover's charges received a wide hearing by virtue of his strong showing. He ran neck and neck with Dolph Briscoe, slipping behind as the late returns were counted. When the final tally was in, Grover received 48.4 percent of the major party vote, 2 percent more than Paul Eggers had received in 1970 and 3 percent more than Jack Cox garnered in 1962. Carrying Dallas, Ector, Harris, Lubbock, Midland, Randall, Smith, Taylor, and sixteen other counties, Henry Grover came within 100,000 votes of becoming governor. It was clear from the returns that the defection of liberal Anglo and Mexican-American Democrats to Ramsey Muniz, the loss of some Wallace Democrats to Grover, and Richard Nixon's broad coattails had brought Henry Grover closer to occupying the Governor's Mansion than a Republican had been in nearly a century. Under the circumstances it was hard to deny that a better financed candidate might well have won—an observation that bred bitterness in the Grover camp and optimism throughout the rest of the party: it might well be accomplished another time.[10]

While Republicans could be amply gratified by the outcomes of three statewide races, encouraging gains were made as well in the Fifth Congressional District and in the lower house of the Texas legislature. In Dallas, Alan Steelman, former executive director of the President's Advisory Council to the Office of Minority Business Enterprise, waged a low-budget shoe-leather effort against Earle Cabell, the Democratic incumbent. Steelman visited 25,000 households in the course of his peripatetic campaign; he hammered away at Cabell's alleged ineffectiveness in Congress, where the congressman sat on the District of Columbia Committee and on the House Select Restaurant Committee. Confident of reelection, Cabell ignored Steelman until late October, when his advisers finally convinced him that he was in deep trouble. By then it was too late: in November, Steelman won with 55 percent of the vote.

The Republican's victory was not entirely of his own making, notwithstanding the hours he spent trudging through the Fifth District. In 1971, the Texas legislature had redrawn district lines, dropping precincts with black majorities and adding precincts with large numbers of conservative white voters, with the aim of creating an apparently safe seat for Cabell, a conservative Democrat. By giving their attention to the dilution of the minority vote, the legislators succeeded in creating a seat which the Republican Steelman was able to win: that a Republican might run for the seat was a matter the Democratic redistricters had not seriously contemplated.[11]

Redistricting also played a part in the additional gains made by the Republican party in the Texas House. Republican Representative Tom Craddick of Midland led a successful effort in 1971 to reverse the legislature's heavy-handed urban gerrymandering, and with federally enforced readjustments in districts in Dallas, San Antonio, and Houston, the GOP picked up seven House seats. At the same time, Mrs. Betty Andujar was elected to the State Senate from Fort Worth, bringing the number of Republicans in that body to three.[12]

After Tower's reelection, Grover's near-miss, and localized victories, it is not surprising that Republican leaders announced the imminent

arrival of two-party politics in Texas. Never before had political developments seemed as promising, and party leaders could not be blamed for
seeing the progress of 1972 as the result of their own efforts. Yet, in
reality, much of what took place in 1972 was less the result of Republican energy than of Democratic misadventure. If the Democrats
could live down Sharpstown, George McGovern, and intraparty feuding,
the next general election would be a real test of apparent Republican
gains. Having profited by tribulation among Democrats, however, the
Republicans were about to encounter their own share of adversity.

Like their fellow party members throughout the nation, the Texas
Republicans could not have foreseen that the grandly triumphant reelection of Richard Nixon would be followed in little more than six
months by a scandal of devastating proportions. When the enormity of
Watergate unfolded and public reaction mounted, the value of Richard
Nixon's leadership of the national Republican party metamorphosed
from overwhelming asset to crushing liability. As John Mitchell, H. R.
Haldeman, John Erlichman, and other officials in the Nixon administration were hustled from the Ervin Committee to John Sirica's federal
court, public confidence in the Republican party faded; Watergate cast
a pall over party prospects throughout America.

No wonder, then, that when Texas party leaders set out to recruit
candidates in November, 1973, they found few takers. Both George
Bush and Ray Hutchison declined to throw their hats in the ring to
challenge Dolph Briscoe. For a time it appeared that party leaders
might concede the gubernatorial nomination to "Gadfly Grover." Despite his impressive performance in 1972, however, Henry Grover decided to withdraw from candidacy in March, 1974, leaving the party
with the unwelcome task of locating a respectable token candidate. They
settled on Jim Granberry, who was the popular mayor of Lubbock but
little known outside his hometown. Granberry won the nomination in
an uneventful primary in which fewer than seventy thousand Republicans
bothered to vote. Once again, the GOP had been relegated to the status
of a sideshow in the arena of Texas politics. Gone was the heady optimism of 1972.[13]

Though his chance for success was negligible, Granberry campaigned
industriously. He had little money; he had to get by with less than half
the inadequate sum Henry Grover had raised two years earlier. Without
funds, Granberry had no chance at securing adequate name recognition.
By election day only 36 percent of the eligible voters knew who he was.

Dolph Briscoe, accurately gauging the futility of the Republican's efforts, stopped campaigning in October and retired to his ranch to await news of reelection. When it arrived, it surpassed even the most optimistic expectations of Briscoe's managers: he was returned to office by a two-to-one margin, this time for a four-year term mandated by legislation passed in 1972. Carrying even such Republican bastions as Dallas and Midland, Briscoe lost only in Lubbock, Tyler, and Amarillo. In the last-named city, the Republican candidate for state treasurer, Robert G. Holt, an Amarillo resident, ran ahead of Granberry, carrying him to local victory.[14]

Though party leaders had never expected Jim Granberry to win, they had expected him to attract at least 40 percent of the vote. Their disappointment at his weak showing was unrelieved as they surveyed the results of two key congressional contests. In the Panhandle, incumbent Republican Congressman Bob Price lost his seat to popular State Senator Jack Hightower. In the second race, the Republicans had a known candidate in Douglas S. Harlan, who had garnered 43 percent of the vote in 1972, running against O. C. Fisher, the sixteen-term incumbent in the sprawling Twenty-first District. Harlan's showing—the best ever against Fisher—convinced the elderly congressman to retire rather than face the physical demands of another strenuous race.

In 1974 Harlan confronted Robert Krueger, winner of the Democratic primary, in what media billed as the battle of the intellectuals, with a Republican with a Ph.D. in political science from Duke University and a law degree from the University of Texas pitted against a Democrat with an Oxford doctorate in English literature and a deanship at Duke. Both candidates put their academic regalia in mothballs and rolled up their shirtsleeves to wage high-powered "just plain folks" campaigns, appearing together in public debates on more than twenty-five occasions. Harlan secured the support of John Tower and obtained funds from the Republican Congressional Campaign Committee, while Krueger had the advantages of considerable personal wealth, a highly polished media campaign, and, of course, the nomination of the majority party. The press noted flaws in both candidates' images: Harlan came over "like a student," while Krueger impressed one liberal journalist as "dudish." On election day, however, the voters preferred the dude to the student as Krueger ran up a seven-thousand-vote margin. Though Harlan carried the Republican precincts in north San Antonio, Krueger won solidly in most rural areas.[15]

Amid these two disappointments in congressional races, there were three successful defenses by Republican incumbents. Jim Collins won again in the Third District with 65 percent of the vote, and W. R. Archer received nearly 80 percent of the vote in the Seventh District. Alan Steelman retained his seat against the challenge of State Senator Mike McKool, despite the redrawing of the lines of the Fifth District by the Democratic legislature to increase the number of Democratic voters within it. Archer's victory in Houston and those of Collins and Steelman in Dallas were accompanied by a scattering of local wins, particularly in Dallas County, which elected its first Republican county judge when John Whittington, a county commissioner, defeated twenty-five-year incumbent Lew Sterrett.

In general, however, there were few grounds for celebration in November, 1974. Most observers agreed with Bo Byers, Austin chief of the *Houston Chronicle*, who prophesied, "The Democratic tradition means the Republicans are wiped out state-wide for the foreseeable future." What there was to recall of the immediate past held little comfort for the GOP: independent voters and most Democrats had fallen back into their habitual loyalty, which Republicans had worked to undermine since 1952. What there was to expect in the near future was no more hopeful: the beaten and demoralized party was still torn by factional divisions that threatened to reduce its faltering electoral effectiveness even further.[16]

As early as August, 1974, it was evident that John Tower's group of party leaders could expect a strong challenge to their control from Republican ranks. Despite a determined attempt by the senator to head them off, delegates to the Republican State Convention passed a number of resolutions critical of the Ford administration. The declarations demonstrated the growing strength of that faction of the party which found Ronald Reagan more attractive presidential timber than Gerald Ford. In early autumn of the following year, a half-dozen Texas Reagan adherents met with the managers of the Californian's national campaign and drew up some preliminary plans. After Texas Representative Ray Barnhart of Houston and Midland Mayor Ernest Angelo, Jr., became co-chairmen of the Texas Reagan group in November, the Reagan backers began their work with organization, establishing a loose network of regional and local coordinators over which little central control was exercised. Early in 1976 the Reagan leaders recruited delegates to run in the May presidential primary; like the regional coordinators, these delegates raised their own funds and ran their own campaigns.[17]

That Texas had a presidential primary in 1976 was in large measure the result of the presidential ambitions of Senator Lloyd Bentsen. The Texas legislature decided for the presidential primary in 1975, as Bentsen made known his interest in the race. Such a primary was calculated to advance Bentsen's progress toward the Democratic nomination in a number of ways. The primary's winner-take-all provision, which gave all delegates in a district to the candidate with the majority vote, would effectively bar liberals from holding a significant fraction of the delegation, as they had in 1972. By shifting from the convention method of selecting delegates to the primary election method, Bentsen would be spared the work of controlling precincts, of which there were more than two thousand in the state. At the precinct level, moreover, conservative Democrats had been known to have difficulties with militant and better-organized liberals. As constructed, then, the new presidential primary was well calculated to work for its conservative Democratic architects.[18]

The presidential primary posed quite a different set of possibilities and problems for Texas Republicans. In contrast to its operation in the Democratic party, the new primary could be used among Republicans to undercut the power of longtime party leaders. Republican chiefs had previously engineered local and state conventions to produce national convention delegations under their control. As was obvious in 1952, the machine was not invulnerable, but it worked most of the time. It was now possible, however, for a dissident faction within the party, like the Reagan advocates of 1976, to win control of the national delegation without battling against party apparatus at work in conventions, the party machinery which, in 1976, was in the hands of the backers of Gerald Ford. Reagan backers would not have to capture the state convention for their candidate in the face of opposition on the state committee or a hostile convention credentials committee. The presidential primary removed entrenched party obstacles to the advance of the Reagan group: and they were prepared to make the most of this novel advantage. They had, after all, cultivated precinct and local support, the sort of backing which was best calculated to elect delegates in the primary.

By March, 1976, the Reagan movement not only had a considerable grass roots following among Republicans, but it was also beginning to pick up adherents from outside Republican ranks as well. Large numbers of conservative Democrats and former Wallace supporters joined it. Like the Goldwater campaign of 1964, Reagan's candidacy brought an important infusion of new blood to the Texas Republican party. Yet established party leaders at work cranking up Gerald Ford's campaign misread the Reagan effort as no more than another quixotic crusade, a movement destined for political dead end. It might exacerbate party divisions—that was no novelty—but how could it come to anything if Ford had the endorsement of Senator John Tower and the overwhelming majority of recognized party leaders? Ford supporters agreed with Beryl Milburn, vice-chairman of the state party and manager of Ford's campaign, that their ranks contained the party's longtime workers. As the primary drew ever nearer, the Ford camp continued to issue confident predictions of victory while the Reagan element developed and expanded grass roots organization. Reagan backers were encouraged by the Californian's advances elsewhere in the nation, particularly in North Carolina, shortly before the Texas primary. In April the group received considerable notice from the press when ten prominent Democrats, most eminent among them St. John Garwood, former associate justice of the Texas Supreme Court, announced their adherence to the Reagan cause. Behind the scenes, Reagan's local organizations were constructing a smoothly engineered bandwagon powered by a mounting grass roots movement for the governor. With good reason, Ron Dear, executive director of Texas Citizens for Reagan, expected his candidate to benefit from the expected large turnout on primary day.[19]

When that day arrived, more than 400,000 voters cast ballots in the Republican contest, six times as many as had participated in 1974. Reagan beat Ford by a two-to-one margin, taking all the district delegates; then, at the state convention, he picked up all the at-large delegates as well. The Ford backers were completely routed. Senator John Tower, who was Gerald Ford's designated floor manager at the national convention, was cut from the list of Texas delegates. So signal an insult gave weight to the argument that Tower, rather than Ford, was the real loser in the primary. Not only had Tower lost control of the Texas GOP, but he also faced a possibility of real trouble for his reelection in 1978. As one Reagan leader put it, "We'll vote for him, but what he needs two years from now is campaign workers, enthusiasm, and our total dedication to his campaign. And it may not be there." What Tower and his friends had seen as a quixotic crusade turned out to be a mass movement like that of the Eisenhower faction in 1952; like Jack

Porter's campaign, that of Barnhart and Angelo delivered a stunning blow to the old guard.[20]

The triumphant Texas Reaganites soon discovered, however, that while their party opponents were in disarray, they were not entirely driven from the field. That the old guard was not demolished was, in part, a result of the course of national politics. With victories in Texas, Indiana, Georgia, and Alabama, the Reagan bandwagon reached its greatest momentum in May. Its progress thereafter was much less exhilarating, and the national convention brought it to a jarring halt. Though Reagan forces could take consolation from the strongly conservative platform adopted by the national party, Gerald Ford succeeded in winning the presidential nomination. If it were not discouraging enough to have been outmaneuvered in Kansas City, the delegates who returned to Texas found that Ford backers were not about to concede the state party management to their group. Though Ernest Angelo, Jr., was now national committeeman, state positions were still in the hands of the old guard. At the September state convention, Ford backers used their control of the rules committee to deprive the national convention delegates of their customary bonus votes; by that strategem, Ray Hutchison, who had avowed neutrality during the Reagan-Ford primary contest, was able to keep the state chairmanship from Ray Barnhart with a handful of votes. With the presidential election two months away, the divisions between Texas Republicans were more bitter than ever.[21]

If such party animosities boded ill for Republican prospects in November, so did developments in Democratic politics. In contrast to the GOP, the Democratic party of Texas faced November, 1976, with a truly exceptional degree of unity and good feeling. Gone were memories of the days of Sharpstown and George McGovern. Jimmy Carter's nomination for President brought Texas Democrats together. Carter, the winner of the Democratic primary designed to promote Lloyd Bentsen, enjoyed the support of urban liberals, racial and ethnic minorities, and rural conservatives. Party leaders rallied to his cause. Governor Dolph Briscoe happily endorsed Carter and enthusiastically joined him on campaign.[22]

By contrast, Gerald Ford's appearances in Texas were of questionable service to the Republican cause. Reminders of preconvention divisions frequently appeared as Reagan supporters offered halfhearted endorsements of Ford and channeled their efforts into local contests. Ford's public appearances were generally well attended, particularly in

Dallas, but he lost the impact on the wider public of upbeat rallies when newspaper and television reporters emphasized his frequent stumbles and misstatements. The bumbling image of Ford, artfully developed by Chevy Chase, then a regular performer on NBC Television's "Saturday Night Live," was reinforced by stories of the President stumbling out of airplanes, helicopters, and limousines as well as by a photo in which he appeared to be eating the corn shuck wrapper along with a tamale at a San Antonio fete. By contrast to his opponent's image of poise, goodwill, and confidence, Ford's image impaired his credibility with the general electorate. Unlike its smooth behind-the-scenes operation in Texas, in public Ford's national campaign gave the appearance of being all thumbs.[23]

It came as no surprise on election day when Jimmy Carter won Texas with 51.6 percent of the major party vote. Ford's votes fell within the classic GOP pattern, for he drew strong support from Houston, North Texas, and West Texas and trailed in San Antonio, El Paso, and South Texas. Democratic unity and a strong rural vote offset Ford's gains in GOP strongholds, and Texas fell squarely into Carter's column. Nor was Carter the only Democratic victor in contests for federal office. Lloyd Bentsen, who had not renounced his Senate seat in his unsuccessful campaign for the presidential nomination, was reelected as Democrats basked in the party amity fostered by Jimmy Carter.[24]

Bentsen's victory was not accomplished without a vigorous challenge from Congressman Alan Steelman. Bentsen and Steelman alike won their parties' nomination with ease; Bentsen had beaten Phil Gramm, Texas A&M economist, by a two-to-one margin, while Steelman amassed a yet greater lead over two primary opponents. In other important regards, they were not evenly matched. Bentsen enjoyed vital assets which Steelman lacked: party unity, money, and name identification. Steelman tried to compensate for the want of all three with sheer campaign effort, much as he had done in winning his congressional seat. He could not run a shoe-leather campaign in a state as vast as Texas, but he could and did take every opportunity to gain press coverage by pitching into his Democratic opponent. He assailed Bentsen's image by dubbing him "loophole Lloyd," a reference to the senator's work on the 1976 Tax Reform Bill, and he sought to weaken the apparently invincible rampart of Democratic unity by reminding liberals of Bentsen's attacks on Ralph Yarborough six years before. To offset the liability of the feuds at work in Republican ranks, Steelman tried to emphasize his independence of party leadership, a step he hoped would appeal to Reagan supporters and political independents.

Steelman's campaign was energetic, but he could not match Bentsen's political strength in Texas. The incumbent senator rarely so much as referred to his Republican opponent; rather than give Steelman much-needed publicity by meeting his challenges head on, Bentsen settled back into comfortable reliance on the party faithful and on his campaign organization, which extended to nearly every Texas county. By the end of October, the *Texas Observer* summed up prevailing political opinion of the contest by noting, "Steelman has been the more interesting and aggressive campaigner; Bentsen is going to win it."[25]

The *Observer's* forecast proved accurate. Alan Steelman emerged from the race for the Senate with 43 percent of the vote, running more than 5 percent behind Gerald Ford and nearly 4 percent behind George Bush's showing against Bentsen in 1970. Steelman carried Dallas, Tyler, Amarillo, and Midland, the last with more than 60 percent of the vote. But he lost Houston and Fort Worth, both of which were usually essential to Republican victories in statewide contests, and he was soundly defeated in El Paso, San Antonio, Waco, Wichita Falls, Corpus Christi, and South Texas. His Dallas congressional seat was lost as well; Democrat Jim Mattox, a liberal member of the Texas House of Representatives, won it in a contest with Mrs. Nancy Judy, an outspoken member of the Dallas school board, who wrote off minority support by campaigning narrowly for the votes of Reagan and Wallace backers. That minority support dismissed from Judy's campaign had previously enabled Steelman to hold the seat. Alan Steelman's unsuccessful Senate race thus ended in double loss for the GOP.[26]

The result of other congressional races was almost as discouraging as the Republican defeat in Dallas. In four other contests the Republicans ran respectably, but not well enough to win. In Houston, for example, Dr. Ron Paul lost the seat he had narrowly won in a special election earlier in the year, to Democrat Bob Gammage, by a margin of less than three hundred votes. In the Nineteenth District former Odessa mayor Jim Reese ran against Capitol Hill veteran George Mahon and received 45.4 percent of the vote; in central Texas's Eleventh District, Jack Burgess won nearly 43 percent of the major party vote in his race against veteran incumbent W. R. Poage, while in the Sixteenth District Vic Shackelford claimed 42.2 percent of the vote in a race with Richard White. None of these candidates did badly; indeed, the chal-

lenges of Reese and Burgess may have influenced both Mahon and Poage
to make the 1976 campaign their last, and thus demonstrated the merit
of the GOP strategy of putting pressure on elderly Democratic incumbents. But not doing badly was certainly not the same as winning. The
only GOP congressional victories were those in the "safe" districts of
Jim Collins and Bill Archer, both of whom were returned to Washington without serious challenge.[27]

Despite considerable energy spent in pursuing places in the state
legislature, Republican gains in this arena were more the result of redistricting than unusual political enterprise. Republican candidates vied
for fifty-four House and nine Senate places. From the creation of single
member districts in Lubbock and Arlington, the GOP picked up two
seats in the House, bringing its total strength in that body to nineteen;
the party's strength in the Senate, however, remained at three. Redistricting was changing the political composition of the House, but as far
as Republicans were concerned, that change was indeed gradual.[28]

Considering only battles won, 1976 was not a memorable year for
the Texas Republican party. It was a year of party division and difficulty, a year whose intraparty feuds were not readily forgotten. Yet
1976 was also a time of important, if less perceptible, changes in Republican fortunes. As divisive as the Reagan candidacy was in Republican ranks, it also resulted in considerable gains in party support at the
grass roots level. Conservatives of a variety of political backgrounds
united to support Ronald Reagan under the Republican banner. As one
journalist described the phenomenon, "Middle-class Anglos discovered
they didn't get warts or become socially ostracized for having voted in
the 1976 Republican presidential primary for Ronald Reagan, so they
were willing to try it again."[29] The growth in its conservative following might tip the balance of political fortune in the GOP's favor, were
it to find an attractive conservative candidate for a statewide contest
in 1978. To the party's great good fortune, just such a candidate did
come forward.

While candidates like Dwight Eisenhower, Barry Goldwater, and
Ronald Reagan could produce temporary surges in GOP grass roots
following, party leaders had long known that other purposeful organizational work was necessary to build permanent party support. As the
Ford-Reagan contest and the intraparty feuding accompanying it became part of the past, the positive gains of constructive Republican
activity were increasingly evident. It was still true that the Texas Re-

publican party itself could not be of great financial assistance to the individual running for office. Despite the recruitment of so prestigious a member as St. John Garwood to serve as party treasurer, there was no ready flow of funds to headquarters for programs in ballot security, absentee and undecided voter contact, and voter turnout efforts. But with the limited funds at its disposal, Texas Republican headquarters nonetheless did conduct a voter registration program which candidate campaign managers found effective in 1978.

Far more important to candidates was the party's ability to train and season volunteer workers; progress in this area was the result above all of the enlistment of women in the Republican cause. By 1978 Republican women, represented on the state level by the Texas Federation of Republican Women, were organized in more than 130 clubs with over 6,000 members on their rolls. In the gubernatorial, senatorial, congressional, and local campaigns of 1978, members of these clubs joined other interested women in giving more than 38,000 hours of volunteer labor to Republican candidates. The bulk of this time was expended in canvassing, direct mailing, and the operation of phone banks; in 1978 there were about 75 of the last-named at work across the state. Women's contributions to Republican politics lent considerable truth to the commonplace that in the Texas GOP the men provide the candidates and raise the money, while the women win elections.[30]

GOP programs directed toward racial and ethnic minority groups could not match the success of the party efforts to enlist Texas women in the Republican cause. Nevertheless, such programs were continued by the state committees. Among Republican candidates, John Tower, in particular, emphasized the need to win more than the usual token 2 percent of the black vote. Attempts to reach black voters had been made during the Eisenhower campaigns and had been given new support and emphasis in the sixties. In 1973 the Black Republican Council was organized to assist efforts to reach conservative black voters. Though such endeavors did not live up to party expectations, in most instances Texas Republicans did not write off blacks as potential supporters. But they worked harder at what seemed a more promising proposition, the attraction of Mexican-American voters. In the course of the sixties, Celso Moreno worked through the party to build permanent support among Spanish-speaking voters and, as he put it, to "develop our own *jefes*."

The Republicans further demonstrated their interest in Mexicanos by occasionally recruiting Mexican-American candidates. Edward M.

Yturri, for example, was the Republican nominee for attorney general in 1970. He ran substantially behind his opponent, but his candidacy made it known that the Republican party had room for middle-class Mexican-Americans, an increasingly important group in urban areas. During the 1960s and 1970s Celso Moreno and other party workers met with locally influential Mexican-Americans, recruited them for party work in campaigns, and attempted to interest them in joining local party organizations. For the most part, GOP field workers succeeded in enlisting middle-class Mexicanos in specific campaigns, particularly those of Richard Nixon in 1968 and 1972, but they enjoyed less success in signing up new Republicans because local organizations, whether led by Anglo-Americans or by Mexican-Americans, were less interested than the emissaries from the Austin headquarters in promoting new *jefes*. By contrast, the separate campaign organizations were open to new Republicans; Amigos for Tower cast its net widely, even if local party organizations did not.[31]

While headquarters worked to build Republican party strength in Texas, the state party did not extend itself to control the campaigns of major candidates in statewide elections. Campaign organizations were separate from the state party organization. Thus, while the party ran canvassing, direct mail, and ballot security programs for John Tower in 1966, the senator's campaign organization was kept separate from party operations. Similarly, in 1978, both Tower and other candidates maintained campaign operations separate and distinct from party machinery. This practice was dictated by the cardinal reality of Texas political life: no Republican candidate could expect to win unless he widened his following beyond that which the party organization could influence. He needed funds, endorsements, and votes from conservative Democrats, and exclusive reliance on the Republican party apparatus and on party leaders might well close off the necessary support of maverick Democrats.

Thus, John Tower's campaign for reelection in 1972 had been captained by two widely known Democrats, former governor Allan Shivers and former ambassador Edward Clark, who were cochairmen of Texans for Tower. Neither Shivers nor Clark was likely to make the leap to organizational affiliation with the GOP, but both were willing and effective leaders of the faction of conservative Democrats who supported Tower. Equally important for a candidate like the senator, campaigns had to take on a bipartisan image to attract some rank and file Democrats and independents, because ticket-splitting would be diminished if voters perceived the contender as more "Republican" than "conservative." Thus while the party was the irreplaceable source of volunteer workers for Tower and other Republican candidates, overly tight identification with it could cost them the Democratic and independent votes they needed to win.[32]

There was also the persistent belief among candidates and their managers that local party organizations were often more preoccupied with "hidden agendas" than with winning elections. Local prominence, personal rivalries, and a striving for a wide miscellany of individual gratifications were characteristic motivations within local organizations of both parties, if the normal conduct at precinct, county, and district conventions were taken as indicative. This wide variety of intentions was always at odds with the more narrowly goal-oriented behavior of campaign managers and workers; hence the preference of John Tower and other candidates in both parties for their own campaign organizations.

The two statewide contests most important to the Texas Republicans in 1978 were the senatorial and gubernatorial races. In the former race, John Tower looked for reelection to his Senate seat; by January, 1978, his advisers, headed by Nola Haerle, a highly respected and successful political consultant, who had directed the senator's campaign in 1972, had worked out a detailed campaign strategy. But it was not as clear at the beginning of the year how the gubernatorial race would develop. The GOP had two likely prospects for the gubernatorial nomination in William P. Clements, Jr., and Ray Hutchison; perhaps more significant, the Democrats also had two strong contenders for their nomination for governor, incumbent Governor Dolph Briscoe and Attorney General John Hill. As Democratic divisions could add up to Republican opportunities, it was possible for Texas Republicans to hope for great things from 1978. It was clear, however, that nothing would be accomplished without great effort. In no political arena was this more evident than in the race for the Senate, for John Tower faced a Democratic challenger who looked like a winner, Congressman Robert Krueger.[33]

In campaigning for reelection, John Tower was not without substantial assets as well as significant liabilities. That large numbers of Texans knew his name was foremost among his advantages. After nearly two decades of media exposure and nearly two million constituent service contacts since his election in 1961, Tower enjoyed widespread name recognition in the state, something no other Republican in Texas had

ever had. Tower's position in national politics was yet another asset in
Texas. His consistently conservative voting record and his articulate
leadership of conservatives in the Senate appealed to conservative voters
of both major parties; by the time he formally announced his candidacy,
on January 11, 1978, his outspoken opposition to the Labor Reform
Act and the Panama Canal Treaty had further enhanced his standing
among conservatives.

If Tower's incumbency and position were important to a successful
campaign, so was his own considerable political skill. No one was better
versed in the rules of Texas politics than John Tower, and he could be
relied upon to leave little to accident. His actions and remarks alike
were planned with near-Teutonic thoroughness. As the manager of his
1972 campaign remarked, "John Tower probably makes fewer blunders
than any candidate I have ever known." Tower also understood and
applied the rules of coalition politics to strengthen his hold on the seat
in the Sam Houston succession. He assembled support from groups of
prominent Democrats, recruiting Allan Shivers and Ed Clark in both
1972 and 1978 in public support of his candidacy.[34]

With such advantages, Tower might have seemed assured of certain
victory. For a member of the Democratic party, such campaign assets
would have made triumph at the polls inevitable. But with all his strong
points, John Tower was still a Republican in Texas. If his long years
in the Senate and at the forefront of the Texas GOP had taught Texans
who John Tower was, they had also served to make some persons aware
that they disagreed with him. Over the years Tower acquired opposition as well as support. Thus, while his stand on issues was conservative,
it was not always conservative enough to please all groups on the right
of the political spectrum. When, for example, the senator withheld an
unqualified commitment to a balanced federal budget, based upon informed apprehension that major cuts would take place in the defense
budget, some conservatives were loud in their displeasure. In another
instance, when concern for the constitutionality of measures promoted
by the powerful "Right to Life" lobby impelled him to agree to support
only part of their program, "Right to Life" adherents stridently denounced his scruples.

If it was impossible to please all conservatives, it was nearly as difficult to please all Texas Republicans. Tower's preeminence in the Texas
GOP had encountered opposition from 1968, when he was first pitted
against a sizable group of Ronald Reagan supporters. Subsequent party

ruptures were plastered over, but they did not mend. Henry Grover, in particular, had not given up the grudge he had developed against Tower in 1972, and he continued to blame the senator for his defeat. With the encouragement of friends among the ranks of Reagan supporters, in 1978 Grover decided to enter the Senate race himself, in effect as a spoiler. Grover was not a likely victor in the Republican primary; he was even less likely to make any major erosion of Tower's backing in the general election. But in a close contest, the defection of even a small number of conservative voters was no trivial matter. At best, if Grover continued to make trouble he would force a damaging diversion of energy necessary to defeat a Democratic opponent. From any perspective, Henry Grover was a threat to John Tower.[35]

Just as not all conservatives could agree with Tower's record in office and party leadership, not all Texans accepted the senator's image. While so nebulous a matter is not subject to precise analysis, there was no doubt that John Tower's personal tastes and life-style presented a contrast to the artfully unsophisticated and folksy image of the conventional Texas politician. Complex, intelligent, and urbane, John Tower was the antithesis of the stereotypical good ol' boy from down home. He seemed more comfortable with the adversary relationship of intellectuals in the Senate than with the small-town haggling of courthouse politicians. For Tower, a savory in the subdued elegance of The Monocle, a restaurant near the Capitol, was far more satisfying than a tepid bowl of mucky chili wolfed down under the broiling Texas sun. Even in so small a matter as dress the senator was different: he preferred the meticulously tailored pin-striped wool suits from London's Savile Row to the bold plaid polyester suits of his rural constituents. The urbanity which appeared to separate John Tower from his small town and rural constituents had been a matter of common observation ever since his election to office. Certainly Tower seemed to devote most attention to larger cities, in particular Dallas and Houston. No country boy, by 1978 Tower was perceived as a big city senator, and that image was both costly and time-consuming to offset.

With all his personal assets and liabilities in his bid for reelection, by mid-1978 Tower's greatest campaign problem was the strength and liveliness of his Democratic opponent. Representative Robert Krueger won an easy victory over former Insurance Commissioner Joe Christie in the Democratic contest for nomination to the Senate. Krueger served only two terms in Congress, but during that time he received extensive publicity in Texas by virtue of his strenuous and near-successful efforts to deregulate the price of natural gas. Texas oil and gas operators, a numerous, wealthy, and powerful group, expressed their appreciation of Krueger's endeavors by subscribing generously to his campaign; some made it clear that they thought Krueger would be an improvement over Tower, whose behind-the-scene actions in their behalf were less widely known.

Krueger was an indefatigable campaigner. While the senator worked in Washington, the "New Braunfels Flash," as journalists dubbed Krueger, appeared at scores of small-town rallies; at the same time, his media consultants produced appealing television spots which showed him as a small-town boy with energy and clout. To this skillful image-building was attached the slogan, "We need more than a vote—we need a voice," stressing Krueger's dynamism once again. By presenting Krueger as a doer, his campaign managers may have slightly overstepped the mark of vote-getting prudence, at least in the opinion of Tower's campaign manager, by reminding the electorate that Tower had voted "right." By stressing the outgoing Krueger's energy, however, the congressman's managers aimed to exploit Tower's apparent aloofness from the daily affairs of Texas voters. They could hope that the Texans who saw little of Tower would believe he cared little for their interests.[36]

While working to hold the unwieldy Democratic coalition together, Krueger tried chipping away at various elements of Tower's support. To undercut Tower's modest following among Mexican-Americans, for example, the congressman stressed Tower's vigorous opposition to the 1965 Voting Rights Act. Tower's forces were quick to raise a defense. They publicized his continued and effective support of bilingual education, through Nosotros Con Tower, an aggressive campaign group headed by Pete Diaz, a Rio Grande Valley merchant, and they trumpeted Tower's endorsement by Juan Garcia of McAllen, the vice-president of the Texas G.I. Forum. Even music was enlisted in the senator's campaign in South and West Texas by "El Corrido de John Tower," a catchy ranchero song which proved to have considerable appeal.

By the last weeks of the campaign, Tower's staff felt that their effort to resist Krueger's advance in Mexican-American communities was generally successful. Indeed, it seemed that in some areas Krueger's forceful courting of the Mexican-American vote was building a backlash of Anglo opposition among traditionally Democratic farmers, ranchers, and merchants. Tower aides could hope that Krueger's try at undermining Tower's support had actually fractured the Democratic coalition to the senator's benefit at the polls.[37]

As the senatorial contest progressed, it was given unexpected drama by political mistakes on both sides. The most highly publicized gaffe was undoubtedly Tower's curt refusal to shake hands with Krueger at a Houston gathering. The incident took place in the presence of photographers, and pictures of Tower's snubbing his opponent were widely reproduced in Texas newspapers, usually without an accompanying explanation of the episode. The immediate effect of what looked like poor sportsmanship on the senator's part was an instant drop in his standing in the polls. Shifting to defensive action, Tower strategists worked to turn the incident to his advantage. Through extensive radio and television advertising, they explained Tower's behavior by charging that the Krueger campaign acted dishonestly in mailing out reprints of a journalistic smear of Tower, which had been accompanied by additional unflattering comments. Much to his chagrin, Krueger had to admit that an aide had sent out the offensive mailing. The episode did neither campaign any good, but in the long run it was perhaps a greater handicap to Krueger than to Tower; it was an embarrassment and a distraction in Krueger's high momentum effort.[38]

If the handshake incident displayed an uncharacteristic lack of finesse on Tower's part, Krueger made occasional blunders of his own. Under the pressure of numerous public appearances before a wide variety of groups, the congressman occasionally misspoke or let fall tactless remarks. Campaigning in Houston, for example, he announced to the Downtown Kiwanis Club, "If you're looking for someone who is just a spokesman for business, you're not looking for me": a startling way to address a group of conservative businessmen! That Krueger bumbled into such *faux pas* was a sign both of fatigue and of his relative inexperience in professional politics.[39]

Before the contest for the Senate ended, two developments were important in affecting its course. The first was the withdrawal of Henry Grover from the race. As late as June, 1978, polls showed Grover to have a following of 2 to 3 percent of respondents; all of that 2 or 3 percent could realistically be charged as a loss to Tower rather than Krueger. But Reagan forces, wishing both to keep Grover supporters within Republican ranks and to demonstrate leadership clout, proceeded to dry up Grover's financial and volunteer support. What Grover suspected had been done to him in 1972 really happened in 1978: he was irresistibly forced to retire. Tower's chance of victory correspondingly improved.[40]

The second significant development in the Senate race was the appearance of national political celebrities on the Texas campaign circuit. Rosalynn Carter, Vice President Walter Mondale, HEW Secretary Joseph Califano, and HUD Secretary Patricia Harris visited Texas to appear with Krueger; John Connally, George Bush, Ronald Reagan, and Gerald Ford appeared with Tower. Though the effect of using national political figures in state campaigns could not be predicted with precision, Krueger hoped that his string of celebrities would bring him votes from racial and ethnic minorities; similarly, Tower could hope to strengthen his standing among conservative Anglos. In all likelihood, neither expectation was fulfilled exactly according to intention. Krueger's identification with national party leaders might have done more to drive conservative votes to Tower than to lure minority voters to the polls, and Tower's celebrities did little more than reinforce the movement of conservative Anglos in a Republican direction, a movement already given impetus by the gubernatorial campaign. In sum, the strategem used by both candidates of bringing in national figures probably tended to work to Krueger's disadvantage. Whatever the differences of opinion which distinguished Texas Republicans in the ranks of their national party, such differences were not as pronounced in 1978 as those between the majority of conservative Texas Democrats and the national Democratic party.[41]

Comparing the overall campaigns of the two leading candidates, the Tower campaign was superior in both planning and operation. Tower's campaign was based on a three-hundred-page plan drawn up by Nola Haerle. Execution of the plan was the responsibility of Ken Towery, the Pulitzer prize-winning journalist who headed Tower's campaign staff in 1966. Both Haerle and Towery were accomplished political managers. By contrast, the Krueger campaign was directed by thirty-year-old Gary Mauro, whose experience was limited to the management of Krueger's successful bid for Congress in 1974. The Krueger campaign crew had a superabundance of youthful energy and enterprise, but it lacked political veterans with a backlog of experience: the oldest staff member was only thirty-three. Krueger's enthusiasts were thus pitted against Tower's seasoned professionals, a telling difference in a close contest.

Krueger's polling and staff operations were less accurate and effective than Tower's, especially during the final month of the campaign. When Tower's polls showed Krueger eroding Tower's backing, the senator's staff responded with highly targeted and localized media expenditure and campaign appearances. At the beginning of October Krueger's polls, inclined to be biased toward Democrats and nonvoters, in the opinion of Tower aides, showed the race in a dead heat, with Krueger gaining momentum in San Antonio and South Texas. At the end of the month, Tower's polling organization, V. Lance Tarrance Associates, found that while Krueger had virtually eliminated Tower's lead, the Krueger bandwagon was stalled; Tower, at the same time, continued to make small localized gains in northern and southern areas of Texas. The Tower leaders responded by committing additional effort and resources to precisely those areas where Tower seemed to be gaining. Such skilled management tipped the balance, to produce an ultimate victory of roughly one half of one percent. Of this breathtakingly close outcome, Tower quipped, "Close is better than losing." In a close contest, professional expertise meant winning.[42]

The most sensational development of the Texas general election of 1978 was not Tower's narrow reelection to his Senate seat but the election of the first Republican in a century to fill the governor's office. The long-awaited triumph came about as the Republicans finally put together all the elements for political success: they found an able and appealing candidate with ample financial backing, they cranked up all the organizational forces they could muster, they put most intraparty differences in the background in the excitement of the campaign, and they were able to exploit division in Democratic ranks. This last element in the political equation was, as usual, the key to GOP opportunity.

The root of Democratic discord was the contest for the party's gubernatorial nomination. Having served a two-year and a four-year term, incumbent Governor Dolph Briscoe decided to run for a second four-year term. Briscoe's style as governor had been low-keyed and understated. If he enjoyed few stunning successes as an administrator, he had few notable failures during his tour of duty, and this might ordinarily have made his reelection trouble-free. But Briscoe's bid for a third term ran up against an aggressive challenge: the incumbent attorney general, John Hill, formerly a highly successful claims lawyer, set his sights on the Democratic nomination. To this end he directed a steady barrage of criticism against Briscoe, equating the governor's reserve and inclination toward indirect administration with inaction and ineffectuality. He pictured Briscoe as a do-nothing in office, a tactic which proved successful on primary election day. Taken along with the apparent reluctance of Texas Democrats to overturn the traditional two-term limitation on their governors, and assiduous courting of the AFL-CIO, the Texas State Teachers' Association, and various other special interest groups, Hill's personal attacks on Briscoe won him the Democratic gubernatorial nomination with a clear margin of victory.

Hill's personal success, however, proved to be his party's disaster. After Hill's aggressive demolition of Briscoe, the incumbent governor's rural supporters were disinclined to exert themselves for Hill: indeed, were an attractive Republican candidate to come along, conservative rural Democratic votes could be pried loose for Hill's opponent in November. As luck would have it, the Texas GOP found just such a candidate in William P. Clements, Jr.[43]

Clements, the founder and chief executive of SEDCO, the world's largest drilling company, had spent most of his life in the business world, taking little active part in campaigns until 1972, when he served as cochairman of the Texas Committee to Re-Elect the President. From 1973 to 1977, he was undersecretary of defense, a post which gave him experience in government and at least occasional visibility in Republican affairs. Though he lacked experience in practical politics, several friends, Peter O'Donnell and George Bush, and his wife, Rita, remedied this deficiency. Rita Clements had long been both active and prominent in Republican party matters in Texas and in Washington. With good reason, a leader of the Republican Reagan group called her "as good a political head as Texas has," for Mrs. Clements was a highly skilled organizational politician. A veteran campaign leader, Rita Clements had few peers in the art of organizing grass-roots politics. Her experience was a major asset to her husband as he entered the race for governor.[44]

Drawing heavily on his own fortune, estimated at thirty million dollars, Clements built a campaign treasury which probably exceeded the amount spent by all prior Republican candidates for the gubernatorial nomination from the party's birth in Texas. He put together a sixty-person campaign staff which was headed by Omar Harvey, a retired IBM executive. Clements spent heavily on advertising and aimed his personal appeals directly at grass roots Republicans; he attended teas, luncheons, and barbecues in twenty-nine targeted counties, making a special effort to meet party workers on the precinct level. It took large sums of money to make the local contacts, and it took considerable determination to endure the strenuous campaign, but Clements was long on cash and will.[45]

Clements's opponent for the Republican gubernatorial nomination was the former state party chairman, Ray Hutchison. A highly regarded member of the state legislature and party leader, Hutchison was widely known through the upper ranks of the party. Though some Reagan supporters mistrusted him, Hutchison emerged from the intraparty warfare in 1976 with relatively little damage to his political standing; he was the obvious choice to run for governor.

But when the polls closed on primary day, Republican voters chose Clements over Hutchison by a margin of roughly three to one, an exceptional outcome which upset the conventional order of insider politics. Clements's victory was in part the result of superior financing; the total amount of Hutchison's campaign contributions would not have equaled the interest payments on the over two million dollars of his own fortune which Clements used to win the nomination. Yet for all his financial resources, Clements's energy and intelligence were also of major importance in his success. They were of even greater interest to the millions of Texans who knew little about him.[46]

Those who knew him realized that Bill Clements was even longer on determination than he was on cash. Journalists' descriptions of him have been similar in content. Writing for the *Dallas Morning News*, George Kuempel described him as an enthusiastic, brash, aggressive, "fast on-the-lip, shoòt-from-the-hip millionaire." A *Washington Post* correspondent described him as "a Randolph Scott with a flat Texas drawl . . . a feisty, shoot-from-the-hip Texan." In their nationally syndicated column Rowland Evans and Robert Novak depicted him as a "dynamic, articulate, compact, combative, blunt, hot-tempered Dallas business tycoon." Clements-watchers generally agreed that he was intelligent, ambitious, and aggressively energetic. Not since Jack Porter's Senate race of 1948 had a Republican candidate so strikingly shown that particular combination of traits.[47]

Though Clements's decisive victory over Ray Hutchison seemed to convince workers in the losing camp that support of Clements was the only sensible course, Clements had a number of important problems to solve before he could be considered a serious challenger to Hill: he had to increase his meager 18 percent name identification, and he had to build a winning coalition of Republicans, conservative Democrats, and independent voters.[48]

His nomination secure, Clements immediately began to work to win the November election. His first step was to reorganize his campaign staff, which he did with the help of Peter O'Donnell and Tom Reed, former secretary of the air force, who had managed Ronald Reagan's first successful gubernatorial campaign. Most of the Clements-paid primary workers were not retained, though Omar Harvey was persuaded to remain with a special assignment. Nola Haerle was brought from the Tower campaign to head operations. Much as she had done for Tower, she began her work for Clements by drawing a 150-page campaign plan, detailing strategy, analyzing the candidates, and organizing fund-raising, budget, cash flow, organizational responsibilities, media commitments, and press operations. Less voluminous than the Tower plan, it outlined operations on lines which would be followed closely during the campaign.

With Clements's approval, Nola Haerle then hired the campaign's principal media consultants, Don Rheem and Company of Boston and V. Lance Tarrance Associates of Houston, public opinion and market experts. Clements recruited Stuart Spencer, a Californian who had devised successful approaches to uncommitted voters, and Mrs. Nancy Brataas, a Minnesota state senator and an expert in the organization and operation of telephone banks. George Strake, Jr., and Mrs. Bobbie Biggart came over from the Tower volunteers to accept assignments in finance and volunteer coordination respectively; Bill Keener, formerly a member of Tower's staff, joined them. Jim Francis, former director of the Dallas GOP, served as finance director, and Mark Heckmann, a reporter for the *Houston Chronicle*, became Clements's press aide. By the consensus of most outside observers, Clements had hired or borrowed the services of the best available political talent for a hell-bent-for-leather campaign.[49]

Even with his blue ribbon campaign organization, Clements had much work to do before he would be seen as a serious threat to John Hill's election. His first goal was to become better known by Texas voters. Six months earlier, Clements's name had been recognized by only 4 percent of the potential voters polled. Even after the primary, he was far less widely known than Hill, who had been in the public eye for six years. The first Clements poll, taken in June, showed him receiving 27 percent approval to Hill's 59 percent, with 14 percent undecided. To compensate, the Clements organization launched a media blitz of ten-second radio and television spots to increase their candidate's name identification and to lay the basis for subsequent issue-oriented commercials. As Hill settled into Austin to observe the conventional summer campaign hiatus, Clements and his team launched a full-scale effort to reach their targeted goals: 52 percent of the vote in the major cities, a break-even showing in the next 28 urban counties, and at least 46 percent of the vote in the rural counties. The last was surely the toughest objective, for the brass-collar old-line Democrats were secure in their control of local politics in the countryside. Gerald Ford, for example, had received only 41 percent of the rural vote two years earlier. Under ordinary circumstances, it would seem virtually impossible to make much progress in the country.[50]

As a series of events began to unfold after the primary elections, Clements's forces realized that country Democrats might be unusually open to Republican advances. Whether by intention or oversight, Hill did little to mend bitter differences with disappointed Briscoe supporters. His victory speech was less than generous; in return, Briscoe's concession was distinctly chilly. In the weeks which followed the primary, Hill generally ignored the governor and his connections, making few effective efforts to unite the party. Quick to take advantage of Hill's snubbing of his most powerful party opposition, Clements moved to pick up support from the Briscoe faction. When the Clements campaign organization moved from Dallas to Austin, in order to gain better access to the capitol press corps, it rented the space previously occupied by Briscoe headquarters; at Briscoe's request, David Dean, his legal counsel and campaign treasurer, was allowed to retain office space until June 1 to wrap up the financial end of the campaign.

By the time June 1 arrived, Clements had succeeded in recruiting Dean to serve as deputy director of his own campaign. Dean's recruitment was a coup indeed, for no one was better placed to be the principal architect of bridge-building between Clements and the conservative Democrats. With rapprochement underway, Omar Harvey launched Project 230, which was designed to carry the campaign into the 230 rural counties. The next step in the long summer campaign in the rural counties was a visit to Uvalde. There Dean lined up a dinner meeting for Clements with about twenty important West Texas Democrats at the home of Edward and Cele Briscoe Vaughn, Dolph Briscoe's son-in-law and daughter. Following the dinner, a large public reception was held for Clements at the First State Bank of Uvalde, Dolph Briscoe's bank. As David Dean intended, the signal went out from the Uvalde gatherings; Clements was acceptable to the conservative Briscoe faction of the Democratic party.[51]

During the next two months, Bill and Rita Clements toured the 230 rural counties in a trailer house, talking with courthouse Democrats and rural voters, spreading word of fiscal conservatism, and capitalizing on anti-Hill and anti-Carter sentiments. Not surprisingly, growing numbers of Briscoe Democrats found Clements's position familiar and appealing, and his take-charge, "Texan to the toenails" personality was familiar and reassuring. Clements's sizable fortune proved to be an advantage in more than just the cost of the campaign: rural Texans accepted it as a legitimate sign of honestly won success and as a guarantee that "he won't need to steal," as innumerable farmers and ranchers put it to members of his campaign staff. In August, Clements's two months of eating dust began to pay off. More than three hundred Briscoe supporters joined his campaign as volunteers, and conservative Democrats signed on to head his campaign operations in 130 rural counties. By election day, more than a thousand Democrats were working for Clements; a majority of his county chairmen had crossed party lines to take their positions. Even rural bankers and road contractors, considered vulnerable to punitive and discriminatory actions by Democratic-controlled state agencies, contributed to the Clements effort. Other conservative Democrats, particularly courthouse leaders, assured Clements that they would not work against him, even if they could not offer public endorsements of him. Large numbers of rural party chiefs who disliked Hill had nothing to fear in the event of Clements's election: they would take a walk on election day.[52]

While Clements was strenuously campaigning for the country vote, John Hill placidly spent most of his time in Austin. Confident of victory, he organized a shadow government, assembled the next biennial budget with the heads of state agencies, worked on the postelection transition, and oversaw the organizational aspects of his inauguration. Complacent about his election, he gave little effort to campaigning during the sweltering summer months. Yet his preoccupation with assuming office was not without political effect. He further alienated Governor Briscoe and his supporters, who resented Hill's "playing governor" a full half-year before the inauguration. Briscoe and his friends did not hide their irritation from rural Democrats, who already disliked Hill. The acme of misunderstanding between Hill and Briscoe factions came about during a special legislative session, called by Briscoe during the summer. Briscoe hoped to effect sweeping tax cuts, intended to be his party victory for the conservative cause. But the legislature failed to respond to his urging, and Briscoe's defeat was blamed squarely on John Hill, whose allies and employees in the legislature talked Briscoe's initiative to death. Resultant ill will among Democrats hurt Hill's popularity, which dropped nine points during June and July; at the same time, it also generated more support for Clements.[53]

In August, as John Hill was mapping out his administration, Clements got his maximum statewide effort underway. The August assault began with John Connally's ringing endorsement of Clements, carried statewide on radio in August and on television in September. Organizational work accelerated; telephone banks were set up in thirty-three locations, and material was distributed to volunteers at county and precinct levels. Voter registration drives were launched in Republican areas, with impressive results. In Harris County, for example, registration in GOP precincts increased 14 percent, while that in the whole county climbed by 7 percent. All of the organizational work, campaigning, and media expenditures started to work to good effect. Clements's name identification increased from 39 percent in July to 58 percent in September, while John Hill's remained at 68 percent throughout the campaign.

Polls showed Clements making small but steady gains through the summer and into September. Then the rate of increase in Clements's support accelerated in response both to planned campaign events and to unexpected assistance from the Briscoes. When a *Dallas Times Herald* reporter called the Briscoe ranch to solicit the governor's view of the candidates and their campaigns, Briscoe did not respond. His wife, Janey, however, said that Clements would make a better governor than Hill, in her opinion, and that party loyalty alone would bring her to vote for the Democrat. It was widely assumed that Mrs. Briscoe was speaking the governor's mind and that her statement was intended to be an understated endorsement of Clements. During the month, most of the presidential hopefuls of the Republican party endorsed Clements and appeared with him. The joint appearance of Governor Reagan and former President Ford at a campaign dinner for Clements in Dallas drew widespread attention in the media, reinforcing Clements's exposure in five-minute biographical ads which showed him as a folksy but hardheaded businessman, an obvious contrast to his diffident lawyer-politician opponent.[54]

During the early fall, Clements's credibility as a candidate grew until it far surpassed that of Republican gubernatorial candidates of the past. By the beginning of October even John Hill began to see him as serious opposition, though both Hill's and Clements's polls indicated that the Democrat seemed to enjoy a safe lead. In mid-October, Hill's polling consultants showed him holding 53.5 percent of the vote, a lead that might well be sustained with an energetic campaign finish. Cranking up a campaign in October, however, proved more easily said than done. Hill's earlier assurance lulled his urban campaign workers into half-efforts; worse yet, it permitted Clements's work in the countryside, which immobilized many of Hill's potential workers or actually brought them into the Republican campaign. By way of compensation, Hill intensified his personal efforts in urban areas, particularly in San Antonio, where he needed a large turnout, and in Houston, his designated home-town, where he trailed in the polls. It was nonetheless clear that his casual campaign in the summer of 1978 would prove costly.[55]

Clements's campaign meanwhile proceeded with hard-punching "issues" commercials on radio and television, targeted with a finely tuned interlock of careful polling and media budgeting. The Hill group apparently ceased its opinion survey work in October, but V. Lance Tarrance Associates continued to follow opinion changes and their apparent causes through 125 daily interviews. In October, Tarrance discovered that nearly half of the likely voters were undecided in regard to the Clements-Hill race, though most had made up their minds in the Tower-Krueger contest. In response to these findings Clements's phone bank operations and door-to-door work were increased. Nearly a million phone calls were made from mid-October to early November, half of them on election day. A quarter of their likely supporters were called by the Clements volunteers on the eve of the election, while Hill's workers reached only 8 percent of theirs. Clements's managers used daily poll results to target media coverage. When it was clear that Clements's margin in Dallas was slipping during early November, as Hill attracted disproportionate numbers of voters who were making up their minds, an additional ten thousand dollars was committed to the Dallas area for media exposure. In short, as the critical number of undecided voters were deciding between Hill and Clements, the Republican campaign was moving in high gear with flawless survey work and carefully measured responses.[56]

During the final week of the campaign, members of the black caucus in the legislature campaigned intensively in East and Gulf Coast areas of Texas, a last-ditch effort to interest their own constituents in the gubernatorial contest. During the same period, Hill campaigned through the precincts of south and west San Antonio in a last minute attempt to rouse Mexican-American voters. After this effort, little more was done; apparently Hill took victory for granted. But the final Clements poll, taken on November 5, showed him ahead of Hill by six-tenths of one percent, a slim lead well within the margin of error. Clements predicted victory in a dead heat race, which was exactly how the race came out: he won by eight-tenths of one percent of the vote for governor.[57]

Reactions to Clements's victory came quickly. One longtime Republican worker exuded delight mingled with disbelief: "Hot damn! Is it for real? I've waited thirty years for this." Understandably, state chairman Ray Barnhart shared the joy: "The Lord smiled on Tuesday!" he said. Billie Carr, liberal Democratic national committeewoman, did not: "It looks like Texas is now a two-party state," she lamented. These reactions anticipated the final tally, for slow counts and recounts dragged through November. Apprehensive of a stolen election, the GOP sent a legal team, headed by Justice Garwood, to every tally session in Austin. According to one party official, the ballot security program was not discontinued until Bill Clements took the oath of office.[58]

Most spur-of-the-moment analyses of Clements's victory fell back on the belief that voter turnout had been abnormally low; John Hill, in other words, had not gotten enough voters to the polls. While low voter turnout had helped the GOP in past elections, however, the turnout of registered voters for the 1978 general election was by no means especially low. Forty-two percent of Texas's registered voters cast ballots in the 1978 gubernatorial race: only 31 percent had done so in the previous off-year election in 1974. Examination of election returns shows that voter turnout was not so much low as uneven. Of the ninety-six counties carried by Clements, only seven had a turnout lower than 40 percent, while nearly half of the Hill counties fell below the 40 percent mark. Of the twenty principal urban counties, Clements carried eleven; none of his counties had a turnout of less than 40 percent. Of the urban counties for Hill, four fell below the mark and five exceeded the statewide average by only a narrow margin. Throughout Texas, in Clements's areas of support a greater percentage of registered voters went to the polls than turned out in areas carried by Hill. Clements was the more successful at turning out his vote.[59]

Various theories were offered to explain the uneven character of turnout in 1978. One argument held that Mexican-American voters let Hill down. Data presented by the well-regarded Southwest Voter Registration Education Project, based in San Antonio, revealed that while the turnout in predominantly Mexican-American precincts was higher in 1978 than it had been in 1974, only 27 percent of registered voters in these precincts went to the polls. But Clements's advisors saw more than a letdown in the data: in their view, Hill failed to rouse Mexican-American loyalties, while Clements was careful not to excite apprehension. Like their Anglo counterparts in rural areas, some lifelong Mexican-American Democrats simply preferred Clements to Hill; they resolved the tension between established voting habits and the appeal of the Republican candidate by deciding not to vote at all. Postelection polling by Tarrance confirmed this point of view.

As for the competition for Mexican-American votes offered by La Raza Unida, that party's candidate, Mario C. Compean, received less than one percent of the total vote. La Raza may have taken some votes from John Hill, but most of its supporters, particularly in Bexar, Reeves, and Zavala counties, were alienated from both major parties. Unlike La Raza's inroads upon Briscoe's vote in 1972, its support in 1978 probably did not represent defection of those who would have supported Hill.[60] But the analysis of election results offered by Democratic State Chairman Billy Goldberg was equally plausible: ". . . we just got outworked and outorganized. They did much better at getting out their votes." The Clements and Tower campaigns were simply more effective where it counted, at precinct level. In this sense, the slow and uncertain work of building grass-roots organization, begun in earnest in 1952 and refined progressively during the 1960s and 1970s, finally paid off in 1978.[61]

A complementary explanation of the outcome of the gubernatorial election may be developed from John Hill's failure to hold the Democratic coalition together. In many instances conservative Democrats, particularly those in rural areas, either stayed at home or voted for Clements. The combined effects of Project 230 and of unsolicited defections, therefore, were probably sufficient to swing thirty-two counties from the Democratic column. Clements carried these counties with the support of rural Democrats; thirty of these same counties had gone for Dolph Briscoe in the Democratic primary. By writing off Briscoe's following, Hill lost votes which might have brought him to victory.[62]

TABLE 1

VOTES FOR REPUBLICAN CANDIDATES IN SELECTED URBAN COUNTIES, 1972-1978

County	1972 President	1972 Governor	1976 President	1978 Governor	1978 U.S. Senator
Bexar	60.0%	44.1%	45.3%	47.6%	48.6%
Bowie	26.2	37.8	43.5	49.3	49.4
Cameron	60.9	47.8	39.4	44.5	48.2
Dallas	70.2	60.4	57.3	58.8	54.9
Ector	79.7	59.7	63.7	72.3	59.7
El Paso	60.6	47.7	48.4	42.5	47.3
Galveston	57.8	49.2	40.0	47.5	41.5
Grayson	70.7	40.8	38.6	47.6	45.8
Gregg	78.9	49.3	64.1	57.5	60.2
Harris	62.9	56.1	52.6	53.2	60.5
Hidalgo	55.5	41.6	35.4	43.4	45.7
Jefferson	60.5	45.5	40.5	40.1	41.3
Lubbock	73.9	52.9	60.8	55.4	58.4
McLennan	67.7	41.0	45.5	48.9	48.9
Midland	81.2	63.1	71.3	74.9	69.9
Nueces	55.6	41.1	38.3	45.5	47.6
Potter	75.1	59.1	53.7	51.0	50.7
Randall	84.2	65.5	65.4	61.3	62.5
Smith	74.6	51.6	56.9	58.0	57.0
Tarrant	68.7	55.7	50.4	52.6	52.4
Taylor	78.8	50.1	57.8	56.9	54.9
Tom Green	72.1	47.3	52.7	53.8	46.6
Travis	56.6	39.9	47.5	44.5	47.0
Webb	41.6	18.1	28.9	35.7	33.0
Wichita	69.7	41.3	46.4	47.8	50.1
TEXAS	66.6	48.4	48.4	50.4	50.3

SOURCES: Richard M. Scammon, ed., *America Votes* 10 (Washington, D.C.: Congressional Quarterly, 1973): 351-58; Richard M. Scammon and Alice V. McGillivray, eds., *America Votes* 12 (Washington, D.C.: Congressional Quarterly, 1977): 352-55; "General Election Returns, November 7, 1978," typescript, Office of the Secretary of State of Texas.

At least part of the explanation of the outcome in 1978, however, rests in the personalities of Clements and Hill. The latter, more conventionally polished and considerably more experienced at the politician's craft, failed to inspire either deep respect or fear among his associates and workers. They neither rose, nor were they driven, to a strenuous second effort when one was needed. By contrast, in the Clements camp the candidate was generally viewed with strong admiration, mingled with legitimate apprehension of the consequences of not doing well. Clements's unwavering confidence and unswerving determination prompted the best efforts of his staff, both paid and volunteer. John Hill's defeat rested on a single remarkable error of judgment: he mounted an unexceptional campaign against an uncommon opponent.

In significant measure, Bill Clements's election was a personal victory, which was based on a commanding personality and a remarkable will to win.

Other Republican candidates for statewide office did not run as well as Clements and Tower. Jim Baker, a prominent Houston attorney and manager of Gerald Ford's presidential campaign in 1976, challenged Mark White for the office of attorney general. With a million-dollar campaign fund and a statewide effort, Baker became the most credible and visible Republican candidate for that post in many years. His opponent, Mark White, enjoyed wider name recognition as the incumbent secretary of state, and he held the unified support of Democrats. Thus, though he added significantly to the "Republican third" of the vote, Baker lost to White by a 12 percent margin. Gaylord Marshall, candidate for lieutenant governor, and Jim Lacy, an independent oilman from Midland who ran for railroad commissioner, ran less well. Marshall was seriously underfunded; he ran a limited campaign against incumbent Bill Hobby, who received nearly two-thirds of the vote. Lacy's opponent, incumbent John Poerner, formerly a state legislator and a member of Dolph Briscoe's staff, took about 62 percent of the vote.

Local contests were, nonetheless, waged by Republican candidates to some advantage. Party nominees ran with opposition for twenty-nine positions in the Texas House of Representatives, winning five of these seats, seventeen that were not contested, and one more in a special election shortly thereafter. By the date of Bill Clements's inauguration, there were twenty-three Republicans in the Texas House and four in the Senate, a record to date. Courthouse victories were recorded in Collin, Lipscomb, Kerr, Gray, Mason, Midland, Randall, and Smith counties, where candidates for county judge won elections. In addition several Republicans, including two GOP candidates in Dallas, were elected to state courts.[63]

In several congressional districts it is possible that local contests turned out additional voters who supported Clements and Tower. Major contests were waged in nine districts, with hot races in Dallas, Houston, the Waco area, in the north San Antonio–West Texas district represented by Bob Krueger, in the Permian Basin, and in the Mid-Cities district of the Dallas–Fort Worth area. In Dallas, Tom Pauken aggressively challenged incumbent Jim Mattox, losing by only nine hundred votes. In a rematch of two previous contests, one of which he had won, Dr. Ron Paul opposed and defeated Bob Gammage. In Central Texas,

Jack Burgess unsuccessfully faced Marvin Leath for the seat held for decades by Omar Burleson, running about 3 percent behind the Democrat. In the 21st District, Tom Loeffler, who had worked for both Gerald Ford and John Tower, ran a tightly organized, well-financed, and victorious campaign against former State Senator Nelson Wolff for the Krueger seat, cutting sharply into whatever coattails effect Krueger's candidacy might have had for other Democrats in that region.

Much the same happened in the Lubbock-Midland-Odessa area, where George Bush, Jr., ran against State Senator Kent Hance for the seat vacated by George Mahon. Bush's campaign helped produce a turnout of 53 percent of the registered voters in Midland County, the highest rate in a major urban center of the state. In the Mid-Cities district, Leo Berman ran again, against Martin Frost, who had defeated Representative Dale Milford in the Democratic primary, winning about 46 percent of the vote. It is likely that all of these contests had some effect on the statewide contests, though it is not possible to determine the extent of it with precision. In themselves, the results of the congressional contests had considerable significance, for two more Republican congressmen were sent to Washington.[64]

What did the general election of 1978 mean? To Texas Democrats it indicated the imperative need to rebuild their party, starting at the precinct level. To Texas Republicans, it signaled a return to the governor's office after an absence of more than a century. Did it signal a long-term reversal of political fortunes? Bo Byers again expressed the reactions of most seasoned observers: "Yes, this is the day of the Republican and Republican Bill Clements should enjoy it. But whether that day evolves into a lasting era is a question not to be answered for some years to come."[65] In some measure, the answer will rest on the course of national politics; perhaps in equal measure it will depend on Bill Clements. In any case, the place of Clements's victory in the longer course of Texas politics will depend on future developments in both parties. If the Democrats succeed in revamping their political machine and construct an effective modern organization from the assorted scraps of the current nineteenth-century model, and if they find candidates who have personal appeal of sufficient strength to hold the ungainly coalition together, Clements's victory may prove to be a short-lived aberration. If, however, the Republicans can both maintain their newly established credibility with conservative rural Democrats and avoid debilitating factional squabbles in their own ranks, the election of Bill Clements might well mark the beginning of a new era in Texas politics. In any event, the election of 1978 signaled the long-awaited arrival of competitive politics in Texas. After the delusions of the 1920s, the slow growth of the 1950s, the mingled hopes and frustrations of the 1960s, the Republicans brought real two-party politics to Texas in 1978.

Notes

CHAPTER ONE

1. *Dallas Times Herald*, September 18, 1920; *Dallas Dispatch*, September 18, 1920.

2. Edgar Eugene Robinson, *The Presidential Vote, 1896-1932* (Palo Alto, California: Stanford University Press, 1933), pp. 178-84; Richard M. Scammon, *America at the Polls* (Pittsburgh: University of Pittsburgh Press, 1965), pp. 426-30; *San Antonio Express*, March 5, 1921.

3. The so-called German counties are Austin, Calhoun, Colorado, Comal, Dewitt, Fayette, Gillespie, Goliad, Guadalupe, Kendall, Kerr, Lavaca, Lee, Mason, Victoria, and Washington. In theory, these counties tend to be Republican through the historical extension of their Unionist sympathy during the Civil War. This notion has been disproved for a later period, 1948 through 1961, by James R. Soukup, Clifton McCleskey, and Harry Holloway in *Party and Factional Division in Texas* (Austin: University of Texas Press, 1964), pp. 37-40.

4. *Who's Who in America* (Chicago: A. H. Marquis Co., 1943), p. 762.

5. The percentage of the popular vote cast for Harding in the various southern states was as follows: Texas 28.5, Arkansas 40.5, Louisiana 30.6, Tennessee 55.4, Kentucky 49.8, Mississippi 14.3, Alabama 32.4, Georgia 44.0, South Carolina 3.9, North Carolina 43.3, and Virginia 38.2; see Scammon, *America at the Polls, passim.*

6. Robert K. Murray, *The Harding Era* (Minneapolis: University of Minnesota Press, 1969), pp. 21, 27. State chairman Phil E. Baer, former national committeeman E. H. R. Green (the son of Hetty Green), and leaders of the Black and Tan faction in the Texas Republican party were inclined to support General Leonard Wood, while McGregor was noncommittal as far as Harding was concerned, until the state convention. See Frank E. Scobey to Warren G. Harding, February 3, 11, 12, 1920; H. F. McGregor to Frank E. Scobey, April 24, 1920; Frank E. Scobey to Warren G. Harding, December 29, 1920, microfilm roll 263, Warren G. Harding

Papers, Ohio Historical Society (hereafter cited as WGH Papers). The conventional wisdom on the subject of trading delegates for patronage was expressed by Victor O. Key, Jr., *Southern Politics* (New York: Alfred A. Knopf, 1949), pp. 34, 287, 292, 294-95.

7. Murray, *The Harding Era*, pp. 4, 32; Malcolm Moos, *The Republicans: A History of Their Party* (New York: Random House, 1956), p. 319.

8. *San Antonio Express*, August 10, 1916.

9. Born in Ohio in 1866, Frank E. Scobey served as sheriff of Miami County in 1902, when Warren G. Harding successfully sought election to the state senate from that area. Through Harding's efforts, Scobey became clerk of the Ohio State Senate in 1902. He held the post until 1906, when he moved to Texas. Harding's long and close association, which included several visits to Scobey in San Antonio, led local newspapermen to speculate that he would become a "Second Colonel House," upon Harding's election in 1920 (*New York Times*, November 4, 1920). Their long association is recorded in the following items: Harding to Scobey, December 7, 1916; Scobey to Arthur W. McMahon, June 12, 1922; Scobey to Harding, December 31, 1914, January 27, 1915, November 9, 1914; Scobey to Harry M. Daugherty, February 23, 1920; Harding to Scobey, December 6, 1917, microfilm roll 263, WGH Papers; *San Antonio Express*, January 27, 1915; *Dallas Morning News*, November 3, 4, 1920. See also Roger M. Olien, "The Man Who Never Became a Colonel House," *West Texas Historical Association Yearbook* (1975), pp. 13-23.

10. Scobey to Harry M. Daugherty, January 8, 1916; Scobey to Harding, November 9, 1914; Harding to Charles D. Hilles, May 27, 1916; Harding general letter of introduction for Scobey, May 27, 1916, microfilm roll 263, WGH Papers; Murray, *The Harding Era*, pp. 21-22.

11. Frank E. Scobey to Malcolm Jennings, July 19, 1922, microfilm roll 263, WGH Papers.

12. Harding to Scobey, December 13, 1915; Scobey to Harding, January 8, 1916; Scobey to Daugherty, January 8, 1916; Daugherty to Scobey, December 4, 1919; Daugherty to Scobey, January 17, 1916, microfilm roll 263, WGH Papers.

13. Creager was the attorney for F. W. Fordyce's American Rio Grande Land Company, with which Scobey did business as the owner of the Rhodes and Saens tracts of the Mercedes Plantation in Hidalgo County. DuVal West, who was appointed United States District Court judge by Woodrow Wilson in 1917, did land work for Fordyce and Creager; see F. W. Fordyce to Scobey, October 25, October 27, 1915, February 18, 1918, December 4, 1918, microfilm roll 263, WGH Papers.

14. Scobey to Harding, June 13, 1918; Harding to Scobey, September 2, 1919; Scobey to Daugherty, December 1, 1919, microfilm roll 263, WGH Papers; Murray, *The Harding Era*, pp. 4-27.

15. *Dallas Times Herald*, September 18, 1920; Scobey to Harding, April 20, May 7, 1921; Harding to Scobey, May 12, 1921; R. B. Creager to Elmer Dover, February 15, 1922, microfilm roll 228, WGH Papers.

16. Scobey to Harding, December 29, 1920, March 18, 1921; W. F. McGregor to Harding, March 17, 1921; Creager to Harding, January 24, 1922; W. H. Hays to Harding, August 29, 1921, microfilm roll 203; Daugherty to Harding, April 26, 1921, microfilm roll 263, WGH Papers; *San Antonio Express*, March 10, 1921.

17. Harding to Will Hays, August 26, 1921, microfilm roll 203; Harding to Scobey, March 21, May 12, 1921, microfilm roll 263; Harding to Creager, May 11, 1921, microfilm roll 228, WGH Papers. In 1921, Harding was making a special effort to get along with the Republican Congress. By the summer of 1922, his natural affability had given way to general frustration and frequent impatience shown even with close friends in the Senate; see Murray, *The Harding Era*, pp. 314-15.

18. Creager to Harding, May 6, 1921, microfilm roll 228; H. F. McGregor to

Harding, April 4, 1921, microfilm roll 203; Harding to Scobey, May 2, 1921, Scobey to Harding, April 20, 1921, microfilm roll 263; Creager to Harding, April 6, 1921, microfilm roll 228; Scobey to Nicholas Longworth, November 24, 1924, Scobey to Calvin Coolidge, February 3, 1925; Scobey to Charles G. Dawes, February 24, February 28, April 9, May 10, May 23, June 18, 1928, microfilm roll 263, WGH Papers; *San Antonio Express*, August 15, 1912, June 12, 14, 1928; *Dallas Times Herald*, December 6, 1946; Daugherty to Harding, April 26, 1921, microfilm roll 203, WGH Papers.

19. Scobey to George Griffith, April 3, 1923; Scobey to I. T. Pryor, April 3, 1923; Scobey to "Fred," November 30, 1926; Scobey to Evaland Scobey (Mrs. Frank E. Scobey), August 29, 1923, microfilm roll 263, WGH Papers.

20. Scobey to Charles G. Dawes, February 24, 1928; Scobey to Calvin Coolidge, February 3, 1925, microfilm roll 262, WGH Papers; *New York Times*, February 7, 1931; Murray, *The Harding Era*, pp. 300-301.

21. The photographs are located in the papers of Eugene Nolte, Sr., San Antonio, Texas. Identification was made by Helen Ackenhausen of Dallas, who held various staff positions and offices in the state party from 1926 to 1933 and from 1936 through 1947.

22. Creager to Harding, September 2, 1920, microfilm roll 72; Scobey to Harding, April 9, 1919, microfilm roll 263, WGH Papers; Sam H. Acheson et al., *Texian Who's Who* (Dallas: Texian Co., 1937), p. 108; interview with Carlos Watson, Brownsville, Texas, May 7, 1971; Joe Robert Baulch, "James B. Wells: South Texas Economic and Political Leader" (Ph.D. diss., Texas Tech University, 1974), pp. 184, 262, 265.

23. H. H. Herren to Herbert Hoover, May 27, 1929, "States-Texas," Subject File: Republican National Committee, Hoover Papers, Herbert Hoover Presidential Library (hereafter cited as HHPL); *Senate Report 272*, 71st Cong., 2d sess., pp. 25, 29.

24. *Official Register, Persons in the Civil, Military, and Naval Services of the United States, and List of Vessels, 1911* (Washington, D.C.: Government Printing Office, 1911, 1: 248; interview with Carlos Watson, Brownsville, Texas, May 7, 1971; "Equity No. 529: Fidelity-Philadelphia *v.* Houston Gas and Fuel Company, United States District Court, Southern District of Texas, September 24, 1932," Box 32046, Federal Records Center, Fort Worth, Texas; Creager to Harding, September 2, 1920, microfilm roll 72; Scobey to Dawes, May 23, 1928, microfilm roll 263, WGH Papers; *Senate Report 272*, 71st Cong., 2d sess., p. 32. There is little concrete evidence to substantiate Scobey's charges.

25. *New York Times*, May 18, 1935; R. B. Creager to Herbert Hoover, February 17, 1935, and November 12, 1938; "R. B. Creager," Post-Presidential Papers, Hoover Papers, HHPL; William J. Hamilton, President and General Manager, Illind Oil Company, to R. Olien, August 27, 1975.

26. Neither the Harding Papers nor the Hoover Papers contain any specific evidence of Creager's having been offered any post in the federal government at any time. The various rumors of appointments appeared in the *Dallas Times Herald*, November 3, 1920, *New York Times*, December 16, 1923, and *San Antonio Express*, November 7, 1928. President Harding was aware that Creager wished to succeed Will Hays as postmaster general, but Harding put him off. Harding to Creager, January 1, 1922, microfilm roll 228, WGH Papers.

27. *Dallas Morning News*, April 17, 1921. A longtime Creager associate, Carlos Watson, remarked, "We put our friends on the Headquarters Committee." Interview, May 24, 1971, Brownsville, Texas.

28. R. B. Creager to Charles Hubbard, February 5, 1922, microfilm roll 228; Creager to Harding, March 8, 1922, microfilm roll 203, WGH Papers; Mrs. Ruby R. Erdwinn to R. Olien, March 18, 1971. Mrs. Erdwinn was the secretary to the director of organization from 1921 until 1926; interview with Helen Ackenhausen,

March 9, 1971, Dallas, Texas; *The Press of Texas Comments on the Patronage Investigation* (Dallas: Republican State Headquarters, 1929).

29. Acheson et al., *Texian Who's Who*, p. 271; *Fort Worth Star-Telegram*, February 3, 1930; *Dallas Morning News*, February 4, 1930; Mrs. Ruby Erdwinn to R. Olien, March 18, 1971.

30. See, for example, the Orville Bullington file, "Judiciary—Judges, Circuit Judge—Circuit 5," Box 175, Presidential Papers, HHPL.

31. *Dallas Times Herald*, June 8, 1931.

32. Murray, *The Harding Era*, pp. 67-68; Victor O. Key, Jr., *Political Parties and Pressure Groups*, 5th ed. (New York: Thomas Y. Crowell Co., 1964), p. 494; "The Press of Texas Comments on the Patronage Investigation"; Mrs. Ruby Erdwinn to R. Olien, March 18, 1971. Republican State Chairman Eugene Nolte signed a note for $1,200 on June 30, 1927, and George Butte paid a regular subscription of $250 on March 14, 1932 (Nolte Papers). Federal employees were commonly asked for "donations." Senator Smith W. Brookhardt reported that 242 out of the 350 signers of notes were employees of the Post Office Department; *Senate Report 272*, 71st Cong., 2d sess., p. 21. Earlier, when funds were raised for the Harding Memorial, employees in the office of the collector of internal revenue, Austin, contributed $5,271.90. Their names and amounts of their contributions went to the state chairman through Collector James W. Bass. This method of raising funds seems to have been common to both political parties. William Mosher found, in 1932, that a large percentage of party members at precinct conventions across the country were government employees; "Party and Government Control at the Grass Roots," *National Municipal Review*, January, 1935, p. 16.

33. This subject is discussed extensively in chap. 2.

34. See "Revised Statutes, 1911; articles 3110 and 3085," *Vernon's Annotated Texas Statutes*, Election Code, 389/519, 478-484; *Acts of the First Called Session of the 37th Legislature*, chap. 60 (Austin: The Secretary of State, 1922), p. 230. The legal decision which summarized previous opinions regarding the Republican party as an unregulated private association was Wall *v.* Currie, (1948), 147, T. 127, 213 SW2d, 816. See also "Opinion of the Attorney General of the State of Texas" (1948, No. 547) and Seay *v.* Latham (1944), 143, T.1, 182 SW2b, 251, 155A, LR180.

35. Scammon, *America at the Polls*, pp. 431-35; Helen Ackenhausen, "Radio Address over KGMB, Honolulu, Hawaii, June 13, 1931," Ackenhausen Papers, Dallas.

36. Interview with Carlos Watson, May 7, 1971, Brownsville, Texas.

37. "Dallas County Republican Executive Committee, Minutes of Meeting Held at Room 206, Hilton Hotel, July 13, 1926, 8 o'clock," George S. Atkinson Papers, Dallas, Texas.

38. Interview with Sarah Menezes, January 27, 1971, Irving, Texas.

39. "List of Republican Primary Election, July 24, 1926," Atkinson Papers; *Dallas Morning News*, November 5, 1924, July 26, 1926.

40. Acheson et al., *Texian Who's Who*, p. 451; Scobey to Dawes, February 8, 1928, microfilm roll 263; Creager to Hubbard, February 5, 1922, microfilm roll 228, WGH Papers; Creager to Hoover, June 1, 1929, "Republican National Committee," President's Personal Files, HHPL.

41. "Official Roster to and including County Chairmen, Republican Party of Texas, October 1, 1928," Eugene Nolte, Sr., Papers (hereafter cited as Nolte Papers); *Registers of Appointments of Postmaster*, Vol. 100 (Texas, 1904-1930), National Archives; *Senate Report 272*, 71st Cong., 2d sess., p. 26.

42. Creager to Hoover, June 1, 1929, "Republican National Committee," President's Personal Files, HHPL.

43. *Texas Almanac and State Industrial Guide, 1941-1942* (Dallas: A. H. Belo Corp., 1941), pp. 309-10.

44. "Minutes of the Republican National Committee" 3 (1924): 439. The

records are housed in Eisenhower Center, Office of the Republican National Committee, Washington, D.C.

45. The 1946 incident is described extensively in chap. 4.

46. "Minutes of a Meeting of the Republican State Executive Committee in the Hotel Adolphus at Dallas, Texas, June 14, 1926," Nolte Papers; *Official Register, 1911,* 1:606.

47. Interview with Sam Acheson, November 3, 1970, Dallas, Texas; interview with Sarah Menezes, January 27, 1971, Irving, Texas. Mrs. Menezes was a delegate to several state conventions.

48. Alexander Heard and Donald S. Strong, *Southern Primaries and Elections, 1920-1949* (University, Alabama: University of Alabama Press, 1950), pp. 163-65; *Dallas Morning News,* November 18, 1932.

49. R. B. Creager to Thomas B. Love, February 17, 1927, June 11, 1927, "Misc. Corres., 1927-1929," Thomas B. Love Papers, Dallas Historical Society, Dallas, Texas.

50. For a general discussion of the Black and Tan party, see Paul Casdorph, *A History of the Republican Party in Texas, 1865-1964* (Austin: Pemberton Press, 1965), pp. 46-97.

51. Interview with Helen Ackenhausen, November 21, 1970, Dallas, Texas; Walter Newton, Memorandum, 11-13-31, "U. S. District Judge: Texas," Box 178, Presidential Papers, HHPL; Hon. Miriam A. Ferguson to Eugene Nolte, March 1, 1926; Hon. Ross Sterling to Eugene Nolte, September 23, 1931, Nolte Papers; Soupkup et al., *Party and Factional Division in Texas,* pp. 67-167; R. B. Creager to Charles D. Hilles, May 29, 1935, Box 204, Charles D. Hilles Papers, Sterling Memorial Library, Yale University (hereafter cited as Hilles Papers); O. B. Colquitt to Herbert Hoover, July 22, 1929; "Texas-C," Box 13, Subject File: Republican National Committee: Texas, Hoover Papers, HHPL.

52. *Dallas Times Herald,* October 22, 1922, November 2, 7, 8, 1922; *Dallas Morning News,* November 2, 1924; *San Antonio Express,* November 1, 2, 4, 5, 7, 9, 1924; *Dallas Times Herald,* October 23, 27, November 1, 1932.

CHAPTER TWO

1. *San Antonio Express,* November 3, 4, 1920; Creager to Harding, March 22, 1922, microfilm roll 228, WGH Papers.

2. *Biographical Directory of the American Congress, 1774-1961* (Washington, D.C.: Government Printing Office, 1962), pp. 1853-54; Creager to Harding, May 15, 1921, microfilm roll 228; Harding to Will H. Hayes, August 16, 1921, microfilm roll 203, WGH Papers; R. B. Creager, form letter to members of the Republican State Executive Committee (Texas), March 27, 1926, "H. W. Wurzbach," Commerce Papers, HHPL.

3. U.S., Congress, *Congressional Record,* 67th Cong., 1st sess., pp. 3571-74; 69th Cong., 1st sess., pp. 449-50; 70th Cong., 1st sess., p. 5516.

4. *Congressional Record,* 67th Cong., 2d sess., pp. 2030, 4208-9, 9341-42; 68th Cong., 1st sess., pp. 2101-3, 3588-89; 71st Cong., 2d sess., pp. 9673-75.

5. *Congressional Record,* 69th Cong., 1st sess., p. 3479; *New York Times,* February 7, 1926; *San Antonio Express,* November 2, 1928; *Congressional Record,* 67th Cong., 2d sess., p. 31; 67th Cong., 3d sess., p. 6; 67th Cong., 4th sess., pp. 2036-38.

6. *Congressional Record,* 68th Cong., 1st sess., pp. 2523-2780; 67th Cong., 2d sess., pp. 1794-95; 69th Cong., 1st sess., p. 4940; *New York Times,* June 8, 1926.

7. Frank E. Scobey to Warren G. Harding, December 29, 1920; Harding to Scobey, January 4, 1921, microfilm roll 263, WGH Papers.

8. *San Antonio Express,* July 21, 1926.

9. Creager to Harding, July 18, 1922, and Harding to Creager, July 31, 1922, microfilm roll 228, WGH Papers; *San Antonio Express,* July 21, 1926; Creager to W. J. Harris, March 27, 1926, Nolte Papers.

10. *San Antonio Express*, November 2, 1922; interview with Joe Sheldon, February 9, 1971, San Antonio, Texas.

11. *San Antonio Express*, November 3, 1922; interview with Joe Sheldon, February 9, 1971, San Antonio, Texas.

12. *San Antonio Express*, November 4, 5, 6, 7, 1922; interview with Joe Sheldon, February 9, 1971, San Antonio, Texas.

13. *San Antonio Express*, July 21, 1926.

14. *New York Times*, January 29, 31, February 10, 15, April 1, 13, 1924.

15. *San Antonio Express*, November 5, 6, 1924; Paul Casdorph, *A History of the Republican Party in Texas, 1865-1964* (Austin: Pemberton Press, 1965), p. 258; interview with Joe Sheldon, February 9, 1971, San Antonio, Texas.

16. *Dallas Morning News*, February 18, 1926; *Dallas Times Herald*, February 12, 1926; *San Antonio Express*, July 13, 1926; Creager to Herbert Hoover, February 23, 1926, copy, Nolte Papers. This charge was picked up later by Senator Smith W. Brookhardt and by the *Dallas Morning News*, Senate Report 272, 71st Cong., 2d sess., p. 20; *Dallas Morning News*, November 18, 1932; *New York Times*, March 4, 15, 23, June 8, 1926.

17. *New York Times*, March 15, 17, 1926, February 4, 1927.

18. *New York Times*, June 23, 1926.

19. "Minutes of a Meeting of the Republican State Executive Committee Held in the Hotel Adolphus at Dallas, Texas, June 14, 1926," Nolte Papers. Creager explained his actions to Herbert Hoover in a letter (February 23, 1926, copy, Nolte Papers); *San Antonio Express*, July 13, 1926; R. B. Creager, form letter to members of the Republican State Executive Committee (Texas), March 27, 1926; "H. W. Wurzbach," Commerce Papers, HHPL.

20. Primary elections in both parties were funded by the collection of filing fees (*San Antonio Express*, July 1, 2, 4, 14, 20, 1926); the Republican party paid the expenses of litigation against Wurzbach (F. L. Thompson to Eugene Nolte, January 20, 1927, Nolte Papers).

21. *San Antonio Express*, July 21, 1926.

22. *San Antonio Express*, July 24, 25, October 27, 31, November 3, 4, 5, 1926.

23. *Congressional Record*, 69th Cong., 1st sess., p. 4940.

24. Creager to Hubbard, February 5, 1922, microfilm roll 228; Creager to Harding, March 8, 1922, microfilm roll 203, WGH Papers.

25. Leonard Withington to Hoover, March 4, 1926, copy, Nolte Papers. At the 1924 Republican National Convention, in league with C. Bascomb Slemp, national committeeman for Virginia and an old-time conventioneer, Creager delivered the old guard delegations from the South to Calvin Coolidge. In return, Creager and other southern party leaders were promised control of federal patronage in their states. Donald R. McCoy, *Calvin Coolidge* (New York: Macmillan Co., 1967), p. 197; Guy B. Hathorn, "The Political Career of C. Bascomb Slemp" (Ph.D. diss., Duke University, 1950), pp. 199, 205.

26. For example, see Leonard Withington to Mark Requa, June 7, 1929, "Republican National Committee—Texas," Box 228, Presidential Papers, HHPL.

27. *San Antonio Express*, May 22, August 15, 1928; *Dallas Journal*, January 16, 1928; McCoy, *Calvin Coolidge*, pp. 64-65; *New York Times*, November 4, December 10, 1927, April 9, 1928; Malcolm Moos, *The Republicans: A History of Their Party* (New York: Random House, 1956), p. 371; Scobey to Dawes, June 18, 1928: "Our friend Wurzbach is absolutely a mess as a leader. He couldn't lead a horse to a trough and have him drink" (microfilm roll 263, WGH Papers). This estimation of Wurzbach's managerial abilities is shared by Joe Sheldon, who managed several of the congressman's campaigns for reelection; interview with Joe Sheldon, February 9, 1971, San Antonio, Texas.

28. Creager to Nolte, January 2, 1928, Nolte Papers; *New York Times*, January 4, 1928; Wurzbach to C. Littleton, March 7, 1928, copy, Nolte Papers; *San Antonio*

Express, February 10, 1928; "Draft of a Resolution written by Harry M. Wurzbach to be introduced by Littleton at the Republican State Executive Committee Meeting before the Convention," n.d., Nolte Papers.

29. *San Antonio Express*, May 10, 1928.

30. *Hearings on Contests before the Republican National Committee*, June 6, 1928, vol. 3, Republican National Committee, Washington, D.C., pp. 537-73, 698; *New York Times*, June 7, 1928.

31. *Official Proceedings of the Nineteenth Republican National Convention* (New York: Tenny Press, 1928), pp. 54-58, 68.

32. Creager to Hoover, June 14, 1929; Clarence E. Linz to Hoover, April 3, 1929; W. E. Talbot to Hoover, April 3, 1929; all in "Republican National Committee—Texas," Box 228, Presidential Papers, HHPL (neither Linz nor Talbot revealed his business association with Creager in Hidalgo County Real Estate); McCoy, *Calvin Coolidge*, pp. 64-65; Robert K. Murray, *The Harding Era* (Minneapolis: University of Minnesota Press, 1969), p. 192; Moos, *The Republicans*, p. 383.

33. Press release of Hoover for President, New York State Committee, April 11, 1928; "Report #5," October 8, 1928, Hoover-Curtis Organizational Bureau; "Report #8," October 27, 1928, Hoover-Curtis Organizational Bureau, Box 91, Pre-Presidential Papers, HHPL.

34. O. Douglas Weeks, "The South in National Politics," in Avery Leiserson, ed., *The American South in the 1960's* (New York: Frederick A. Praeger, 1964), pp. 224-25; Charles C. Alexander, *Crusade for Conformity: The Ku Klux Klan in Texas, 1920-1930* (Houston: Texas Gulf Coast Historical Association, 1962), p. 179.

35. *Dallas Morning News*, November 17, 1928; J. V. Hardy to George W. Armstrong, December 19, 1930, File A, Miscellaneous Correspondence, 1930, Thomas B. Love Papers, Dallas Historical Society (hereafter cited as Love Papers); interview with Helen Ackenhausen, March 9, 1971, Dallas, Texas.

36. Richard M. Scammon, ed., *America at the Polls* (Pittsburgh: University of Pittsburgh Press, 1965), pp. 431-35; Moos, *The Republicans*, pp. 375-76.

37. *Biographical Directory of the American Congress, 1774-1961*, p. 1286; *San Antonio Express*, November 2, 1928; interview with Joe Sheldon, February 9, 1971, San Antonio, Texas.

38. *San Antonio Express*, November 7, 8, 9, 10, 11, 13, 15, 16, 18, 21, 1928, January 9, 10, 1929. It was possible for the number of actual voters to exceed the number of voters who had paid poll taxes because those exempt from the tax did not appear on the poll tax rolls as registered. There is, however, no indication that this argument was used by the Democrats in their defense.

39. *San Antonio Express*, January 11, February 21, 23, 24, 25, 1929.

40. *San Antonio Express*, February 21, 23, 25, 27, 28, March 1, 8, 1929.

41. *San Antonio Light*, February 23, 1929; *San Antonio Express*, February 25, 1929.

42. *New York Times*, November 19, 1928, February 11, 1930; *Congressional Record*, 71st Cong., 2d sess., pp. 3383-84; *San Antonio Express*, February 2, 4, 8, 11, 1930.

43. *San Antonio Express*, February 11, November 4, 5, 6, 1930.

44. Walter Newton to Mrs. J. C. Griswold, November 13, 1931, "Texas G," Subject Files: Republican National Committee, Box 13, HHPL.

45. Walter Newton to Mrs. J. C. Griswold, November 15, 1931; Larry [Richey] to Walter [Newton], March 19, 1929, both in "Texas G," Box 13, Presidential Papers, HHPL. Representative Lehlbach furnished Newton with evidence against Creager (Lehlbach to Newton, October 29, 1929, "Republican National Committee—Texas," Box 13, Presidential Papers, HHPL). For Walter Newton's congressional career, see the *Biographical Directory of the American Congress*, 1937. Senator Brookhardt conferred with President Hoover in February; the next month Hoover issued a statement regarding the Republican parties in the South, implying a critical view

of the Texas party; *New York Times*, February 24, March 27, 1929. At the time of the Brookhardt-Hoover meeting, Creager requested an appointment to see Hoover regarding the Brookhardt charges. He was put off and received no specific answer (Creager to Hoover, telegram, February 24, 1929, "Texas," Box 7, Pre-Presidential General Correspondence, HHPL). The official letter of introduction for Orville Bullington was written by Captain J. F. Lucey; J. F. Lucey to Walter H. Newton, November 22, 1929, "Orville Bullington," Secretary's File, Box 87, Presidential Papers, HHPL.

46. *San Antonio Express*, February 11, 22, 25, March 1, 2, 3, 14, April 12, 1929; *New York Times*, March 2, 3, 24, April 6, October 29, November 30, December 29, 1929, February 25, 1930; Creager to Hoover, June 1, 1929; Brookhardt to Hoover, April 12, 1929; Creager to Lawrence Richey, April 13, 1929 (telegram); William D. Mitchell to Creager, April 18, 1929, all in "Republican National Committee—Texas," Box 191, Subject Files, Presidential Papers, HHPL.

47. *New York Times*, November 3, 7, 9, 1931.

48. William G. Shepherd, "Getting a Job for Jack," *Collier's*, June 15, 1929, pp. 8-9.

49. Owen P. White, "High-Handed and Hell-Bent," *Collier's*, June 22, 1929, pp. 8-9; Owen P. White, *The Autobiography of a Durable Sinner* (New York: G. P. Putnam's Sons, 1942), pp. 219-44; interview with Mrs. Owen P. White, Southold, New York, December 28, 1974.

50. White, "High-Handed and Hell-Bent," p. 9.

51. White, *Autobiography*, pp. 223-41; *New York Times*, August 4, 1929, May 16, December 4, 1930.

52. *San Antonio Express*, February 2, 4, 8, 11, November 4, 5, 6, 1930; *Senate Report No. 46*, 71st Cong., 2d sess., p. 2.

53. Sam H. Acheson et al., *Texian Who's Who* (Dallas: Texian Co., 1937), pp. 66-67. For the record of correspondence regarding the Bullington nomination, see "Orville Bullington," "Judiciary—Judges Fifth Circuit," Presidential Papers, HHPL.

54. Wurzbach to Newton, October 26, 1931, "Judiciary—Judges—U.S. District, Texas," Presidential Papers, HHPL. Wurzbach also put himself in contention for the vacancy on the U.S. District Court, Western Texas, upon the retirement of DuVal West. Creager scotched Wurzbach's chances for the appointment, as one might expect (Creager to Newton, telegram, July 12, 1930, "Judiciary—Judges—U.S. District, Texas," Presidential Papers, HHPL).

55. Acheson et al., *Texian Who's Who*, pp. 230-31; Tom Connally to R. O. Kenley, June 17, 1929, telegram, "Judiciary—Judges—Circuit 5," Presidential Papers, HHPL.

56. J. F. Lucey to Newton, July 19, 1930; Orville Bullington to Lucey, June 28, 1930; both in "Orville Bullington, Judiciary—Judges—5th Circuit (Texas)," Presidential Papers, HHPL; *Dallas Times Herald*, June 8, 1931. Remnants of the Wurzbach faction used this issue against Creager in 1932. See *Texas Republican* (Fort Worth), no. 5 (May 5, 1932), Nolte Papers.

CHAPTER THREE

1. Alexander Heard and Donald S. Strong, *Southern Primaries and Elections, 1920-1949* (University, Alabama: University of Alabama Press, 1950), pp. 186-89.

2. *Dallas Morning News*, July 28, 1930; *Dallas Times Herald*, June 8, 1931; *Dallas Morning News*, September 10, 1930.

3. J. F. Lucey to Eugene Nolte, October 13, 1930, Nolte Papers.

4. Heard and Strong, *Southern Primaries and Elections*, pp. 143-45; *Dallas Times Herald*, June 8, 1931.

5. *Dallas Times Herald*, June 8, 1931.

6. *Dallas Morning News*, July 22, 1932; interview with Helen Ackenhausen, November 7, 1971, Dallas, Texas; interview with Carlos Watson, May 7, 1971, Brownsville, Texas.

7. *Dallas Morning News*, September 10, 11, 1930; Mrs. Charles S. Riley to Walter Newton, telegram, "Texas-R," Box 13, Republican National Committee, HHPL; interview with Mrs. George S. Atkinson, November 20, 1969, Dallas, Texas.

8. *Dallas Morning News*, January 23, July 22, July 31, 1932; Creager to Nolte, August 19, 1932, Nolte Papers.

9. *Dallas Times Herald*, August 8, 1932; interview with Carlos Watson, May 7, 1971, Brownsville, Texas; Sam H. Acheson et al., *Texian Who's Who* (Dallas: Texian Co., 1937), p. 67; *Dallas Times Herald*, August 12, 1942; *Texas Almanac*, 1940-41, p. 406.

10. *Dallas Times Herald*, August 28, 1928; Heard and Strong, *Southern Primaries and Elections*, p. 146; *Dallas Morning News*, September 14, 25, October 23, 1932; *Dallas Times Herald*, October 23, 27, November 1, 1932.

11. Interview with Helen Ackenhausen, November 5, 1971, Dallas, Texas; interview with Carlos Watson, May 7, 1971, Brownsville, Texas.

12. Heard and Strong, *Southern Primaries and Elections*, p. 146; Richard M. Scammon, ed., *America at the Polls* (Pittsburgh: University of Pittsburgh Press, 1965), pp. 431, 435.

13. General Elections in Texas, 1934-48:

GOVERNOR

	DEMOCRATS		REPUBLICANS	
1934	J. V. Allred	428,734	D. E. Waggoner	13,703
1936	J. V. Allred	782,083	C. O. Harris	58,842
1938	W. Lee O'Daniel	358,943	Alex. Boynton	11,309
1940	W. Lee O'Daniel	1,019,338	George C. Hopkins	59,885
1942	Coke Stevenson	280,735	C. K. McDowell	9,204
1944	Coke Stevenson	1,007,826	B. J. Beasley	100,287
1946	Beauford Jester	345,513	Eugene Nolte, Jr.	33,231
1948	Beauford Jester	1,024,160	Alvin E. Lane	177,399

U.S. SENATE

1948	Lyndon B. Johnson	785,335	H. J. Porter	381,110

SOURCE: Heard and Strong, *Southern Primaries and Elections*, pp. 148-86.

14. Interview with Helen Ackenhausen, November 5, 1970, Dallas, Texas; interview with Carlos Watson, May 7, 1971, Brownsville, Texas.

15. *San Antonio Express*, September 12, 1934.

16. *Dallas Journal*, August 12, 1934; *Dallas Times Herald*, September 12, 1934; *Dallas Morning News*, January 23, 1932, September 11, 1934; interview with Ralph Currie, March 20, 1971, Dallas, Texas.

17. *Dallas Journal*, August 12, 1934.

18. *San Antonio Express*, September 12, 1934.

19. Donald R. McCoy, *Landon of Kansas* (Lincoln: University of Nebraska Press, 1966), p. 209; Creager to Hoover, May 17, 1934, "R. B. Creager," Post-Presidential Papers (hereafter cited as PPP), HHPL.

20. Malcolm Moos, *The Republicans* (New York: Random House, 1956), p. 395; Creager to Hoover, May 10, 17, 29, July 8, 22, December 2, 1935, January 4, 14, 1936; Hoover to Creager, January 19, February 10, 1936, "R. B. Creager," PPP, HHPL. For Creager's position on national party factions, see R. B. Creager to Charles D. Hilles, June 21, 1935, Box 205, November 8, 1935, Box 206, Hilles Papers, Yale University.

21. McCoy, *Landon of Kansas*, p. 213; Donald Bruce Johnson, *The Republican Party and Wendell Willkie* (Urbana: University of Illinois Press, 1960), p. 14.

22. McCoy, *Landon of Kansas*, pp. 231, 216; Hoover to Creager, January 19, 1936, "R. B. Creager," PPP, HHPL; Creager to Hilles, June 21, 1935, Box 205, Hilles Papers.

23. Creager to Henry Fletcher, December 23, 1935, "Texas File," Alfred Landon Papers, Kansas State Historical Society; Creager to Henry P. Fletcher, February 19, 1935, "R. B. Creager," PPP, HHPL.

24. McCoy, *Landon of Kansas*, pp. 212, 253, 260-61; Hoover claimed that the Hearst movement for Landon was dangerous, that the regular organization would push for uncommitted delegations (Hoover to Creager, February 10, 1936, "R. B. Creager," PPP, HHPL).

25. McCoy, *Landon of Kansas*, pp. 218, 245, 210-11; *New York Times*, December 18, 1935; Orville Bullington to Hoover, June 12, 1935, February 22, 1936, "Orville Bullington," PPP, HHPL.

26. *San Antonio Express*, August 11, 12, 1936; interview with Ralph Currie, March 20, 1971, Dallas, Texas.

27. McCoy, *Landon of Kansas*, pp. 258-61, 271, 363; Moos, *The Republicans*, p. 401; Johnson, *The Republican Party and Wendell Willkie*, pp. 10-13; *New York Times*, January 6, March 5, 10, 1937, February 17, 1940. The debt was not paid until 1940. See Louise Overacker, "Campaign Finance in the Presidential Election of 1940," *American Political Science Review* 35 (August 1941): 703.

28. McCoy, *Landon of Kansas*, pp. 270, 301, 338; Moos, *The Republicans*, p. 401.

29. McCoy, *Landon of Kansas*, pp. 310, 342; *New York Times*, December 1, 1935.

30. Scammon, *America at the Polls*, pp. 436-40; Sam Lubell uncovered evidence of concentrated and significant upper-income support for Alf Landon in Houston in 1936; Bernard Cosman, *The Case of the Goldwater Delegates* (University, Alabama: University of Alabama Bureau of Public Administration, 1966), pp. 52-53; John O. King, *J. S. Cullinan* (Nashville: Vanderbilt University Press, 1971), pp. 210-12; James A. Clark, *Marrs McLean* (Houston: James A. Clark Books, 1969), p. 118; *Dallas Times Herald*, August 12, 1942; Richard Nowinson et al., *Who's Who in United States Politics* (Chicago: Capitol House, 1950), p. 591; Creager to Hilles, November 24, 1936, Box 210, Hilles Papers.

31. McCoy, *Landon of Kansas*, pp. 350, 363; Creager to Landon, November 20, 1936, "Texas File," Landon Papers, Kansas State Historical Society.

32. *New York Times*, November 7, 1937, November 30, 1938; McCoy, *Landon of Kansas*, pp. 367, 376, 365; Hoover to Creager, November 21, 1938, "R. B. Creager," PPP, HHPL.

33. *New York Times*, November 27, 1938; Moos, *The Republicans*, p. 408; Henry O. Evjen, "The Willkie Campaign: An Unfortunate Chapter in Republican Leadership," *Journal of Politics* 14 (May 1952): 242.

34. McCoy, *Landon of Kansas*, p. 398.

35. Adolph K. Barta to David S. Ingalls, September 21, 1939; Creager to Ingalls, August 8, 1939; Darrell H. Hamric to Thomas W. Bowers, January 21, 1940, all in "Politics—1940—Texas," Box 87; Bowers to F. M. Mayer, May 9, 1940, "Political —Campaign Miscellany—C," Box 92, Robert A. Taft Papers (hereafter cited as Taft Papers), Library of Congress.

36. Barta to Ingalls, October 1, 6, 1939; Philip Lee Eubank to Taft, June 1, 1940, Box 87, Taft Papers.

37. Louis V. Howe to Taft, June 14, 1940, "Politics—1940—Campaign," Box 87, Taft Papers.

38. Taft to Helen Ackenhausen, February 23, 1940; Marrs McLean to Taft, October 18, 1939, May 8, 1940; Barta to Ingalls, September 28, 1939, May 29, 1940,

"Politics—Texas—1940," Box 87, Taft Papers; Creager to Harrison E. Spangler, June 1, 1940, "Politics—1940—Campaign," Box 119, Taft Papers; *Dallas Times Herald*, December 1, 1938.

39. Moos, *The Republicans*, pp. 409, 412; Johnson, *The Republican Party and Wendell Willkie*, pp. 64, 72, 80, 90; *New York Times*, June 27, 1940.

40. Interview with Helen Ackenhausen, November 21, 1970, Dallas, Texas.

41. *Amarillo Daily News*, September 18, 1940; Clark, *Marrs McLean*, p. 121; interview with Carlos Watson, May 7, 1971, Brownsville, Texas.

42. Scammon, *America at the Polls*, pp. 436-40.

43. Johnson, *The Republican Party and Wendell Willkie*, pp. 49, 175; Moos, *The Republicans*, p. 422; Evjen, "The Willkie Campaign," pp. 241, 242, 246, 247; McCoy, *Landon of Kansas*, p. 447; Overacker, "Campaign Finance in the Presidential Election of 1940," p. 711.

44. *Chicago Tribune*, March 25, 1941; Johnson, *The Republican Party and Wendell Willkie*, pp. 160-87.

45. Clark, *Marrs McLean*, p. 123; *Houston Post*, October 10, 1946; Marrs McLean to Mike Nolte, "Sunday 1946," Nolte Papers.

46. *Dallas Times Herald*, August 10, 1938; Barta to Ingalls, October 6, 1939, "Politics—Texas—1940," Box 87, Taft Papers; Clark, *Marrs McLean*, pp. 14, 56; interview with Helen Ackenhausen, March 7, 1971, Dallas, Texas.

47. *Dallas Times Herald*, August 10, 1938; Barta to Ingalls, October 6, 1939, "Politics—Texas—1940," Box 87, Taft Papers; interview with Carlos Watson, May 7, 1971, Brownsville, Texas; interview with Joe Ingraham, March 25, 1971, Houston, Texas. The Nolte Papers contain various items of correspondence between Nolte and Zweifel relating to personal notes taken out by the latter during the period 1926-28.

48. The scant literature on the subject of the entry of the Texas oilmen into politics, in general, is highly biased against them, generally written from the "good government" viewpoint. *The Empire of Oil* by Harvey O'Connor (New York: Monthly Review Press, 1955) is dedicated "To Henry Demarest Lloyd, Pioneer in Exploring the Public Interest in a Basic Natural Resource." Chapter 19, "The Province of Texas," pp. 200-208, tells "the whole story." The same general approach marks Robert Engler's *The Politics of Oil: A Study of Private Power and Democratic Directions* (New York: Macmillan Co., 1961). To this date, the soundest study of the relationship of oil interests and politics is to be found in two brief chapters, 9 and 10, of *United States Oil Policy, 1890-1964* by Gerald D. Nash (Pittsburgh: University of Pittsburgh Press, 1968).

CHAPTER FOUR

1. Alexander Heard and Donald S. Strong, *Southern Primaries and Elections, 1920-1949* (University, Alabama: University of Alabama Press, 1950), pp. 158-60; Sarah Menezes to Robert A. Taft, November 7, 1942; Taft to Marrs McLean, November 30, 1942; McLean to Taft, July 11, 1942; J. F. Lucey to Taft, April 13, 1942, all in "Political—Texas—1942," Box 110, Taft Papers. In New Mexico, twice-elected Governor Richard Dillon observed that "the Republican Party is in a bad way and I do not see any future for them, and have made up my mind that it is a hopeless task to try to help them out in any way" (Richard Dillon to Tom Hughes, March 20, 1941, quoted in Charles B. Judah, *The Republican Party in New Mexico* [Albuquerque: Division of Research, Department of Government, University of New Mexico, 1949]), p. 112.

2. *New York Times*, January 13, 31, 1941; April 21, November 13, 26, December 3, 4, 5, 1942; Henry O. Evjen, "The Willkie Campaign: An Unfortunate Chapter in Republican Leadership," *Journal of Politics* 14 (May 1952): 253-54.

3. R. B. Creager to Robert A. Taft, April 13, 1942; Taft to Creager, telegram, April 16, 1942, both in "Political—Campaign—1944," Box 110, Taft Papers; *New York Times*, June 9, 1941, April 21, 1942.

4. *New York Times*, April 21, 1942; George H. Mayer, *The Republican Party, 1854-1964* (New York: Oxford University Press, 1967), p. 462.

5. Creager to Taft, June 1, 1943, "Political—Campaign—1944," Box 110, Taft Papers; *Dallas Times Herald*, May 23, 24, 1944.

6. The menu is in the Nolte Papers.

7. Sam Rayburn to W. H. Kittrell, Jr., September 22, 1943, File: 1943: Politics; Alvin Wirtz to Harold Ickes, May 25, 1944, copy, File: 1944: Politics, both in the Sam Rayburn Library. For general information on the American Liberty League, see George F. Wolfskill, *The Revolt of the Conservatives* (Boston: Houghton Mifflin, 1962). Specific references to the revolt within the Texas party by Liberty Leaguers are found in Seth Shepard MacKay, *Texas Politics, 1906-1944* (Lubbock: Texas Tech Press, 1952), pp. 405-6.

8. MacKay, *Texas Politics*, pp. 391-466. A useful brief summary of major developments in the Democratic party in Texas will be found in James R. Soukup, Clifton McCleskey, and Harry Holloway, *Party and Factional Division in Texas* (Austin: University of Texas Press, 1964), pp. 67-167.

9. Three days before Creager's announcement, the *Dallas Morning News*, which usually reflected the conservative Democratic viewpoint editorially, endorsed Dewey (*Dallas Morning News*, October 14, 15, 16, November 4, 1944); Alvin Wirtz to Harold L. Ickes, May 25, 1944, copy, File: 1944: Political: National, Sam Rayburn Library.

10. *Dallas Morning News*, October 19, 1944; *New York Times*, July 21, 1929.

11. *Dallas Morning News*, October 29, November 1, 5, 1944; interview with Ralph Currie, March 20, 1971, Dallas, Texas.

12. Richard M. Scammon, ed., *America at the Polls* (Pittsburgh: University of Pittsburgh Press, 1965), p. 441; *Dallas Morning News*, November 8, 1944; interview with Ralph Currie, March 20, 1971, Dallas, Texas.

13. Svend Petersen, *A Statistical History of the American Presidential Elections* (New York: Frederick Ungar Publishing Co., 1963), pp. 98, 101.

14. David M. Olsen, Wilfred O. Webb, and Murray C. Havens, *Texas Votes: Selected General and Special Elections Statistics, 1944-1963* (Austin: Institute of Public Affairs, University of Texas, 1964), pp. 1-4.

15. *Amarillo Daily News*, November 1, 4, 5, 1946; *Amarillo Sunday News-Globe*, November 3, 1946.

16. *Amarillo Daily News*, November 6, 1946.

17. Ibid., November 7, 1946, November 3, 1948.

18. *New York Times*, June 30, July 6, 1944, February 26, April 3, 1946, May 26, June 26, 1948, January 28, July 10, August 5, 1949, October 29, 1950.

19. *Dallas Times Herald*, May 22, August 9, 1944; interview with Helen Ackenhausen, March 9, 1971, Dallas, Texas.

20. W. C. "Collie" Briggs to "Hobart, the Judge and Mike," December 17, 1944, Nolte Papers.

21. Interview with Eugene "Mike" Nolte, Jr., February 11, 1971, San Antonio, Texas.

22. Malcolm Moos, *The Republicans: A History of Their Party* (New York: Random House, 1956), p. 436; interview with Mike Nolte, February 11, 1971, San Antonio, Texas; interview with Ralph Currie, March 20, 1971, Dallas, Texas; interview with Helen Ackenhausen, November 21, 1970, Dallas, Texas.

23. *Dallas Morning News*, May 15, 1946; interview with Ralph Currie, March 20, 1971, Dallas, Texas; interview with Helen Ackenhausen, November 21, 1970, Dallas, Texas.

24. *San Antonio Express*, August 16, 19, 1946; interview with Joe Ingraham, March 25, 1971, Houston, Texas.

25. *Austin American*, September 20, 1946; *Dallas Morning News*, August 14, 1946; interview with Helen Ackenhausen, November 21, 1970, Dallas, Texas. C. K.

McDowell wrote Nolte a "feeler" letter in 1946 (C. K. McDowell to George C. Hopkins, January 7, 1946, copy, Nolte Papers).

26. *Dallas Times Herald*, August 12, 14, 1946; *Dallas Morning News*, August 13, 14, 1946. The *San Antonio Express*, August 14, 1946, carried the United Press International story which described "Creager's setback."

27. "Headquarters Committee Meeting, November 29, 1946, Baker Hotel, Dallas, Texas," Carlos Watson, Sr., Papers, Brownsville, Texas; Collie Briggs to Mike Nolte, August 18, 1946; George C. Hopkins to Mike Nolte, October 18, 1946, and R. B. Creager to George Hopkins, December 26, 1946, copy, both in the Nolte Papers; *Dallas Times Herald*, December 6, 1946; interview with Helen Ackenhausen, November 21, 1970, Dallas, Texas.

28. Gerald Cullinan, "Republican Activity in Texas," *Southern Weekly*, January 18, 1947, pp. 3-4.

29. *Dallas Morning News*, January 3, 10, 21, 1947; *Austin American*, February 1, 1947.

30. *The Two Party News* 1, no. 8 (September 1947): 1. Copies of this publication are in the Nolte Papers. *San Antonio Express*, April 10, 12, 1947; Tom Bowers to Taft, July 14, 1947, "1948—Texas—XYZ"; Bowers to Taft, September 10, 1948, "1948—Texas—Lists," both in Box 188, Taft Papers.

31. McLean to Creager, October 6, 1947, copy; McLean to Clarence J. Brown, October 11, 1947, both in "1948—Texas—C," Box 186, Taft Papers; Gerald Cullinan, "G.O.P. Revolt in Texas," *Scene* 1, no. 1 (October 1947): 34-35.

32. *San Antonio Light*, October 9, 10, 1947.

33. Marrs McLean to Clarence J. Brown, October 22, 1947; Orville Bullington to Robert A. Taft, November 3, 1947; McLean to Clarence J. Brown, November 10, 1947; Brown to McLean, October 30, November 15, 1947, "1948—Texas—C," Box 186; McLean to Brown, March 24, 1948; Creager to McLean, November 29, 1947, copy, "1948—Campaign—Texas, D-P," Box 187, Taft Papers; *New York Times*, April 15, 1948.

34. McLean to Clarence J. Brown, November 19, 1947, "1948—Texas—Confidential," Box 188, Taft Papers; interview, Gerald Cullinan, April 20, 1971, Washington, D.C.

35. Creager to Robert A. Taft, February 17, 1948; Brown to Creager, February 19, 1948; Creager to Taft, March 19, 1948, "1948—Texas—C," Box 186; McLean to Brown, March 24, 1948, "Texas, D-P," Box 187; McLean to Taft, August 11, 1951, "Presidential Campaign 1952—Texas—Mc," Box 390, Taft Papers.

36. *San Antonio Evening News*, April 8, 1948; *New York Times*, April 15, 1948; "Minutes, State Headquarters Committee Meeting, San Antonio, Texas, April 15, 1948," typescript, Carlos Watson, Sr., Papers.

37. *Corpus Christi Caller*, April 24, 25, 26, 1948; *New York Times*, May 26, 1948.

38. *Austin American*, August 11, 1948; Creager to Brown, July 7, 1948, "1948 —Texas—C," Box 186, Taft Papers. One party leader recalled that after the convention and Dewey's nomination, Hopkins seemed to expect Creager and his associates to step aside. Hopkins was genuinely puzzled by their refusal to do so. Baffled but determined, George Hopkins refused to accept the Creager group's leadership in the conduct of the Dewey-Warren campaign. He insisted on setting up a rival organization, presumably in an effort to maintain his patronage rights in the event of a Dewey victory in November. As Hopkins and Creager continued their feud, Hopkins charged that Creager attempted to purge Dewey men; Creager replied that Hopkins's "small, incompetent, politically inept minority" had removed itself from the Republican party in Texas. See R. B. Creager to George C. Hopkins, August 1, 1948, copy, "1948—Campaign—Texas, D-P," Box 187, Taft Papers.

39. *Dallas Morning News*, August 10, 11, 1948; *Austin American*, August 11, 1948.

40. Heard and Strong, *Southern Primaries and Elections*, pp. 182-84; *Dallas Times Herald*, August 17, 1948.

41. Heard and Strong, *Southern Primaries and Elections*, pp. 182-86.

42. Interviews with H. J. Porter, February 16, 1971, May 18, 1971, Houston, Texas. For a discussion of federal gas policy, with little direct attention to Texas politics, see Gerald D. Nash, *United States Oil Policy, 1890-1964* (Pittsburgh: University of Pittsburgh Press, 1968), pp. 181, 209-37.

43. Evelyn Miller Crowell, ed., *Men of Achievement* (Dallas: John Moranz Assoc., 1948), p. 228; interview with H. J. Porter, May 18, 1971, Houston, Texas.

44. Interview with H. J. Porter, May 18, 1971, Houston, Texas; *Houston Press*, November 1, 1948; *New York Times*, October 14, 1948.

45. *New York Times*, October 14, 1948; Heard and Strong, *Southern Primaries and Elections*, pp. 184-86; *Amarillo News*, November 3, 7, 1948; interview with H. J. Porter, May 18, 1971, Houston, Texas.

46. Heard and Strong, *Southern Primaries and Elections*, pp. 184-86; interview with Alvin H. Lane, December 8, 1970, Dallas, Texas.

47. Interview with H. J. Porter, February 16, 1971, Houston, Texas.

48. *Texas Almanac, 1952-1953*, p. 488; interview with H. J. Porter, May 18, 1971, Houston, Texas.

49. Interview with H. J. Porter, May 18, 1971, Houston, Texas; H. J. Porter to General Dwight D. Eisenhower, November 9, 1952, "Geog: Texas, Mc-Z," Pre-Inaugural Files, Box 13, Dwight D. Eisenhower Papers, Dwight D. Eisenhower Presidential Library (hereafter cited as DDEPL), Abilene, Kansas; *Dallas Morning News*, August 8, 1950.

50. *Biographical Directory of the American Congress* (Washington: Government Printing Office, 1961), p. 982. *Dallas Times Herald*, May 10, 28, 1950; *Amarillo Sunday News-Globe*, April 9, 1950; *Dallas Morning News*, May 9, August 7, 1950; interview with Ben Guill, April 19, 1971, Washington, D.C.; interview with H. J. Porter, February 16, 1971, Houston, Texas.

51. *Pampa News*, November 2, 1950; interview with Ben Guill, April 19, 1971; interview with Gerald Cullinan, April 20, 1971, Washington, D.C.; Waco *News-Tribune*, November 8, 1950.

52. *New York Times*, January 23, 28, August 5, 1949; *Dallas Morning News*, August 7, 8, 1950.

53. *New York Times*, October 29, 1950; *Dallas Morning News*, November 1, 1950; *Austin American*, October 29, 1950; interview with Ralph Currie, March 20, 1971, Dallas, Texas.

54. *San Antonio Express*, November 19, 1950; *Austin American*, November 21, 1950.

CHAPTER FIVE

1. On Eisenhower's campaign for the American Assembly see the *New York Times*, October 31, November 13, 23, 1951; February 16, 1952; for the Texas correspondence: H. J. Porter to Dwight D. Eisenhower, December 20, 1949, June 26, 1950, December 20, 1950, "H. J. Porter," Box 85, President's Personal Papers (hereafter cited as EPP); Invitation List, "Jesse Jones," Box 57; Sid W. Richardson to Eisenhower, March 23, 1952, Box 90; Dillon Anderson to Eisenhower, December 13, 1960, Box 127, EPP, Dwight D. Eisenhower Presidential Library (hereafter cited as DDEPL); *Houston Post*, November 21, 1950.

2. Porter to Eisenhower, August 30, 1950; "H. J. Porter," Box 85, EPP, DDEPL.

3. Malcolm Moos, *The Republicans: A History of Their Party* (New York: Random House, 1956), pp. 459-60; interview with Harry Darby by Ed Edwin, October 5, 1957, Kansas City, Kansas, p. 10, DDEPL.

4. David Ingalls to Marrs McLean, May 17, 1951; Marrs McLean to Joseph W. Martin, August 8, 1951, "Presidential Campaign—Texas—1952 Mc," Box 390;

"Political Survey of Texas," Box 391, Taft Papers; "Minutes of Meeting of Dallas County Republican Executive Committee, May 19, 1951," typescript, George S. Atkinson Papers, Dallas, Texas.

5. McLean to Henry Zweifel, August 2, 1951; Marrs McLean to Robert A. Taft, August 11, 1951, "Presidential Campaign—1952—Texas Mc," Box 390, Taft Papers; *Dallas Morning News*, July 5, 1951.

6. McLean to Taft, August 11, 1951, "Presidential Campaign—Texas—1952 Mc," Box 390, Taft Papers.

7. Porter to Eisenhower, September 13, 1951; Eisenhower to Porter, September 22, 1951; Porter to Eisenhower, February 18, March 24, 1952, "H. J. Porter," Box 85, DDEPL.

8. Ingalls to Zweifel, September 4, 1951; Ingalls to Howard Wrentmore, November 5, 1951, "Presidential Campaign—1952—Texas M," Box 389, Taft Papers.

9. *San Antonio Express*, December 21, 1951.

10. Porter to Eisenhower, December 14, 1951, "H. J. Porter," Box 85, EPP, DDEPL; *Dallas Morning News*, January 12, February 4, 1952; *New York Times*, January 7, 18, 1952; interview with Alvin H. Lane, December 8, 1970, Dallas, Texas.

11. "Letters Asking for Support—Texas," Box 391, Taft Papers; interview with Joe Ingraham, March 25, 1971, Houston, Texas; *New York Times*, March 13, 16, 1952; *Dallas Times Herald*, March 11, 1952; *Dallas Morning News*, March 12, 1952. William S. White characterizes Taft's staff as loyal but none too competent (*The Taft Story* [New York: Harper & Row, 1954], pp. 174-85). James T. Patterson also attributed Taft's defeat at the national convention to inept management and disorganization. See Patterson, *Mr. Republican: A Biography of Robert A. Taft* (Boston: Houghton Mifflin, 1972), pp. 553, 555, 559; Oliver Douglas Weeks, *Texas Presidential Politics in 1952* (Austin: University of Texas, Institute of Public Affairs, 1953), p. 55.

12. Frank Blankenbeckler to Carroll Reece, February 18, 1952; Blankenbeckler to I. Jack Martin, January 18, 28, 1952, "Presidential Campaign—1952—Texas B," Box 388; Dudley Lawson, A. W. Orr, E. P. Beck, H. D. Rakeshaw, and Jesse Garoun to "Dear Fellow Republicans," December 15, 1951, "Presidential Campaign—1952—Texas L," Box 389, Taft Papers; Porter to Eisenhower, December 14, 1951, February 14, 1952, "H. J. Porter," Box 85, EPP, DDEPL.

13. Porter to Eisenhower, December 14, 1951, "H. J. Porter," Box 85, EPP, DDEPL; "List of Precinct Chairmen, April 1, 1952," Atkinson Papers; *Dallas Morning News*, May 28, 1952; *Houston Post*, February 29, 1952; James A. Clark, *Marrs McLean* (Houston: James A. Clark Books, 1969), p. 127. On the early optimism of Taft leaders, see Patterson, *Mr. Republican*, p. 540.

14. McLean to Ingalls, May 7, 1952, "Presidential Campaign—1952—Texas Mc," Box 390, Taft Papers; *San Antonio Express*, May 3, 4, 1952; *Dallas Morning News*, May 3, 1952; interview with Joe Sheldon, February 9, 1971, San Antonio, Texas; interview with Eugene "Mike" Nolte, February 11, 1971, San Antonio, Texas.

15. Porter to Eisenhower, May 9, 1952; "H. J. Porter," Box 85, EPP, DDEPL; *Houston Press*, May 4, 25, 1952; *Houston Post*, May 25, 1952; *Dallas Morning News*, April 23, 1952.

16. *Dallas Morning News*, May 1, 4, 7, 1952.

17. *Fort Worth Star-Telegram*, May 5, 1952; *Lubbock Avalanche-Journal*, May 4, 6, 1952; *Beaumont Enterprise*, May 4, 1952; *Dallas Times Herald*, May 4, 1952; *Corpus Christi Caller*, May 4, 1952; *Brownsville Herald*, May 4, 1952; *Midland Reporter-Telegram*, May 3, 4, 1952.

18. *Dallas Morning News*, February 17, April 21, May 1, 7, 8, 1952; interview with Alvin H. Lane, December 8, 1970.

19. See, for example, advertisements in the *Lubbock Avalanche-Journal*, May 1, 2, 1952; *Dallas Morning News*, May 1, 1952; *Dallas Morning News*, April 21, 1952; interview with Alvin H. Lane, December 8, 1970, Dallas, Texas; *Houston Chronicle*,

April 29, 1952; Dickson *v.* Taylor, 105F Supp. 251 (Texas, 1952). State Chairman Orville Bullington took a broad view of party membership, telling the *New York Times* reporter: "If the party started purging Democrats, there wouldn't be enough purging power to go around" (*New York Times*, May 27, 1952).

20. *Houston Post*, May 7, 25, 1952; *Brownsville Herald*, May 7, 1952; *Beaumont Enterprise*, May 7, 1952; *Dallas Morning News*, May 7, 1952.

21. *Dallas Morning News*, May 7, 8, 11, 20, 23, 27, 1952; *San Antonio Express*, May 7, 1952; *Dallas Times Herald*, May 7, 1952; *Fort Worth Star-Telegram*, May 7, 9, 1952; *Austin Statesman*, May 6, 1952.

22. *Dallas Morning News*, May 14, 1952.

23. *Houston Post*, May 24, 1952; *Dallas Morning News*, May 14, 18, 21, 28, 1952.

24. *Houston Post*, May 26, 1952; *New York Times*, May 25, 1952; *Dallas Morning News*, May 22, 24, 26, 27, 1952; *Dallas Times Herald*, May 27, 1952; *Time*, June 9, 1952; Neil C. Erwin to Eisenhower, June 17, 1952, "Texas, 1952-53," Box 530, EPP, DDEPL.

25. Erwin to Eisenhower, June 17, 1952, "Texas, 1952-53," Box 530, EPP, DDEPL; *Dallas Morning News*, May 28, 29, 1952; *Houston Post*, May 26, 27, 1952; interview with Helen Ackenhausen, November 21, 1970, Dallas, Texas. William S. White blames Taft personally for the "Texas steal" strategy (White, *The Taft Story*, p. 177), while James T. Patterson limits Taft's "culpability" to his failure to stop Zweifel and McLean (Patterson, *Mr. Republican*, pp. 541-43).

26. *Houston Post*, May 26, 27, 1952.

27. *Time*, June 9, 1952.

28. *Dallas Morning News*, May 28, 1952; *Cincinnati Post*, May 28, 1952.

29. *Houston Post*, May 27, 1952; *New York Times*, May 25, 26, 28, 1952; *Dallas Morning News*, May 26, 1952; interview with Alvin H. Lane, December 8, 1970, Dallas, Texas.

30. *Dallas Morning News*, May 22, 23, 1952; *New York Times*, May 26, 1952; see also Patterson, *Mr. Republican*, p. 542.

31. *Dallas Morning News*, May 23, 1952; Moos, *The Republicans*, p. 468; interview with Frederick A. Zaghi of Young, Rubicam, by Ed Edwin, November 5, 1968, New York, p. 5, DDEPL.

32. *Dallas Times Herald*, May 29, 1952; see also *Time*, June 9, *Newsweek*, July 9, *Life*, June 9, *New York Times*, May 25, 26, 1952.

33. *New York Times*, June 9, 1952.

34. *Dallas Morning News*, May 11, 1952.

35. *Time*, July 7, 1952; *Dallas Morning News*, July 1, 1952.

36. "Brief for the Delegates of the Regular Republican Organization of Texas," "Brief of H. J. (Jack) Porter, *et al.*, Delegates-at-Large and Alternate Delegates-at-Large, Elected at the Lawful Republican State Convention held in Mineral Wells, Texas, on May 27, 1952," Porter Papers; *Dallas Morning News*, July 10, 1952.

37. On the Democratic precinct conventions see Sam Rayburn to Jonathan Mitchell, June 7, 1952, "Political National, 1952," Sam Rayburn Library, Bonham, Texas; Richard M. Scammon, *America at the Polls* (Pittsburgh: University of Pittsburgh Press, 1965), p. 445.

38. *Dallas Morning News*, July 1, 2, 4, 8, 1952.

39. *New York Times*, June 4, 1952; Taft to Guy G. Gabrielson, July 3, 1952, "Presidential Campaign—1952—Texas E," Box 389, Taft Papers; *Dallas Morning News*, July 3, 4, 5, 1952; *Chicago Daily News*, July 9, 1952; Moos, *The Republicans*, p. 473. Herbert S. Parmet claims Lee was tricked into this statement; see his *Eisenhower and the American Crusades* (New York: Macmillan, 1972), pp. 81-82.

40. *Dallas Morning News*, July 3, 4, 1952.

41. *New York Times*, July 7, 1952; *Dallas Morning News*, July 8, 1952; Parmet, *Eisenhower and the American Crusades*, pp. 85-87.

42. *New York Times*, July 7, 1952; *Dallas Morning News*, July 8, 1952.

43. *Dallas Morning News*, July 8, 9, 10, 1952.

44. *New York Times*, July 11, 1952; Moos, *The Republicans*, pp. 477-78.

45. *New York Times*, July 12, 1952; *Dallas Morning News*, July 12, 13, 1952.

46. *Dallas Morning News*, July 11, 1952.

47. McLean to Taft, August 23, 1952, "Presidential Campaign—1952—Texas Mc," Box 298, Taft Papers; *Dallas Morning News*, July 14, 1952; Clark, *Marrs McLean*, pp. 128, 129, 145; *Dallas Morning News*, July 20, 1952; "Minutes of Dallas County Executive Committee, June 19, 1952," Atkinson Papers.

48. *Dallas Morning News*, July 12, 1952.

49. *New York Times*, July 15, 22, 1952; *Dallas Morning News*, July 11, 16, 18, 21, 22, 1952.

50. *Brownsville Herald*, July 26, 1952; *Dallas Morning News*, July 21, 22, 1952; interview with Carlos G. Watson, May 6, 1971, Brownsville, Texas.

51. *Vernon's Annotated Texas Statutes*, Election Code, Article 6.01; *El Paso Times*, July 13, 1952; *Dallas Times Herald*, July 11, 1952; *Houston Post*, August 26, 1952.

52. *Dallas Morning News*, July 19, 22, 24, 26, 27, 28, August 3, 1952.

53. *Dallas Morning News*, August 22, 24, 25, 1952.

54. *San Antonio Express*, August 26, 1952; *Houston Post*, August 26, 1952; *Dallas Morning News*, August 27, 1952; interview with Carlos G. Watson, May 7, 1971, Brownsville, Texas.

55. *Houston Post*, August 27, 1952; *San Antonio Express*, August 17, 1952; *Dallas Morning News*, August 27, 1952.

56. *New York Times*, May 24, 25, August 27, 1952.

57. Scammon, *America at the Polls*, pp. 441-45; *Dallas Morning News*, August 27, 1952; *Austin American Statesman*, October 1, 1952; *Dallas Times Herald*, October 5, 1952; *Houston Post*, August 18, 1952; *Denison Herald*, September 14, 1952; *Dallas Morning News*, October 11, 1952; interview with Gerald Cullinan, April 20, 1971, Washington, D.C.

58. Eisenhower to Lane, September 18, 1952, Alvin H. Lane Papers, Dallas, Texas; interview with Gerald Cullinan, April 20, 1971, Washington, D.C.

59. *Dallas Morning News*, September 17, 1952, "Texas Democrats for Eisenhower," Box 1, Oveta Culp Hobby Papers, DDEPL; Ben Guill to Sherman Adams, October 1, 1952, "Texas," Box 36, Sherman Adams Papers, DDEPL.

60. Scammon, *America at the Polls*, pp. 446-50.

61. Weeks, *Texas Presidential Politics in 1952*, pp. 107, 108; *Dallas Times Herald*, November 5, 1952.

CHAPTER SIX

1. Donald S. Strong, "Alabama: Transition and Alienation," in William C. Havard, ed., *The Changing Politics of the South* (Baton Rouge: Louisiana State University Press, 1972), p. 410.

2. This account of the 1954 campaign is based on Bernard Cosman, "The Republican Congressman from Dallas, Texas: An Analysis of Urban Republicanism in the South" (M.A. thesis, University of Alabama, 1958), pp. 20, 23-32, 36, 37, 40, 52, 60, 74, 122, supplemented by the following materials: *San Antonio Express*, November 2, 1954; interview with H. J. Porter, May 18, 1971, Houston, Texas; memorandum, Charles F. Willis, Jr., to Sherman Adams, April 20, 1954, "Texas 1954 (1)," Box 530, General Files, DDEPL; *Dallas Morning News*, October 31, November 2, 3, 4, 1954; interview with Frank Crowley, March 23, 1971, Dallas.

3. *San Antonio Express*, November 1, 2, 3, 1954; *Texas Almanac—1956-1957* (Dallas: A. H. Belo Corp., 1955), p. 522; Oliver Douglas Weeks, *Texas One-Party Politics in 1956* (Austin: University of Texas, Institute of Public Affairs, 1957), p. 5; interview with John G. Tower, March 8, 1971, Dallas, Texas.

4. Minutes of the Republican State Executive Committee 1: 109 (hereafter cited as RSEC Minutes), available at Republican State Headquarters, Austin, Texas.

5. Oliver Douglas Weeks, "The South in National Politics," in Avery Leiserson, ed., *The American South in the 1960's* (New York: Frederick A. Praeger, 1964), p. 233; Porter to Eisenhower, January 17, 1955, May 1, 1956; both letters are in "Texas 1," Box 696, General Files, DDEPL; Eisenhower invited Shivers to play golf a year earlier and Shivers declined (Shivers to Eisenhower, March 11, 1955, "Shivers," Box 954, General Files, DDEPL).

6. Interview with Alvin H. Lane, December 8, 1970, Dallas, Texas.

7. Interview with Frank Crowley, March 23, 1971, Dallas, Texas.

8. *San Antonio Express*, June 27, 1954.

9. Interview with H. J. Porter, May 18, 1971, Houston, Texas.

10. *Houston Post*, August 19, 1956; *Dallas Morning News*, July 17, 1959.

11. *Houston Post*, May 22, 23, 1956; *Dallas Morning News*, November 7, 1956; Weeks, *Texas One-Party Politics in 1956*, p. 43; Richard M. Scammon, ed., *America at the Polls* (Pittsburgh: University of Pittsburgh Press, 1965), p. 447.

12. *Dallas Morning News*, June 1, August 22, November 1, 2, 4, 7, 1956.

13. Ibid., November 7, 1956; *San Antonio Express*, November 6, 7, 1956.

14. W. H. Francis to Sherman Adams, July 25, 1956, "Texas 1956 (1)," Box 539, General Files, DDEPL; interview with Albert B. Fay, February 18, 1971, Houston, Texas.

15. *Houston Post*, August 28, 1956; interview with Thad Hutcheson, February 18, 1971, Houston, Texas.

16. Thad Hutcheson to Sherman Adams, November 9, 1956, telegram, "Texas 1956 (2)," Box 531, General Files, DDEPL; interview with Thad Hutcheson, February 18, 1971, Houston, Texas; "The President's News Conference of November 14, 1956," in *Public Papers of the President: Dwight D. Eisenhower*, 1956, vol. 2 (Washington: Government Printing Office, 1961), p. 1102.

17. Ibid., interview with Florence Atherton, May 19, 1971, San Antonio, Texas; interview with Joe Sheldon, February 9, 1971, San Antonio, Texas.

18. Thad Hutcheson, "Newsgram," April 5, 1957, Thad Hutcheson Papers, Houston, Texas; interview with Thad Hutcheson, February 18, 1971, Houston, Texas; Richard M. Scammon, ed., *America Votes* 4 (Pittsburgh: University of Pittsburgh Press, 1962): 398-402.

19. *Austin American*, May 10, 1957; Hutcheson, "Newsgram," April 5, 1957; interview with Thad Hutcheson, February 18, 1971, Houston, Texas; interview with John G. Tower, March 8, 1971, Dallas, Texas; RSEC Minutes 1:261-63, 1968; 2:32. Available at state headquarters, Austin, Texas.

20. Interview with Albert B. Fay, February 18, 1971, Houston, Texas; interview with Thad Hutcheson, February 18, 1971, Houston, Texas.

21. *Dallas Morning News*, July 19, 26, August 1, 12, September 10, 1958; *Texas Almanac—1961-1962* (Dallas: A. H. Belo Corp., 1960), p. 489.

22. *Dallas Morning News*, November 5, 1958; interview with Peter O'Donnell, December 13, 1972, Dallas, Texas.

23. *Dallas Morning News*, July 19, November 1, 2, 3, 5, 1958.

24. *VIM*, Number 13 (December 1965); H. J. Porter to Lance Tarrance, January 13, 1966, Porter Papers, Houston, Texas.

25. "Eisenhower Administration Appointments by Department and Agency. Republican National Committee, June 9, 1953," Box 75; H. J. Porter to Dwight D. Eisenhower, April 2, 1953, "Texas," Box 723, General Files, DDEPL.

26. H. J. Porter to Sherman Adams, February 5, 1953; W. H. Francis to Arthur E. Summerfield, January 8, 1953, both in "Texas," Box 723, DDEPL.

27. John A. Donaldson to Daniel G. Gainey, n.d. (probably October or November, 1953); Frank T. O'Brien to Gainey, November 10, 1953, both in "Texas, 1952-53," Box 530, DDEPL. On the national patronage situation see Herbert S.

Parmet, *Eisenhower and the American Crusade* (New York: Macmillan Co., 1972), pp. 104, 216.

28. Parmet, *Eisenhower and the American Crusade*, pp. 104, 216; Sherman Adams, *Firsthand Report: The Story of the Eisenhower Administration* (New York: Harper & Row, 1961), pp. 18-25.

29. Thad Hutcheson to Eisenhower, October 7, 1958; David W. Kendall to Potter, June 12, 1958, "Texas Eastern District Endorsement," Box 90, General Files, DDEPL; Porter to Eisenhower, August 21, 1959, Porter Papers; interview with John G. Tower, May 14, 1971, Dallas, Texas. See endorsement files for L. J. Benckenstein, Enoch Fletcher, William Steger, and John G. Tucker, Box 90, General Files, DDEPL.

30. Alvin H. Lane to Sherman Adams, November 19, 1954; Bruce Alger to Eisenhower, November 26, 1954, "Ralph Currie Endorsement"; Porter to Adams, December 1, 1954, "Texas Endorsements"; Porter to Herbert Brownell, June 14, 1955, "J. D. Estes Endorsements." See also endorsement files for M. Sims Davidson and A. W. Walker; and Porter to Eisenhower, April 2, 1953, "Texas North District Endorsements"; all files are in Box 90, General Files, DDEPL.

31. Porter to Eisenhower, April 2, 1953, "Texas Northern District Endorsements," Box 90, DDEPL. Of 174 appointments to circuit and district courts, Eisenhower named only nine Democrats—eight of them in the South and two of this number in Texas. See *Congressional Quarterly Almanac, 1971* (Washington, D.C.: Congressional Quarterly, 1971), p. 117.

32. George S. Atkinson to Richard Simpson, January 23, 1959, Atkinson Papers, Dallas, Texas.

33. Gerald D. Nash, *United States Oil Policy, 1890-1964* (Pittsburgh: University of Pittsburgh Press, 1968), pp. 181-83.

34. Ibid., pp. 197, 201, 206-8, 229.

35. Eisenhower to Porter, March 28, 1952; Arthur J. Vandenburg to Porter, telegram, June 18, 1952, Porter Papers.

36. Nash, *United States Oil Policy*, pp. 197-201, 206-8, 193-94.

37. Ibid., pp. 235-36; *Washington Post*, February 11, 1958; U.S. Congress, *Congressional Record*, 84th Cong., 2d sess., February 17, 1956, pp. 2793, 2796.

38. Porter to Eisenhower, March 19, 1956; Bernard Shanley to Porter, March 21, 1956; Porter to Adams, March 26, 1956, all in "P," Box 726, Official Files, DDEPL.

39. *Houston Post*, February 8, 1959; Porter to Eisenhower, February 16, 1955, "Republican National Committee: 1955," Box 709, DDEPL; interview with H. J. Porter, May 18, 1971, Houston, Texas.

40. *Washington Post*, February 11, 1958.

41. Ibid., February 11, 12, 1958.

42. Ibid. Porter's shaky relationship with Eisenhower may well have grown largely from Eisenhower's general disdain for partisan politicians, with whom his relations were "superficially cordial," according to Adams, *Firsthand Report*, pp. 18-19, 25.

43. *Washington Post*, February 12, 13, 1958; *Dallas Morning News,* February 12, 1958.

44. *Washington Post*, February 14, 1958.

45. *Houston Post*, May 10, 1958.

46. Paul G. Hoffman, "How Eisenhower Saved the Republican Party," *Collier's* (October 26, 1956): 44-47; Goldwater to Sherman Adams, November 12, 1956, "Campaign G," Box 712, General Files, DDEPL. On reactions to the Hoffman article and attitudes toward Sherman Adams by party conservatives see Parmet, *Eisenhower and the American Crusade*, pp. 462-63, 521.

47. *Public Papers of the President: Dwight D. Eisenhower, 1956*, vol. 2 (Washington: U.S. Government Printing Office, 1961), p. 1103; *New York Times*, November 15, 1956; *Dallas Morning News*, November 15, 16, 1956.

48. Interview with Frank Crowley, March 23, 1971, Dallas, Texas.
49. *Houston Post*, May 23, 1956.
50. RSEC Minutes, 1: 220, 250; *Dallas Morning News*, March 3, 1958; *Dallas Times Herald*, September 8, 1958; Thad Hutcheson to Eisenhower, May 15, 1957, "Texas 1957," Box 531, DDEPL.
51. RSEC Minutes 2:116.
52. Interview with I. Lee Potter, April 22, 1971, Washington, D.C.; Meade Alcorn to Eisenhower, November 12, 1957, "1957—RNC," Box 710; Mrs. Dick Elam to Alcorn, February 20, 1958, "Texas—1958," Box 531, both in DDEPL; *Dallas Morning News*, November 2, 1959.
53. James E. McKillips, Jr., to Robert T. Jones, October 19, 1953; Charles F. Willis to Herbert Brownell, October 27, 1953, both in "Republican Party (T)," Box 696, Pre-Inaugural Files, DDEPL; interview with H. J. Porter, May 18, 1971, Houston, Texas.
54. *Dallas Morning News*, November 2, 1959; interview with I. Lee Potter, April 22, 1971, Washington, D.C.
55. RSEC Minutes 2:27-29.

CHAPTER SEVEN

1. *Dallas Times Herald*, November 17, 1957.
2. See various items in the papers of Maurice I. Carlson, Dallas, Texas.
3. *Dallas Times Herald*, November 17, 1957; see various items in the Maurice I. Carlson Papers, Dallas, Texas.
4. *New York Times*, July 24, 1960; *Dallas Morning News*, November 4, 1960; *Texas Republican* 1, no. 2 (July 22, 1960), published by the Headquarters Committee, Austin, Texas; interview with John G. Tower, March 8, 1971, Dallas, Texas.
5. *Dallas Morning News*, November 4, 1960; interview with Frank Crowley, March 23, 1971, Dallas, Texas.
6. *Dallas Morning News*, November 5, 1960; interview with Frank Crowley, March 23, 1971; interview with John G. Tower, March 8, 1971.
7. *Dallas Morning News*, November 5, 8, 1960.
8. Richard M. Scammon, ed., *America at the Polls* (Pittsburgh: University of Pittsburgh Press, 1965), p. 455; Richard M. Scammon, ed., *America Votes* 4 (Pittsburgh: University of Pittsburgh Press, 1962): 400.
9. Interview with John G. Tower, March 8, 1971.
10. *Dallas Morning News*, November 4, 1960; Scammon, *America Votes* 4: 396-400; interview with Joe Sheldon, February 9, 1971, San Antonio, Texas; interview with John G. Tower, March 8, 1971.
11. *San Antonio Express*, April 6, 1961; *Dallas Morning News*, April 6, 1961.
12. *Fort Worth Star-Telegram*, May 29, 1961; *Wall Street Journal*, May 25, 1961.
13. *New York Herald Tribune*, June 7, 1961; *Dallas Morning News*, June 24, 1961; Porter to Eisenhower, May 16, 1961, Porter Papers; interview with Barry Goldwater, April 20, 1971, Washington, D.C.; interview with Albert B. Fay, February 18, 1971, Houston, Texas; Scammon, *America Votes* 4: 404-8.
14. Interview with John Goode, February 11, 1971, San Antonio, Texas; *Biographical Directory of the American Congress, 1774-1971* (Washington, D.C.: United States Government Printing Office, 1971), p. 1012.
15. *Dallas Morning News*, June 16, 1961; *San Antonio Express*, October 1, 2, 4, 8, 13, 19, 24, 1961. During their only public debate, Goode apparently bettered Gonzalez; thereafter Gonzalez prudently avoided public debates (interview with John Goode, February 11, 1971).
16. *San Antonio Express*, October 20, 22, 24, 27, 28, 29, 31, November 1, 2, 3, 4, 1961.

17. *San Antonio Express*, November 5, 1961; interview with Florence Atherton, May 19, 1971, San Antonio, Texas.

18. *Houston Post*, September 16, 18, 1962; *San Antonio Express*, November 3, 1961.

19. *Texas Observer*, May 26, August 17, 1962; *New York Times*, June 4, 1962.

20. *Dallas Morning News*, May 30, June 4, 5, 1962; *Texas Observer*, December 27, 1962; *Texas Almanac—1964-1965* (Dallas: A. H. Belo Corp., 1963), p. 497.

21. *Houston Post*, September 16, 18, 1962; *Dallas Morning News*, October 3, 30, 1962.

22. *New York Times*, October 2, 28, 1962; *Midland Reporter-Telegram*, October 3, 5, 1962; *San Antonio Express*, October 4, 1962.

23. *Midland Reporter-Telegram*, October 14, 17, 31, 1962.

24. *San Antonio Express*, October 28, 1962.

25. *Midland Reporter-Telegram*, October 14, 17, 18, 19, 1962; *San Antonio Express*, October 29, 1962.

26. *Midland Reporter-Telegram*, October 18, November 1, 1962.

27. Ibid., October 18, 19, 31, November 2, 1962.

28. *Midland Reporter-Telegram*, October 26, November 7, 1962; *San Antonio Express*, November 7, 1962.

29. *Midland Reporter-Telegram*, October 28, 1962; *Dallas Morning News*, November 7, 1962; Laveta Larie Amsler, "Ed Foreman: A Conservative Republican" (M.A. thesis, Texas Tech University, 1969), pp. 7, 19, 39, 44.

30. *Dallas Morning News*, November 7, 1962.

31. Ibid.; *Midland Reporter-Telegram*, November 7, 1962.

32. RSEC Minutes 1 (March 3, 1958): 306-8.

33. Stephen Shadegg, *What Happened to Goldwater?* (New York: Holt, Rinehart & Winston, 1965), p. 62.

34. RSEC Minutes 2:255.

35. *Wall Street Journal*, May 25, 1961; *Texas Observer*, February 7, 1963.

36. RSEC Minutes 2: 225; John H. Kessel, *The Goldwater Coalition* (Indianapolis: Bobbs-Merrill Co., 1968), pp. 41-42, 128.

37. Shadegg, *What Happened to Goldwater?*, p. 60.

38. Kessel, *The Goldwater Coalition*, p. 49.

39. *Dallas Morning News*, November 1, 1964; interview with Peter O'Donnell, December 13, 1972, Dallas, Texas.

40. Shadegg, *What Happened to Goldwater?*, p. 273.

41. *Dallas Morning News*, February 4, November 1, 1964; *Houston Post*, August 21, 1964; *Houston Chronicle*, August 21, 1964; *New York Times*, November 1, 1964.

42. *Dallas Morning News*, November 1, 1964.

43. Ibid., July 21, November 7, 8, 21, 22, 1964.

44. Larry Goodwyn in the *Texas Observer*, December 13, 1962; interview with Mrs. Rita Clements, May 24, 1973, Dallas, Texas; interview with Mrs. J. C. Mann, Jr., May 15, 1973, Dallas, Texas.

45. Interview with John G. Tower, March 13, 1971, Dallas, Texas; interview with George Bush, April 7, 1971, New York.

46. Richard M. Scammon, ed., *America Votes* 6 (Washington, D.C.: Congressional Quarterly, 1966): 404-8; *Midland Reporter-Telegram*, November 1, 4, 1964; *Dallas Morning News*, November 4, 1964.

47. *Dallas Times Herald*, November 8, 1964.

48. Joseph L. Bernd, "The 1964 Presidential Election in Texas," in John M. Claunch, ed., *The 1964 Presidential Election in the Southwest* (Dallas: Arnold Foundation, Southern Methodist University, 1966), pp. 7-32.

49. Victor O. Key, Jr., *Southern Politics* (New York: Alfred A. Knopf, 1949), pp. 280, 669, 674; Kevin P. Phillips, *The Emerging Republican Majority* (New Rochelle, New York: Arlington House, 1969), pp. 270-87.

50. Scammon, *America Votes* 4:404-8.

51. Scammon, *America Votes* 4:404-8; Alexander Heard and Donald S. Strong, *Southern Primaries and Elections, 1920-1949* (University: University of Alabama Press, 1950), pp. 184-85. For comparative comments on Republicanism in the urban South, see Ralph Eisenberg, "Virginia, the Emergence of Two-Party Politics," p. 87; Manning Dauer, "Florida, a Different State," p. 126; Preston W. Edsall and J. Oliver Williams, "North Carolina: Bipartisan Paradox," pp. 395-96, 399, 400; Donald S. Strong, "Alabama: Transition and Alienation," pp. 436-37; Perry Howard, "Louisiana: Resistance and Change," pp. 530, 564-65; Richard E. Yates, "Arkansas: Independent and Unpredictable," p. 281, all in William C. Havard, ed., *The Changing Politics of the South* (Baton Rouge: Louisiana State University Press, 1972).

52. Donald S. Strong, "Alabama: Transition and Alienation," pp. 437-38; Richard E. Yates, "Arkansas: Independent and Unpredictable," p. 281; Joseph L. Bernd, "Georgia: Static and Dynamic," p. 311; Perry H. Howard, "Louisiana: Resistance and Change," p. 534; and Preston W. Edsall and J. Oliver Williams, "North Carolina: Bipartisan Paradox," p. 396, all in William C. Havard, *The Changing Politics of the South.*

53. U.S. Bureau of the Census, *U.S. Census of Population and Housing: 1960. Census Tracts. Final Report PHC (1)-34* (Washington: Government Printing Office, 1962), pp. 15-29; James R. Soukup, Clifton McCleskey, and Harry Holloway, *Party and Factional Division in Texas* (Austin: University of Texas Press, 1964), p. 51; for a comparison with Virginia, see Ralph Eisenberg, "Virginia: The Emergence of Two-Party Politics," in Havard, *Changing Politics of the South*, p. 188.

54. Charles P. Elliot, "Democratic and Republican County Party Chairmen in Texas," in Richard H. Kraemer and Philip W. Barnes, eds., *Texas: Readings in Politics, Government and Public Policy* (San Francisco: Chandler Publishing Co., 1971), pp. 40-49.

55. Soukup et al., *Party and Factional Division in Texas*, pp. 43-44; Manning J. Dauer, "Florida: The Different State," in Havard, *Changing Politics of the South*, p. 99.

56. Soukup et al., *Party and Factional Division in Texas*, pp. 43-44.

57. On the basis of voting in the presidential elections of 1952, 1956, 1960, 1964, and 1972; United States senatorial elections in 1961, 1966, 1972; elections for governor in 1962, 1970. Counties which voted Republican in six or more of these contests were classified "Republican"; the converse standard was used to identify Democratic counties; those counties which did not cast six ballots for either party in the elections considered were designated "marginal." The Republican counties are Dallas, Ector, Gregg, Harris, Midland, Potter, and Smith; the Democratic counties are Galveston, Grayson, Jefferson, McLennan, Nueces, Travis, Webb, and Wichita; the "marginal" counties are Bexar, Cameron, El Paso, Hidalgo, Lubbock, and Tarrant (*Texas Almanac—1972-1973*, pp. 185-222).

58. Soukup et al., *Party and Factional Divisions in Texas*, p. 45.

59. Harold A. Stone, Donald K. Price, Kathryn H. Stone, *City Manager Government in Nine States* (Chicago: Public Administration Service, 1940), pp. 280-90, 304, 352; Harold Zink, *Government of Cities in the United States* (New York: Macmillan Co., 1939), pp. 172, 300. For El Paso, see Edward C. Banfield, *Big City Government* (New York: Random House, 1965), p. 70; interview with Joe Sheldon, February 9, 1971.

60. This theory receives support in Bernard R. Berelson, Paul F. Lazarsfeld, and William N. McPhee, *Voting: A Study of Opinion Formation in a Presidential Campaign* (Chicago: University of Chicago Press, 1954), pp. 77-87.

61. Eisenberg, "Virginia," in Havard, *Changing Politics of the South*, p. 188.

62. *RSEC Minutes* 2 (May 15, 1962): 188.

63. Interviews with Florence Atherton, May 19, 1971, San Antonio, Texas; Mrs.

J. C. Mann, Jr., May 15, 1973, Dallas, Texas; Rita Clements, May 24, 1973, Dallas, Texas.

64. Interviews with John G. Tower, March 13, 1971, Dallas, Texas; Peter O'Donnell, December 13, 1972, Dallas, Texas; Florence Atherton; Rita Clements; RSEC Minutes 2: 165, 170 A-K, 171.

65. RSEC Minutes 2: 234, 266.

66. Ibid., pp. 242, 275, 293.

67. Interviews with Peter O'Donnell, Mrs. J. C. Mann, Jr., Florence Atherton.

68. Interview with Peter O'Donnell.

69. Dallas County Election Returns, vol. 4, pp. 1-21; these records are kept by the Clerk of the Commissioners Court.

70. Ibid., pp. 1-5.

71. U.S. Bureau of the Census, *U.S. Census, Final Report PHC (1)-34*, pp. 15-29; Soukup et al., *Party and Factional Division in Texas*, pp. 32-36, 47, 50, 63; for a general opinion of the importance of education and income as demographic characteristics, see V. O. Key, Jr., *Politics, Parties and Pressure Groups*, 5th ed. (New York: Thomas Y. Crowell Co., 1964), pp. 586-89.

CHAPTER EIGHT

1. *Houston Post*, November 1, 1966; *Dallas Morning News*, November 3, 1966.

2. *San Antonio Express*, November 3, 7, 8, 1966; *Houston Post*, November 1, 2, 4, 6, 8, 1966.

3. *Texas Observer*, June 10, 1966.

4. *San Antonio Express*, September 8, 9, 1966.

5. *Houston Post*, November 2, 3, 6, 1966.

6. *San Antonio Express*, November 6, 8, 1966; *Houston Post*, November 7, 8, 10, 1966; *Texas Observer*, June 9, 1966; V. Lance Tarrance, Jr., ed., *Texas Precinct Votes, '66* (Austin: Politics, Inc., 1967), p. 19.

7. *New York Times*, March 4, September 21, 1966; *Houston Post*, November 3, 1966; *Texas Observer*, January 21, March 4, September 2, October 28, 1966.

8. *San Antonio Express*, November 3, 1966; *Texas Observer*, November 25, August 19, 1966; interview with John G. Tower, March 13, 1972, Dallas, Texas.

9. *Texas Observer*, April 1, December 9, 1966; Tony Castro, *Chicano Power: The Emergence of Mexican America* (New York: Saturday Review Press, 1974), pp. 175-77.

10. *Houston Post*, November 10, 1966; *Texas Observer*, November 25, 1966.

11. *Houston Post*, November 3, 4, 9, 1966); *Texas Observer*, October 14, November 25, 1966.

12. *Houston Post*, November 3, 10, 1966; *Dallas Morning News*, November 4, 1966; *Midland Reporter-Telegram*, November 4, 1966.

13. *New York Times*, July 4, 1966; *Houston Post*, November 9, 1966; *Texas Observer*, May 23, 1966.

14. *New York Times*, June 12, 1968; *Corpus Christi Caller*, June 9, 10, 11, 12, 1968.

15. *New York Times*, September 29, 1968; *Fort Worth Star-Telegram*, September 16, 17, 18, 1968.

16. *New York Times*, September 29, 1968.

17. For a useful summary of the conventions and campaigns, see Herbert E. Alexander, *Financing the 1968 Election* (Princeton: Citizen's Research Foundation, 1971), pp. 79-141.

18. *Dallas Morning News*, October 30, 1968.

19. *Texas Observer*, October 18, 1968.

20. *Houston Post*, November 1, 2, 1968; *Dallas Morning News*, October 4, 9, 16, 30, 1968; *El Paso Times*, November 1, 2, 1968; *Midland Reporter-Telegram*, November 1, 1968; *Texas Observer*, October 18, 1968.

21. *Dallas Morning News*, October 24, 29, November 1, 1968.

22. *El Paso Times*, November 2, 1968; *Dallas Morning News*, October 23, 1968; *Texas Observer*, November 15, 1968.

23. *Dallas Morning News*, October 13, November 2, 1968.

24. Ibid., October 29, 1968; *Houston Post*, November 3, 1968.

25. *Dallas Morning News*, August 25, 1968; interview with Peter O'Donnell, December 13, 1972, Dallas, Texas; interview with James M. Collins, April 7, 1971, Washington, D.C.; *The Congressional Directory*, 94th Cong., 1st sess. (Washington, D.C.: United States Government Printing Office, 1975), p. 172.

26. V. Lance Tarrance, Jr., ed., *Texas Precinct Votes '68* (Dallas: Southern Methodist University Press, 1970), pp. 4-8, 10-14, 190.

27. *Houston Post*, November 1, 1968; *Dallas Morning News*, November 1, 1968.

28. *Texas Observer*, May 23, 1969.

29. *Dallas Morning News*, November 2, 4, 1970; *Midland Reporter-Telegram*, November 4, 1970.

30. *New York Times*, September 28, 1969; interview with George Bush, April 14, 1971, New York City.

31. *Dallas Morning News*, October 9, 1970; *El Paso Times*, October 18, 1970.

32. *Dallas Morning News*, October 6, 1970; *El Paso Times*, October 18, 1970.

33. *Dallas Morning News*, October 10, 17, 20, November 1, 1970; *El Paso Times*, October 30, 1970.

34. *Dallas Morning News*, October 2, 8, 1970.

35. Ibid., October 2, 7, 1970; *Texas Observer*, October 30, 1970.

36. *Dallas Morning News*, October 4, November 1, 1970; *El Paso Times*, October 15, 1970.

37. *Dallas Morning News*, October 1, 3, 4, 1970; *El Paso Times*, October 15, 1970; *Texas Observer*, October 30, November 27, 1970.

38. *Dallas Morning News*, October 18, 1970; *Texas Observer*, October 30, 1970; *Houston Post*, November 3, 1970.

39. *El Paso Times*, October 16, 18, 1970; *Houston Post*, November 1, 1970; *Dallas Morning News*, November 1, 2, 1970; *Midland Reporter-Telegram*, November 4, 1970.

40. V. Lance Tarrance, Jr., ed., *Texas Precinct Votes '70* (Austin: University of Texas Press, 1972), pp. 11-15, 16-20; *Texas Almanac—1972-1973* (Dallas: A. H. Belo Corp., 1972), pp. 537, 544-49, 640-41. In predominantly black Dallas precincts, the turnout for 1180 (numbered 122 in 1970) and 332 (326 in 1970) increased from 54.9 percent in 1966 to 70.9 percent in 1970 as Bush's vote trailed Tower's. In San Antonio's Mexican-American precincts, the same development is evident. In precincts 15 (numbered 107 in 1970) and 192 (112 in 1970) turnout increased from 20.3 percent in 1966 to 40.4 percent in 1970 and from 28.9 percent in 1966 to 43.1 percent in 1970. Whereas Tower received 27.1 percent and 28.9 percent of the vote in 1966, Bush won only 19.6 percent and 10.5 percent in the same precincts in 1970. See Tarrance, *Texas Precinct Votes '70*, pp. 58-64.

CHAPTER NINE

1. "The Role of Information in the Election of John Tower," Decision-Making Information, 2700 North Main Street, Suite 800, Santa Ana, California 92701. It is not possible to determine the number of Republican voters with precision because Texas voters do not indicate party preference when they register to vote.

2. Ibid.

3. *New York Times*, August 1, 14, 15, 1971; Harvey Katz's *Shadow on the Alamo* (Garden City: Doubleday & Co., 1972) is a slick and occasionally inaccurate version of the scandal. A more reliable version is Sam Kinch, Jr., and Ben Procter, *Texas under a Cloud* (Austin: Jenkins Publishing Co., 1972). For a recent

summary see Richard West, "Ben Barnes Is Still Running," *Texas Monthly* (June 1979), pp. 196-97.

4. *Texas Observer*, August 25, September 22, 1972, November 29, 1974.

5. *Midland Reporter-Telegram*, November 5, 8, 1972; *Texas Observer*, June 12, 1972.

6. *Dallas Morning News*, June 5, November 1, 1972; *Midland Reporter-Telegram*, November 5, 8, 1972.

7. *Dallas Morning News*, November 12, 1972; *Midland Reporter-Telegram*, November 2, 9, 1972.

8. *New York Times*, October 18, November 8, 1972; *Midland Reporter-Telegram*, October 26, November 8, 1972; *Dallas Morning News*, November 5, 8, 1972; Theodore H. White, *The Making of a President, 1972* (New York: Atheneum, 1973), p. 11.

9. Richard M. Scammon, ed., *America Votes* 10 (Washington, D.C.: Congressional Quarterly, 1973): 349, 354-58; *Dallas Morning News*, November 1, 1972; *Midland Reporter-Telegram*, November 9, 1972; *Texas Observer*, December 1, 1972.

10. Scammon, *America Votes* 10:355-58.

11. *Dallas Morning News*, November 8, 1972; *Texas Observer*, December 1, 1972.

12. RSEC Minutes, October 9, 1971; *Midland Reporter-Telegram*, November 8, 1972; *Fort Worth Star-Telegram*, November 9, 1972.

13. *Texas Observer*, March 29, 1974; Richard M. Scammon, ed., *America Votes* 11 (Washington, D.C.: Congressional Quarterly, 1975): 316.

14. Scammon, *America Votes* 11:311-14; *Dallas Morning News*, November 3, 4, 7, 1974; *Midland Reporter-Telegram*, November 6, 1974.

15. *Texas Observer*, November 1, 1974; *New York Times*, June 16, 1974; Scammon, *America Votes* 11:315.

16. Byers was quoted in the *Texas Observer*, November 29, 1974. *Dallas Morning News*, November 6, 1974; *Midland Reporter-Telegram*, November 6, 1974.

17. Interview with Ernest Angelo, Jr., March 20, 1979, Midland, Texas; *New York Times*, September 19, 1974.

18. *Texas Observer*, March 14, May 23, 1975.

19. *Houston Post*, January 12, March 2, 18, 24, 27, 1976.

20. *Dallas Morning News*, May 3, 1976; *Midland Reporter-Telegram*, May 4, 1976; *Houston Post*, May 3, September 3, 1976; *Texas Observer*, May 21, September 3, 1976.

21. *RSEC Minutes*, September 10, 1976; *Dallas Morning News*, September 10, 11, 1976; *New York Times*, September 12, 1976.

22. *Texas Observer*, May 21, November 26, 1976; *Dallas Morning News*, November 4, 1976.

23. *Dallas Morning News*, November 3, 1976.

24. Richard M. Scammon and Alice V. McGillivray, eds., *America Votes* 12 (Washington, D.C.: Congressional Quarterly, 1977): 352-55.

25. *Texas Observer*, September 17, October 29, 1976; *Midland Reporter-Telegram*, November 3, 1976; Scammon and McGillivray, *America Votes* 12:15, 350; *Dallas Morning News*, November 3, 1973.

26. *Midland Reporter-Telegram*, November 3, 1976; Scammon and McGillivray, *America Votes* 12:360.

27. Scammon and McGillivray, *America Votes* 12:360.

28. *Dallas Morning News*, November 3, 4, 12, 1976; *Midland Reporter-Telegram*, November 3, 1976; *Texas Observer*, November 26, 1976.

29. *Dallas Morning News*, November 12, 1978.

30. *New York Times*, April 29, 1978; *RSEC Minutes*, May 16, 1972, February 10, 1973, December 9, 1978; *Texas Advocate*, April, July, August, 1978; interview with Nola Haerle, March 23, 1979, Austin, Texas; interview with Juandelle Lacy,

April 11, 1979, Midland, Texas; interview with Ernest Angelo, Jr., March 20, 1979, Midland, Texas.

31. *RSEC Minutes*, January 16, 1965, November 19, 1973; *Texas Advocate*, September, 1978; interview with Ernest Angelo, Jr., March 20, 1979, Midland, Texas.

32. Interview with Senator John G. Tower, April 25, 1979 (telephone).

33. *Houston Post*, January 12, 1978; *Texas Observer*, February 3, June 23, 1978; interview with Nola Haerle, March 23, 1979, Austin, Texas; interview with Ken Towery, March 23, 1979, Austin, Texas.

34. Interview with Nola Haerle, March 23, 1979, Austin, Texas.

35. Interview with Ken Towery, March 23, 1979, Austin, Texas.

36. Interview with John Tower, April 28, 1979, Dallas, Texas; interview with Ken Towery, March 23, 1979, Austin, Texas; interiew with Nola Haerle, March 23, 1979, Austin, Texas; *Dallas Morning News*, November 1, 4, 1978; *Texas Observer*, October 23, 1977, March 17, May 12, 1978; *Midland Reporter-Telegram*, November 5, 1978.

37. *Dallas Morning News*, November 2, 1978; interview with Ken Towery, March 23, 1979, Austin, Texas; *Midland Reporter-Telegram*, November 4, 1978.

38. *Dallas Morning News*, November 2, 1978; interview with Ken Towery, March 23, 1979, Austin, Texas; *Beaumont Enterprise*, November 4, 1978.

39. *Houston Post*, November 1, 1978.

40. *Texas Observer*, June 23, 1978; interview with Ken Towery, March 23, 1979, Austin, Texas; interview with Ernest Angelo, Jr., March 20, 1979, Midland, Texas.

41. *Dallas Morning News*, November 1, 2, 1978; *Midland Reporter-Telegram*, November 5, 1978.

42. *Houston Chronicle*, November 12, 1978; *Dallas Morning News*, November 26, 1978; *Texas Observer*, July 7, 1978; interview with Ken Towery, March 23, 1979, Austin, Texas; *Austin American-Statesman*, December 10, 1978.

43. *Texas Observer*, November 4, 1977, March 31, 1978.

44. *Washington Post*, February 28, 1979, *Texas Observer*, February 3, 1978; Richard H. Rovere, *The Goldwater Caper* (New York: Harcourt, Brace & World, 1965), p. 181; interview with Ernest Angelo, Jr., March 20, 1979, Midland, Texas; interview with Rita Clements, May 24, 1973, Dallas, Texas; *Texas Advocate*, January 16, 1979.

45. Douglas S. Harlan in the *Texas Observer*, February 3, April 28, 1978; interview with William P. Clements, Jr., April 24, 1979, Austin, Texas.

46. *New York Times*, May 7, 1978; *Texas Observer*, May 26, 1978.

47. *Dallas Morning News*, January 8, 1979; *Washington Post*, February 28, 1979; *Houston Post*, January 3, 1979.

48. *New York Times*, May 7, 1978; *Texas Observer*, May 26, 1978; interview with Nola Haerle, March 23, 1979, Austin, Texas.

49. Interview with Nola Haerle, March 23, 1979, Austin, Texas; *Austin American-Statesman*, November 12, 1978; *Texas Advocate*, November-December 1978; *Houston Chronicle*, November 12, 1978; *Dallas Morning News*, November 26, 1978.

50. *Beaumont Enterprise*, November 15, 1978; *Dallas Morning News*, December 19, 1978; interview with W. P. Clements, Jr., April 24, 1979, Austin, Texas; interview with Nola Haerle, March 23, 1979, Austin, Texas.

51. Interview with Nola Haerle, March 23, 1979, Austin, Texas; interview with David Dean, April 24, 1979, Austin, Texas.

52. Interview with David Dean, April 24, 1979, Austin, Texas; interview with Nola Haerle, March 23, 1979, Austin, Texas; *Houston Post*, August 26, 1978.

53. *Houston Chronicle*, November 9, 1978; *Dallas Morning News*, November 12, 1978; *Houston Post*, September 6, 1978; interview with David Dean, April 24, 1979, Austin, Texas.

54. *Texas Advocate*, August 1978; *Houston Post*, August 4, September 29,

1978; interview with David Dean, April 24, 1979, Austin, Texas; "Address of Mr. Thomas Reed to the National Press Club, Washington, D.C., December 18, 1978," typescript.

55. Interview with Nola Haerle, March 23, 1979, Austin, Texas; "Address of Mr. Thomas Reed."

56. "Address of Mr. Thomas Reed"; interview with David Dean, April 24, 1979, Austin, Texas; interview with Nola Haerle, March 23, 1979, Austin, Texas; interview with William P. Clements, Jr., April 24, 1979, Austin, Texas; *Houston Chronicle*, December 8, 1978.

57. *Dallas Morning News*, November 1, 1978; *Midland Reporter-Telegram*, November 5, 1978; Office of the Secretary of State of Texas, "General Election Returns, November 7, 1978," typescript.

58. *Dallas Morning News*, November 12, 1978; *Austin American-Statesman*, November 9, 1978; *Washington Post*, November 9, 1978; interview with Ernest Angelo, Jr., March 20, 1979, Midland, Texas.

59. Scammon and McGillivray, *America Votes* 12:309; "General Election Returns," November 7, 1978.

60. Southwest Voter Registration Education Project, "Mexican-American Voting in the 1978 Texas General Election," December 1, 1978, pp. 4-5; "Address of Mr. Thomas Reed"; interview with David Dean, April 24, 1979, Austin, Texas; interview with Nola Haerle, March 23, 1979, Austin, Texas.

61. *Houston Post*, November 10, 1978.

62. "General Election Returns, November 7, 1978"; interview with David Dean, April 24, 1979, Austin, Texas; interview with Nola Haerle, March 23, 1979, Austin, Texas.

63. Douglas S. Harlan in the *Texas Observer*, October 7, 1977; *Dallas Morning News*, November 1, 1978; *Texas Advocate*, July 1978, February-March 1979.

64. *Texas Observer*, June 9, 1978; *Dallas Morning News*, November 1, 4, 1978.

65. *Houston Chronicle*, January 7, 1979.

Bibliography

In addition to the works listed here, the author consulted selected news-papers and documents and conducted numerous interviews; to list them here would be of little aid to the reader.

MANUSCRIPT COLLECTIONS

ADAMS, SHERMAN. Papers. Dwight D. Eisenhower Presidential Library, Abilene, Kansas.

EISENHOWER, DWIGHT D. Papers. Dwight D. Eisenhower Presidential Library, Abilene, Kansas.

HARDING, WARREN G. Papers. Ohio Historical Society, Columbus.

HILLES, CHARLES D. Papers. Sterling Memorial Library, Yale University, New Haven, Connecticut.

HOBBY, OVETA CULP. Papers. Dwight D. Eisenhower Presidential Library, Abilene, Kansas.

HOOVER, HERBERT. Papers. Hoover Presidential Library, West Branch, Iowa.

LANDON, ALFRED. Papers. Kansas State Historical Society, Topeka.

LOVE, THOMAS B. Papers. Dallas Historical Society.

RAYBURN, SAM. Papers. Sam Rayburn Library, Bonham, Texas.

SCOBEY, FRANK E. Papers. Ohio Historical Society, Columbus.

TAFT, ROBERT A. Papers. Library of Congress, Washington, D.C.

UNPUBLISHED DISSERTATIONS AND PAPERS

AMSLER, LAVETA LARIE. "Ed Foreman: A Conservative Republican." Master's thesis, Texas Tech University, 1969.

BAULCH, JOE ROBERT. "James B. Wells: South Texas Economic and Political Leader." Ph.D. dissertation, Texas Tech University, 1974.

COSMAN, BERNARD. "The Republican Congressman from Dallas, Texas: An Analysis of Urban Republicanism in the South." Master's thesis, University of Alabama, 1958.

GREEN, GEORGE NORRIS. "The Far Right Wing in Texas Politics, 1930's-1960's." Ph.D. dissertation, Florida State University, 1966.

HATHORN, GUY B. "The Political Career of C. Bascomb Slemp." Ph.D. dissertation, Duke University, 1950.

PATENAUDE, LIONEL V. "The New Deal and Texas." Ph.D. dissertation, University of Texas, 1953.

REED, THOMAS. "Address of Mr. Thomas Reed to the National Press Club, Washington, D.C., December 18, 1978." Typescript.

SANFORD, WILLIAM REYNOLDS. "History of the Republican Party in the State of Texas." Master's thesis, University of Texas, 1955.

THOMPSON, HARRY J. "Senator John Goodwin Tower of Texas." Master's thesis, University of Maryland, 1968.

BOOKS

ACHESON, SAM H.; GAMBRELL, HERBERT P.; TOOMEY, MARY CARTER; and ACHESON, ALEX H. *Texian Who's Who.* Dallas: Texian Co., 1937.

ADAMS, SHERMAN. *Firsthand Report: The Story of the Eisenhower Administration.* New York: Harper & Row, 1961.

ALEXANDER, CHARLES C. *Crusade for Conformity: The Ku Klux Klan in Texas, 1920-1930.* Houston: Gulf Coast Historical Association, 1962.

ALEXANDER, HERBERT E. *Financing the 1968 Election.* Lexington, Mass.: Heath Lexington Books, 1971.

BANFIELD, EDWARD C. *Big City Politics: A Comparative Guide to the Political Systems of Atlanta, Boston, Detroit, El Paso, Los Angeles, Miami, Philadelphia, St. Louis, and Seattle.* New York: Random House, 1965.

BARTLEY, ERNEST R. *The Tidelands Oil Controversy: A Legal and Historical Analysis.* Austin: University of Texas Press, 1953.

BARTLEY, NUMAN V., and GRAHAM, HUGH D. *Southern Politics and the Second Reconstruction.* Baltimore: Johns Hopkins University Press, 1975.

BASS, JACK, and DE VRIES, WALTER. *The Transformation of Southern Politics: Social Change and Political Consequence since 1945.* New York: Basic Books, 1976.

BERELSON, BERNARD R.; LAZARSFELD, PAUL F.; and McPHEE, WILLIAM N. *Voting: A Study of Opinion Formation in a Presidential Campaign.* Chicago: University of Chicago Press, 1954.

BURTON, ROBERT E. *Democrats of Oregon: The Pattern of Minority Politics, 1900-1956.* Eugene: University of Oregon Books, 1970.

CASDORPH, PAUL D. *A History of the Republican Party in Texas, 1865-1965.* Austin: Pemberton Press, 1965.

CASTRO, TONY. *Chicano Power: The Emergence of Mexican America.* New York: Saturday Review Press, 1974.

CLARK, JAMES A. *Marrs McLean: A Biography.* Houston: Clark Book Co., 1969.

CLAUNCH, JOHN M., ed. *The 1964 Presidential Elections in the Southwest.* Dallas: Arnold Foundation, Southern Methodist University, 1966.

COSMAN, BERNARD. *The Case of the Goldwater Delegates: Deep South Republican Leadership.* University, Ala.: Bureau of Public Administration, University of Alabama, 1966.

—————, and HUCKSHORN, ROBERT J., eds. *Republican Politics: The 1964 Campaign and Its Aftermath for the Party.* New York: Frederick A. Praeger, 1968.

CROWELL, EVELYN MILLER, ed. *Men of Achievement.* Texas ed. Dallas: John Moranz Associates, 1948.

DAVID, PAUL T.; MOOS, MALCOLM; and GOODMAN, RALPH M. *Presidential Nominating Politics in 1952.* 5 vols. Vol. 3, *The South.* Baltimore: Johns Hopkins University Press, 1954.

DOROUGH, C. DWIGHT. *Mr. Sam.* New York: Random House, 1962.

DOWNES, RANDOLPH C. *The Rise of Warren Gamaliel Harding, 1865-1920.* Columbus: Ohio State University Press, 1970.

EISENHOWER, DWIGHT D. *The White House Years: Mandate for Change, 1953-1956.* Garden City, N.Y.: Doubleday, 1963.

—————. *The White House Years: Waging Peace, 1956-1961.* Garden City, N.Y.: Doubleday, 1965.

ENGLER, ROBERT. *The Politics of Oil: A Study of Private Power and Democratic Directions.* New York: Macmillan Co., 1961.

FREIDEL, FRANK. *F.D.R. and the South.* Baton Rouge: Louisiana State University Press, 1965.

HARBAUGH, WILLIAM HENRY. *The Life and Times of Theodore Roosevelt.* New, rev. ed. New York: Collier Books, 1963.

HAVARD, WILLIAM C., ed. *The Changing Politics of the South.* Baton Rouge: Louisiana State University Press, 1972.

HEARD, ALEXANDER, and STRONG, DONALD S. *Southern Primaries and Elections, 1920-1949.* University, Ala.: University of Alabama Press, 1950.

HUGHES, EMMET JOHN. *The Ordeal of Power: A Political Memoir of the Eisenhower Years.* New York: Atheneum, 1963.

JOHNSON, DONALD BRUCE. *The Republican Party and Wendell Willkie.* Urbana: University of Illinois Press, 1960.

JUDAH, CHARLES B. *The Republican Party in New Mexico.* Albuquerque: Division of Research, Department of Government, University of New Mexico, 1949.

KATZ, HARVEY. *Shadow on the Alamo: New Heroes Fight Old Corruption in Texas Politics.* Garden City, N.Y.: Doubleday & Co., 1972.

KESSEL, JOHN H. *The Goldwater Coalition: Republican Strategies in 1964.* Indianapolis: Bobbs-Merrill Co., 1968.

KEY, V. O., JR. *Politics, Parties, and Pressure Groups.* 5th ed. New York: Thomas Y. Crowell Co., 1964.

———————. *Southern Politics in State and Nation.* New York: Alfred A. Knopf, 1949.

KINCH, SAM, JR., and PROCTER, BEN. *Texas under a Cloud.* Austin: Jenkins Pub. Co., 1972.

KING, JOHN O. *Joseph Stephen Cullinan: A Study of Leadership in the Texas Petroleum Industry, 1897-1937.* Nashville: Vanderbilt University Press, 1970.

KRAEMER, RICHARD H., and BARNES, PHILIP W., eds. *Texas: Readings in Politics, Government, and Public Policy.* San Francisco: Chandler Pub. Co., 1971.

LEISERSON, AVERY, ed. *The American South in the 1960's.* New York: Frederick A. Praeger, 1964.

McCOY, DONALD R. *Calvin Coolidge: The Quiet President.* New York: Macmillan Co., 1967.

———————. *Landon of Kansas.* Lincoln: University of Nebraska Press, 1966.

McKAY, SETH SHEPARD. *Texas Politics, 1906-1944: With Special Reference to the German Counties.* Lubbock: Texas Tech Press, 1952.

MARTIN, JOSEPH W. *My First Fifty Years in Politics.* As told to Robert J. Donovan. New York: McGraw-Hill, 1960.

MAYER, GEORGE H. *The Republican Party, 1854-1964.* New York: Oxford University Press, 1964.

MOOS, MALCOLM. *The Republicans: A History of Their Party.* New York: Random House, 1956.

MURRAY, ROBERT K. *The Harding Era: Warren G. Harding and His Administration.* Minneapolis: University of Minnesota Press, 1969.

NASH, GERALD D. *United States Oil Policy, 1890-1964: Business and Government in Twentieth Century America.* Pittsburgh: University of Pittsburgh Press, 1968.

NOWINSON, RICHARD; POTTER, RUTH THORNQUIST; SPENCE, NICOLAS; and KELLA, JOAN DUNCAN. *Who's Who in United States Politics*. Chicago: Capitol House, 1950.

O'CONNOR, HARVEY. *The Empire of Oil*. New York: Monthly Review Press, 1955.

OLSEN, DAVID M.; WEBB, WILFRED O.; and HAVENS, MURRAY C. *Texas Votes: Selected General and Special Elections Statistics, 1944-1963*. Austin: Institute of Public Affairs, University of Texas, 1964.

PARMET, HERBERT S. *Eisenhower and the American Crusades*. New York: Macmillan Co., 1972.

PETERSEN, SVEND. *A Statistical History of the American Presidential Elections*. New York: Frederick Ungar Pub. Co., 1963.

PHILLIPS, CABELL B. *The Truman Presidency: The History of a Triumphant Succession*. New York: Macmillan Co., 1966.

PHILLIPS, KEVIN P. *The Emerging Republican Majority*. New Rochelle, N.Y.: Arlington House, 1969.

ROBINSON, EDGAR EUGENE. *The Presidential Vote, 1896-1932*. Palo Alto: Stanford University Press, 1934.

ROVERE, RICHARD H. *The Goldwater Caper*. New York: Harcourt, Brace, & World, 1965.

RUSSELL, FRANCIS. *The Shadow of Blooming Grove: Warren G. Harding in His Times*. New York: McGraw-Hill, 1968.

SCAMMON, RICHARD M., ed. *America at the Polls*. Pittsburgh: University of Pittsburgh Press, 1965.

_____, ed. *America Votes*. Vols. 1, 2. New York: Macmillan Co., 1956, 1958.

_____, ed. *America Votes*. Vols. 3, 4, 5. Pittsburgh: University of Pittsburgh Press, 1959, 1962, 1964.

_____, ed. *America Votes*. Vols. 6, 7, 8, 9, 10, 11. Washington, D.C.: Congressional Quarterly, 1966, 1968, 1970, 1972, 1973, 1975.

_____, and McGILLIVRAY, ALICE V., eds. *America Votes*. Vol. 12. Washington, D.C.: Governmental Affairs Institute, Elections Research Center, 1977.

SHADEGG, STEPHEN. *What Happened to Goldwater?* New York: Holt, Rinehart & Winston, 1965.

SHERMAN, RICHARD B. *The Republican Party and Black America from McKinley to Hoover, 1896-1933*. Charlottesville: University Press of Virginia, 1973.

SOUKUP, JAMES R.; McCLESKEY, CLIFTON; and HOLLOWAY, HARRY. *Party and Factional Division in Texas*. Austin: University of Texas Press, 1964.

STAVE, BRUCE M. *The New Deal and the Last Hurrah: Pittsburgh Machine Politics*. Pittsburgh: University of Pittsburgh Press, 1970.

STONE, HAROLD A.; PRICE, DON K.; and STONE, KATHRYN H. *City Manager Government in Nine Cities*. Chicago: Public Administration Service, 1940.

STRONG, DONALD S. *Urban Republicanism in the South*. University, Ala.: University of Alabama Bureau of Public Administration, 1957.

——————. *The 1952 Presidential Election in the South*. University, Ala.: University of Alabama Bureau of Public Administration, 1955.

TARRANCE, V. LANCE, ed. *Texas Precinct Votes '66*. Austin: Politics, Inc., 1967.

——————, ed. *Texas Precinct Votes '68*. Dallas: Southern Methodist University Press, 1970.

——————, ed. *Texas Precinct Votes '70*. Austin: University of Texas Press, 1972.

Texas Almanac, 1940-41, 1952-53, 1956-57, 1961-62, 1964-65, 1972-73. Dallas: A. H. Belo Corp., 1940, 1952, 1956, 1961, 1964, 1972.

THOMSON, CHARLES A. H., and SHATTUCK, FRANCES M. *The 1956 Presidential Campaign*. Washington, D.C.: Brookings Institution, 1960.

WEEKS, OLIVER DOUGLAS. *Texas Presidential Politics in 1952*. Austin: Institute of Public Affairs, University of Texas, 1953.

——————. *Texas One-Party Politics in 1956*. Austin: Institute of Public Affairs, University of Texas, 1957.

——————. *Texas in the 1960 Presidential Election*. Austin: Institute of Public Affairs, University of Texas, 1961.

——————. *Texas in 1964: A One-Party State Again?* Austin: Institute of Public Affairs, University of Texas, 1965.

WHITE, OWEN P. *The Autobiography of a Durable Sinner*. New York: G. P. Putnam's Sons, 1942.

WHITE, THEODORE H. *The Making of the President, 1972*. New York: Atheneum, 1973.

WHITE, WILLIAM S. *The Taft Story*. New York: Harper & Row, 1954.

Who's Who in America. Chicago: A. H. Marquis Co., 1943.

WOLFSKILL, GEORGE F. *The Revolt of the Conservatives: A History of the American Liberty League, 1934-1940*. Boston: Houghton Mifflin, 1962.

ARTICLES IN PERIODICALS

CULLINAN, GERALD. "GOP Revolt in Texas." *Scene*, October 1947, pp. 34-35.

——————. "Republican Activity in Texas." *Southern Weekly*, January 18, 1947, pp. 3-4.

CUTRIGHT, PHILLIPS. "Measuring the Impact of Local Party Activity on the General Election Vote." *Public Opinion Quarterly* 27 (Fall 1963): 372-87.

DABNEY, VIRGINIUS. "What the GOP Is Doing in the South." *Harper's* 226 (May 1963): 86-94.

EVJEN, HENRY O. "The Willkie Campaign: An Unfortunate Chapter in Republican Leadership." *Journal of Politics* 14 (May 1952): 241-56.

FLINN, THOMAS A., and WIRT, FREDERICK M. "Local Party Leaders: Groups of Like-Minded Men." *Midwest Journal of Political Science* 9 (1965): 77-98.

HOFFMAN, PAUL G. "How Eisenhower Saved the Republican Party." *Collier's*, October 26, 1956, pp. 44-47.

KATZ, SAMUEL, and ELDERSVELD, SAMUEL J. "The Impact of Local Party Activity upon the Electorate." *Public Opinion Quarterly* 25 (Spring 1961): 1-24.

McCLOSKEY, HERBERT; HOFFMAN, PAUL J.; and O'HARA, ROSEMARY. "Issue Conflict and Consensus among Party Leaders and Followers." *American Political Science Review* 54 (June 1960): 406-27.

MOSHER, WILLIAM. "Party and Government Control at the Grass Roots." *National Municipal Review* 24 (January 1935): 37-49.

OLIEN, ROGER M. "The Man Who Never Became a Colonel House." *West Texas Historical Association Yearbook*, 1975, pp. 13-23.

OVERACKER, LOUISE. "Campaign Finance in the Presidential Election of 1940." *American Political Science Review* 35 (August 1941): 35.

PIERCE, JOHN C. "Party Identification and the Changing Role of Ideology in American Politics." *Midwest Journal of Political Science* 14 (February 1970): 25-42.

SHANNON, J. B. "Presidential Politics of the South." *Journal of Politics* 1 (May 1939): 146-70.

SHEPHERD, WILLIAM G. "Getting a Job for Jack." *Collier's*, June 15, 1929.

"Texas Convention." *Time*, June 9, 1952, p. 20.

Texas Republican, July 22, 1960.

"Tumult in Texas Leads to a Republican Breach." *Life*, June 19, 1952, pp. 41-42.

Two Party News, September 1947.

WEEKS, OLIVER DOUGLAS. "Republicanism and Conservatism in the South." *Southwestern Social Science Quarterly* 36 (December 1955): 248-56.

WEST, RICHARD. "Ben Barnes Is Still Running." *Texas Monthly*, June 1979, pp. 196-97.

WHITE, OWEN P. "High-Handed and Hell-Bent." *Collier's*, June 22, 1929.

WHITE, WILLIAM S. "An Attempt to Define Our Party Lines." *New York Times Magazine*, May 5, 1957, p. 19.

WILDAVSKY, ADAM. "The Goldwater Phenomenon: Purists, Politicians, and the Two-Party System." *Review of Politics* 27 (1965): 386-413.

Index